The Practice of Social Influence in Multiple Cultures

Applied Social Research

Marlene Turner and Anthony Pratkanis, Series Editors

The Practice of Social Influence in Multiple Cultures

Edited by

Wilhelmina Wosinska
Arizona State University, West

Robert B. Cialdini
Arizona State University

Daniel W. Barrett
Arizona State University

Janusz Reykowski
Polish Academy of Science

LEA LAWRENCE ERLBAUM ASSOCIATES, PUBLISHERS
2001   Mahwah, New Jersey   London

The final camera copy for this work was prepared by the author,
and therefore the publisher takes no responsibility for consistency
or correctness of typographical style. However, this arrangement
helps to make publication of this kind of scholarship possible.

Lawrence Erlbaum Associates, Inc., Publishers
10 Industrial Avenue
Mahwah, NJ 07430

Cover design by Suzanne Lehman

Library of Congress Cataloging-in-Publication Data

The practice of social influence in multiple cultures / edited by
    Wilhelmina Wosinska ... [et al.].
            p. cm.
Includes bibliographical references and index.
ISBN 0-8058-3279-3
1. Multiculturism–Research. 2. Social influence–Research.
    I. Wosinska, Wilhelmina.
HM1271 .P73 2000
306'.07–dc21
                                        00-037527
                                            CIP

Books published by Lawrence Erlbaum Associates are printed
on acid-free paper, and their bindings are chosen for strength
and durability.

Printed in the United States of America
10 9 8 7 6 5 4 3 2 1

To Marek, Marta, Zosia, and Magda Lena
and to the memory of the beloved daughter Alunia

To Bobette, Christopher, and Jason

To Leslie and Madeline

To Zula and Dorotka

Contents

Part II. Social Influence and Social Change Across Cultures

Part III. Culture and Moral Perspective in the Social Influence Process

Preface

Wilhelmina Wosinska
Robert B. Cialdini
Daniel W. Barrett

The 1990s witnessed the evolution of increasingly sophisticated theories and rapidly growing empirical support for the impact of cross-cultural factors on attitudes, beliefs, and behaviors. One of the areas in which the cross-cultural focus in social psychology holds great promise is the study of social influence. However, although recent published research has clearly demonstrated the need to consider the interactions between cultural differences and social influence processes, no volume reflecting the depth and breadth of this work has previously been available. The purpose of this book is to provide, in a single volume, a diverse collection of studies reporting the effects of social influence processes in multiple cultures, at both the universal and culture-specific levels.

This volume is characterized by three novel and distinct features. The first major feature is that the social influence process is considered to be a ubiquitous and pervasive characteristic of human interaction. This means that, first, social influence is conceptualized in terms of a few general governing principles that work universally for all people, although the magnitude of the impact of these principles may be culture- and context-bound. Second, this volume underscores the pervasiveness of the social influence process by expanding its connotation beyond the dynamics of individual persuasion: Influence is considered a process for generating large-scale social change. Third, and finally, social influence is approached from a moral perspective, which incorporates practices that range from the manipulative to the ethically desirable.

The second feature of our volume is that it represents a multiple cultural approach. That is, the book is largely composed of original data collected via two separate but complementary research approaches to the social influence process. One is the cross-cultural approach. Many of the chapters presented here contain analyses of different national cultures. Some of the cross-cultural chapters focus on a particular phenomenon studied simultaneously in more than one society, whereas others investigate a social influence issue within a single culture and compare their data with findings from other cultures. The second culture-focused approach may be called *multicultural*: The chapters incorporating this approach examine social influence as it applies to different subcultures within a single society rather than cultures in different nations.

Thus, as the title of the volume indicates, we are dealing with the social influence process in multiple cultures, both between and within societies. In our view, this volume represents a unique and important contribution in two ways. First, the populations that are studied herein are broadly based. This is in contrast to previous research on social influence that has, for the most part, used White, middle-class college students or, less frequently, representatives of the general population of North America. Second, this collection of studies includes examinations of Central and Eastern European cultures that, because of political and language barriers, were not previously accessible to most foreign scholars. In the past, much of the non-American research published in English language outlets has focused on Asian cultures. Virtually none investigated cultures from Central and Eastern Europe. Now that the political barriers in this region have been lowered, valuable research that emerged in the 1990s can be more widely disseminated. In part, this volume represents an attempt to do just that by widening the potential audience for research conveying insights into the social psychological processes occurring in emerging democracies. However, we did include both Western European as well as Asian cultures. All in all, this volume incorporates Hungarian, Polish, German, Turkish, Spanish, Japanese, Chinese, Mexican-American, and EuroAmerican cultures and subcultures in the original research and includes numerous reference to additional research conducted in many more nations.

The third distinctive feature of our volume is its emphasis on the practical implications of the research presented herein. The reader not only learns how the principles and mechanisms of social influences operate powerfully in various cultures and contexts, but sees specific applications of the research data in given domains. Each chapter ends with a brief (or, in some cases, more extended) discussion of the major practical implications for its findings.

Combining these three approaches to the social influence process within an overall cultural theme allowed us to arrange the chapters into the three following sections: Part I: Principles of Social Influence Across Cultures, Part II: Social Influence and Social Change Across Cultures, and Part III: Culture and Moral Perspective in the Social Influence Process.

Part I provides analyses of how the six general principles of social influence described by Cialdini (1993; i.e., commitment/consistency, social proof, authority, scarcity, reciprocity, and liking) work universally across cultures and how cultural factors may mold the impact of the principles in specific contexts. The power of commitment/consistency (the tendency to remain consistent with one's previous actions or beliefs) is analyzed in the chapter by Iyengar and Brockner (chap. 1) in research on how the opportunity to choose their task (which affected commitment to the task) differentially impacted school performance by Asian and American children. The same principle is studied by Cialdini, Wosinska, Barrett, Butner, and Górnik-Durose (chap. 2), who examine readiness to participate in a consumer survey in Polish and

American culture. Another approach to commitment is undertaken by Spangenberg and Greenwald (chap. 3), who analyze its effects within the self-prophecy paradigm. Liking (the tendency to be favorably impacted by those who are perceived as likable), which is partially produced by perceived similarity, was studied (along with empathy and perceived responsibility) by Miller, Kozu, and Davis (chap. 4). Their meta-analytic approach covers several European, Asian, and American cultures and deals—as did Iyengar and Brockner's research—with a class of subjects relatively neglected in social influence research—children. Cialdini et al. also investigate a second principle, social proof (the tendency to behave as referent others do), which Pietras (chap. 5) analyzes in a different consumer context. Pietras extends her research, conducted on a general population of Poles, to two more principles: authority (the tendency to comply to the expectations of others with higher status or greater expertise) and scarcity (the tendency to perceive scarce objects or situations as more desirable). The operations of the reciprocity principle (the tendency to return a favor received from another) in a specific organization located in four diverse cultures are discussed by Morris, Podolny, and Ariel (chap. 6). The final chapter in Part I, written by Gutierres and Van Puymbroeck (chap 7.), considers the impact of different types of influence and various cultural factors on illicit drug misuse and reactions to therapeutic assistance by Euro-American and Mexican-American women.

These six general principles of social influence were researched in various cultures, in different contexts, and on different representatives of the national cultures. Several aspects of cross-cultural differences are addressed in these chapters. Individualism/collectivism, which has been considered by many researchers as a core dimension of cultural variability, is one such construal of cross-cultural differences discussed in the volume. Other dimensions, such as universalism/particularism and power distance, are also considered, although to a lesser degree. In addition, historic national experiences such as communist governments or scarcity-based economies are also included as factors contributing to the specificity of the social influence principles' impact. Finally, both national and individual differences in cultural orientation are considered in terms of how they might differentially impact the effectiveness of the social influence principles.

Part II is devoted to the social influence processes that are based not on interpersonal exchange (which can lead to more or less momentary acts of compliance)—as was the case for most of the research in Part I—but to those that generate more permanent change of the sort observed typically in larger audiences. In other words, in this section, authors deal with the influences that lead to social change. Nowak and Vallacher (chap. 8) apply a dynamical systems perspective to structural changes and to resulting widespread attitude change in Poland. Wojciszke (chap. 9) reflects on the consequences of a strong political minority on abortion-related laws in Poland; Klinger and Bierbrauer (chap. 10) discuss acculturation and conflict resolution among Turkish immigrants living in Germany; Kopp, Skrabski, and Szedmák (chap. 11) describe increased morbidity and mortality rates in Hungary that were produced by dramatic socioeconomic changes following the fall of the communist system; and Górnik-Durose (chap. 12) examines Westernized patterns of consumption among Polish youth.

Influences that lead to such diverse examples of social change may be termed *structural* in contrast to interpersonal or mass-mediated influences. Here, the source of the influence is neither typically an individual (although sometimes this may be a case, for instance, when a leader of the political opposition triggers an avalanche of changes) nor mass-mediated (although again mass-mediated influences may overlap with structural ones, as in the case where a radical new government commandeers major media outlets and uses them as part of a strategy to affect social change).

Although some of these chapters are primarily based on data collected in a single culture, the authors attempt to examine the implications for their findings for other cultures by discussing the potential universal and culture-specific aspects of their research.

Part III of the volume assumes yet another approach to the social influence process. Namely, it looks at it in terms of its moral aspects. There is a deeply rooted conviction—shared by representatives of the general population and also by some scholars—that social influence implies machiavellian manipulations that benefit only those who employ them. Certainly, knowledge of social influence, when combined with the ability to exert influence, can result in the manipulation of others' perceptions and opinions. Sometimes, however, strategies designed to produce one set of outcomes may inadvertently also lead to unintended and perhaps even unwanted consequences. For example, Dolinski and Kofta (chap. 13) describe some unintended consequences of the break that media often insert between the presentation of a story headline about a person and his or her alleged involvement in a crime and the description of the details of the story: Attributions of responsibility to the named person turn out to be greater simply because the break occurred. The break is designed to retain viewers by providing a tease, yet it can produce the side effect of biasing perceptions of culpability. Manipulations may also occur on a larger scale with more serious implications. For instance, Pratkanis (chap. 14) describes the substitution of political propaganda for deliberative persuasion in established and emerging democracies, which severely hinders the actualization of democratic principles. In contrast to these two chapters, three others describe how social influence may be involved in prosocial activities. Snyder and Omoto (chap. 15) examine the role of social influence processes in volunteering to help persons suffering from AIDS. Ohme (chap. 16) depicts mass-mediated efforts to reduce the prevalence of smoking and reveals some interesting paradoxes embedded within some antismoking advertisements, crafted by a tobacco company, that may undermine their effectiveness. In the final chapter of Part III, Cody and Seiter (chap 17) suggest how deliberate manipulations by sales clerks in retail outlets may benefit both the store and the customer. Again, as in the earlier sections, if some authors primarily focus on a single culture, they nevertheless discuss the generalizability of their findings and/or hypothesize outcomes for other (contrasting) cultures.

In conclusion, this volume collects a diverse set of readings that are united in their attention to the intersection of social influence and culture. Research is drawn from multiple cultures and spans three broad sources of influence: interpersonal, mass-mediated, and structural. Although these sources of influence may be conceptually distinguishable, any single instance of social influence can easily involve all three sources. For example, illicit drug use may be a product of the confluence of structural influences (e.g., poverty), mass-mediated influences (portrayals of drug use on television), and interpersonal influences (e.g., spousal modeling). However, in a given instance, one source is often more impactful than others and may be appropriately allotted more emphasis than the others.

Because each of the three parts of the book encompasses a considerable variety of research methodologies, social contexts, and cultures, each is proceeded by an integrative commentary authored by one of the book editors, Janusz Reykowski. These essays provide syntheses of the topics and themes within the corresponding sections and within the book as a whole. In addition to drawing out common themes in the chapters, they offer critical commentaries on both theoretical and methodological issues. Furthermore, they raise suggestions for future research and focus on practical applications.

All in all, this book is intended for scholars interested in cross- and multicultural research into the mechanisms of the social influence process. It is also designed for the professional whose mission is to make planned changes in a society. Knowledge about the influence process, especially regarding how it works in different cultures and within several cultural groups, should facilitate this goal. The practical implications ending each chapter may serve as encouraging instructions for such applications.

ACKNOWLEDGMENTS

We would like to end our introductory comments by acknowledging the tremendous organizational, financial, and moral support we have received from Dr. Jay Braun, former Chair of the Department of Psychology at Arizona State University, and Dr. Gary Krahenbuhl, Dean of the College of Liberal Arts and Sciences at this university. Both of these leaders warmly embraced the novel idea of conducting cross-cultural research within the Psychology

Department and thus affirmed its importance in the future of psychology through their words and deeds. Such support for cross-cultural research is an especially timely response to the demands and challenges of humanity at this historical moment of the break of the millennia.

REFERENCE

Cialdini, R. B. (1993). *Influence: Science and practice.* New York: Harper.

About the Editors

Wilhelmina Wosinska graduated from the University of Warsaw and received her doctoral degree from the Jagiellonian University in Krakow, Poland. She founded the Department of Social Psychology at the University of Silesia in Katowice, Poland, and chaired it for several years. Since immigrating to the United States in 1991, she has taught at Arizona State University West, where she introduced a new course on cross-cultural social psychology. This course reflects her area of expertise, and she is particularly interested in the study of social influence across cultures. She has published in both Polish and English. Her Polish publications include the book *Leadership in the Organization from the Perspective of Social Psychology*. Her publications in English deal with different principles and factors determining compliance in various cultures, especially in an organizational context.

Robert B. Cialdini is a regents professor at Arizona State University, where he has also been named Graduate Distinguished Professor. He received his undergraduate degree from the University of Wisconsin and his graduate degrees from the University of North Carolina. He is a past president of the Society for Personality and Social Psychology. His research has appeared in numerous publications, including the *Handbook of Social Psychology, Advances in Experimental Social Psychology, Journal of Personality and Social Psychology,* and *Journal of Experimental Social Psychology*. His book *Influence: Science and Practice* (1993) has been translated into seven languages.

Daniel W. Barrett is a doctoral student in the social psychology program at Arizona State University and is currently a National Science Foundation Graduate Research Fellow. He received his bachelor's degree in the College of Social Studies at Wesleyan University in Middletown, Connecticut, and his master's at Arizona State. His research interests include social influence and culture, the antecedents and consequences of epistemic doubt, religion and cognition, and belief perseverance.

Janusz Reykowski graduated from the University of Warsaw in Poland. For the past several years, he has served as the Director of the Institute of Psychology at the Polish Academy of Science and is a member of both this Academy and the European Academy of Science. During 1990 to1991, he was a visiting fellow at Stanford University. In 1989, he was a co-chairman of the Round Table political negotiations in Poland. In concert with this role, his recent research focus has been the changes in sociopolitical mentality related to social change in the emerging democracies and sociopolitical conflicts. His more recent publications include *Social and Moral Values: Individual and Societal Perspectives* (1989; co-editor along with Nancy Eisenberg and Ervin Staub), "Why Did The Collectivist State Fail?" (1994; *Theory and Society*), and "Belief System and Collective Action" (1998; *Applied Psychology: An International Review*).

Part I: Principles of Social Influence Across Cultures

Janusz Reykowski

Polish Academy of Science

Overview and Commentary

Most of the research on social influence has been conducted in Western countries and primarily within the United States. Nevertheless, many people regard the basic principles of influence to be universal. In other words, they assume that the principles operate in similar ways in divergent cultures. This seems to be a latent assumption not only among authors who have described these principles, but also among many readers in various countries who accepted, with enthusiasm, translations of Cialdini's (1993) book *Influence: Science and Practice* into their respective languages. One question should be asked: To what extent can one generalize the findings concerning the mechanisms of social influence beyond the original milieu in which they were discovered and successfully applied? Relatedly, what is the role of cultural factors in people's reactions to various influence strategies? The first part of this volume discusses these very questions.

The first three chapters of Part I are focused primarily, but not solely, on one important mechanism of social influence that has been called the *principle of commitment*. A plethora of research has demonstrated that people who are led to commit themselves to certain behavior are likely to perform it when requested, despite mounting difficulties and decreasing attractiveness of the goal. Is this mechanism equally effective in various cultures?

In the first chapter, Iyengar and Brockner review research concerning this issue. First, they summarize many studies that show that when individuals commit to a certain activity, they develop attitudes consistent with such commitment, which then sustain this activity. Such commitment is stronger if it was public, if the corresponding activity required much effort, if it was irrevocable, and if it was freely chosen. Free choice appears to be an especially potent factor. Researchers found that every time people were convinced that *they* made the choice, they became much more persistent in their efforts. Do these results apply to people in general?

Iyengar and Brockner (chap. 1) point out that free choice holds a high position in the hierarchy of American values. It is related to the self-conception of the American people, especially to the ideal of the independent self, which is characteristic of this individualistic culture. However, the ideal of the independent self is not universal. As Markus and Kitayama (1991) explained, in collectivistic cultures, such as those in the Far East, people strive for interconnectedness and belonging. This striving is one reason that the interdependent self seems more malleable across contexts and why self-consistency may be less important for them. On the basis of this reasoning, Iyengar and Brockner hypothesize that the provision of personal choice can be more motivating for American individualists than for Asian collectivists. Their research reported in chapter 1 supports this hypothesis. In fact, choice was a much more effective manipulation for American children than for their Asian counterparts. At the same time, they found that Asian children were more motivated when the choice was made by an important ingroup member—the children's mothers; the Asian children did significantly worse when they made their own choices. The latter result also indicates that there must be important cultural differences in the operation of the social proof principle on behavior. For a collectivist, social proof can be a potent mechanism of influence, provided that it comes from ingroup members.

The theoretical analysis and the data provided by Iyengar and Brockner clearly show that cultural differences do matter as far as social influence processes are concerned. However, the authors formulate some warnings. In particular, they underscore that cultures are not homogenous and members of a given society are not all alike. In other words, the same dimensions of comparison that distinguish people between cultures may also differentiate people within a given culture. Therefore, to account for differences in people's reactions to particular forms of social influence, one should not depend solely on knowledge of cultural membership—one also has to take into account the specific position of the given persons on the specific dimension of comparison that is relevant for the given principle of influence. For the principles of commitment and social proofs, the relevant dimension is individualism/collectivism (I/C).

The significance of this postulate is well illustrated in chapter 2 by Cialdini, Wosinska, Barrett, Butner, and Górnik-Durose. It reports their research concerning the effectiveness of two social influence principles—commitment/consistency and social proof—in two different cultural contexts: individualistic and collectivistic. The authors hypothesize that in societies where collectivistic tendencies are relatively strong, social proof may affect compliance to a greater degree than in societies where individualism predominates. The opposite should be true about the commitment/consistency principle. The authors also expect that it would not be sheer national belonging and national I/C orientation that crucially influences compliance, but rather personal I/C orientation. They tested their hypotheses by recruiting subjects in two countries: the United States and Poland. Their data support previous research that indicated that collectivistic tendencies are more prevalent and of greater intensity in Poland than in the United States. Their main findings confirmed the hypotheses formulated by the authors. In particular, the evidence suggests that the strength of personal I/C orientation differentiates susceptibility to the two social influence procedures.

Thus, taking together the analyses and data provided in first two chapters of this part of the volume, one may conclude that the same social influence principles operate in various cultures but with unequal strength: In some cultures, some of the principles appear to be more potent than in others. The specific characteristic of the culture that was found to be responsible for this difference was individualism/collectivism. It was also found that the location of an individual on this dimension tends to determine his or her reactions to the various forms of social influence rather than his or her national culture.

The Cialdini et al. research also produced some unexpected results. One was that collectivists in both countries tended to comply more than individualists, independent of influence principle. The authors conjecture that it may be because collectivists possess a stronger social responsibility norm than do individualists and found empirical support for it in an additional experiment described in the chapter. Nonetheless, one may still wonder whether this is a universal truth. On the basis of I/C theory (Triandis, 1990, 1994), one might expect that, for collectivists, the social responsibility norm has a rather narrow range of application—it is limited to ingroups. Moreover, this norm is also respected by individualists, although its motivational basis may be different than for collectivists. With this in mind, one has to be cautious about emphasizing the role of the social responsibility norm in this instance. Other plausible explanations could probably be generated here that could be explored in future research. However, this commentary is not the place for extensive speculations on why, in this research, collectivists manifested a higher degree of compliance than individualists.

Another unexpected result of the Cialdini et al. research concerned Polish individualists: They were not affected by the manipulations based on the commitment/consistency principle. These authors operationalized commitment/consistency as information about one's past behavior. It should be taken into consideration, however, that information about one's own past behavior may have different meaning for different people. Some people would understand it as evidence concerning their internal attributes and thus feel obliged to maintain self-consistency by behaving in the same way, whereas others may regard such information—especially when provided by someone whose strategic intentions are not concealed—as a manipulation impinging on their freedom of choice. In such a case, reactance may be a likely response. Thus, individualists who regard freedom of choice as an important value may, in some circumstances, react paradoxically to the information about their own past activities. As a matter of fact, commonsense knowledge about the Polish character suggests that reactance is a frequent reaction among Poles.

There is still another aspect of the commitment/consistency principle that should be considered here. Cialdini et al. maintain that the motivating power of the practices based on this principle comes from information about one's own past behavior. However, they would probably not argue against the proposition that the concept of commitment could be extended to include other behavior. This is in fact what Spangenberg and Greenwald (chap. 3) do in their chapter on self-prophecy. On the basis of previous research and their own studies, they suggest that predictions concerning one's own future action increase the probability of executing the given action. The authors mention two conditions that have to be met for the self-prophecy effect to occur consistently: The given action is socially desirable, and subjects are unable to make confident self-predictions based on their past behavior.

As to the first condition, it may require a fairly liberal interpretation. In one of the experiments, the self-prophecy effect was found for a rather odd kind of behavior—namely, singing on the phone. It is difficult to assume that singing on the phone is socially desirable behavior unless one agrees that social desirability can be defined in a concrete situation by specific persons or a group. The second condition indicates that there might be a competition between self-prophecy and well-established patterns of behavior. In such a competition, the well-established patterns are bound to win, indicating that consistency with past behavior has priority over consistency with situationally evoked predictions.

Spangenberg and Greenwald argue that the self-prophecy effect is robust in both the magnitude of the effect size and the variety of contexts in which it has been observed. Therefore, it can be used as an effective tool of social influence. Although they explain this phenomenon by referring to value-action discrepancy, it can also be seen as another instance of the commitment/consistency principle. Still there are questions about its applicability in various cultural contexts. The authors consider that cultural differences in normative systems may play an important mediating role. That is, the strength of the norm associated with the given behavior may influence the self-prophecy effect concerning that behavior. Another cultural difference that is taken into consideration is the method of evoking the predictions. The authors believe that the standard American approach—using telephones or paper-and-pencil technique—would not be feasible in many countries.

However, the problem runs deeper than that. As discussed earlier and in the first two chapters, there are good reasons to doubt whether consistency appeals engender equally strong motivation in different cultural contexts. On the basis of this reasoning, one can expect that consistency effects should be much stronger in cultures where an independent construal of the self predominates than in cultures where the interdependent construal does—or, in other words, in individualistic rather than collectivistic contexts.

The role of the individualistic versus collectivistic cultural contexts in determining the effectiveness of social influence is not limited to the commitment/consistency and social proof principles. Data and analyses presented in chapter 4 by Miller, Kozu and Davis, show that several other factors of social influence can be modified by cultural context. These authors focus on how empathy and sympathy are affected by three different factors of social influence: beliefs about similarity to a target person, observational set (focusing attention on psychological states—feelings and thoughts of a target person vs. focusing it on the objective situation), and beliefs about responsibility for the predicament of a target person (the target person's responsibility for his or her condition vs. external, uncontrollable causes). One may notice that only the first factor is somewhat related to the principles of social influence described by Cialdini (1993)—the similarity manipulation tends to evoke liking that facilitates social impact. The two others are more specific: They regard instances where the influence consists of evoking affective responses toward exigencies of a particular person.

The authors' present a meta-analysis of studies conducted in the United States and several countries in Europe and Asia. The results of this analysis indicate, first of all, that the three factors of social influence operate cross-culturally (i.e., it may be reasonable to contend that evoking beliefs about similarity to a given person, focusing attention on his or her psychological states, or providing information that a target person is not responsible for his or her negative situation tend to facilitate empathetic and sympathetic responding across cultures). In discussing their results, the authors point out that similarity appeared to have the least influence in eliciting the prosocial effect, but this observation is rather ambiguous. To make a direct comparison of various social influence factors, one should have a common measure of the strength of these factors. Unfortunately, no such measure is available. Therefore, it is unclear whether the weaker effect of the similarity manipulation is due to the fact that it is a less potent factor or because the given similarity manipulations were not meaningful for the subjects.

Despite the fact that the three influence factors appear to have effects in various cultures, there were also some culturally determined differences. One difference concerns the interpretation of responsibility for one's own predicament. In collectivistic cultures, a person tends to be perceived as less responsible for his or her misfortune than in individualistic ones. In the former, a group is supposed to assume responsibility for an individual, whereas in the latter, the responsibility is attributed to a given person. It explains previous findings that show that the helping behavior of Indian subjects (representing a collectivistic culture) was not affected by information about target responsibility for his or her misfortune. It can be added that the same subjects were more empathetic if the cause of someone's plight was personally uncontrollable. It probably means that normative demands of the given culture may override differences in affective responses.

Another point where cultural differences are likely to appear is in the perception of similarity. Some of the data quoted by Miller et al. indicate that, in collectivistic cultures, ingroup/outgroup differentiation may play a significant role in evoking empathy: It is much more likely for an ingroup member. One may conjecture that group belonging may determine, to a major degree, who is perceived as similar and dissimilar.

The data provided up to this point seem to support the notion that, as far as responses to various social influence principles are concerned, I/C is a valid dimension for comparison. Nevertheless, using culture as a unit of analysis can only give us gross approximation to the phenomena one is interested in. In fact, societies belonging to the same category of cultures (individualistic or collectivistic) may still differ in their reactions to social influence, in part due to their differential historical experiences. For example, one can conjecture that extended periods of economic deprivation may sensitize members of a society to information about scarcity. Moreover, there may exist systematic differences among people representing different social categories (e.g., socioeconomic status [SES]) within a given culture in their reactions to various principles.

These ideas are investigated in chapter 5 by Pietras. Her focus is on the effects of three social influence principles (scarcity, social proof, and authority) on Polish consumer behavior. Pietras argues that I/C should have some bearings on the impact of the social proof principle. At the same time, societal experience—a long period of economic shortage—can increase susceptibility to a scarcity appeal. Moreover, she takes into account the role of sociodemographic categories (age, gender, income) and a psychological variable (locus of control) when testing these principles. In her field experiment, reactions were obtained from people chosen randomly from adults in shops and on the streets to leaflets advertising a new product. The leaflets differed with respect to the kind of appeal they contained. The appeals reflected three social influence principles: scarcity, social proof, authority. The dependent measures were attitudes toward the product and intentions of buying it.

The author hypothesized that the relatively higher level of collectivism in Poland should make the social proof tactics more effective than the others. Moreover, the 40 years of experience of shortage of the most of ordinary goods should make Poles especially sensitive to the information about scarcity. Unfortunately, the author's hypotheses could not be tested directly because she lacked comparison groups. Therefore, she has tested the tactics against each other. Surprisingly, she found that social proof was less effective than authority and scarcity. Nevertheless, it is difficult to interpret this finding. Does it mean that the collectivistic participants were not sensitive to information about others' preferences and behavior or, as the author suggests was more likely the case, that the operationalization of this tactics was inappropriate? It is doubtful that telling Poles "that people all over the world like this product" suggested a reference group that was sufficiently relevant to invoke social proof. Collectivists are more likely to react to the opinions of their ingroup rather than of people in general. Therefore, one should not be surprised that collectivistic subjects would not be impacted by such information.

Interestingly enough, social proof information was more persuasive for people with high income, suggesting that *people all over the world* was a better reference group for more affluent consumers. This finding is an illustration of the thesis that, when considering the role of cultural differences on social behavior, one should take into account social categories within the culture.

It should be stressed that one may not formulate, on the basis of these data, general statements about differences in effectiveness of the three social influence principles. The main difficulty consists in the fact that the effectiveness of the message depends not only on the underlying principle, but also on its specific content. Therefore, one does not know whether the greater effectiveness of a particular principle in comparison to the other ones was related to the greater sensitivity of the given group to this kind of tactic or due to the more or less adequate translation of the principles into specific messages.

However, one can compare the effectiveness of the same messages for different kinds of people. Thus, Pietras' data indicate that men manifested less compliance than women (or that the product was intrinsically more attractive for women than for men), that older people were more influenced by the authority principle than younger people (either because an authority played a greater role for the older people or because they were more susceptible to a specific kind of authority—in this case, the authority of a physician), and that people with a higher income were more likely to be influenced by the behavior of an international reference group. These data also suggest that people with external locus of control were more susceptible to all kinds of influences than people with internal locus of control.

Obviously it is difficult to formulate firm conclusions from these data. However, at least one can say that the effectiveness of the social influence principles was modified by a number of sociodemographic and cultural factors (such as age, gender, income) and psychological factors (such as locus of control). Thus, all of these kinds of variables should be considered in future research regarding the impact of culture on social influence processes. This claim is consistent with Diaz-Guerrero's (1993) speculation regarding the need to include sociohistorical precursors when examining national cultures.

Another approach to cultural differences in response to social influence is presented in chapter 6 on feelings of obligation in the workplace in several countries. In this chapter, Morris, Podolny, and Ariel compare responses to an imagined request for assistance in performing a dull task. Their subjects were from four countries: Germany, Hong Kong, Spain, and the United States. The main finding of this research was that various channels of influence were differentially effective in these nations. Three such channels were investigated in this research: power, friendship, and formal position in an organization. In other words, the request for assistance came from people with high or low power, from people who were or were not identified as friends, or from someone who belonged to the same or a different branch of the organization and had a designated location in the command structure. For the U.S. participants, the most influential channel was power, whereas in Germany it was formal position in the organization, in Spain, friendship and formal position, and in Hong Kong, power and formal position. Not surprisingly, in each sample, other channels were also effective, albeit to a lesser degree. In some countries, some channels were apparently altogether closed.

The extent to which these findings are generalizable is not clear. For instance, do the same channels operate in the case of other types of influence, such as inducing a political action or a purchase or altering one's beliefs? One also does not know whether people would display the same pattern of responses in real-life situations as opposed to the *imagine* scenarios used in this study. These uncertainties notwithstanding, there is good reason to expect that individuals from different cultures manifest differential susceptibility as a function of the source and character of the influence attempts. What are the possible sources of his differential susceptibility? At least two dimensions of cultural differences postulated by Hofstede (1983) can be considered. One is the previously mentioned I/C dimension. Assuming that Spain is a relatively collectivistic country, one may not be surprised that friendship played a significant role there. What about Hong Kong? Chinese people are allegedly highly collectivistic, so why has friendship not appeared there as an important channel? Does it mean that Hong Kong workplace ingroups are not defined in terms of friendship, at least not in the terms that were used in the study? Or is it that, as the authors suggest, in the Chinese context, attitudes toward persons in power have a collectivistic connotation—they represent filial relationship?

Another dimension that is likely to be relevant for differences in compliance is power distance. However, the two countries where power channels were the most effective—the United States and Hong Kong—are not high on this dimension (Hofstede, 1983; Schwartz, 1994). Therefore, it seems that widely known, general characteristics of a culture do not provide easy explanation of the obtained findings. The authors propose their own classification of the differences between cultures and argue that their data are consistent with it.

It seems that there is a common message in the five chapters of Part I: All the major factors of social influence considered here operate in various cultures, but there are culturally related significant differences in their effectiveness as well as in the specific conditions of their operation. Some of the observed differences can be explained, at least partially, as the result of differences in culturally bound normative systems that can be accounted for by means of one important dimension—individualism and collectivism. These normative systems affect the construal of the self-concept, which partially determines the differential susceptibility of individuals to various social influence factors.

The role of cultural determinants, however, is broader than that. In chapter 7 Gutierres and Van Puymbroeck discuss other consequences of cultural differences. The problem they identify is the differential responses to treatment for substance misuse among people belonging to divergent cultural groups. Their data show that Mexican-American women have significantly lower prospects of recovery from drug misuse than Euro-American women and both Mexican- and Euro-American men. What makes this particular group more resistant to the therapeutic influences than other groups?

First of all, the authors indicate that there are strong cultural expectations concerning abstinence from substance use for the Mexican-American women. The dominant cultural pattern is that they are more likely than other groups to abstain from alcohol use; when they do use it, they do so in much lower quantities and frequencies. This is true for women in urban and rural communities, for recent immigrants, and for second and later generations as well. The strong normative barriers against substance misuse among these women provide a kind of a shield protecting them from the pressures existing in their milieu. This shield is highly effective in contemporary societies where these women are exposed to many pressures and temptations to use substance. Once these normative barriers are broken (the authors describe a number of factors that contribute to such breakdown), recovery is difficult. Gutierres and Van Puymbroeck label this as the *cultural abstinence violation effect*.

This phenomenon is probably a more general one and has some bearings for a theory of social influence. Namely, one can expect that strong culturally enforced norms can provide effective protection against counternormative social influences, but they make it much more difficult to save the transgressors. The authors mention internal and external sources of this difficulty. The internal source is the strong feeling of shame that prevents the afflicted women from seeking help from family and friends. There is also an external factor—stigmatization. Mexican-American women who abuse alcohol are considered black sheep in their environment. According to the authors, a special therapeutic program needs to be developed for the Mexican-American women that takes into consideration conditions unique to their substance misuse experience.

In conclusion, one may suggest that, although there are several general mechanisms of social influence, their specific characteristics can be distinct in different cultures. In attempting to account for these differences, one must consider that the dynamics and effects of the social influence processes may depend not only on the content of the beliefs, normative systems, and values dominant in the given culture, but also on the formal characteristics of the normative systems—their strength and rigidity.

It is apparent that differences in the effectiveness of social influence principles across cultures is partially dependent on one major dimension of culture variability: individualism/collectivism. Evidence presented in this volume suggests that at least some social influence principles have different effects on individualistic and collectivistic contexts. Some additional comments concerning the nature of the I/C dimension should be added.

First, it should be borne in mind that individualism/collectivism may not be a one-dimensional construct, because a number of studies have demonstrated its multidimensionality. For example, in their recent article, Triandis and Gelfand (1998) argued that there are two kinds of individualism and two kinds of collectivism: horizontal—emphasizing equality—and vertical—emphasizing hierarchy. The authors provide some theoretical and empirical arguments supporting this claim. Obviously the differences in the characteristics of the I/C construct may have some bearing on the theory of social influence (e.g., one can expect that reactions to various social influence tactics would differ in people representing vertical vs. horizontal collectivism—or individualism). Other authors describe still other dimensions of I/C (e.g., Bierbrauer, Meyer, Wolfradt, 1994; Kim, 1994; Reykowski, 1998).

Second, societies are not homogenous in terms of their mapping on the I/C dimension. A single society may contain major variations in I/C orientation depending on sociodemographic categories as well as territorial ones. For example, in the United States, collectivistic tendencies are strongest in the Deep South and individualistic tendencies are greater in the Mountain West and Great Plains (Vandello & Cohen, 1999).

Third, the I/C construct can be analyzed on both the societal (cultural) and individual levels, and there may be important differences between the two. On the societal level, the I/C construct refers to systems of dominant beliefs, norms, and values, as well as to institutions and cultural products. It is a kind of a broad context in which the lives of society members are conducted. The role of the cultural context was considered in chapter 7, where the authors, although not explicitly dealing with I/C, clearly demonstrate how the cultural context can affect the individual's behavior—in this case, susceptibility to social influence. On the individual level, the I/C construct refers to the structure of beliefs and values in the minds of individual persons. Cialdini et al. demonstrate that the individual's position on the I/C dimensions plays a more important role in his or her reaction to social influence tactics than does national I/C. In other words, information concerning the characteristics of the culture (societal level) is not sufficient if one wants to predict behavior of a concrete member of the culture (individual level). There may be another problem as well, for which existing data are insufficient to suggest a clear resolution: Can one assume that reactions to social influence are independent of context? In other words, is there no difference in the functioning of an individualist (or, respectively, the collectivist) in the individualistic and collectivistic cultural milieus? Apparently a clear answer to this question is not currently possible, although there have been some attempts at looking at this issue (Sinha & Tripathi, 1994).

Fourth, it should be stressed that, although the I/C construct is an important dimension of cultural differences that mediates the effects of social influence, it is not the only dimension. In this part of the volume, several other impactive dimensions are discussed (e.g., in chap. 6). Moreover, as suggested earlier, specific sociohistorical experiences can also affect people's reactions to social influence. An example of such societal experience is going through a long period of economic shortage. Some other important dimensions of culture comparison have been described by Hofstede (1980) and Schwartz (1994). Of course, there are others that might also be considered. This multidimensionality of cultural differences becomes a theoretical challenge because it necessitates the development of a comprehensive model that could account for interactions between various dimensions.

The role of content-related cultural differences notwithstanding, there are also important differences in the formal characteristics of normative systems. The data analyzed in Part I (e.g., chap. 7) indicate that the effects of social influence also appear to depend on the strength and rigidity of the normative systems operating in a given culture. If the normative systems are strong (consequently supported by the members of the society) and rigid (not allowing even minor departures), they may effectively prevent counternormative influences. Of course, the social influence process is culturally embedded: The strength and rigidity of societal norms can be viewed as the specific effects of social influence existing in a particular cultural milieu.

REFERENCES

Bierbrauer, G., Meyer, H., & Wolfradt, U. (1994). Measurement of normative and evaluative aspects of individualistic and collectivistic orientations: The Cultural Orientation Scale (COS). In U. Kim, H. C. Triandis, C. Kagitcibasi, S.-C. Choi, & G. Yoon (Eds.), *Individualism and collectivism: Theory, methods and applications* (pp. 189–194). Thousand Oaks, CA: Sage.

Cialdini, R. B. (1993). *Influence: Science and practice.* New York: Harper.

Diaz-Guerrero, R. (1993). Mexican ethnopsychology. In U. Kim & J. W. Berry (Eds.), *Indigenous psychologies: Research and experience in cultural context* (pp. 44–55). Newbury Park, CA: Sage.

Hofstede, G. (1980). *Culture's consequences: International differences in work-related values.* Beverly Hills: Sage.

Hofstede, G. (1983). Dimensions of national cultures in fifty countries and three regions. In J. Deregowski, S. Dzuirawiec, & R. Annis (Eds.), *Explications in cross-cultural psychology* (pp. 335–555). Lisse: Swets & Zeitlinger.

Kim, U. (1994). Individualism and collectivism: Conceptual clarification and elaboration. In U. Kim, H. C. Triandis, C. Kagitcibasi, S.-C. Choi, & G. Yoon (Eds.), *Individualism and collectivism: Theory, methods and applications* (pp. 19–40). Thousand Oaks: Sage.

Markus, H., & Kitayama, S. (1991). Culture and the self: Implications for cognition, emotion and motivation. *Psychological Review, 98,* 224–253.

Reykowski, J. (1998). Belief system and collective action: Changes in Poland from the psychological perspective. *Applied Psychology: An International Review, 47* (1), 89–109.

Schwartz, S. (1994). Beyond individualism/collectivism: New cultural dimensions of values. In U. Kim, H. C. Triandis, C. Kagitcibasi, S.-C. Choi, & G. Yoon (Eds.), *Individualism and collectivism: Theory, methods and applications* (pp. 85–119). Thousand Oaks: Sage.

Sinha, D., & Tripathi, R. C. (1994). Individualism in a collectivist culture: A case of coexistence of opposites. In U. Kim, H. C. Triandis, C. Kagitcibasi, S.-C. Choi, & G. Yoon (Eds.), *Individualism and collectivism: Theory, methods and applications* (pp. 123–136). Thousand Oaks: Sage.

Triandis, H. C. (1990). Cross-cultural studies of individualism and collectivism. *Nebraska Symposium on Motivation 1989.* Lincoln, NE: University of Nebraska Press.

Triandis, H. C. (1994). Theoretical and methodological approaches to the study of collectivism and individualism. In U. Kim, H. C. Triandis, C. Kagitcibasi, S.-C. Choi, & G. Yoon (Eds.), *Individualism and collectivism: Theory, methods and applications* (pp. 41–51). Thousand Oaks, CA Sage.

Triandis, H. C., & Gelfand, M. J. (1998). Converging measurements of horizontal and vertical individualism and collectivism. *Journal of Personality and Social Psychology, 74,* 118–129.

Vandello, J. A., & Cohen, D. (1999). Patterns of individualism and collectivism across the United States. *Journal of Personality and Social Psychology, 77,* 279–292.

1

Cultural Differences in Self and the Impact of Personal and Social Influences

Sheena S. Iyengar

Joel Brockner

Graduate School of Business

Columbia University

ABSTRACT

A long and rich tradition in Western-dominated social psychology has examined the effects of people's observations of their own behavior on their subsequent attitudes and behaviors. Studies in this tradition examine and find moderating effects of various contextual factors (e.g., volition and publicness) on people's tendencies to align their attitudes/behaviors with their observed behaviors. Conversely, there has been a historical tradition for examining the effects of social influences and group pressure on human thought and behavior. Recent findings reviewed in this chapter suggest that cultural differences in independence and interdependence moderate the relative impact of one's own and other's behavior. People from cultures stressing independence are more influenced by observations of their own behaviors, whereas people from cultures stressing interdependence are more influenced by observations of their peers' behaviors.

Historically, there have been two research traditions in the study of influence: one focusing on the effects of personal information and the other dealing with the effects of social information. Influence based on personal information refers to people being affected by their observations of what they have said and done in the past. Influence based on social information refers to people being affected by their observations of others' attitudes and behaviors. This chapter considers how the impact of these two forms of influence varies across cultures.

THE POWER OF PERSONAL INFORMATION

> The last of the human freedoms is to choose one's attitudes.
> —Victor Frankl

Much theory and research on influence suggest that people are more committed to behaviors they have chosen. One of the first to draw on this insight, Lewin (1952), the father of experimental social psychology, demonstrated that housewives could be persuaded to purchase otherwise undesirable meats (e.g., sweetbreads) if they were convinced not of the benefits of consuming such meats, but instead that they had chosen and publicly committed to purchase and consume these meats. Since Lewin's seminal studies, decades of research have repeatedly shown that people are influenced by personal information (i.e., their observations of what they said and did in the past).

In particular, studies indicate that when individuals behaviorally commit to a situation, they tend to develop attitudes consistent with their commitment (e.g., Kiesler, 1971; Salancik, 1977). Moreover, research has identified four variables that moderate the effect of behavioral commitment on subsequent attitudes. First, people are more persuaded by acts they engaged in publicly rather than privately (cf. Hovland, Campbell, & Brock, 1957). Second, people make judgments about how committed they are to a particular belief based on past efforts exerted in support of their belief. In other words, people make attitude inferences based partly on the frequency of the acts of commitment in which they have already engaged (cf. Sherif, Sherif, & Nebergall, 1965). Third, people are compelled by those commitments that are irrevocable (see Gerard, 1968). Fourth, people are persuaded by those acts that they perceived to have been volitional or freely chosen (cf. Freedman & Steinbruner, 1964). Essentially, after committing themselves to a particular position that is public, effortful, irrevocable, and freely chosen, people are likely to think and act congruently with that position (Aronson, 1992; Cialdini, 1993).

Although the influence of these four moderating variables often coexist, it is the last variable—that of perceived choice—that has received by far the most theoretical and empirical consideration. Salancik (1977) theorized

that, without choice, people need not infer that their behavior has any implication for their attitudes. Publicness, effortfulness, and irrevocability bind
individuals to their behaviors, forcing them to come to terms with their previously committed deeds. However, their perception that they have freely
elected to act in a particular way instigates the degree to which they give
credence to their earlier commitments. Thus, although the publicness, effortfulness, and irrevocability of one's behavior may enhance its impact on subsequent attitudes and behaviors, the influential determinant may be volition
or perceived choice.

THE INFLUENCE OF CHOICE

Give me liberty or give me death!

—Patrick Henry

Since the beginning of American political and legal history, the concept of *choice*
has been drawn on as a persuasive device for influencing social ideology. Not
surprisingly, psychological research and theory have also manipulated choice to
illustrate its merits as a powerful influencing weapon on human thought and
behavior. In fact, the provision of choice has proved to be so powerful that the
motivational consequences of choice extend even to contexts in which the choice
is trivial, incidental, or entirely illusory.

In the clearest demonstration of the relationship between choice and
human motivation, researchers have repeatedly shown that the provision of
choice is linked to intrinsic motivation, which in turn is correlated with greater
commitment. Specifically, the provision of choice increases levels of intrinsic
motivation and enhances performance on a variety of tasks (Deci, 1975, 1981;
Deci & Ryan, 1985). In a typical study, the intrinsic motivation of participants is
compared across two conditions, one in which participants are given a choice
("Which one of the following six puzzles would you like to do?") and a second
in which participants are told by an experimenter which puzzle to undertake
(Zuckerman, Porac, Lathin, Smith, & Deci, 1978). Findings consistently indicate
that, when given a choice, people tend to do better and persevere more at these
activities—both of which may reflect greater commitment.

More recent findings suggest that the opportunity to make a choice
need not be directly linked to the central activity at hand to be associated with
increased levels of intrinsic motivation. Even the provision of small and instructionally irrelevant choices can increase intrinsic motivation and learning
(Cordova & Lepper, 1996). The Cordova and Lepper study showed that when students work on a computer math game, even trivial choices, such as the option to

select the name by which they would be addressed during the game, increased intrinsic motivation and learning of mathematical concepts.

Indeed, even a pure illusion of choice has powerful motivating effects. Consider one of the theoretical cornerstones of social psychology—cognitive dissonance. When individuals perceive themselves as choosing to engage in counterattitudinal behavior, such as writing essays, subsequent changes in attitudes are observed. In contrast, when they perceive themselves to have been forced into that same behavior, their attitudes do not change (e.g., Collins & Hoyt, 1972; Cooper & Fazio, 1984; Festinger, 1957; Goethals & Cooper, 1972; Linder, Cooper, & Jones, 1967; Sherman, 1970). Likewise, as long as individuals believe that they have chosen to undertake an unpleasant activity, such as administering electric shocks to oneself or eating grasshoppers, they will tend to perceive these behaviors as less unpleasant (Zimbardo, Weisenberg, Firestone, & Levy, 1965).

Researchers have even argued that the illusion of choice can influence the quality of human life (e.g., Rotter, 1966; Taylor, 1989; Taylor & Brown, 1988). One particularly compelling demonstration conducted by Langer and Rodin (1977) suggested that the health of elderly patients in a nursing home could be significantly improved—even leading to decrements in mortality rates—if the elderly patients were led to perceive themselves as having choices over relatively trivial matters within the institution. Perhaps Lefcourt (1973) best summed up the essence of this research when he concluded that, "the sense of control, the illusion that one can exercise personal choice, has a definite and a positive role in sustaining life" (p. 424).

In summary, the positive effects of choice appear ubiquitous. The provision of choice seems inherently linked with intrinsic motivation, perceived control, and personal commitment, all of which are in turn correlated with numerous psychological benefits. One explanation for the importance of choice may be its concomitance with self-responsibility. As long as people perceive their behaviors to be volitional, they presume responsibility for their actions and, consequently, their behaviors can serve as a source of information for constructing personal attitude statements (Bem, 1972; Bem & McConnell, 1970; Jones & Harris, 1967). Individuals may ask themselves, "What must my attitude have been if I was willing to perform this behavior in this situation?" Such a theory might suggest that a necessary factor underlying the power of choice is that an individual's drive for consistency will take precedence over his or her convictions.

Support for this theory comes from one of the most reliable compliance techniques—the commitment/consistency principle (also known as the foot-in-the-door technique; Dillard, 1991; Freedman & Fraser, 1966). This technique begins with a request that is so small that it almost always elicits compliance. After initial compliance is attained, a larger, related request is then made. Agreement to perform the second request is usually enhanced by this technique and is often interpreted as resulting from a desire to be consistent with the initial commitment (Cialdini, 1993). Thus, one's perception of choice may be inextricably linked to one's desire to be consistent. Just how central is the power of choice and how pervasive is the desire for internal consistency, especially in societies less permeated by the rhetoric of personal freedom?

CULTURE AND CHOICE

In the world, there are two great decrees. One is fate and the other is duty. That a son should love his parents is fate: you cannot erase this from his heart. That a subject should serve his ruler is duty: there is no place he can go and be without his ruler-no place he can escape to between Heaven and Earth.

—Confucius, Analects

Just as the cultural ideals of individual freedom and liberty are reflected in the way Americans are influenced by the provision of choice and personal history, so too might the ideals of duty and fate mitigate the effects of such powerful influencing tools in cultures less individualistic than our own. In particular, although the provision of choice is an integral part of American ideals, one might wonder what role it plays in contexts less individualistic—contexts that emphasize social interdependence over personal autonomy.

Drawing on the cultural analysis of Markus and Kitayama (1991), one may expect members of more collectivist cultures to be less influenced by their personal histories. Indeed, the findings regarding the effects of freely chosen behaviors on subsequent attitudes and behaviors might be particularly applicable to North Americans and Western Europeans. Markus and Kitayama's theory regarding self-systems argues that, although personal agency and internal consistency are essential elements of the self-concept of American individualists, it may be less relevant to the self-concepts of members of more collectivist cultures (characteristic of Asia and elsewhere).

Markus and Kitayama (1991) suggest that Americans possess a model of the self as fundamentally independent. Such individuals desire a sense of autonomy and seek to express their internal attributes to establish their distinctness from others in their environment. For Americans, then, it is important to be consistent with what one has done in the past to establish one's own stable internal attributes. Consequently, making a choice provides an opportunity to display one's preferences, express one's internal attributes, assert one's autonomy, and fulfill the goal of being unique. Thus, for Americans, internal consistency and personal agency may be deeply intertwined with their sense of self-identity.

Now consider a different cultural context—one in which the members possess a more interdependent model of the self. In contrast to American individualists, Markus and Kitayama (1991) theorized that members of more interdependent cultures (most non-Western cultures) strive for interconnectedness and belonging with their social ingroups by maintaining harmony and endeavoring to fulfill the wishes of their social ingroups (DeVos, 1985; Hsu, 1985; Miller, 1988; Shweder & Bourne, 1984; Triandis, 1990, 1995). Moreover, because the superordinate goal for interdependent selves is to strive for interconnectedness, they possess a more malleable self-identity across contexts, suggesting that how they behaved in the past may not be an accurate reflection of their current or future preferences. For such individuals, the exercise of personal choice may be considerably less significant.

Recent research has provided strong empirical support for this hypothesis (Iyengar & Lepper, 1999; Iyengar, Lepper & Ross, 1999). In two studies, the provision of personal choice motivated American individualists more than Asian collectivists. In the first experiment (Iyengar & Lepper, 1999), patterned after traditional choice paradigms, Asian- and Euro-American children were exposed to either a choice condition, in which they were offered an option of engaging in one of six activities, or a no-choice condition, in which they were told by an experimenter which of the six activities to undertake. Subsequent findings revealed that, although performance on the activity did not vary by culture, Euro-American children proved significantly more committed to personally chosen activities than were the Asians.

A second study conducted by Iyengar and Lepper (1999) showed even more powerful cultural differences in circumstances in which the actual choices involved seemed quite trivial. Using a paradigm patterned after the one employed by Cordova and Lepper (1996), both Asian- and Euro-American fifth graders engaged in a computer math game in either a personal choice condition or a no-choice condition. In the personal choice condition, participants were given half a dozen instructionally irrelevant and seemingly trivial choices (e.g., "Which icon would you like to have as your game piece?"). In the no-choice condition, participants were assigned the same icons as the ones selected by participants in the choice condition. Once again, compared with the Asian participants, Euro-American children preferred more challenging math problems, showed more task engagement, and actually reported liking the subject of mathematics more when they had been allowed to make such seemingly trivial choices. Indeed, what is intriguing about the findings resulting from these two studies is not just the observed cultural differences in the power of choice, but the observed cultural differences in the power of externally dictated preferences on human motivation. We elaborate on cultural differences in the no-choice condition later in this chapter.

One explanation for these cultural differences is that internal consistency is not as relevant for members of more interdependent cultures. Specifically, collectivists may be less committed to their previously stated preferences because there is no expectation for past preferences to be reflected in current ones. Consider the study conducted by Cialdini, Wosinska, Barrett, Butner, and Gornik-Durose (chap. 2, this volume) in which Euro-American and Polish participants reported their willingness to comply with a request to fill out a survey after considering their past compliance to similar requests. The results show that one's past actions have relatively more impact on Americans (the more individualistic culture) than on the Polish (the more collectivistic culture). More specifically, researchers found that it was not the nation of origin, but rather the extent to which persons are individualistic or collectivistic, that moderates the likelihood of those persons being influenced by past deeds.

THE POWER OF SOCIAL INFORMATION

That we have found the tendency to conformity in our society so strong that reasonably intelligent and well-meaning young people are willing to call White Black is a matter of concern.

—Asch (1955, p.34)

Once more, psychologists' understanding of the determinants of human thought and behavior is shaped by societal preoccupations. Just as the American ideals have glorified the concept of independence, so too do American values renounce the existence of social influence. In parallel with the research on the power of personal information, there has been a tradition of examining the consequences of social information, which is the extent to which people are influenced by their knowledge of what others have said and done. The prospect that individuals may yield to group pressure and may sacrifice their individuality in the face of social norms has dismayed many psychologists, including Asch (1955). There are several examples of such research traditions, but perhaps the most outstanding are the studies of conformity.

In his seminal study, Asch (1952) examined the influence of social information on compliance. In the presence of nine other confederates who all provided the wrong answer, Asch asked Euro-American male participants to name which of three comparison lines was the same length as a standard. To his chagrin, Asch found that 36% of his subjects conformed to group pressure. Subsequently, over 100 studies have been conducted to examine the pervasiveness of and factors affecting conforming behavior. Recent meta-analyses indicate that the greater the size of the majority, the greater the likelihood of conformity (Bond & Smith, 1996). Additionally, research on conformity and social comparison theory (Festinger, 1954) suggests that the more ambiguous the stimulus, the greater the likelihood for people to rely on their peers for making judgments.

Despite the apparent pervasiveness of the influence of social information, it may be argued that Americans are not as subject to committing to attitudes and behaviors instigated through social influence when compared with other cultural groups. Not to be understated is the fact that 64% of Asch's (1952) participants did not submit in the face of social opposition. Moreover, although the participants in the Asch experiments complied with the dictates of their social situation, there is little evidence to suggest that their compliance demonstrated in the laboratory led to long-term commitment and internalization of attitudes. Might we observe a greater prevalence of reliance on social information in more socially interdependent cultures?

CULTURE AND SOCIAL INFORMATION

Filial piety and fraternal submission! Are they not the root of all benevolent action?

—Confucius, Analects

Just as the ideals surrounding personal choice and independence are reflected in Americans' greater commitment to personal information, so too might the ideals of sacrifice and submission suggest the increased persuasiveness of social information among people from more interdependent societies. A growing body of research provides support for this hypothesis.

Drawing once more on the theory of Markus and Kitayama (1991), one might argue that people possessing interdependent self-models will be more receptive to the imposition of others' attitudes when making judgments about personal attitudes and behaviors. Because interdependent selves strive not for autonomy and independence, but rather interconnectedness, they might actually prefer the choices selected by others, especially if the social context enables them to fulfill the superordinate cultural goal of belonging.

The aforementioned study by Cialdini et al. (chap. 2, this volume) on social proof provides some initial insights about this phenomenon. Building on their previous research, Cialdini and his colleagues surveyed the willingness of Euro-American and Polish participants to fill out a questionnaire when considering the prior compliance rates among their peers. Social proof was shown to be a more powerful compliance technique in Poland than in the United States.

Additionally, a recent meta-analysis on conformity tested the hypothesis that collectivists would conform more than individualists (Bond & Smith, 1996). Findings from this meta-analysis suggest that participants from collectivist countries tended to show higher levels of conformity than participants from individualist countries. If conformist behavior is strongly related to collectivism, then the decline in conformist behavior among Americans since the 1950s observed in the meta-analysis of Bond and Smith might suggest an increase in individualism in the United States.

Although the evidence suggesting collectivists' greater tendency for conformity is substantial, more refined experimentation suggests that it may be too simplistic to contend that interdependent selves are invariably more conformist than independent selves. In particular, for individuals possessing interdependent selves, the effects of having one's preferences dictated by others should depend on the identity of the chooser. Given that the identity of an interdependent self is fused with ingroup members, a choice that conforms to the selection of an ingroup member should provoke significantly more commitment. The same selection made by an outgroup member, however, may be just as uninspiring as other-choice contexts are for American independent selves. Depending on the degree of closeness between the chooser and the self, a person making choices for another can be perceived either as a benevolent agent or an arrogant usurper of an individual's right to choose.

The previously described studies conducted by Iyengar and Lepper (1999) tested the hypothesis that members from more interdependent cultures will be more intrinsically motivated by the choices made by others as compared with their own choices. Earlier we discussed the differential effects on Euro- and Asian-American children of the choice and no-choice conditions. Now we consider the cultural difference within the (two) no-choice conditions. For half of the students in the no-choice conditions, the person making the choice for them was a previously unencountered adult (i.e., the experimenter), whereas for the other students, the person making the choice was a person with whom participants shared a close and interdependent relationship (i.e., their mothers). Results show that, in contrast to the Euro-American participants, Asians were much more motivated and performed the best when their mothers had made the selection.

Iyengar and Lepper (1999) conducted a second cross-cultural study in which participants' closeness to the source of social influence varied. Specifically, it was hypothesized that the effect of social information on the intrinsic motivation level of individualistic persons would be relatively unaffected by whether the source of the social information were members of an ingroup or an outgroup. In contrast, the identity of the source of social information was expected to be much more pronounced among collectivistic persons. In this study Asian- (collectivistic) and Euro-American (individualistic) fifth graders encountered either a choice or a no-choice manipulation while playing a computer math game. Participants were given trivial, instructionally irrelevant choices or had their selections assigned to them by either an equal-status peer group (i.e., their classmates) or a lower status group (third graders at a rival school). The findings were striking. They showed that, in contrast to Euro-Americans, Asians were more intrinsically motivated and learned more when the choices had been made by their classmates than when they made their own choices, which in turn produced better results than when the choices had been made for them by unfamiliar and lower status others. In contrast, for Euro-Americans, the critical distinction proved to

be between having a choice and not having a choice. That is, they showed significantly more commitment, more motivation, and higher learning in the context offering
them trivial choices as compared with either of the two no-choice contexts.

In summary, two major research streams in American social psychology have investigated the effects of: (a) one's own behavior—especially freely
enacted deeds—on subsequent attitudes and behavior (Bem, 1972; Festinger,
1957), and (b) other people's behaviors on individuals' subsequent attitudes and
behaviors (for a review, see Salancik & Pfeffer, 1978). Recent findings reviewed
here suggest that the relative impact of one's own behavior and the behavior of
others are moderated by cultural differences in individualism/collectivism.
Individualists tend to be more influenced by their own behavior relative to collectivists, whereas collectivists are more influenced by other people's behavior
relative to individualists, especially those exhibited by people who are close to
the target individual.

THEORETICAL IMPLICATIONS AND SUGGESTIONS FOR FUTURE RESEARCH

The fact that cultural differences in individualism/collectivism moderate the
impact of one's own behaviors and other people's behaviors underscores the
need for further research. We discuss herein five potentially fruitful avenues
for future investigation, including: (a) operationalizing the psychological factors presumed to mediate the relationships between culture and
attitudes/behaviors; (b) articulating the aspect of individualism/collectivism
that is most operative in a given situation; (c) distinguishing the impact of
individualism/collectivism from that attributable to other cultural dimensions;
(d) identifying moderating influences on the tendency for individualists to be
more affected by their own behaviors than collectivists; and (e) identifying
moderating influences on the tendency for collectivists to be more affected by
other people's behaviors than individualists.

Operationalizing the Psychological Mediator

Many studies examining cross-cultural differences are predicated on the
assumption that participants' culture (or nation) is a proxy for some psychological factor that influences their attitudes or behaviors. However, researchers
often fail to measure the relevant psychological factor. In many cross-nation
studies, researchers (e.g., Morris & Peng, 1994; Iyengar & Lepper, 1999) do
not assess the psychological factor presumed to account for their findings; that
is, psychological measures related to individualism/collectivism often are not
included in their studies.

It is important that future research include operationalizations of the psychological variables hypothesized to account for cross-nation differences (e.g., Cialdini et al., chap. 2, in this volume). To begin with, there is often considerable within-culture variability in the relevant dimensions: All people from Asia are not collectivistic—or *allocentric* in Triandis' (1995) terms—nor are all people from Western cultures individualistic—or *idiocentric* in Triandis' terms. By measuring the psychological factors, future researchers will be able to evaluate their underlying assumptions that the participants in their studies exhibit beliefs/values associated with their respective nations. More important, researchers will also be able to evaluate whether the psychological factors presumed to differ by nation actually account for observed differences between nations on the relevant dependent variables.

A recent study by Chen, Brockner, and Katz (1998) provided a demonstration of the procedure we advocate. The study was designed to examine conditions under which collectivists showed greater ingroup favoritism than individualists. Specifically, participants from the People's Republic of China (the collectivistic nation) and the United States (the individualistic nation) worked on a task and were given feedback about their individual performance. Half were told that they had performed well (individual success condition, whereas half were told they had performed poorly (individual failure condition). Cross-cutting the individual feedback induction was an orthogonal manipulation of ingroup performance. Half were told that their ingroup had performed well (ingroup success condition), whereas half were told that their ingroup had performed poorly (ingroup failure condition). A three-factor analysis of variance (ANOVA; nation x individual feedback x group feedback) yielded a significant triple interaction effect. The only condition to produce a cultural difference in ingroup favoritism was the individual success/ingroup failure condition, in which participants from the People's Republic of China showed greater ingroup favoritism than did those from the United States.

Additionally, participants also completed self-report measures tapping their individualistic versus collectivistic beliefs. When people were classified as individualistic (I) or collectivistic (C) based on their beliefs (rather than the nation from which they came), a triple interaction among I/C beliefs, individual feedback, and group feedback also emerged. The form of the interaction revealed that it was only in the individual success/group failure feedback condition that participants with relatively collectivistic beliefs showed greater ingroup favoritism than those with more individualistic beliefs.

To evaluate whether the effect of nation was mediated by people's I/C beliefs, an additional regression analysis was conducted in which both triple interaction effects (nation x individual feedback x group feedback and I/C beliefs x individual feedback x group feedback) were entered simultaneously into the equation. The results show that the triple interaction involving nation no longer was significant, whereas the triple interaction involving I/C beliefs remained significant.

Thus, the pattern of findings observed by Chen et al. (1998) suggests that it was participants' I/C beliefs that accounted for the observed differences between cultures in participants' ingroup favoritism.

Delineating the Germane Aspect of Individualism/Collectivism

A second mandate for future research stems from the multifaceted nature of individualism/collectivism. Markus and Kitayama (1991) and Triandis (1995) have noted that the construct actually consists of a number of related but conceptually distinct dimensions, including individual–collective primacy (i.e., whether people put more emphasis on their individual versus their social ingroup's interests, especially when the two are in conflict), independent versus interdependent self-construal (whether people define themselves based on their distinctiveness from others or their connectedness to others), self-reliance, and sociability, to name just a few. It is likely that certain aspects of I/C beliefs are more significant in some situations than in others.

To illustrate this point, consider again the study by Chen et al. (1998). In their study, participants completed multiple measures of I/C beliefs, including Triandis' (1995) scale of horizontal and vertical individualism and collectivism, Singelis' (1994) measure of interdependent self-construal, and a shortened version of the Triandis et al. (1986) idiocentrism–allocentrism scale (previously used by Brockner & Chen, 1996). When participants were classified on the basis of preexisting categories based on the survey instruments, no mediating effects of I/C beliefs on the impact of nation were observed.

In fact, the Chen et al. conceptualization suggested that it was the participants' I/C primacy beliefs in particular that should have a moderating influence on their reactions to personal and ingroup feedback. Accordingly, the authors selected those items from the previously existing scales that seemed to most closely correspond to the notion of individual-collective primacy (e.g., "I usually sacrifice my self-interests for the benefit of the group I am in" and "I will stay in a group if they need me, even if I am not happy"). The results show that it was only participants' responses to the items tapping I/C primacy that accounted for the relationship between culture and ingroup favoritism.

Furthermore, there were substantial differences between participants from the two nations in their responses to the previously existing scales. For example, participants from the People's Republic of China had significantly greater levels of interdependent self-construal (Singelis, 1994) than those from the United States. However, responses to the previously existing scales did not explain the relationship between nation and ingroup favoritism. In other words, even if one were to find national differences on certain dimensions, it is still necessary to evaluate whether differences between nations along these dimensions actually account for differences between nations on the main dependent variables.

Distinguishing the Impact of Individualism/Collectivism From Other Constructs

Our third recommendation for future research pertains to distinguishing the mediating effects of individualism/collectivism beliefs from other factors that may differ between nations. Consider, for example, Hofstede's (1980) notion of power distance, which refers to the extent to which people perceive differences between persons in their level of formal authority to be a natural and even desirable aspect of the social order. In high power distance nations, people with less formal authority believe that it is appropriate and useful to make clear distinctions between those who have authority versus those who do not. The opposite is found in low power distance nations, in which people share in the power maintained by those in high-authority positions. Although power distance is conceptually distinct from I/C beliefs, the two tend to be empirically related to a modest degree. Collectivists tend to have high power distance beliefs, whereas individualists generally have low power distance beliefs. Just as we recommend that future research include measures of I/C beliefs (to evaluate whether such beliefs account for the relationship between the nation from which people come and their responses to the primary dependent variables), so too is it important to measure other psychological factors showing between-nation differences. This is done to evaluate whether these factors provide an alternative explanation of observed relationships between participants' nation and their responses to the primary dependent variables.

When Are Individualists Influenced by Their Own Behavior?

One of our primary assertions is that the attitudes of people from individualistic cultures are more likely to be influenced in the direction of espoused behaviors, relative to collectivists'. Moreover, we have asserted that cultural differences in the tendency for attitudes to become aligned with actions are especially pronounced for behaviors enacted with perceived choice (Iyengar & Lepper, 1999). Choice was one of several contextual factors identified by Kiesler (1971) and Cialdini (1993) as moderators of the influence of behavior on subsequent attitudes. Others include publicity, effortfulness, and irrevocability. The common principle underlying the hypothesized moderating influence of the various contextual factors is *retrospective rationality* (Salancik, 1977). When people see themselves performing behaviors that are volitional, public, irrevocable, or effortful, they are likely to infer in retrospect that they truly believe in those behaviors.

Although contextual factors other than choice have been hypothesized to moderate the impact of people's behaviors on their attitudes, social psychologists have devoted far more attention to the choice factor than all others combined.

Perhaps the tendency to focus on choice—a concept linked to individual free-dom—is the product of an individualistic orientation on the part of Western social psychologists. Similarly, the handful of studies that have examined how cultural variables moderate the impact of people's behavior on their attitudes have also focused on the choice factor (Iyengar & Lepper, 1999). Yet it is impor-tant for future researchers to evaluate whether the observed tendency for indi-vidualists to be more influenced than collectivists by behaviors enacted volition-ally also would apply to behaviors enacted publicly, irrevocably, and effortfully. In other words, is there something unique to high-choice conditions that cause the attitudes of individualists to be more influenced by their behaviors relative to collectivists? Or are Iyengar and Lepper's (1999) findings part of a more gener-al phenomenon in which the conditions hypothesized to moderate the impact of people's behavior on their attitudes (e.g., publicity) are more applicable to those from individualistic than collectivistic cultures?

When Are Collectivists Influenced by Other People's Behavior?

Just as it is important to identify moderating influences on the tendency for indi-vidualists to be more swayed by their behavior, so too is it important to delineate the conditions under which collectivists are more affected by other people's atti-tudes and behaviors. Previous theory and research suggest that the closeness of the relationship between the target person and the other parties moderate the influence of the latter on the former. To be a collectivist does not mean that the person feels highly connected to other people and groups in general. Rather, col-lectivists feel more of a bond with, and therefore are more likely to be influenced by, others who are members of their ingroup (Markus & Kitayama, 1991). Indeed, it appears that collectivists generally make more of a psychological dis-tinction than do individualists between others deemed to be members of their ingroup versus those perceived to be in their outgroup.

One implication of these findings is that the tendency for collec-tivistic participants to be more influenced than individualists in the Asch (1952) conformity paradigm should be more pronounced when the others are ingroup members. Bond and Smith (1996) offered a similar prediction in their meta-analytic review, but to date this worthwhile hypothesis has not been tested.

APPLIED IMPLICATIONS

The findings of the Iyengar and Lepper (1999) studies are also of considerable practical significance. As in previous research (Cordova & Lepper, 1996; Lepper & Cordova, 1992), the findings suggest that seemingly trivial manipulations of instructionally incidental features of an educational activity may produce power-ful differences in student motivation and learning. Considerable research shows that students permitted to make actual choices involving instructionally central decisions often make dysfunctional decisions that can interfere with learning (Lepper & Malone, 1987; Steinberg, 1989, 1991). Thus, it is significant that many of the substantial benefits of choice may be obtained by offering choices along instructionally irrelevant dimensions without the attendant risk that students may inadvertently sabotage their own learning. Such findings may be of particular value in the development of teaching strategies or the design of educational software, in which the choices may be offered to students to maximize learning, especially across diverse student populations (Lepper, Woolverton, Mumme, & Gurtner, 1993; Malone & Lepper, 1987).

Similarly, the findings from the Iyengar and Lepper (1999) studies may be helpful in understanding issues related to worker motivation and performance in culturally diverse organizations and globalized corporations. Organizational psychologists have long been interested in the effects of employees' self-determination at work on their productivity and morale. Self-determination is inherent in such concepts as participatory management, empowerment, and the high-involvement workplace (e.g., Vroom & Jago, 1988). The Iyengar and Lepper (1999) findings suggest that, in individualistic cultures, employees' motivation (particularly intrinsic motivation) may well be enhanced by giving them greater control, choice, and decision-making authority. The same types of self-determination may be less apt to have similarly enhancing effects on people from collectivistic cultures. This is not to say that employees in collectivistic cultures never appreciate self-determination at work. It just may be that they prefer different forms of self-determination relative to their individualistic counterparts. Perhaps a form of self-determination in which collectivists participate along with ingroup members—in which they perceive that *we* participated, rather than *I* participated—would have positive effects on the productivity and morale of employees from collectivistic cultures.

Several studies suggest that, although American employees tend to prefer individualized goals, collectivistic employees tend to perform better when engaged with group goals (e.g., Chatman & Barsade, 1995; Earley, 1989, 1993, 1994). In short, cultural differences in the preference for choice may also have significant motivational and performance consequences in organizations.

CONCLUDING COMMENT

A long-standing debate in social psychology centers on the relative importance of personal versus situational factors as determinants of people's beliefs and behaviors (e.g., Mischel, 1968). More recently, the debate has taken a different and, we believe, more productive approach, in which the goal is to identify the conditions under which personal versus situational variables are more influential.

Our analysis is consistent with this latter approach to the person–situation debate. Situational factors (most notably, the behaviors of other people) appear to be particularly significant among collectivists, whereas personal variables (most notably, one's own behaviors) are especially influential among individualists.

REFERENCES

Aronson, E. (1992). The return of the repressed: Dissonance theory makes a comeback. *Psychological Inquiry, 3*, 303–311.

Asch, S. E. (1952). Effects of group pressure on the modification and distortion of judgments. In G. E. Swanson, T. M. Newcomb, & E. L. Hartley (Eds.), *Readings in social psychology* (2nd ed., pp. 2–11). New York: Holt.

Asch, S. E. (1955). Opinions and social pressure. *Scientific American, 193*, 33–35.

Bem, D. J. (1972). Self-perception theory. In L. Berkowitz (Ed.), *Advances in experimental social psychology* (Vol. 6, pp. 1–62). New York: Academic Press.

Bem, D. J., & McConnell, H. K. (1970). Testing the self-perception explanation of the dissonance phenomena: On the salience of premanipulation attitudes. *Journal of Personality and Social Psychology, 14*, 23–31.

Bond, R., & Smith, P. B. (1996). Culture and conformity: A meta-analysis of studies using Asch's (1952, 1956) line judgment task. *Psychological Bulletin, 119*, 111–137.

Brockner, J., & Chen, Y. (1996). The moderating effects of self-esteem and self-construal in reaction to a threat to the self: Evidence from the People's Republic of China and the United States. *Journal of Personality and Social Psychology, 71*, 603–615.

Chatman, J. A., & Barsade, S. G. (1995). Personality, organizational culture, and cooperation: Evidence from a business simulation. *Administrative Science Quarterly, 40*, 423–443.

Chen, Y., Brockner, J., & Katz, T. (1998). Towards an explanation of cultural differences in ingroup favoritism: The role of individual vs. collective primacy. *Journal of Personality and Social Psychology, 75*, 1490–1502.

Cialdini, R. B. (1993). *Influence: Science and practice* (3rd ed.). New York: HarperCollins.

Collins, B. E., & Hoyt, M. G. (1972). Personal responsibility for consequences: An integration and extension of the "forced compliance" literature. *Journal of Experimental Social Psychology, 8*, 558–593.

Cooper, J., & Fazio, R. H. (1984). A new look at dissonance theory. In L. Berkowitz (Ed.), *Advances in experimental social psychology* (Vol. 17, pp. 229–266). Orlando, FL: Academic Press.

Cordova, D. I., & Lepper, M. R. (1996). Intrinsic motivation and the process of learning: Beneficial effects of contextualization, personalization, and choice. *Journal of Educational Psychology, 88*, 715–730.

Deci, E. L. (1975). *Intrinsic motivation.* New York: Plenum.

Deci, E. L. (1981). *The psychology of self-determination.* Lexington, MA: Heath.

Deci, E. L., & Ryan, R. M. (1985). *Intrinsic motivation and self-determination in human behavior.* New York: Plenum.

De Vos, G. A. (1985). Dimensions of the self in Japanese culture. In A. J. Marsella, G. De Vos, & F. L. K. Hsu (Eds.), *Culture and self* (pp. 149–184). London: Tavistock.

Dillard, J. P. (1991). The current status of research on sequential-request compliance techniques. *Personality and Social Psychology Bulletin, 17*, 283–288.

Earley, P. C. (1989). Social loafing and collectivism: A comparison of the United States and the People's Republic of China. *Administrative Science Quarterly, 34*, 565–581.

Earley, P. C. (1993). East meets West meets Mideast: Further explorations of collectivistic and individualistic work groups. *Academy of Management Journal, 36*, 319–348.

Earley, P. C. (1994). Self or group? Cultural effects of training on self-efficacy and performance. *Administrative Science Quarterly, 39*, 89–117.

Festinger, L. (1954). A theory of social comparison processes. *Human Relations, 7*, 117–140.

Festinger, L. (1957). *A theory of cognitive dissonance.* Stanford, CA: Stanford University Press.

Freedman, J. L., & Fraser, S. C. (1966). Compliance without pressure: The foot-in-the-door technique. *Journal of Personality and Social Psychology, 4*, 195–202.

Freedman, J. L., & Steinbruner, J. D. (1964). Perceived choice and resistance to persuasion. *Journal of Abnormal and Social Psychology, 68*, 678–681.

Gerard, H. B. (1968). Basic features of commitment. In R. P. Abelson et al. (Eds.), *Theories of cognitive consistency: A sourcebook* (pp. 456–463). Chicago: McNally.

Goethals, G. R., & Cooper, J. (1972). The role of intention and postbehavioral consequences in the arousal of cognitive dissonance. *Journal of Personality and Social Psychology, 3*, 293–301.

Hofstede, G. (1980). *Culture's consequences: International differences in work-related values.* Beverly Hills, CA: Sage.

Hovland, C. I., Campbell, D. H., & Brock, T. C. (1957). The effects of "commitment"on opinion change following communication. In C. I. Hovland et al. (Eds.), *The order of presentation in persuasion* (pp. 23–32). New Haven, CT: Yale University Press.

Hsu, F. L. K. (1985). The self in cross-cultural perspective. In A. J. Marsella, G.

De Vos, & F. L. K. Hsu (Eds.), *Culture and self* (pp. 24–55). London: Tavistock.

Iyengar, S. S., & Lepper, M. R. (1999). Rethinking the value of choice: A cultural perspective on intrinsic motivation. *Journal of Personality and Social Psychology, 76,* 349–366.

Iyengar, S. S., Lepper, M. R., & Ross, L. (1999). Independence from whom? Interdependence with whom? A cultural perspective on ingroups and outgroups. In D. Prentice & D. Miller (Eds.), *Cultural divides.* New York: Sage.

Jones, E. E., & Harris, V. A. (1967). The attribution of attitudes. *Journal of Experimental Social Psychology, 3,* 2–24.

Kiesler, C. (1971). *The psychology of commitment: Experiments linking behavior to belief.* New York: Academic Press.

Langer, E. J., & Rodin, J. (1977). The effects of choice and enhanced personal responsibility for the aged: A field experiment in an institutional setting. *Journal of Personality and Social Psychology, 34,* 191–198.

Lefcourt, H. M. (1973). The function of the illusions of control and freedom. *American Psychologist, 28,* 417–425.

Lepper, M. R., & Cordova, D. I. (1992). A desire to be taught: Instructional consequences of intrinsic motivation. *Motivation and Emotion, 16,* 1–22.

Lepper, M. R., & Malone, T. W. (1987). Intrinsic motivation and instructional effectiveness in computer-based education. In R. E. Snow & M. J. Farr (Eds.), *Aptitude, learning and instruction: Vol. 3. Cognitive and affective process analysis* (pp. 255–286). Hillsdale, NJ: Lawrence Erlbaum Associates.

Lepper, M. R., Woolverton, M., Mumme, D. L., & Gurtner, J. (1993). Motivational techniques of expert human tutors: Lessons for the design of computer-based tutors. In S. P. LaJoie & S. J. Derry (Eds.), *Computers as cognitive tools* (pp. 75–105). Hillsdale, NJ: Lawrence Erlbaum Associates.

Lewin, K. (1952). Group decision and social change. In G. E. Swanson, T. M. Newcomb, & E. L. Hartley (Eds.), *Readings in social psychology* (pp. 459–473). New York: Henry Holt.

Linder, D. E., Cooper, J., & Jones, E. E. (1967). Decision freedom as a determinant of the role of incentive magnitude in attitude change. *Journal of Personality and Social Psychology, 6,* 245–254.

Malone, T. W., & Lepper, M. R. (1987). Making learning fun: A taxonomy of intrinsic motivations for learning. In R. E. Snow & M. J. Farr (Eds.), *Aptitude, learning and instruction: Vol. 3. Cognitive and affective process analysis* (pp. 223–253). Hillsdale, NJ: Lawrence Erlbaum Associates.

Markus, H., & Kitayama, S. (1991). Culture and the self: Implications for cognition, emotion and motivation. *Psychological Review, 98,* 224–253.

Miller, J. G. (1988). Bridging the content-structure dichotomy: Culture and the self. In M. H. Bond (Ed.), *The cross-cultural challenge to social psychology* (pp. 266–281). Beverly Hills, CA: Sage.

Mischel, W. (1968). *Personality and assessment.* New York: Wiley.

Morris, M., & Peng, K. (1994). Culture and cause: American and Chinese attributions for social and physical events. *Journal of Personality and Social Psychology, 67,* 949–971.

Rotter, J. B. (1966). Generalized expectancies for internal versus external locus of control of reinforcement. *Psychological Monographs, 80,* 1–28.

Salancik, G. (1977). Commitment and the control of organizational behavior. In B. M. Staw & G. Salancik (Eds.), *New directions in organizational behavior* (pp. 1–27). Chicago: St. Clair Press.

Salancik, G., & Pfeffer, J. (1978). A social information processing approach to job attitudes and task design. *Administrative Science Quarterly, 23,* 224–253.

Sherif, C. W., Sherif, M., & Nebergall, R. E. (1965). *Attitude and attitude change.* Philadelphia: Saunders.

Sherman, S. J. (1970). Effects of choice and incentive on attitude change in a discrepant behavior situation. *Journal of Personality and Social Psychology, 15,* 245–252.

Shweder, R. A., & Bourne, E. J. (1984). Does the concept of the person vary cross-culturally? In R. A. Shweder & R. A. LeVine (Eds.), *Culture theory: Essays on mind, self, and emotion* (pp. 158-199). Cambridge, England: Cambridge University Press.

Singelis, T. M. (1994). The measurement of independent and interdependent self-construals. *Personality and Social Psychology Bulletin, 20,* 580–591.

Steinberg, E. R. (1989). Cognition and learner control: A literature review, 1977–1988. *Journal of Computer-Based Instruction, 16,* 117–121.

Steinberg, E. R. (1991). *Computer-assisted instruction.* Hillsdale, NJ: Lawrence Erlbaum Associates.

Taylor, S. E. (1989). *Positive illusions: Creative self-deception and the healthy mind.* New York: Basic Books.

Taylor, S. E., & Brown, J. D. (1988). Illusion and well-being: A social-psychological perspective on mental health. *Psychological Bulletin, 103,* 193–210.

Triandis, H. C. (1990). Cross-cultural studies of individualism and collectivism. In J. Berman (Ed.), *Nebraska symposium of motivation: Vol. 38. Perspectives in motivation* (pp. 41–133). Lincoln, NE: University of Nebraska Press.

Triandis, H. C. (1995). *Individualism and collectivism*. Boulder, CO: Westview.

Triandis, H. C., Bontempo, R., Betancourt, H., Bond, M., Leung, K., Brenes, A., Georgas, J., Hui, C. H., Marin, G., Setiadi, B., Sinha, J. B. P., Verma, J., Spangenberg, J., Touzard, H., & de Monmollin, G. (1986). The measurement of etic aspects of individualism and collectivism across cultures. *Australian Journal of Psychology, 38*, 257–267.

Vroom, V. H., & Jago, A. G. (1988). *The new leadership: Managing participation in organizations*. Englewood Cliffs, NJ: Prentice-Hall.

Zimbardo, P. G., Weisenberg, M., Firestone, I., & Levy, M. (1965). Communicator effectiveness in producing public conformity and private attitude change. *Journal of Personality, 33*, 233–255.

Zuckerman, M., Porac, J., Lathin, D., Smith, R., & Deci, E. L. (1978). On the importance of self-determination for intrinsically motivated behavior. *Personality and Social Psychology Bulletin, 4*, 443–446.

2

The Differential Impact of Two Social Influence Principles on Individualists and Collectivists in Poland and the United States

Robert B. Cialdini

Wilhelmina Wosinska

Daniel W. Barrett

Jonathan Butner

Arizona State University

Malgorzata Gornik-Durose

University of Silesia

ABSTRACT

Research examined the impact of two social influence principles (com-mitment/consistency and social proof) on U.S. and Polish residents' will-ingness to participate in a marketing survey. Both principles were effec-tive in both cultures. However, the commitment/consistency principle (wherein people are motivated to behave in ways consistent with their own past behavior) had a greater impact on Americans, whereas the social proof principle (wherein people are motivated to behave as impor-tant referent others behave) had a stronger effect on Poles. This pattern was attributable principally, but not entirely, to participants' personal individualistic/collectivistic orientation, rather than to the dominant indi-vidualistic/collectivistic orientation of their nations.

There can be little doubt that the influence process is a universal feature of human social experience. Many times a day, people of all cultures and groups are both the initiators and targets of attempts to influence perceptions, beliefs, attitudes, and behaviors. What is more, the influence process is not limited to any one arena of human social exchange: It is embedded in close personal relationships (e.g., among family and friends), political contexts (e.g., in election campaigns, international negotiations, government efforts at structural change within whole societies), commercial endeavors (e.g., as embodied in sales, marketing, and advertising appeals), and a multitude of other settings. As such, a thorough understanding of the workings of the social influence process would be of immense value to those who wish to create change in others as well as those wishing to block change.

One systematic attempt to understand the process of successful social influence was undertaken by Cialdini (1987, 1993), who examined the most prevalent and effective compliance-gaining strategies of influence professionals. Influence professionals are those individuals—such as salespeople—fundraisers, recruiters, lobbyists, and negotiators, whose economic welfare depends on the success of the influence tactics they employ. Adopting a survival-of-the-fittest-like logic, Cialdini argued that an informed understanding of the influence process could be developed, in part, by observing the regular influence practices of effective influence professionals. After a period of such observation, Cialdini listed a relatively small set of psychological principles that appeared to empower many of these practices—commitment/consistency, social proof, reciprocity, authority, scarcity, and liking. However, because he based his observations solely on U.S. samples, Cialdini's conclusions should be received with caution as to their generalizability to other cultures. Regrettably, such caution is appropriate for many of the conclusions derived from academic research into the influence process.

Indeed, most social psychological research on social influence has been conducted by North Americans on North Americans (Smith & Bond, 1998). Milgram's experiments on obedience to authority and Asch's conformity experiments, which have been replicated in many nations other than the United States, are notable exceptions (Bond & Smith, 1996; Furnham, 1984; Smith & Bond, 1998).

Similarly, the individualism/collectivism (I/C) dimension, the most studied cross-cultural variable in social psychological research in the last decade (e.g., Hofstede, 1980; Kim, Triandis, Kagitcibasi, Choi, & Yoon, 1994; Triandis, 1995), has been little examined for its effects on persuasion (Han & Shavitt, 1994). Bond and Smith's (1996) meta-analysis of conformity studies (using the Asch line judgment task in 17 countries) provided insight into the relationship between conformity and individualism/collectivism. However, it introduced individualism/collectivism as a mediator in a post facto manner, because the original researchers did not include this variable in their analyses.

The main purpose of the present research was to investigate the effect of individualistic versus collectivistic tendencies on the effectiveness of selected principles of social influence.[1] We begin by briefly describing some of the defining attributes of the I/C dimension. We then introduce two principles of social influence (social proof and commitment/consistency) that we hypothesize will be differentially affected by I/C orientation.

INDIVIDUALISM/COLLECTIVISM AS A CULTURAL AND PERSONAL DIMENSION

Individualism/collectivism is considered a core dimension of cultural variability (Han & Shavitt, 1994; Hofstede, 1980; Kim et al., 1994; Smith & Bond, 1998). Members of individualistic societies tend to define the self as autonomous and independent from groups, whereas in collectivistic societies the self is defined more in terms of group membership (Kim, 1994). Differences are also found in the relationship between personal goals and ingroup goals. On the one hand, personal goals tend to be distinct from and prioritized above ingroup goals in an individualistic society. On the other hand, in a collectivistic culture, personal goals and communal goals are more closely related and, when discrepant, the former are subordinated to the latter (Triandis, 1995, 1996). In individualistic nations, attitudes typically take precedence over norms as determinants of social behavior, whereas the opposite is true in collectivistic nations.

Although conceptualizations of I/C were initially applied at the level of nation or culture (Hofstede, 1980), these constructs can also be operationalized at the individual level and have been labeled *idiocentrism* and *allocentrism* (Triandis, Bontempo, Villareal, Asai, & Lucca, 1988; Triandis et al., 1993) or *independent* and *interdependent* construals of the self, respectively (Markus & Kitayama, 1991). Within either an individualistic or collectivistic society, people may differ from one another with regard to their personal I/C orientation. Thus, any investigation of individualism/collectivism should take into account both the dominant cultural orientation and the personal I/C orientation of research participants. Because nations demonstrate variability in their proportions of individualistic and collectivistic citizens, an interesting question arises, hinted at by Triandis, Leung, Villareal, and Clack (1985): Would an individualist in an individualistic culture (or a collectivist in a collectivistic culture) respond like an individualist in a collectivistic culture (or a collectivist in an individualistic culture)? That is, is I/C-based responding attributable entirely to the dominant cultural orientation of one's society or is there an additional, unique impact due to one's personal I/C orientation? The answer to this question, as it pertained to principles of successful social influence, was one focus of the present research project.

[1] A fuller description of this work is provided in Cialdini, Wosinska, Barrett, Butner, and Gornik-Durose (1999).

Compliance-gaining strategies may be categorized according to the underlying psychological principles through which they operate. Of the six fundamental psychological principles of social influence identified by Cialdini (1987, 1993), two seemed especially linked to collectivistic and individualistic motivations; social proof and commitment/consistency, respectively.

SOCIAL PROOF

According to the principle of social proof, one way individuals determine appropriate behavior for themselves in a situation is to examine the behavior of others there—especially similar others (Cialdini, 1993; Goethals & Darley, 1977; Miller, 1984). It is through social comparison with these referent others that people validate the correctness of their opinions and decisions (Festinger, 1954). Consequently, people tend to behave as their friends and peers have behaved.

Because the critical source of information within the principle of social proof is the responses of referent others, compliance tactics that employ this information should be especially effective in collectivistically oriented nations and persons. Some evidence in this regard comes from a study by Han and Shavitt (1994) showing that advertisements that promoted group benefits were more persuasive in Korea (a collectivistic society) than in the United States (an individualistic society). These data must be seen as only suggestive for our hypothesis, however, because the selected (and successful) advertisements in Korea encouraged purchases by pointing out the advantages to one's group of buying the advertised product rather than by pointing out that one's group had a history of buying it. It is this latter information that would directly reflect on our hypothesis. Regrettably, neither the Han and Shavitt study nor any other study of which we are aware has investigated the relative impact of purely social proof-based appeals across cultures or persons differing in individualistic/collectivistic orientation.

COMMITMENT/CONSISTENCY

Social psychologists have long considered the desire for consistency within one's attitudes, beliefs, and actions a central motivator of human conduct (Festinger, 1957; Heider, 1946, 1958; Newcomb, 1953). Most people prefer to be consistent with what they have already said and done. Thus, after committing themselves to a particular position—especially when the commitment is active, public, and freely chosen—people are more likely to behave in ways that are congruent with that position (Aronson, 1992; Cialdini, 1993). As a consequence, future behavior is likely to resemble past behavior because this past behavior occurred.

As opposed to the social proof principle (wherein motivating information comes from the prior responses of one's peers), within the commitment/consistency principle, the motivating information comes from one's own prior responses. Accordingly, the impact of social influence practices that embody the commitment/consistency principle should be especially strong in indvidualistically oriented cultures and individuals. That is, where the individualized self is both the focus and the standard, one's own behavioral history should be heavily weighted in subsequent behavior.

OVERVIEW AND PREDICTIONS

Our overall purpose was to investigate the differential effects of individualism and collectivism on compliance resulting from the principles of social proof (SP) and commitment/consistency (C/C) in a pair of cultures expected to differ in the I/C orientation (Poland and the United States). To do so, we inquired into the willingness of Polish and U.S. college students to participate in a 40-minute marketing survey. They did so while taking into account information about prior compliance with such requests of either their peers or themselves. Prior compliance was varied along a continuum ranging from *complete past compliance* to *no past compliance*.

Poland was selected for inclusion because, along with other Central and Eastern European nations, it has largely been ignored in previous cross-cultural research on individualism/collectivism. Yet despite popular belief that there has been a dramatic shift toward individualism in Poland, strong collectivistic elements have persisted (Reykowski, 1994, 1998). As this author has documented, an individualistic orientation has become more prevalent at the manifest level, whereas a collectivistic orientation predominates at a deeper level.

We had three main hypotheses. First, we expected that information about peers' prior compliance (SP) would affect participants' compliance levels more in the collectivistic nation of Poland than in the individualistic United States, whereas information about one's own prior compliance (C/C) would have the opposite effect, exerting more influence in the United States than in Poland. It is important to note that we did not expect that the principles would operate in an either–or fashion, with the influence of one excluding the influence of the other. Rather, we anticipated that both principles would be effective in both cultures, but that their relative impact would differ in the two countries.

Second, we expected that, within a culture, willingness to comply based on one's peers' (SP) or one's own (C/C) prior compliance would be determined by the participants' personal I/C orientation. That is, we predicted that collectivists in both countries would be more affected than individualists by peers' compliance histories, but that individualists in both countries would be more affected by their own histories. Unknown was the extent to which participants' willingness to comply would be accounted for by their personal I/C orientations versus the dominant I/C orientation of their nation. The lack of a clear prediction in this regard was due to our failure to locate prior systematic evidence on the question. However, our third hypothesis was that the majority of the I/C effect would be attributable to the personal dimension. This expectation was based on our view that even societal-level forces affect behavior through their influence on one's personal psychology. This third hypothesis can be seen as integrative of the first two in that it sets them in relation to one another.

METHOD

Participants

Five hundred and five undergraduates in several psychology classes at Arizona State University in the United States and at the University of Silesia in Poland participated in a study described as a twofold investigation into factors affecting (a) willingness to participate in a survey, and (b) perceptions of social relationships.

Procedure

After the study was introduced in class, each participant read the following scenario in his or her native language:

> Imagine that you are walking out of the student union at your university and that an individual approaches you. This person is a representative from the Coca Cola Company and asks you to participate in a survey. The representative explains that Coca Cola is studying consumer preferences for a particular brand of soft drink. You will be asked to answer a few questions about the product, taste a small amount of it, and answer more questions such as: How familiar are you with this brand of soft drink? Have you heard or seen advertisements for it? When was the last time you saw this brand at the store? And a variety of similar questions. The representative asks you to participate in the survey today, which will take approximately 40 minutes.

At the completion of the scenario, participants responded anonymously to a questionnaire that incorporated the major independent and dependent variables. All written materials were translated into Polish by a bilingual, native Polish speaker and were reviewed and validated by a second bilingual, native Polish speaker.

Independent Variables

Nation. Participants' nation of origin was varied by administering the experimental materials to native students in the United States and Poland.

Personal I/C Orientation. Participants' personal I/C orientation was measured by the Cultural Orientation Scale (COS) developed by Bierbrauer et al. (1994). Bierbrauer et al. (1994) reported a total Cronbach's alpha reliability of .86 for this scale. We opted for the COS because it was been validated as a measure of personal I/C orientation on European respondents. For the current study, the COS was utilized without modification (see Bierbrauer et al., 1994), and the overall measure of I/C orientation, which averages responses to all 26 items, was used.

Type of Social Influence Principle. Approximately half of the participants were instructed to rate their willingness to comply with the survey request while taking into account information about their peers' (SP) prior compliance with such survey requests and about half while considering information about their own (C/C) prior compliance with such survey requests.

Intensity of the Social Influence Principle. Participants in the SP condition indicated their willingness to comply with the survey request three times: once when considering that in the past all their classmates had complied with similar requests (high intensity), once when considering that about half had complied (moderate intensity), and once when considering that none had complied (low intensity). Similarly, participants in the C/C condition indicated their willingness to comply when considering that in the past they had always complied, had complied about half of the time, and had never complied with similar requests. Thus, the intensity variable was manipulated as a within-subjects factor.[2]

Dependent Variable

Willingness to Comply. Participants indicated their willingness to comply with the marketing survey request first on 9-point scales ranging from 0 (*no likelihood*) to 8 (*very high likelihood*). They did so three times—once for each level of the intensity factor.

RESULTS

A general linear model was used for all of the analyses.

---

[2]To ensure that the invariant presentation order of the intensity levels (from high to moderate to low) did not affect our results, we exposed a sample of 58 U.S. participants to a pair of alternate orders (low, moderate, high and moderate, high, low). When their compliance responses were compared to those of participants in our main study, no order effects approached significance.

Nation and Compliance

Our first hypothesis was that the effect of a manipulation of the SP principle would be stronger in Poland (a more collectivistic culture) than in the United States (a more individualistic culture), whereas the effect of a manipulation of the C/C principle would be stronger in the United States than in Poland.[3] This hypothesis was tested as a three-way interaction among the variables of nation, type of social influence principle, and intensity of the principle. That interaction proved significant [F (2, 1002) = 4.36, $p <$ .05]. The lower level, two-way interactions showed that, as predicted, the effect of the SP manipulation was stronger in Poland than in the United States [F (2, 428) = 3.48, $p <$ .05], and that the effect of the C/C manipulation was marginally stronger in the United States than in Poland [F (2, 574) = 2.31, $p =$ .12]. The analysis also revealed a highly significant main effect for intensity of the principle [F (1, 501) = 181.91, $p <$ .001]. An examination of the compliance data depicted in Figs. 1a and 1b shows that both principles had linear effects on compliance decisions in each nation. In all four comparisons (two nations, two conditions), the most compliance appeared at the highest level of principle intensity (in the all/always conditions), and the least compliance appeared at the lowest level of principle intensity (in the none/never conditions). All ps for these linear trend comparisons wer less than .001. None of the nonlinear trend effects approached significance (all Fs < 1). In summary, although both SP and C/C had a significant impact on compliance in both nations, their relative strengths differed such that SP was more effective in Poland than in the United States and C/C was more effective in the United States than in Poland.

[3]An analysis of COS data on Polish and U.S. participants confirmed that average COS scores were significantly higher (more collectivistic) in Poland (M = 92.61; SD = 8.07) than in the United States [M = 87.60; SD = 10.39, F (1, 494) = 36.54, $p <$ .001].

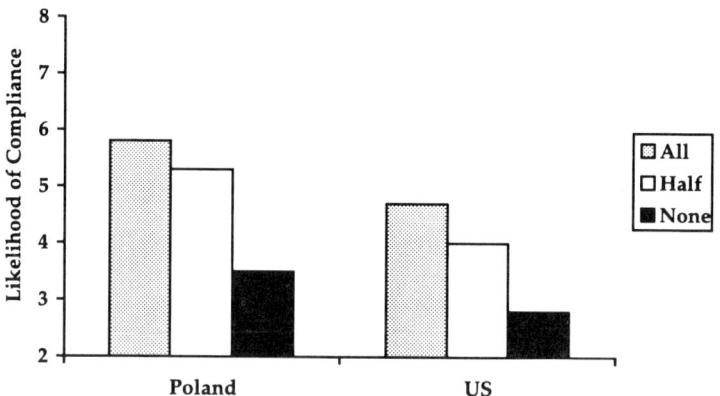

FIG. 2.1a. Effect of social proof on likelihood of compliance in Poland and the United States.

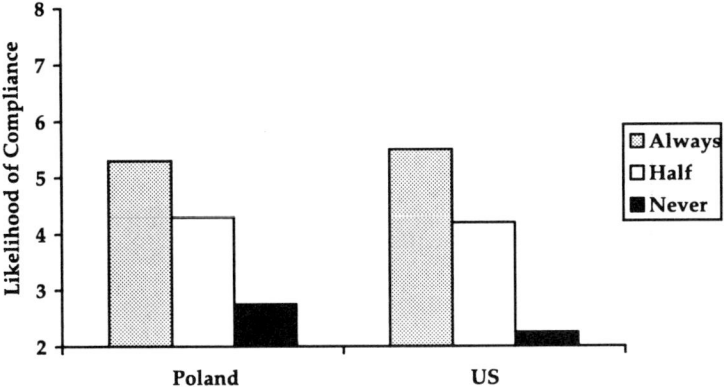

FIG. 2.1b. Effect of commitment/consistency on likelihood of compliance in Poland and the United States.

Individualism/Collectivism and Compliance

Our second and third hypotheses were that, across cultures, participants' willingness to comply on the basis of SP versus C/C information would be affected by their personal I/C orientations and that the effect of personal I/C orientation would account for the majority of the effect observed for national I/C orientation. To test these hypotheses, we included personal I/C orientation (as measured by COS score) in the general linear model along with nation, type of social influence principle, and intensity of the principle. We found, in support of our third hypothesis, that nation no longer predicted compliance; indeed, no main effect or interaction involving nation remained significant once personal I/C was included in the model. Instead, the three-way interaction that had included nation was replaced by a three-way interaction that included personal I/C score [F (2, 976) = 4.64, p < .05]. The three-way interaction was composed of a pair of two-way interactions, both of which were consistent with our second hypothesis. First, collectivists were more likely to make their decisions to comply on the basis of SP principle intensity than were individualists [F (2, 420) = 6.62, p < .01]. Second, individualists were marginally more likely to make their own decisions to comply on the basis of C/C principle intensity than were collectivists [F (2, 564) = 2.07, p = .14]. These interaction patterns are presented in Figs. 2a and 2b.

The marginal character of the interaction between personal I/C orientation and C/C principle intensity spurred us to look separately at the form of the interaction among Polish and American participants. The interaction pattern was close to conventional significance and as predicted in the United States, in that individualists were more affected by information concerning their own past compliance than were collectivists [F (2, 226) = 2.82, p = .08].

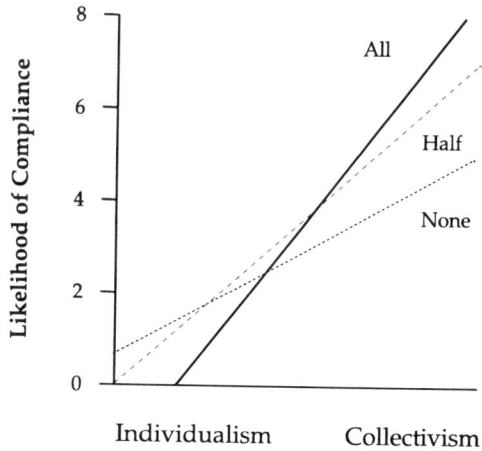

FIG. 2.2a. Effect of social proof and individualism/collectivism on likelihood of compliance.

In Poland, however, the interaction did not approach significance [F (2, 334) < 1]. Instead, there was only a significant main effect for I/C orientation [F (1, 167) = 4.48, $p < .05$], such that collectivists were more likely to comply than individualists. To explore whether comparable national differences occurred within the SP condition data, we examined the personal I/C orientation by SP intensity interactions in Poland and the United States. Both interaction patterns were similar and as predicted, with information regarding the compliance his-

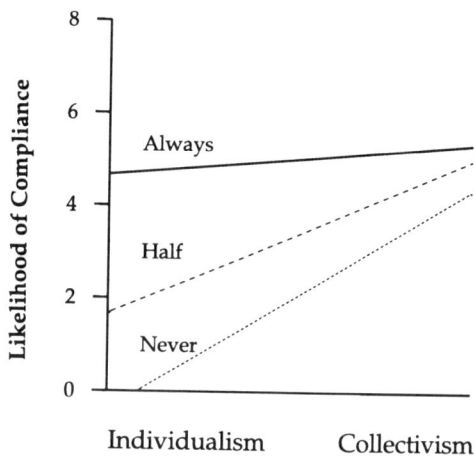

FIG. 2.2b. Effect of commitment/consistency and individualism/collectivism on likelihood of compliance

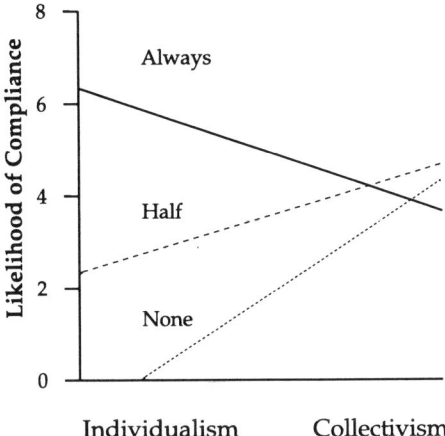

FIG. 2.3a. Effect of commitment/consistency and I/C on likelihood of compliance in the United States.

tory of one's group having more of an impact on collectivists' than individualists' compliance decisions in the United States [F (2, 220) = 3.43, p < .05], and in Poland [F (2, 196) = 3.33, p < .06]. The patterns for all four of the interactions are presented in Figs. 3a, 3b, 3c, and 3d.

In summary, for the most part, the relationships between personal I/C orientation and the two influence principles appeared as anticipated: Compared with individualists, collectivists' compliance decisions were more affected by the

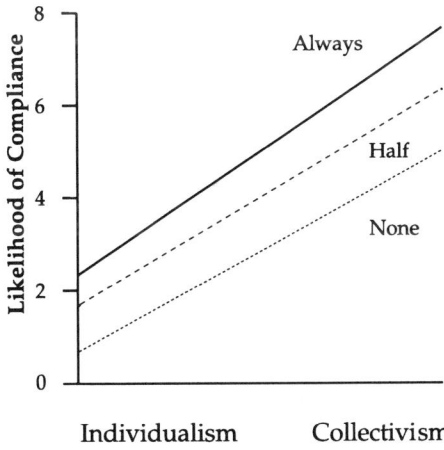

FIG. 2.3b. Effect of commitment/consistency and I/C on likelihood of compliance in the Poland.

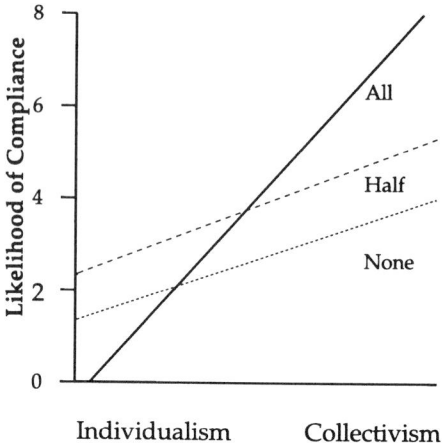

FIG. 2.3c. Effect of social proof and I/C on likelihood of compliance in the United States.

compliance histories of their peers, and this was the case in both the United States and Poland. In contrast, compared with collectivists, individualists' compliance decisions were more affected by their own compliance histories, unexpectedly, this was only the case in the United States.

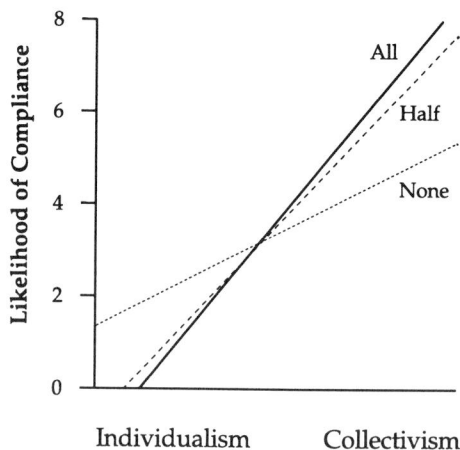

FIG. 2.3d. Effect of social proof and I/C on likelihood of compliance in Poland.

Investigation of a Puzzling Result

Overall, there was a main effect of collectivism on compliance such that collectivists tended to comply more than individualists [F (1, 488) = 15.18, p < .001]. As hypothesized, in the SP conditions, collectivists tended to comply more than individualists in both the all/always and half conditions. This was expected, because collectivists should naturally be more responsive to evidence of peers' prior compliance than individualists. However, it was surprising that, in the none condition for SP, in which participants learned that none of their classmates had agreed to participate in previous similar surveys, collectivists still complied more than individualists [F (1, 492) = 6.38, p < .05].

One possible explanation for this anomaly is that, because of their orientation toward social interdependency (Triandis et al., 1988), collectivists may possess a stronger social responsibility norm than individualists. According to this norm, people should give aid to those who are dependent on them for it (Berkowitz, 1972) or compensate for those who are less efficient or less able (Smith & Bond, 1998). That is, they should assume the responsibility for helping others, especially when no one else has agreed to help. If collectivists feel more social responsibility than individualists, perhaps they were more willing to comply in the none condition of our study precisely because no one else had been willing to help the survey requester. This left them with the social responsibility for helping. To test our hypothesis, we conducted a follow-up investigation that was designed to examine the possibility that collectivists' willingness to comply in the none condition occurred, in part, out of a desire to be socially responsible by helping when no one else had been willing to help.

The sample for our follow-up investigation consisted of 73 male and female undergraduates from Arizona State University who were exposed to the same experimental materials as participants in the original SP intensity conditions of our study with one exception: The original SP intensity condition materials varied the proportion of classmates who had participated in previous similar surveys, whereas the materials of the modified SP intensity conditions varied the proportion of classmates who indicated that they liked participating in such surveys. Participants were asked to consider that, after several classmates participated in similar types of surveys in the past, each of them, about half of them, or not one of them said that they liked participating in the surveys. In this way, with the amount of prior helping held constant, participants could respond more directly to information about the reactions of similar others.

Our hypothesis was tested through a comparison of trends between the two types of SP information in the all, half, and none conditions. Although the trends for the all and half conditions did not differ between the two kinds of SP information [F all (1, 187) = .8, ns; F half (1, 187) = 2.17, p = .14], they did differ for the none condition [F none (1, 187) = 25.13, p < .001], such that collectivists were no longer more willing to comply than

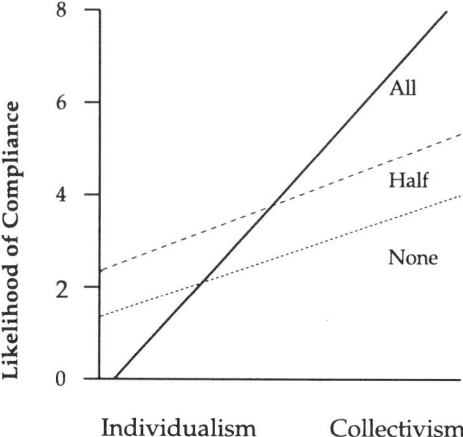

FIG. 2.4a. Compliance based on information about others' compliance.

individualists. Figures 4a and 4b present the form of these effects. Thus, when participants were exposed to social comparison information that did not imply differences in the amount of helping still needed, this unconfounded information guided their responding commensurately.

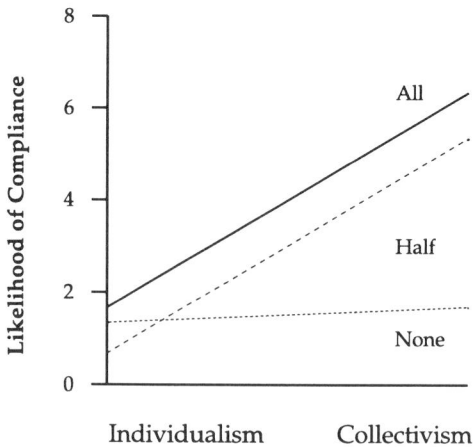

FIG. 2.4b. Compliance based on whether others liked their own experience of compliance.

DISCUSSION

Several insights emerge from the results of this research. First, information about one's own and one's peers' histories of compliance had powerful effects on future willingness to comply with a related request in Poland and the United States. Thus, the principles of social proof and commitment/consistency appear to be important determinants of compliance decisions in each society. Nonetheless, the decisional weight assigned to these two kinds of information differed depending on the participants' nationality. Evidence of what one had done in the past was relatively more impactful in the United States than in Poland, whereas evidence of what one's peers had done was relatively more impactful in Poland than in the United States. This pattern can be understood in terms of the greater tendencies toward individualism in the United States and toward collectivism in Poland.

Indeed, when participants' personal individualism/collectivism scores were included in the data analysis, all statistical differences in compliance patterns between the two nations were eliminated. Thus, the majority of the I/C-based effect on our compliance data can be attributed to participants' personal I/C orientations rather than to the dominant I/C traditions of their respective nations. In general, irrespective of nationality, collectivists were more influenced by their peers' compliance histories and individualists were more influenced by their own compliance histories in deciding how to respond to a new compliance opportunity. A close analysis of the data revealed one exception to this general conclusion, however. Unlike their U.S. counterparts, Polish individualists and collectivists were not differentially influenced by information about their prior compliance decisions.

Why should this be? Although our study provided no data directly relevant to this question, we can offer a speculation based on prior research. An examination of Fig. 3b indicates that the data pattern of the Polish participants differed from that of U.S. participants (and from prediction) primarily because Polish individualists did not base their compliance estimates on their compliance histories. This may have been the case because, in a collectivistic society, how one has behaved in the past may not be an accurate reflection of one's own preferences. Because of strong pressures to conform to group norms and foster group goals, even individualistic members of collectivistic societies may have frequently failed to act in accord with their personal norms and goals (Triandis, 1995, 1996). Hence, they may not see a strong correlation between their prior actions and personal predilections.

Thus, individualists may not have been highly informative as to what they would decide when asked to comply under little group pressure, as in our study. Regardless of whether our speculation is correct, future research should examine this intriguing feature of our data, because it suggests that I/C-based behavior is best understood as a joint function of cultural and personal I/C orientations.

PRACTICAL IMPLICATIONS

The clearest practical implication of our results may be derived from the fact that individualists and collectivists are likely to be differentially responsive to influence attempts that engage the principles of commitment/consistency and social proof. Thus, advertisements, marketing strategies, sales appeals, and even propaganda efforts are more likely to succeed in individualistically oriented societies (e.g., the United States, United Kingdom, Canada, Western Europe) by linking a recommended action to the relevant histories, private attitudes, and personal values of individual audience members. In contrast, influence attempts that link a recommended action to group histories, norms, and values are more likely to succeed in more communal societies. Of course, as our findings indicate, these receptivities will not apply to all members of a national group. Even within highly individualistic and collectivistic societies, there will exist members whose personal orientation runs counter to the predominant cultural orientation. The wise agent of influence, then, must recognize this complexity and tailor messages to the likely personal I/C orientation of particular influence targets.

REFERENCES

Aronson, E. (1992). The return of the repressed: Dissonance theory makes a comeback. *Psychological Inquiry, 3*, 303–311.

Berkowitz, L. (1972). Social norms, feelings, and other factors affecting helping behavior and altruism. In L. Berkowitz (Ed.), *Advances in experimental social psychology* (Vol. 6, pp. 66–108). New York: Academic Press.

Bierbrauer, G., Meyer, H., & Wolfradt, U. (1994). Measurement of normative and evaluative aspects in individualistic and collectivistic orientations: The cultural orientation scale (COS). In U. Kim, H. Triandis, C. Kagitcibasi., S. Choi, & G. Yoon, (Eds.), *Individualism and collectivism: Theory, method, and applications* (pp. 189–194). Thousand Oaks, CA: Sage.

Bond, R., & Smith, P. B. (1996). Culture and conformity: A meta-analysis of studies using Asch's (1952b, 1956) line judgment task. *Psychological Bulletin, 119*, 111–137.

Bontempo, R., Lobel, S., & Triandis, H. (1990). Compliance and value internalization in Brazil and the United States: Effects of allocentrism and anonymity. *Journal of Cross-Cultural Psychology, 21*, 200–213.

Cialdini, R. B. (1987). Compliance principles of compliance professionals: Psychologists of necessity. In M. P. Zanna, J. M. Olson, & C. P. Herman (Eds.), *Social influence: The Ontario Symposium* (Vol. 5, pp. 165–184). Hillsdale, NJ: Lawrence Erlbaum Associates.

Cialdini, R. B. (1993). *Influence: Science and practice* (3rd ed.). New York: HarperCollins.

Cialdini, R. B., Wosinska, W., Barrett, D. W., Butner, J., & Gornik-Durose, M. (1999). Compliance with a request in two cultures: The differential influence of social proof and commitment/consistency on collectivists and individualists. *Personality and Social Psychology Bulletin, 25,* 1242–1253.

Festinger, L. (1954). A theory of social comparison processes. *Human Relations, 7,* 117–140.

Festinger, L. (1957). *A theory of cognitive dissonance.* Stanford: Stanford University Press.

Furnham, A. (1984). Studies of cross-cultural conformity: A brief and critical review. *Psychologia, 27,* 65–72.

Goethals, G. R., & Darley, J. M. (1977). Social comparison theory: An attributional approach. In J. M. Suls & R. L. Miller (Eds.), Social comparison processes: *Theoretical and empirical perspectives,* (pp. 259–278). Washington, DC: Hemisphere/Halsted.

Han, S., & Shavitt, S. (1994). Persuasion and culture: Advertising appeals in individualistic and collectivistic societies. *Journal of Experimental Social Psychology, 30,* 326–350.

Heider, F. (1946). Attitudes and cognitive organization. *Journal of Psychology, 21,* 107–112.

Heider, F. (1958). *The psychology of interpersonal relations.* New York: Wiley.

Hofstede, G. (1980). *Culture's consequences: International differences in work-related values* (Abridged ed.). Beverly Hills, CA: Sage.

Kim, U. (1994). Individualism and collectivism: Conceptual clarification and elaboration. In U. Kim, H. Triandis, C. Kagitcibasi., S. Choi, & G. Yoon, (Eds.), *Individualism and collectivism: Theory, method, and applications* (pp. 189–194). Thousand Oaks, CA: Sage.

Kim, U., Triandis, H. C., Kagitcibasi, C., Choi, S.-C., & Yoon, G. (Eds.).(1994). *Individualism and collectivism: Theory, method, and applications.* Thousand Oaks, CA: Sage.

Markus, H., & Kitayama, S. (1991). Culture and the self: Implications for cognition, emotion and motivation. *Psychological Review, 98,* 224–253.

Miller, J. (1984). Culture and the development of everyday social explanation. *Journal of Personality and Social Psychology, 46,* 961–978.

Newcomb, T. M. (1953). An approach to the study of communicative acts. *Psychological Review, 60,* 393–404.

Reykowski, J. (1994). Collectivism and individualism as dimensions of social change. In U. Kim, H. Triandis, C. Kagitcibasi., S. Choi, & G. Yoon, (Eds.), *Individualism and collectivism: Theory, method, and applications* (pp. 276–292). Thousand Oaks, CA: Sage.

Reykowski, J. (1998). Belief systems and collective action: Changes in Poland from the psychological perspective. *Applied Psychology: An International Review, 47,* 89–108.

Smith, P. B., & Bond, M. H. (1998). *Social psychology across cultures: Analysis and perspectives*. Needham Heights, MA: Allyn & Bacon.

Triandis, H. C. (1995). *Individualism and collectivism*. Boulder, CO: Westview.

Triandis, H. C. (1996). The psychological measurement of cultural syndromes. *American Psychologist, 51*, 407–415.

Triandis, H. C., Bontempo, R., Villareal, M. J., Asai, M., & Lucca, N. (1988). Individualism and collectivism: Cross-cultural perspectives on self-ingroup relationships. *Journal of Personality and Social Psychology, 54*, 232–328.

Triandis, H. C., Leung, K., Villareal, M. J., & Clack, F. L. (1985). Allocentric versus idiocentric tendencies: Convergent and discriminant validation. *Journal of Research in Personality, 19*, 395–415.

Triandis, H. C., McCusker, C., Betancourt, H., Iwao, S., Leung, K., Salazar, J. M., Setiadi, B., Sinha, J. B. P., Touzard, H., & Zaleski, Z. (1993). An etic-emic analysis of individualism and collectivism. *Journal of Cross-Cultural Psychology, 24*, 366–383.

3

Self-Prophecy as a Behavior Modification Technique in the United States

Eric R. Spangenberg
Washington State University
Anthony G. Greenwald
University of Washington

ABSTRACT

The self-prophecy effect consists merely of a request to predict one's own behavior in a possible future situation, resulting in a change in the performance of that future behavior. Among other applications, self-prophecy has been used successfully in the United States. to increase the probability of voting, to reduce classroom cheating, and to increase adherence to long-term physical exercise. This chapter reviews all known research on the self-prophecy effect. Significant challenges remain in finding a theoretical interpretation that will describe the common ingredient of the class of techniques and identification of the limiting conditions for the effect's occurrence. Toward this end, self-prophecy is discussed within the contexts of objective self-awareness (e.g., Duval & Wickland, 1972) and Aronson's (1992) recent interpretation of cognitive dissonance—the basis of a new class of findings labeled induced hypocrisy *with effects strikingly similar to those of self-prophecy. The chapter ends by discussing some practical implications of these findings in the context of cultural variability.*

Although the act of making a prediction about one's own behavior seems itself benign, several researchers have shown in multiple contexts that predicting one's own behavior can induce subsequent action consistent with the prediction, yet different than would otherwise have been observed (see Spangenberg & Greenwald, 1999, for a review). In other words, the prediction becomes a self-fulfilling prophecy. This self-prophecy effect gives rise to a straightforward influence strategy, as Greenwald, Carnot, Beach, and Young (1987) stated: "The influence technique is remarkably simple: It involves asking people to predict whether they will perform the target action (p. 315)."

Although exploration of the self-prophecy effect has been limited to a small group of scholars in the United States, its robustness—regarding both the magnitude of the effect size and the variety of contexts in which it has been observed—is compelling. To date there are no cross-cultural demonstrations of the effect. However, we have no reason to believe that the effect would not manifest in various cultures. Lacking a solid theoretical explanation for the effect, some research suggests interesting cross-cultural applications of the effect. As is discussed, one seemingly consistent characteristic of successful demonstrations of the self-prophecy effect is a relationship of the predicted behavior to social norms. Therefore, differing norms may be relevant to application of the effect across cultural contexts.

This chapter provides a review of self-prophecy research—work spanning a wide variety of laboratory and field behaviors, yet reliably showing substantial effect sizes. Empirical evidence is followed by the currently most convincing theoretical explanations for this novel social influence technique. Finally, practical applications of the effect across differing contexts are presented.

EXISTING EVIDENCE FOR THE
SELF-PROPHECY EFFECT

The modest number of known self-prophecy studies conducted by a small group of investigators might lead one to believe that this is a research program of little consequence. We feel, however, that self-prophecy has remained subterranean for too long. A brief review of all known work suggests that it is a behavior modification technique holding much promise.

Sherman (1980) introduced the self-prophecy effect with three experiments (see Table 3.1 for summary of these and all known self-prophecy studies discussed herein). Depending on the context, the prediction request had the ability to decrease (i.e., singing over the phone and writing a counterattitudinal essay) as well as increase (i.e., volunteering for charity work) the probability of the predicted action.

In seeking to determine whether the self-prophecy effect could be consequential in an important nonlaboratory setting, several tests have been conducted in relation to public elections. In their first study, Greenwald et al. (1987) reported a directionally consistent, but not statistically significant self-prophecy effect for Ohio State University dormitory residents contacted by telephone with to registering to vote. In their second study, these authors showed a significant self-prophecy effect regarding actual voting behavior for the same population. For both of these studies, initial contact was made 1 or 2 days prior to the behavioral opportunity; the naturally occurring dependent measures (using official precinct and poll records) regarded the 1984 U.S. presidential election.

Using procedures similar to those of Greenwald et al. (1987), two studies were conducted by Greenwald, Klinger, Vande Kamp, and Kerr (1988) in relation to (a) voting in a closely contested 1986 U.S. Senate race, and (b) voting in a relatively unimportant 1987 State House of Representatives election. Spangenberg and Greenwald (1999) provided details regarding these unpublished studies. In Greenwald et al. (1988; Exp. 1), socioeconomically diverse subjects were selected from registered voters in the city of Seattle, Washington. Failure to find a significant self-prophecy effect in this study is convincingly explained by the high turnout level in both the control (81.7%) and prediction conditions (86.3%). The turnout rate appeared to have created a ceiling effect, leaving little opportunity to observe treatment effects.

In their second study (Greenwald et al., 1988; Exp. 2), subjects were selected from registered voters in the State of Washington's 43rd legislative district. Finding no main effect across all voters, a significant interaction showed that the magnitude of the self-prophecy effect varying significantly as a function of subjects' prior voting record. Low- and high-prior-turnout voters showed no effect of prediction, whereas a significant self-prophecy effect held for the moderate-prior-turnout group. Prediction request brought turnout of moderate-prior-turnout voters up to a level indistinguishable from that of high-prior-turnout voters.

Spangenberg and Obermiller (1996) found a statistically significant self-prophecy effect in reducing undergraduate cheating behavior. Of students not asked to make a prediction, less than a third avoided the temptation to cheat on a take-home exam. Of those asked to predict, a majority said that they would resist the temptation to cheat, and over half of this latter group subsequently did behave honestly when provided the opportunity to cheat. Spangenberg (1997) demonstrated the self-prophecy technique's ability to increase attendance at a health club for members that had not used club facilities for at least a month prior to experimental contact. Although not statistically significant, there was a self-prophecy effect in the expected direction in the 10 days following initial contact. However, this study was the first demonstration of the self-prophecy effect over an extended time period. In the 6-month period following initial contact, subjects making a prediction used their club at double the rate of control subjects.

Obermiller, Spangenberg, and Atwood (1992) examined a direct fundraising appeal using a self-prophecy technique: Would university alumni

TABLE 3.1
Review of Self-Prophecy Research

Study	Prediction Task	Study N[a]	Summary Statistics[b]	Effect Size(r)
Sherman (1980; Exp. 1)	Agreeing to write a counter attitudinal essay.	36	Control: 67%; Prediction: (29%) 33%	.329
Sherman (1980; Exp. 2)	Singing the "Star Spangled Banner" over the telephone.	52	Control: 68%; Prediction: (44%) 42%	.300
Sherman (1980; Exp. 3)	Volunteering to work 3 hours for the American Cancer Society.	91	Control: 4%; Prediction: (48%) 31%	.352
Greenwald, Carnot, Beach, & Young (1987; Exp. 1)	Registering to vote prior to 1984 U.S. presidential election.	46	Control: 9%; Prediction: (71%) 21%	.167
Greenwald, Carnot, Beach, & Young (1987; Exp. 2)	Voting in 1984 U.S. presidential election.	56	Control: 62%; Prediction: (100%) 87%	.289
Greenwald, Klinger, Vande Kamp, & Kerr (1988; Exp. 1)	Voting in 1986 U.S. Senate race (Seattle, WA).	1139	Control: 87%; Prediction: (100%) 86%	.011
Greenwald, Klinger, Vande Kamp, & Kerr (1988; Exp. 2)c	Voting in 1987 primary for seat in the State House of Representatives.	346	Control: 35%; Prediction: (83%) 44%	.089
Obermiller, Spangenberg, & Atwood (1992)	Making a donation pledge in a college fundraising campaign.	390	Control: 46%; Prediction: (53%) 46%	.007
Spangenberg (1997): Short term	Using health club in the next week.	142	Control: 7%; Prediction: (61%) 14%	.089
Long term	Using health club over 6 months.	95	Visits: Control = 5.1; Prediction = 10.25d	.202
Spangenberg & Obermiller (1996)	Refraining from cheating on a take-home quiz.	81	Control: 29%; Prediction: (59%) 51%	.232
Spangenberg & Greenwald (1999; Exp. 1)	Reduction of a gender-based stereotype (w/gender monitoring).	331	Error Index: Control = -0.42;Prediction =-0.39e	.077
Spangenberg & Greenwald (1999; Exp. 2)	Reduction of a gender-based stereotype (w/past experience).	406	Error Index: Control = -0.55;Prediction =-0.45f	.220
Sprott, Spangenberg, & Perkins (1999; Exp. 1)	Engaging in aluminum can recycling by dormitory floors.	14	Number Recycled: Control = 18.11;Prediction = 30.53g	.397
Sprott, Spangenberg, & Perkins (1999; Exp. 2)	Self-report of engaging in recycling behaviors.	126	Self-report recycling scale: Control = 9.47;Prediction = 8.99h	.034
			Average effect size (15 studies) ip	**.132**
			(12 studies) jp	.193

[a] Cell sizes in all studies were approximately equal for Control (no-prediction) and Prediction conditions.

[b] Categorical dependent variables are summarized as: (a) % of control group performing target action; (b) % of prediction group (in parentheses) predicting they would perform the action; and (b) % of prediction group performing action. For intervally scaled dependent measures, means are provided for respective conditions.

[c] Self-prophecy varied as a function of subjects' prior voting record [$F(2,439) = 2.98, p = .05$]. Effect sizes were $Z_r = .044$, $Z_r = .249$, and $Z_r = .017$, respectively, for low, moderate, and high-prior-turnout voters. The only significant self-prophecy effect was for the moderate group, ($\chi^2 = 5.96$, df = 1, $p = .015$).

[d] Average number of visits differed significantly between the two conditions [$F(1,93) = 3.78, p = .05$].

[e] Difference in error index (i.e., more positive numbers indicate more female names when guessing) was consistent with self-prophecy, but not significantly different across conditions, [$F(1,323) = 1.94, p = .16$].

[f] The error index was significantly different between conditions, [$F(1,381) = 17.42, p = .0005$].

[g] Average cans recycled (for 13 weeks) was significantly different between with floor size included as a covariate, [$t(11) = 5.89, p = .03$].

[h] The self-report scale of recycling (with higher numbers indicating more recycling behavior) was not significantly different between the control and prediction conditions, [$t (124) = 0.38, p = .35$].

i Effect sizes were weighted by the square root of respective study Ns to avoid a disproportionate effect of one or more studies with large samples.

[j] The subset of 12 out of the 15 studies omitted Greenwald et al. (1988; Exp. 1), Obermiller et al. (1992), and Sprott et al. (1999; Exp. 2) for theoretical and empirical reasons discussed in text.

overpredict their response to a request for a donation pledge, perhaps resulting in increased giving in a subsequent campaign? In their failure to find a statistically significant self-prophecy effect, these authors provided post hoc empirical evidence suggesting that reactance (Brehm, 1966) may have overpowered the self-prophecy manipulation. Because both the prediction and pledge requests were identified with the same university, subjects appeared to have regarded the prediction request as an attempt to manipulate them into making a donation.

Employing a laboratory name-generation task, Spangenberg and Greenwald (1999) demonstrated the efficacy of self-prophecy to reduce expression of an implicit gender stereotype (errors in judging fame of last names revealed a stereotype that associates males [more than females] with fame-deserving achievement). These authors found that reminding subjects of the nature of their prediction at the time of the behavioral opportunity served to reduce gender stereotyping much like the self-prophecy request alone. However, there was no interaction between these two variables. In their second study, they found no more than slight support for their hypothesis that the self-prophecy effect would be stronger if subjects lacked prior experience with the task for which a prediction was requested. More important, these studies showed that the self-prophecy effect could be successfully produced in a single-session procedure, both in an after-only design and in a repeated measures (pretest–posttest) design. Development of the single-session procedure considerably increased the efficiency of conducting theory testing regarding the effect.

Sprott, Spangenberg, and Perkins (in press) demonstrated the effect in the socially relevant context of aluminum can recycling. Prediction request resulted in significantly increased recycling participation over a 13-week period in student dormitories. In a second experiment, these authors found no effect of prediction for self-report of recycling. Explanations for the null effect included: (a) self-report elicited *good* behavior responses (whether honest or not), (b) self-deception at the time of self-report to avoid cognitive dissonance (Festinger, 1957), and (c) self-report occurred so frequently (weekly) in all conditions that respondents were primed to engage in the socially sensitive behavior, thereby creating a ceiling effect.

Meta-Analytic Summary of Existing Evidence

Regardless of the relative lack of scholarly attention, meta-analysis of the existing work confirms the consistency of occurrence and size of the self-prophecy effect. The set of 15 studies included in Table 3.1 was homogenous with regard to effect size (average $r = .13$) and p values. A defendable subset of 12 studies omits the three studies (with relatively large sample sizes) whose authors provide sound methodological and theoretical explanations for their failure to find significant self-prophecy effects (i.e., Greenwald et al., 1988, Exp. 1; Obermiller et al., 1992; Sprott et al., in press; Exp. 2). The average $r = .19$, and p values are homogenous for this 12-study subset. Thus, existing empirical evidence leaves little doubt as to the size and robustness of the effect associated with the self-prophecy technique. Therefore, the significant remaining challenges are identification of the limiting conditions for the effect and theoretical explanation for its occurrence.

EMPIRICAL CONSISTENCIES IN OBTAINED EFFECTS

Theory-relevant generalizations that appear to be supported by characteristics of situations in which self-prophecy effects have been demonstrated are that (a) the target action for the self-prophecy has most often been a socially desirable action, and (b) the self-prophecy effect has been observed chiefly in situations in which subjects cannot make confident self-predictions based on past experience.

Social Desirability of Target Actions

Registering to vote and voting (Greenwald et al., 1987, 1988), volunteering to do charitable work (Sherman, 1980), resisting the temptation to cheat

(Spangenberg & Obermiller, 1996), exercising at a health club (Spangenberg, 1997), avoiding a gender-based stereotype (Spangenberg & Greenwald, 1999), and recycling (Sprott et al., in press) all appear to be socially desirable behaviors. In fact, although not all demonstrations of the effect clearly have this underlying normative support, existing empirical evidence suggests that the social desirability of target actions is likely a necessary condition for the effect.

A socially normative precondition for the effect to occur suggests that prediction request could elicit behaviors consistent with different sets of social norms depending on the cultural context. Socially normative behaviors in one culture may be neutral or even negative in other cultures. For example, although self-prophecy has been shown to affect recycling behavior of U.S. residents (Sprott et al., in press), there may be (assuming a socially normative component to the effect) no such self-prophecy effect for individuals in most Third World countries—people of those cultures may not exhibit any normative behavior with regard to recycling. Thus, the impacts of social desirability and cross-cultural differences on the self-prophecy effect remain significant questions for future research.

Nonconfident Self-Predictions

In most self-prophecy studies, the target action was either completely unfamiliar to subjects [e.g., Sherman (1980)—singing on the phone and agreeing to write a counterattitudinal essay; Greenwald et al. (1987)—registering to vote and first-time voting] or was one for which subjects' past performance could not provide a basis for confident self-prediction [Spangenberg (1997)—exercising at a health club that one had joined but not regularly used; Greenwald et al. (1988)—voting in a primary election by moderate-prior-turnout voters]. A few of the null findings appear to be in situations for which subjects have had enough past experience to confidently predict their future performance. Perhaps the most informative null result was the Greenwald et al. (1988) null finding for low-prior-turnout voters in a low-turnout election. When asked to predict their voting/nonvoting in the upcoming election, these voters may have known from past experience that they would not vote. Interestingly, a majority of these low-prior-turnout voters predicted that they would vote (75%), although only a small proportion of the 75% did vote. A substantial fraction of these subjects apparently succumbed to the social desirability pressure to declare that they would vote while apparently knowing that this was unlikely. The issue of familiarity with the target action, however, remains unresolved. Recent published and unpublished experimental evidence suggests that prediction and prior experience with the task do not significantly interact (Spangenberg & Greenwald, 1999; Spangenberg, Sprott, & Fisher, 1999).

THEORETICAL INTERPRETATION OF THE
SELF-PROPHECY EFFECT

As noted, prior research has not convincingly established the theoretical process(es) underlying self-prophecy. Sherman's (1980) best explanation for the effect was script evocation. However, we feel that the most compelling interpretation is suggested by a new group of findings related to cognitive dissonance—induced hypocrisy—and the well-established program of research on objective self-awareness.

Cognitive Dissonance

Self-prophecy shares procedural elements with some well-established cognitive dissonance experimental procedures. For example, the classic induced compliance experiment (e.g., Festinger & Carlsmith, 1959) used the implicit authority of an experimenter to elicit agreement to perform a counterattitudinal action. Subjects are then likely to show attitude change consistent with the induced action. As with self-prophecy, there is a social influence on response to an initial request and subsequent change consistent with that response. There is a long history of controversy over theoretical interpretation of the cognitive changes induced by such dissonance experiments. One recently successful theoretical view of these results is Aronson's (1992) proposal that the experiment induces a discrepancy between the subject's self-concept and the induced action. The opinion change serves to restore consistency by providing a self-concept-preserving justification for the induced action.

Aronson's position is the basis of a relatively recent class of findings labeled *induced hypocrisy* (e.g., Aronson, Fried, & Stone, 1991; Dickerson, Thibodeau, Aronson, & Miller, 1992; Stone, Aronson, Crain, Winslow, & Fried, 1994; Fried & Aronson, 1995; Stone, Wiegand, Cooper, & Aronson, 1997), which converges nicely with results of the self-prophecy research reviewed. In this work, *induced hypocrisy* has been defined as (a) advocating a position one supports, and (b) being made mindful of one's failure to act in accordance with that advocacy. In all of these experiments, subjects make proattitudinal speeches that they are led to believe will have a positive impact on others. Subjects are also reminded of their history of failing to live up to the standards they advocate in their speeches. These studies have shown that the combination of these two factors appears to arouse dissonance, but either factor in isolation does not. Enough important similarities between the experimental procedures of induced hypocrisy and self-prophecy exist to suggest that the latter effect also works by motivating subjects to reduce a values-action discrepancy made salient by the self-prediction procedure accompanied by reminder of their past failures to act in the predicted direction.

Self-Awareness

Also arguably related to dissonance theory, the theory of self-awareness (Duval & Wicklund, 1972) suggests that the presence of self-focusing stimuli (often cameras or mirrors in laboratory studies) heighten self-focused attention, producing a state of objective self-awareness that involves attention to discrepancies between actual and ideal selves. The theory further supposes that negative affect results from perception of such discrepancy (Gibbons, 1990), in turn leading to attempts to reduce the discrepancy. Direct comparison suggests that self-awareness theory is probably not distinguishable from the induced-hypocrisy work; the two are highly similar theories experimentally accounting for approximately the same dissonance-related conclusions. Similarity between dissonance and self-awareness research can also be seen in the observation that both lines of research show individuals to be strongly influenced by norms—heightened self-awareness may either increase or decrease pro- or antisocial behavior depending on what is considered more normatively desirable (Carver, 1974; Rule, Nesdale, & Dyck, 1977; Wegner & Schaefer, 1978). Thus, if the relationship between self-hypocrisy and self-prophecy is accepted, the relationship between self-prophecy and self-awareness is straightforward.

PRACTICAL IMPLICATIONS

The robustness of the self-prophecy effect suggests substantial effects for several practical applications. Recall that these applications may be moderated by the strength of the norm associated with the behavior, and these norms may differ widely by culture. For example, self-prophecy could be used to influence the outcome of an election if the electorate is clearly segmented into partisan groups (not an unrealistic scenario in many cultures). By targeting the self-prophecy effect at an appropriately sympathetic portion of the electorate (e.g., a well-defined racial, ethnic, or socioeconomic segment), the effect on turnout should favor candidates or ballot alternatives preferred by that segment. If one could call 10,000 voters who could be counted on to vote for one's preferred candidate, an effect of the average strength observed across self-prophecy research (approximate r = .20) would increase that candidate's vote total by about 2,000 votes— not an insubstantial contribution to many election outcomes.

Other practical concerns across diverse cultures would appear to be ripe for application of the self-prophecy technique. In more developed cultures, self-prophecy might be used to address social problems including drinking and driving, blood donation, recycling behaviors, and organ donation, among several others. Additionally, in less affluent cultures, simple, yet serious concerns like infant immunization and disease control could be addressed using the technique.

Implementation of self-prophecy in differing cultures raises the unanswered question regarding the mode of prediction elicitation. Existing research has demonstrated the efficacy of interpersonal telephone and paper-and-pencil techniques for obtaining predictions and subsequent behavior changes on an individual basis. Although these methods of prediction request may be viable in the United States, one can easily think of other cultures in which neither of these methods would be practicable for a significant portion of the population. Further, a mass-mediated contact would be more economically implemented than individual contact in any culture. A compelling question for future research should ask: Can self-prophecy effects be elicited using a mass-mediated form of prediction request? Were this question answered affirmatively, for example, a local culture could utilize billboards to ask people to predict (to themselves) whether they would take the necessary precautions to prevent spread of a communicable disease or take precautions against threatening natural disasters.

CONCLUSION

It is hoped that this chapter effectively demonstrates the substantive importance and theoretical intrigue of the self-prophecy effect. Some of the most powerful and enduring persuasion techniques from social psychology have been drawn from theory and research on cognitive dissonance (Festinger, 1957). We suggest that the effects of self-prophecy on subsequent behavior may be a unique dissonance-evoking technique that few investigators have explored. Existing self-prophecy research suggests some plausible theoretical interpretations and provides research tools that can be used for needed further investigation.

The self-prophecy technique is noncoercive and free of ethical objections. People can be expected to make predictions that present themselves favorably. Therefore, a socially objectionable behavior is unlikely to be elicited by the technique. Indeed, a self-prophecy technique is likely to create a situation in which people are induced to act more acceptably or less hypocritically to the benefit of themselves and society.

ACKNOWLEDGMENTS

The authors would like to thank David E. Sprott for his helpful comments. Preparation of this chapter was facilitated by support provided by National Science Foundation (Grant SBR-9710172) and National Institute of Mental Health (Grant MH-41328).

REFERENCES

Aronson, E. (1992). The return of the repressed: Dissonance theory makes a comeback. Psychological Inquiry, 3(4), 303–311.

Aronson, E., Fried, C. B., & Stone, J. (1991). Overcoming denial and increasing the intention to use condoms through the induction of hypocrisy. American Journal of Public Health, 81, 1636–1638.

Brehm, J. W. (1966). A theory of psychological reactance. New York: Academic Press.

Carver, C. S. (1974). Facilitation of physical aggression through objective self-awareness. Journal of Experimental Social Psychology, 10, 365–370.

Dickerson, C. A., Thibodeau, R., Aronson, E., & Miller, D. (1992). Using cognitive dissonance to encourage water conservation. Journal of Applied Social Psychology, 22, 841–854.

Duval, S., & Wicklund, R. A. (1972). A theory of objective self-awareness. New York: Academic Press.

Festinger, L. (1957). A theory of cognitive dissonance. Stanford, CA: Stanford University Press.

Festinger, L., & Carlsmith, J. M. (1959). Cognitive consequences of forced compliance. Journal of Abnormal Social Psychology, 58, 203–211.

Fried, C. B., & Aronson, E. (1995). Hypocrisy, misattribution, and dissonance reduction. Personality and Social Psychology Bulletin, 21, 925–933.

Gibbons, F. X. (1990). Self-attention and behavior: A review and theoretical update. In L. Berkowitz (Ed.), Advances in experimental social psychology (Vol. 23, pp. 249–303). San Diego, CA: Academic Press.

Greenwald, A. G., Carnot, C. G., Beach, R., & Young, B. (1987). Increasing voting behavior by asking people if they expect to vote. Journal of Applied Psychology, 72, 315–318.

Greenwald, A. G., Klinger, M. R., Vande Kamp, M. E., & Kerr, K. L. (1988). The self-prophecy effect: Increasing voter turnout by vanity-assisted consciousness raising. Unpublished manuscript.

Obermiller, C., Spangenberg, E. R., & Atwood, A. (1992). Getting people to give more: A telephone funds-soliciting strategy based on the self-erasing nature of errors of prediction. In C. T. Allen et al. (Eds.), Marketing theory and applications (Vol. 3., pp. 339–345). Chicago, IL: American Marketing Association.

Rule, B. G., Nesdale, A. R., & Dyck, R. (1977). Objective self-awareness and differing standards of aggression. Representative Research in Social Psychology, 8, 89–96.

Sherman, S. J. (1980). On the self-erasing nature of errors of prediction. Journal of Personality and Social Psychology, 39, 211–221.

Spangenberg, E. R. (1997). Increasing health club attendance through self-prophecy. Marketing Letters, 8, 23–32.

Spangenberg, E. R., & Greenwald, A. G. (1999). Social influence by requesting self-prophecy. Journal of Consumer Psychology, 8, 61–89.

Spangenberg, E. R., & Obermiller, C. (1996). To cheat or not to cheat: Reducing cheating by requesting self-prophecy. Marketing Education Review, 6(3), 95–103.

Spangenberg, E. R., Sprott, D. E., & Fisher, R. J. (1999). Effects of self-prophecy on product evaluation and choice. Unpublished raw data.

Sprott, D. E., Spangenberg, E. R., & Perkins, A. W. (in press). Two more self-prophecy experiments. In E. Arnould & L. Price (Eds.), Advances in consumer research (Vol. 25). Provo, UT: Association for Consumer Research.

Stone, J., Aronson, E., Crain, A. L., Winslow, M. P., & Fried, C. B. (1994). Inducing hypocrisy as a means of encouraging young adults to use condoms. Personality and Social Psychology Bulletin, 20, 116–128.

Stone, J., Wiegand, A. W., Cooper, J., & Aronson, E. (1997). When exemplification fails: Hypocrisy and the motive for self-integrity. Journal of Personality and Social Psychology, 72, 54–65.

Wegner, D. M., & Schaefer, D. (1978). The concentration of responsibility: An objective self-awareness analysis of group size effects in helping situations. Journal of Personality and Social Psychology, 36, 147–155.

4

Social Influence, Empathy, and Prosocial Behavior in Cross-Cultural Perspective

Paul A. Miller
Arizona State University West
Junko Kozu
Arizona State University
Amy C. Davis
Sojourner Center, Phoenix, Arizona

ABSTRACT

In this chapter we discuss an important social affective process, its influence on prosocial actions, and how social influence factors may facilitate this process in cross-cultural interpersonal relationships. Specifically, in a series of meta-analyses, we first examine whether prosocial emotions, such as empathy and sympathy, promote altruistic and related other-oriented social behaviors across multiple cultures. If such an association exists, the second question, and the major focus of this chapter, addresses whether empathetic or sympathetic responding can be elicited by interpersonal social influence factors (i.e., similarity, observational set, and controllability) that would presumably be extant in these emerging cross-cultural relationships. Finally, we discuss our findings in terms of cultural differences in conceptions of the self, and how an awareness of these differences may contribute to a better understanding of the role of social influence in promoting prosocial emotions and behavior in cross-cultural interactions.

CROSS-CULTURAL RELATIONS BETWEEN PROSOCIAL EMOTION AND BEHAVIOR

Over a decade ago, Eisenberg and Miller (1987) conducted a meta-analysis to examine whether various indexes of empathy and sympathy were related to indexes of prosocial behavior in children and adults. *Empathy* was defined as a vicarious emotional response (e.g., facial indexes or self-reports of sadness, happiness, etc.) to another person's emotion or situation. *Sympathy* was considered an emotional response involving concern or pity for the emotional state or circumstances of the other person. *Prosocial behavior* was broadly defined to include social behaviors oriented to benefit another, regardless of potential outcomes for oneself. Overall, they found that empathetic and sympathetic responding, as measured by self-report in experiments and on questionnaires, facial and gestural measures, and physiological indexes, were significantly and positively associated with prosocial behavior in children and adults. Nonsignificant associations with prosocial behavior were found when children's empathy or sympathy was assessed through picture/story methods or self-report in experiments.

With the exception of a few isolated studies, however, virtually all of the studies they examined involved U. S. participants, and there were no studies from non-Western countries. From a cross-cultural perspective, limiting theoretical and empirical work to data from a single culture runs the serious risk of creating parochial theories about the development of empathy and prosocial behavior (Stevenson, 1991). Thus, it is unclear whether these findings simply reflect U.S. cultural conceptions of emotional and behavioral responding or more basic and universal aspects of human emotional and behavioral capacity. On the one hand, theory and empirical work from a variety of fields, including sociobiology (Hamilton, 1964; Trivers, 1971), ethology (MacDonald, 1984), temperament (Rothbart & Derryberry, 1981), neuropsychophysiology (MacLean, 1967), personality (McCrae & Costa, 1997), and twin studies of empathy in adults (Matthews, Batson, Horn, & Rosenman, 1981) and children (Zahn-Waxler, Robinson, & Emde, 1992), support the notion that there may be a universal human capacity for prosocial emotions and behavior.

Conversely, Jain (1994) cautioned against making an uncritical assumption of the presence of universal laws of human behavior, which may simply reflect a Western model of individualism. There are profound cultural variations about the self (e.g., along dimensions of individualism vs. collectivism) and psychological interdependencies between the self and social group (Markus & Kitayama, 1991; Triandis, 1991) and notions of personal responsibility and control (Miller & Bersoff, 1992). These cultural variations, in turn, influence the construction, interpretation, and meaning of emotions and prosocial behavior (Misra, 1991; Nakasoto & Matsui, 1996), their phenomenological locus within the individual or social group (Lutz, 1983; Markus & Kitayama, 1991), and the contexts in which they occur (Fiske, 1991; Stevenson, 1991).

Consequently, we initiated a worldwide search for published articles that examined the relation of empathy and sympathy to prosocial responding in adults and children. We used the same definitions for *empathy, sympathy*, and *prosocial behavior* as Eisenberg and Miller (1987). Multiple search strategies were used to locate relevant English and non-English language articles, including Ulrich's International Periodical Directory, standard CD-ROM research databases (e.g., PsychLit, Social Sciences Citation Index), mailings to psychological organizations internationally, and the Internet. We also directly contacted researchers to request their assistance in identifying relevant articles and other researchers with interests in empathy and prosocial behavior. Thirty-four articles (involving 50 data samples) were located from 14 different countries (Australia, Canada, China, Finland, Germany, Greece, India, Japan, Mexico, the Netherlands, Poland, Romania, Spain, and Sweden). Bilingual graduate students or faculty completed the translations of non-English language articles.

In conducting a meta-analysis of these data sets, we followed the same procedures outlined in the meta-analysis of Eisenberg and Miller (1987) and described in Hedges and Olkin (1986). Briefly, we converted various test statistics (e.g., ANOVAs, T tests, etc.) for each sample in the articles to a correlation coefficient using standard formulas (e.g., epsilons for F statistics). Each sample correlation coefficient was transformed into a z statistic using a standard r-to-z transformation table, and each z value and individual sample size was used to compute a weighted estimate of the common correlation ($z+$). These resulting $z+$ values across the study samples were then tested for homogeneity of variance. The summed estimate of the common correlation was then tested to determine whether it differed significantly from zero using a two-tailed critical value of the standard normal curve (for $p = .05$, $z = 1.96$). Confidence intervals for the common correlation and a population estimate of the common correlation were then computed.

The results indicate that the estimate of the common correlation across the studies was $z+ = .24$, yielding a z value of 17.16, which was highly significant ($p < .0001$). The test of homogeneity of variance was significant ($\chi^2 = 152.92$, $p < .001$), indicating that the various samples were likely not representative of a common population. This was expecte, given the differences in sample sizes, research designs, methodologies, and measures of empathy and prosocial behavior across the study samples. The population estimate of the common correlation coefficient was nearly identical ($z+ = .23$). *The confidence interval for the estimate of the common correlation r*anged from .20 to .25. Because the confidence interval was well above 0, these results suggest that empathetic and sympathetic responding is associated with prosocial behavior across the particular culture sampled.[1]

---

[1] Miller, P.A., Kozu, J., & Davis, A. (in preparation). *Interrelations among social influence, prosocial emotions and behavior in cross-cultural perspective*. Arizona State University West.

SOCIAL INFLUENCE FACTORS THAT ELICIT PROSOCIAL EMOTIONS

Given that empathetic and sympathetic emotions appear to be associated with various forms of prosocial responding across multiple cultures, we became interested in examining how social influence factors elicit sympathy and empathy across cultures. Social influence refers to the various ways in which individuals' assumptions, attitudes, and behavior in social interactions are shaped and manipulated through cultural and social group beliefs and values (Myers, 1999). In particular, we were interested in interpersonal influence factors (i.e., those occurring between individuals either directly or indirectly) that evoked changes in individuals' overt behaviors or behavioral intentions toward another person (Kenrick, Neuberg, & Cialdini, 1999). Specifically, the question was this: Might evoking certain beliefs or values in an observer, or focusing an observer's attention on particular characteristics of individuals or their situations be more likely to elicit that observer's feelings of empathy or sympathy, and thereby influence their prosocial behavior toward those individuals?

In studies of the role of interpersonal social influence factors on prosocial emotions or behavior, three factors have received considerable study. They include perceptions of interpersonal similarity or familiarity, observational set (i.e., focusing attention on an individual's emotions or thoughts in a situation vs. taking a nonemotional, objective perspective toward them), and beliefs or attributions about an individual's perceived controllability over or responsibility for their plight or need state. Generally, the outcome variable of interest in these studies has been prosocial behavior, and participants' empathy or sympathy was experimentally manipulated using one or more of these three factors. For our purposes, however, we were not interested in whether these social influence factors were associated with prosocial responding, but whether there was evidence to indicate that these factors reliably elicited empathetic or sympathetic emotions. Thus, we were interested in examining the effectiveness of researchers' experimental manipulations of similarity, observational set, and attributions of controllability in eliciting study participants' empathetic and sympathetic emotions.[2]

Similarity to Another

Studies across multiple cultures suggest that individuals and groups are more inclined to like those that they perceive as similar to themselves (Osbeck,

---

[2] We looked at whether these experimental manipulations led to differences in participants' reported empathetic or sympathetic feelings. We did not examine whether study participants reported behavior consistent with their experimental manipulation (e.g., felt more similar, observed feelings vs. objective facts, or saw another's plight as more or less controllable).

Moghaddam, & Perreault, 1997). Consequently, might individuals be more likely to feel prosocial emotions toward those to whom they feel more similar? Eisenberg and Miller (1987) reviewed the research in which similarity between study participants and a target person were manipulated to assess its effects on prosocial responding. They found that individuals were more likely to respond prosocially toward others with whom they believed they shared similar interests or preferences. With the exception of a single study in their review, however, tests of the similarity manipulation on empathetic responding were not conducted. Consequently, it was not clear whether similarity with another actually elicited one's sympathetic or empathetic emotions, and thus could account for the effects on prosocial responding.

To test this question, we located 16 studies involving 22 samples. The similarity manipulations in these studies were designed to create the belief in adult or child participants that they shared some attribute (gender, age, name), personality characteristic (values, beliefs, preferences), or outcome (success or failure on a task, job loss) with the target person. Cognitive or emotional empathy or sympathy was assessed by a variety of measures, including self-report of matching affect, emotion adjective checklists, and two to three item rating scales or questionnaires.

The samples were homogenous with respect to their estimates of the correlation between perceptions of similarity and empathy [χ^2 (23) = 33.11, ns]. The estimate of the common correlation ($z+$) across all samples was .15, with z = 5.68 ($p < .001$). Ninety-five percent confidence intervals for $z+$ were .10 and .20. The population estimate for $z+$ was identical to the sample estimate.

Overall, these findings indicate that, across a variety of different experimental manipulations, perceived similarity with another was associated with feelings of sympathy or empathy in children and adults. The strongest associations were found for conditions involving similarity of personal experiences (e.g., success or failure, some past event) or personality characteristics (age, gender, identity) and weakest when the similar target was not in need or experiencing positive affect. In studies involving children in the United States and one study in Japan (Asakawa & Matsuoka, 1987), nonsignificant relations were more often observed when empathy was assessed using picture story methods rather than self-reports of affect or rating scales. The validity of picture story methodology for eliciting empathetic affect has been questioned among U.S. researchers (Strayer, 1987) and is less often used in contemporary empathy research with children. With the exception of three samples, sympathy between an observer and target person was generally positively related when assessed with emotion adjective checklist measures.

However, some caution should be noted because the relations between empathy and similarity were reported as nonsignificant in nearly 39% of the samples. This may suggest that either the empathy or sympathy measures were insufficient to detect the effect or that the particular similarity manipulation condition failed. Theoretically, it also may mean that the perception of similarity to some-one alone may be a less reliable mechanism of social influence.

Focusing on the Feelings or Perspective of the Person in Need

In addition to aspects of a person whom we judge similar to ourselves, anoth-er source of information about others that appears to influence our empathetic or sympathetic feelings toward them is when we focus on their emotional state or perspective when they are in need. In this research, participants are instruct-ed to focus on either the target person's emotional state or condition (e.g., imagine how the target feels/take perspective of the target) or imagine oneself as the target (e.g., imagine yourself how would you would feel if) or to focus on nonemotive, nonpersonal aspects of the person or situation (e.g., watch or think about the target, or evaluate the situation objectively). In their review, Eisenberg and Miller (1987) found that instructing participants to focus on or imagine the feelings of a target person in need versus objectively focusing on the facts of the situation was significantly more likely to lead to increases in prosocial responding. They also noted that the experimental manipulations were effective in some studies but not in others, but they did not statistically assess whether these manipulations significantly affected the level of partici-pants' empathetic or sympathetic responding.

Nineteen studies involving 26 samples were located. The samples were not homogenous in their estimates of the common correlation ($\chi^2 = 138.560$. The lack of homogeneity again was likely due to the different observational set manipulations and measures of empathy used in the various studies. The estimate of the common correlation ($z+ = .28$) was significant ($z = 12.94$ ($p < .001$). Confidence intervals for $z+$ ranged from .24 to .33. The population estimate for the common correlation was $z+ = .27$.

These findings indicate that the types of information a person focuses on in a social situation involving someone in need exert a relatively powerful effect on their subsequent affective response. There are positive effect sizes in 86% of the sample estimates. Thus, individuals appear much more likely to increase empathetic and sympathetic responding when they are asked to imagine themselves in the situation or emotional state of another person in need or to imagine the feelings or perspective of the person in need. These effect sizes are consistent for children and adults and across self-report and adjective checklist measures of prosocial emotions. The flip side of this relation is equally impor-tant. When people only focus objectively on the person's behavior or the facts of their situation, they are much less likely to experience prosocial emotions. Cross-culturally, two studies involving Japanese children (Shutoh, 1994) are consistent with these results, whereas a single study involving Croatian college students reported no effect of the observational set manipulation (Raboteg-Saric, 1986).

Perceptions of Controllability and Responsibility About Another's Plight

A third social influence factor that may influence the course of cross-cultural interpersonal interactions are the causes or attributions that people generate when attempting to explain the reason for events or outcomes that they or others experience in their everyday lives (Heider, 1944). In fact, social psychological research on attributional processes has supported the notion that they play a central role in social interactions of individuals and groups (Hewstone, 1990; Hilton, Smith, & Kin, 1995) and occur across multiple interpersonal situations (Graham & Folkes, 1990) and cultures (Moghaddam, 1998).

In determining whether individuals' attributions might exert a significant influence on their prosocial emotions in cross-cultural interactions, our objective was to examine whether there was a systematic and significant effect of attributional processes on individuals' empathetic and sympathetic emotional reactions. Of the various attributional models, Weiner's (1985) cognition (attribution)-emotion-action (behavior) model has been applied extensively in U.S. and cross-cultural research (Moghaddam, 1998).

According to this model, when an observer is faced with a person in a help-giving context, causal judgments or attributions made about the degree of the person's control over their plight lead to different affective and behavioral reactions. Here, *controllability* refers to internal characteristics of individuals (e.g., degree of effort, motivational state) over which they are presumed to have some volitional control (Weiner, 1985). In this model, the more a person's need state is perceived to be due to a cause that was uncontrollable or unpredictable, the more likely an observer will experience empathetic emotions, which, in turn, increase the likelihood of helping (Betancourt, 1990). Thus, observers will be more likely to experience empathetic or sympathetic feelings if a person's need for assistance (e.g., exam notes, injury) is due to an event beyond his or her control (e.g., illness, accident) versus one under his or her control (e.g., went to the beach instead of class, drank too much). As with the previous two social influence variables, researchers primarily have analyzed attribution-affect-behavior models in relation to help-giving, but have not systematically reviewed the effect of perceived controllability manipulations on observers' empathetic or sympathetic responding.

We located 18 studies involving 20 samples. Controllability was manipulated by depicting the target person's condition as the result of intentional or self-serving behavior (e.g., drunkenness, vacationing, not working, spending freely, refusing to cooperate, aggressiveness) or unintended, unavoidable factors (e.g., accident, injury, eye problem, inability to read, physical characteristic, and lack of opportunity, jobs, or nearby relatives). Emotional empathy or sympathy was assessed primarily by emotion adjective checklists and two- and three-item rating scales.

The samples were not homogenous with respect to their estimates of the correlation between perceptions of controllability and empathy [$\chi^2(20) = 119.23$, $p < .001$]. The estimate of the common correlation ($z+$) across all samples was .33 [with $z = .22$, $p < .001$)]. Ninety-five percent confidence intervals for $z+$ were .30 and .35. The population estimate for $z+$ is virtually identical to the sample estimate (.32).

With the exception of two samples, children and adults consistently reported feeling much less empathetic or sympathetic for individuals perceived as responsible for or having control over their plight or need state across a wide variety of conditions. These conditions included situation-specific needs (e.g., falling down or needing class notes), enduring personal characteristics or social conditions (e.g., deviant behavior, poverty), or personal injury, victimization, or deprivation (e.g., physical abuse, needing food or monetary assistance, victimized by rape). Effects were equally strong in one study involving college students in Croatia (Raboteg-Saric, 1986) and another involving children in Japan (Watanabe & Eto, 1990). It is interesting to note that, in all the studies, the target was a specific individual, not a family or particular social group. The implications of this fact are taken up in the following section.

DISCUSSION

These findings indicate that empathetic and sympathetic responding are positively associated with prosocial behavior in children and adults in the 14 Western and non-Western countries sampled. Individual estimates of the common correlation were consistently positive across study samples, and estimates that were negative or zero order were not associated with a particular country or method of measuring empathy or prosocial behavior. Given that the majority of studies used questionnaires or self-reports in experiments to assess empathy, the overall estimate of the common correlation was similar in magnitude to that found in Eisenberg & Miller's (1987) study, which used the same modes of empathy assessment in U.S. participants.

Similarly, inducing individuals to think of themselves as similar to another, focus on another's perspective or emotional state, or perceive another's plight as due to uncontrollable causes all led to increased reports of empathetic and sympathetic responding. Perceived similarity to another appeared to have had the least influence in eliciting prosocial affect, whereas focusing one's attention on the perspective or feelings of another and perceiving their plight as uncontrollable produced the largest and most consistently positive effect sizes. Although these findings for social influence factors primarily involved U.S. participants, results for eight study samples from Croatia, Germany, and Japan were generally consistent with the U.S. samples and support the notion that some principles of social influence appear to operate similarly across cultures (Moghaddam, 1998). There are a number of implications of these findings for both universal and culture-specific notions of relations between prosocial emotions and behavior and social influence factors that may influence their expression.

First, prosocial emotions likely play an important role in regulating social behavior across cultures, but how they do this may vary according to cultural definitions of the self. Markus and Kitayama (1991) postulated that individuals in individualistic cultures emphasize interpreting and explaining reasons for feeling, thinking, and acting in terms of attributes perceived to be internal to oneself and independent of external, social forces. In collectivistic cultures, however, one's thoughts, feelings, and behavior are organized, experienced, and explained in terms of social relationships, roles, and responsibilities.

Consequently, because of the cultural emphasis on interdependence and connectedness among individuals in collectivistic cultures, we may expect to find higher levels of empathetic sensitivity and prosocial behavior. Thus, although the estimate of the common correlation was similar to that observed by Eisenberg and Miller (1987), the countries examined in this study varied considerably in individualistic and collectivistic orientations (Hofstede, 1980). In cultures with higher ratings on collectivism, such as in Japan or India, relations between prosocial emotions and behavior might be higher.

Enhanced responsiveness toward others in collectivistic cultures, however, may be highly selective and only expressed toward others sharing a common situation, such as one's kin group, school, or employer (Markus & Kitayama, 1991). Less responsiveness may be expected and practiced toward individuals perceived or delegated to outgroups (Stevenson, 1991). Conversely, in individualistic cultures, people attribute their experience of prosocial emotions and behavior toward others to internal traits or principles, thus they likely perceive themselves as freer to choose (or not choose) to respond to others regardless of others' social status or expectations.

Second, it is important not to blankly categorize cultures' respective orientations to prosocial emotion and behavior as wholly individualistic or collectivistic, but to consider the relative emphasis attributed to individual versus social-contextual factors within various cultures. A notion of an individual self"with invariant personality characteristics is not ignored by cultures with collectivistic notions of the self (Markus & Kitayama, 1991). Similar factor structures across multiple Western and Eastern countries, for example, have been found in studies of the Big Five personality traits (McCrae & Costa, 1997; Yang & Bond, 1990) and altruism (Nakasoto & Matsui, 1996). Conversely, social psychological research involving individuals in the United States, a culture rated as the most individualistic in the world (Hofstede, 1980), clearly demonstrates that social, group, and contextual factors influence, persuade, and motivate individuals' prosocial thoughts, feelings, and behavior.

The need to examine both individualistic and collectivistic orientations to prosocial emotions and behavior is especially relevant to the three social influence factors investigated in this study. All three constructs are conceptualized and operationalized as internal, dispositional characteristics typical of cultural assumptions implicit in U.S. psychological research. That is, whether we experience empathy or sympathy for someone is assessed in terms of how similar someone might be to ourselves as individuals, whether we try to imagine their feelings or take their perspective as our own, and how culpable we perceive them to be for their own plight. It would be interesting if Western researchers incorporated social groups and role obligations into their investigations of the effects of social influence factors on prosocial emotions and behavior. For example, Batson et al. (1995) found that individuals higher in dispositional empathy or those who have been asked to imagine the feelings of another increase donations to a person in need at a cost to the collective good. It would be interesting to replicate this study in a highly collectivistic society or social group. In general, the point is that more social psychological research needs to be conducted that frames research on social influence in terms of social and contextual factors (Moghaddam, Taylor, & Wright, 1993).

In one area where cross-cultural research has been conducted on social influence, we do begin to see how collectivistic orientations of the self influence prosocial emotions and behavior. Betancourt, Hardin, and Manzi (1992) proposed that variations in values, social beliefs, and norms are likely to give rise to cross-cultural differences in perceptions of controllability. Because of the emphasis on individuals forming a group or social identity in collectivistic cultures, individuals may be perceived as less in control of circumstances that befall them. Thakkar and Kanekar (1989) found that Indian participants were more empathetic if the cause of someone's plight was uncontrollable, but that individuals higher in empathy helped equally as much regardless of controllability. Miller and Bersoff (1992) found that Indian participants were much more likely to attribute both spontaneous helping and helping in response to a reciprocity norm to endogenous factors. However, U.S. participants only attributed endogenous motivation to individuals in scenarios in which helping was spontaneous and discounted the altruistic nature of helping in response to a reciprocity norm. In a similar study, Indian participants evaluated the failure to help others as morally sanctionable across multiple contexts. However, U.S. participants only saw failure to aid others as morally sanctionable when the situation was life threatening or when parents did not respond to the serious needs of their children (Miller, Bersoff & Harwood, 1990). These findings make sense if we view others and our relationships with them in terms of collectivistic responsibility. That is, empathy for others may be experienced despite their culpability, and prosocial behavior in response to social norms may be perceived as self-motivated because others and oneself are seen as fundamentally interconnected and interdependent.

Finally, if oneself and others are perceived as sharing a common social identity, this has profound implications for how motivational and personality constructs are conceptualized and operationalized. That is, motivational states attributed to the social group or context (rather than to internal states) that lead to altruistic behavior can be experienced by individuals as phenomenologically genuine emotional states (Markus & Kitayama, (1991). Lutz's (1983) ethnopsychological research of the Ifaluk culture in Micronesia reveals that emotions are defined in terms of and attributed to the social situations with others that elicit them, rather than as feeling states internal to oneself. This orientation is consistent with Jain's (1994) discussion of cultural constructions of emotion and, by implication, prosocial emotions and behavior and the factors that elicit them. That is, in some cultures, prosocial, emotional, or motivational states may not be instantiated within individuals, but ontologically defined and phenomenologically experienced within the context of their social roles and responsibilities.

Teasing out such culturally nuanced phenomenological and ontological meanings of prosocial emotions and behavior and related social influence factors, however, may be facilitated by developmental research. For example, Miller (1986) found that U.S. children from ages 8 to 15 gradually increased their use of dispositional factors in their explanation of others' everyday prosocial and deviant behaviors, whereas Indian children made increasing reference to contextual factors in their explanations. Stevenson (1991) pointed out that prosocial behavior in China, Japan, and Taiwan is defined similarly to that in Western countries. The conception of individual's the role as an interdependent member of society, however, results in quite different socialization processes regarding prosocial emotions and behavior. Specifically, children are expected to identify strongly with their social group (family, school), perceive group goals as one's own, obligate themselves to creating harmony within the social group, and understand that one's failures and successes are attributed to the character of one's social group. In this context, then, it may not be surprising to find that empathy increases with age to ingroup members but decreases to outgroup members among Japanese elementary school children (Asakawa & Matsuoka, 1987).

Overall, these findings illustrate the necessity of examining psychological constructs, such as empathy, or processes, such as social influence, theoretically and empirically from a cross-cultural perspective. Researchers must examine the ways in which they are socially constructed and linked to particular experiences, the rules for their interpretation and expression, and how they function to serve pragmatic and social goals (Shweder, 1993). Limiting research endeavors to either Western or Eastern constructions of social reality and methods of inquiry can only serve to limit our science.

PRACTICAL IMPLICATIONS

As illustrated in Miller's (1986) work, it is important to make explicit the ways in which interpersonal social influence mechanisms operate within different cultures. For example, *similarity to another* messages likely need to be construed in terms of shared internal states or characteristics to elicit prosocial emotions or behavior among individuals, social groups, or countries more individualistic in orientation. Among more collectivistically oriented individuals, social groups, and countries, however, *similarity* messages likely need to be framed in terms of shared social role expectations and responsibilities to elicit prosocial affect and behavior. A corollary principle is that the individualistic or collectivistic orientation of the similarity message may depend on the type of issue or problem. For example, *individualistic* similarity messages may be most useful for eliciting prosocial emotions between individuals cross-culturally, whereas *collectivistic* similarity messages may be most influential when attempting to elicit prosocial affect between social institutions cross-culturally.

Second, too often social and emotional identities of individuals and social groups are constructed in terms of differences from rather than similarities with others. Identities based on differences from others are likely a prime source of mutual intolerance and rejection observed within and across cultures. Social institutions (e.g., families, schools, and political groups) need to be taught how to use social influence principles to increase their members' capacity to respond compassionately and prosocially toward social outgroups. Thus, children's and adults' empathetic and prosocial responsiveness might be fostered by identities based on similarities with, rather than their differences from, other individuals, social groups, or cultures. Third, mass media- and government-based interventions could incorporate messages that ask individuals to focus on the feelings, needs, and perspectives of these others and that interpret problems befalling them in terms of situational rather than dispositional causes (e.g., in terms of factors beyond their intention or control).

Finally, the globalization of market economies, the emergence of democracies in Eastern Europe, and the concomitant shifting of political and social ties among nations have resulted in a pace of cross-cultural interactions that is unprecedented, and they make such interventions all the more urgent and necessary. Individuals, groups, and governmental institutions must quickly learn about their respective rules of social exchange and influence, such as those illustrated in this and other chapters in this volume, if cross-cultural interactions are to reflect a compassionate and peaceful character.

ACKNOWLEDGMENTS

This work was supported by a University grant to the first author.

REFERENCES

Asakawa, K., & Matsuoka, S. (1987). A developmental study of empathy in childhood. *Japanese Journal of Educational Psychology, 35*, 231–240.

Batson, C. D., Batson, J. G., Todd, R. M., Brummett, B. H., Shaw, L. L., & Aldeguer, C. M. R. (1995). Empathy and the collective good: Caring for one of the others in a social dilemma. *Journal of Personality and Social Psychology, 68*(4), 619–631.

Betancourt, H. (1990). An attribution-empathy model of helping behavior: Behavioral intentions and judgments of help-giving. *Personality and Social Psychology Bulletin, 16*(3), 573–591.

Betancourt, H., Hardin, C., & Manzi, J. (1992). Beliefs, value orientation, and culture in attribution processes and helping behavior. *Journal of Cross-Cultural Psychology, 23*(2), 179– 195.

Eisenberg, N., & Miller, P. A. (1987). The relation of empathy to prosocial and related behaviors. *Psychological Bulletin, 101*, 91–119.

Fiske, A. P. (1991). The cultural relativity of selfish individualism: Anthropological evidence that humans are inherently sociable. In M. S. Clark (Ed.), *Prosocial behavior: Volume 12* (pp. 176–214). Newbury Park, CA: Sage.

Graham, S., & Folkes, V. S. (Eds.). (1990). *Attribution theory: Applications to achievement, mental health, and interpersonal conflict.* Hillsdale, NJ: Lawrence Erlbaum Associates.

Hamilton, W. D. (1964). The genetical evolution of social behavior. *Journal of Theoretical Biology, 7*, 1–16.

Hedges, L. V., & Olkin, I. (1986). *Statistical methods for meta-analyses.* New York: Academic Press.

Heider, F. (1944). Social perception and phenomenal causality. *Psychological Review, 51*, 358–374.

Hewstone, M. (1990). *Causal attributions: From cognitive processes to collective beliefs.* Oxford: Blackwell.

Hilton, D. J., Smith, R. H., & Kin, S. H. (1995). Processes of causal explanation and dispositional attribution. *Journal of Personality and Social Psychology, 68*, 377–387.

Hofstede, G. (1980). *Culture's consequences.* Beverly Hills, CA: Sage.

Lutz, C. (1983). Parental goals, ethnopsychology, and the development of emotional meaning. *Ethos, 11*, 246–262.

Jain, U. (1994). Socio-cultural construction of emotions. *Psychology and Developing Societies, 6*(2), 151–168.

Kenrick, D. T., Neuberg, S. L., & Cialdini, R. *(1999). Social psychology: Unraveling the mystery.* Boston: Allyn & Bacon

MacDonald, K. (1984). An ethological-social learning theory of the development of altruism: Implications for human sociobiology. *Ethology and Sociobiology, 5*, 97–109.

MacLean, P. D. (1967). The brain in relation to empathy and medical education. *Journal of Nervous and Mental Disease, 144*, 374–382.

Markus, H. R., & Kitayama, S. (1991). Culture and the self: Implications for cognition, emotion, and motivation. *Psychological Review, 98*, 224–253.

Matthews, K. A., Batson, C. D., Horn, J., & Rosenman, R. H. (1981). "Principles in his nature which interest him in the fortune of others...": The heritability of empathetic concern for others. *Journal of Personality, 49*, 237–247.

McCrae, R. R., & Costa, Jr., P. T. (1997). Personality trait structure as a human universal. *American Psychologist, 52*(5), 509–516.

Miller, J. G. (1984). Culture and the development of everyday social explanation. *Journal of Personality and Social Psychology, 46*(5), 961–978.

Miller, J. G (1986). Early cross-cultural commonalities in social explanation. *Developmental Psychology, 22*, 514–520.

Miller, J. G., & Bersoff, D. M. (1992). Cultural influences on the moral status of reciprocity and the discounting of endogenous motivation. *Journal of Personality and Social Psychology Bulletin, 20*, 592–602.

Miller, J. G., Bersoff, D. M., & Harwood, R. L. (1990). Perceptions of social responsibilities in India and in the United States: Moral imperatives or personal decisions? *Journal of Personality & Social Psychology, 58*, 33–47.

Misra, G. (1991). Socio-cultural influences on moral behaviour. *The Indian Journal of Social Work, 52*(2), 179–194.

Moghaddam, F. M. (1998). *Social psychology: Exploring universals across cultures.* New York: W. H. Freeman.

Moghaddam, F. M., Taylor, D. M., & Wright, S. C. (1993). *Social psychology in cross-cultural perspective.* New York: W. H. Freeman and Company.

Myers, D. G. (1999). *Social psychology, (6th ed.).* Boston: McGraw-Hill.

Nakasoto, Y., & Matsui, H. (1996 August). *A structure of altruistic attitudes: A comparison of American, Chinese, Korean, Turkish, and Japanese youths.* Paper presented at the 26th International Congress of Psychology, Montreal, Canada.

Osbeck, L. M., Moghaddam, F. M., & Perreault, S. (1997). Similarity and attraction among majority and minority groups in a multicultural context. *International Journal of Intercultural Relations, 21*(1), 113–123.

Raboteg-Saric, Z. (1986). Distress attributions: Effects on altruistic behavior. ZAdar: Filozofski fakultet, Odsjek za psihologiju. In I. Manenica (Ed.), *Fifth psychology days* (pp. 275–283).

Rothbart, M. K., & Derryberry, D. (1981). Development of individual differences in temperament. In M. E. Lamb & A. L. Brown (Eds.), *Advances in developmental psychology* (Vol. 1, pp. 37–86). Hillsdale, NJ: Lawrence Erlbaum Associates.

Shutoh, T. (1994). *yoji/jido no aitakodo o kiteisuru kyokan to kanjo yokino yakuwari* [*The roles of empathy and empathetic expectation that determine altruistic behavior*]. Tokyo: Kusamashobo.Shweder, R. A. (1993). The cultural psychology of the emotions. In M. Lewis & J. Haviland (Eds.), *The handbook of emotion* (pp. 417–431). New York: Guilford.

Shweder, R. A. (1993). The cultural psychology of the emotions. In M. Lewis & J Haviland (Eds.), *The Handbook of Emotion*. New York: Guilford.

Stevenson, H. W. (1991). The development of prosocial behavior in large-scale collective societies: China & Japan. In R. A. Hinde & J. Groebel (Eds.), *Cooperation and prosocial behavior* (pp. 89–105). Cambridge: Cambridge University Press.

Strayer, J. (1987). Picture-story indices of empathy. In N. Eisenberg & J. Strayer (Eds.), *Empathy and is development* (pp. 351–355). Cambridge: Cambridge University Press.

Thakkar, B. M., & Kanekar, S. (1989). Dispositional empathy and causal attribution as determinants of estimated willingness to help. *The Irish Journal of Psychology, 10*(3), 381–387.

Triandis, H. C. (1991). Cross-cultural differences in assertiveness/competition vs. group loyalty/cooperation. In R. A. Hinde & J. Groebel (Eds.), *Cooperation and prosocial behaviour* (pp. 78–88). Cambridge: Cambridge University Press.

Trivers, R. L. (1971). The evolution of reciprocal altruism. *Quarterly Review of Biology, 46*, 33–37.

Watanabe, Y., & Eto, C. (1990). The influence of empathy and controllability on prosocial behavior in children. *Japanese Journal of Educational Psychology, 38*, 151–156.

Weiner, B. (1985). An attributional theory of achievement motivation and emotion. *Psychological Review, 92*(4), 548–573.

Yang, K., & Bond, M. H. (1990). Exploring implicit personality theories with indigenous or imported constructs: The Chinese case. *Journal of Personality and Social Psychology, 58*(6), 1087–1095.

Zahn-Waxler, C., Robinson, J. L., & Emde, R. N. (1992). The development of empathy in twins. *Developmental Psychology, 28*, 1038–1047.

5

Social Influence Principles in Polish Advertising and Consumer Decision Making

Maria Pietras
University of Silesia

ABSTRACT

Cialdini (1993) hypothesized and garnered substantial evidence for the notion that six psychological principles underlie most social influence attempts. The relative efficacy of these principles in mass-mediated influences has not previously been examined. The present study tested the impact of three of these six principles on Polish consumers' reactions to an advertised product. The principles of social proof, authority, and scarcity were manipulated in advertisements designed to persuade consumers to buy a new product. As hypothesized, the effectiveness of the principles varied depending on the consumers' demographic and psychological characteristics. Among the three principles, the scarcity principle proved to be particularly effective. The results are viewed in terms of individualism/collectivism and the scarcity economy in Poland's recent history. The practical implications of these findings for future advertising campaigns are discussed.

MASS-MEDIATED INFLUENCES ON CONSUMER BEHAVIOR

Economic behavior involving such activities as shopping and buying is shaped by different types of social influences. Attempts at influencing consumers may take an interpersonal form (e.g., sales clerks interactions with shoppers), may result from structural influences (e.g., economic or political conditions), or may operate through more indirect routes, such as the mass media (Warneryd, 1988). The current study examined mass-mediated influence on consumer behavior in Poland.

There is a great deal of evidence of the mass media's influence on consumer behavior (see Roberts & Bachen, 1981, for a review). It could be said that consumers act in *mass-mediated social reality* (O'Guinn & Shrum, 1991). Advertising is one of the most powerful instruments of mass-mediated influences; its persuasive or compliance-gaining effects have been of major interest to researchers and practitioners alike. A vast number of investigations into the factors involved in successful advertising have been conducted. They have examined advertisements' form and content (Crowley & Hoyer, 1994; Petty, Cacioppo, & Schumann, 1983), advertising strategies (Maccoby & Alexander, 1980), the specificity of the persuasion process (Gotlieb & Sarel, 1991; Petty & Cacioppo, 1981), the social context of advertising (Baran & Blasko, 1984), demographic variables (Guy, Rittenburg, & Hawes, 1994; Melville & Cornish, 1993) and the impact of various psychological features of target persons (Haugtvedt, Petty, & Cacioppo, 1992; Shavitt, Lowrey, & Han, 1992).

However, little is known about the relative efficacy of various social influence tactics commonly used in advertising. One of the most useful recent conceptualizations of these tactics was proposed by Cialdini (1993), who found that thousands of different compliance tactics fall into six basic categories governed by six fundamental psychological principles: reciprocation, commitment/consistency, social proof, liking, authority and scarcity. Although these principles have not frequently been pitted against one another, some researchers have examined their relative strength in interpersonal settings (Brock, Good, & Brannon, 1989; Cialdini, Wosinska, Barrett, Butner, & Gornik-Durose, 1997, chap. 2, this volume; Cody & Seiter, chap. 17, this volume). To date, the efficacy of these six principles in a mass-mediated environment has not been systematically studied.

Another crucial issue is to what extent these principles can be considered universal rules of advertising (i.e., whether they are applicable to different cultures). Previous cross-cultural research indicates that implementing effective advertising across cultural boundaries is a rather difficult and challenging task. For instance, consumers from various nations, cultures, and subcultures show differences in their perception of ads (McDonald, 1994; Parekh & Kanekar, 1994), their reactions to appeals used in ads (Aaker & Williams, 1998; Alden, Hoyer, & Lee, 1993; McCullough, 1993), and to emotional expression in ads (Hong, Muderrisoglu, & Zinkhan, 1987).

Although the effectiveness of social influence tactics employed in advertising across cultures and nations has not been extensively explored, some suggestions regarding the importance of cultural differences may be drawn from related studies, such as studies examining cultural variability in persuasion. Research on cultural patterns and the persuasion process describes differences in the vulnerability of different nations and cultures to various advertised messages (Han & Shavitt, 1994). It is assumed that differences in culturally endorsed attitudes and values may be reflected in varying vulnerabilities to persuasive appeals that emphasize these values. One core dimension of cultural variability, individualism/collectivism

(Triandis, 1995), appears to play an important role in the persuasion process, influencing the effectiveness of different types of advertising appeals (Aaker & Williams, 1998; Han & Shavitt, 1994). Han and Shavitt (1994) found that members of an individualistic society (United States) were more persuaded by ads appealing to individualistic benefits, whereas those from a collectivistic country (South Korea) appeared more influenced by ads emphasizing family or ingroup benefits, at least for shared products.

The postsocialistic countries of Central and Eastern Europe, like Poland, have been considered to be collectivistically oriented (Hofstede, 1983). Recent Polish investigations show that, although general economic and political changes in Poland are conducive to individualistic tendencies, they are largely manifested only at a superficial level, whereas more deeply rooted values tend to be collectivistic (Reykowski, 1994).

One may speculate that, for Polish consumers, appeals to others in ads (e.g., using a social proof-type tactic) should be very persuasive. The assumption that social proof would be effective in a collectivistic nation was tested and largely supported in the Cialdini et al. (chap. 2, this volume) cross-cultural investigation, although this research was conducted on interpersonal, as opposed to mass-mediated, influence. Yet one could also expect that, given Polish history, especially the difficult period of the "shortage economy" in the 1980s, consumers would be sensitive to information about the scarcity or unavailability of products so that employing the scarcity principle would also be effective. In addition, it is possible that—taking into account the relatively high level of authoritarianism in Polish society (Korzeniowski, 1993)—appealing to the authority principle would induce a high level of compliance among Polish consumers: Compliance to authority has been seen as a core feature of authoritarianism (Gabennesch, 1972; Miller, Slomczynski, & Schoenberg, 1981).

Existing evidence does not suggest a clear set of predictions as to the relative efficacy of the three principles of social proof, scarcity, and authority. The current study is designed to break new ground by examining the responses of Polish consumers to three compliance-eliciting tactics employing the three principles in a field investigation.

THE CURRENT STUDY

The primary focus of the current study was the impact of the social proof (SP), authority (AU), and scarcity (SC) principles among Polish consumers introduced to a new product. Four potential moderating variables (gender, age, income level, and locus of control) were measured in the study, as described next. The study included 278 Polish respondents (146 females, 132 males) chosen randomly from adults in shops and on the streets (92 in the SP condition, 86 in the AU condition, and 100 in the SC condition).

Experimental Materials and Independent Variables

In this study, the principles of social proof, authority, and scarcity were manipulated in three advertising leaflets created by the experimenter and designed to persuade customers to buy a newly introduced product (a self-massage device). Each of the three advertisements was constructed so that the main part of the information was identical, whereas the beginning and end of the leaflet were changed to reflect the three different social influence principles. Consequently, the first (social proof) ad contained information about other people's positive reactions to the product. These others were described as "people living all over the world" who use the product, especially in Western Europe and America. The reason that this group was selected to represent social proof instead of the more logical (and potentially more powerful) use of friends, neighbors, or families is that subjects would have independent knowledge about the lack of use of the product by these persons and therefore would dismiss the ad as inaccurate. The product was fictional, but in the flood of new, different products that washed throughout the Polish market in recent years with the onset of the market economy, consumers might easily believe that it was a real product.

In the second leaflet, utilized in the authority condition, the device was recommended by a doctor. To avoid the danger of inducing a foreign/domestic endorsement as a moderating factor, the physician was described as working in a Western (non-Polish) clinic. The third leaflet, corresponding to the scarcity condition, contained information about the limited quantity of the product, stating that it was distributed exclusively by a single, foreign firm.

Moderating Variables

The effect of the independent variable was examined in isolation as well as in relation to three potential demographic moderators and one possible psychological moderator. The impact of the demographic variables of gender, age, and income level on the perception of advertisements has been demonstrated in numerous studies (e.g., Guy, Rittenburg, & Hawes, 1994; Melville & Cornish, 1993). The psychological moderator—locus of control (LOC)—was selected from the vast number of potentially influential psychological traits in large part because the generalized expectancy for internal versus external locus of control of reinforcement (Rotter, 1966) has been shown to be relevant to a number of economic behaviors, including consumer behavior (Foxal & Goldsmith, 1988; Warneryd, 1988). Additionally, there is empirical evidence about differences in reactions to social pressure between internal versus external LOC individuals (see Phares, 1976). In the present study, LOC was measured with the Delta-questionnaire developed by Drwal (1979), which is based on the Rotter Internal–External Control Scale (Rotter, 1966).

Dependent Variables

The dependent measures were related to three aspects of the customers' decision-making process: initial product perception, assessment of product desirability, and the actual decision to purchase the product (Hawkins, Best, & Coney, 1995). Respondents were asked to answer questions corresponding to each of these three stages. The measures of the decision-making process, evaluated on 5-point scales, were as follows: (a) perception of the product with regard to 10 product attributes (e.g., aesthetic, clever, or healthy), (b) desire to have the product, and (c) declaration of intention to order the product immediately. The product attributes items were combined to form the overall product evaluation measure (i.e., the arithmetic mean for the 10 product attributes). Desirability of the product and strength of the intention to order it were thought to be reflected in respondents' choice of 1 to 5 points on the scales. Thus, these three dependent measures reflected favorability of the product for consumers.

RESULTS

Effects of the Social Influence Principles

The results show that consumers' perception and reactions to the advertised product differed with regard to type of social influence principle. Significant differences between the SP condition, on the one hand, and AU and SC, on the other, were found with regard to arithmetic means concerning product evaluation and desirability (see Fig. 5.1).[1] Namely, consumers in the SC condition evaluated the product significantly more positively than respondents exposed to the SP leaflet ($t = 4.53$, df-190, $p < .001$); they also showed tendency to desire product more ($t = 1.47$, df-190, $p < .1$). Respondents who read the authority-related ad also perceived the product in a much more positive way than those influenced by SP leaflet ($t = 2.59$, df-176, $p < .01$). They were also significantly more willing to purchase the device ($t = 5.13$, df-176, $p < .001$).

When customers were pressed to show their more concrete intentions by declaring whether they were willing to order the self-massage appliance immediately, only about 20% were ready to do this. For this third dependent measure, there were no significant differences between arithmetic means for the three groups of respondents.

The limited effectiveness of the social proof principle as a compliance-gaining tactic came as a surprise. This principle is expected to be particularly effective when the individual is confronted with uncertainty or when similar others serve as social comparisons. One might expect that, in this study, the newly

---

[1]The t test of significance of independent samples was utilized.

FIG. 5-1. Product favorability in conditions of scarcity, authority, and social proof appeal.

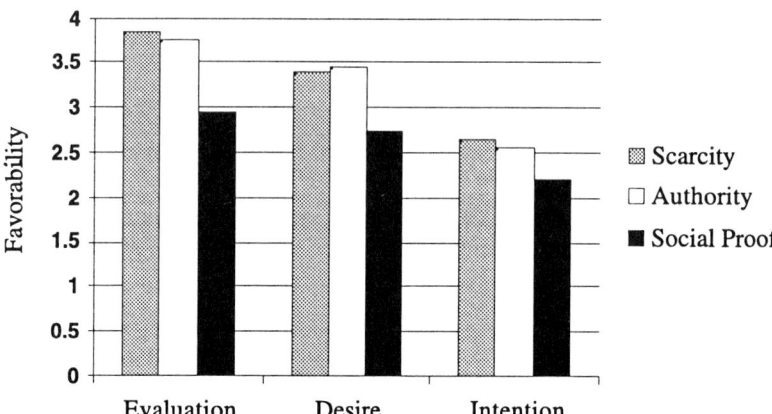

introduced product would evoke some degree of uncertainty and propel consumers to look for additional information for guidance, including information about other people's reactions. Perhaps the *others* described in the leaflets— Western Europeans and Americans—did not, in this case, represent a proper reference group for Polish consumers. It is commonly known that, for many people living in Central and Eastern Europe, Western patterns of consumption and styles of life are tempting and eagerly imitated; therefore, the *others* described in the advertisement could serve as a reference group to which many Polish consumers aspire. Unfortunately, the extent to which the *others* represented a proper reference group was not tested in this study.

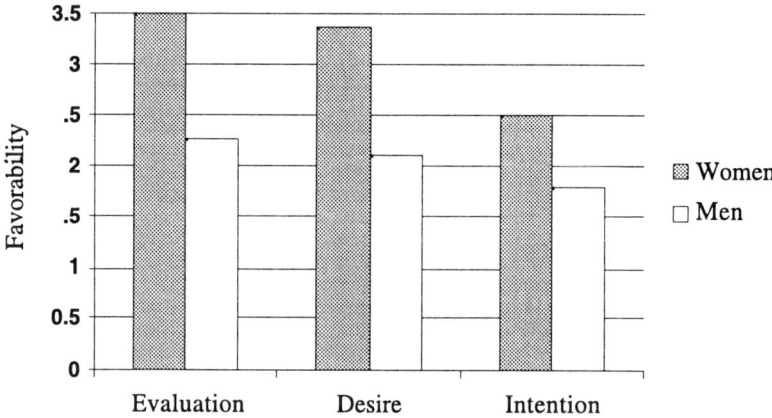

FIG. 5-2a. Product favorability with social proof appeal among women and men.

FIG. 5-2b. Product favorability with scarcity appeal among women and men.

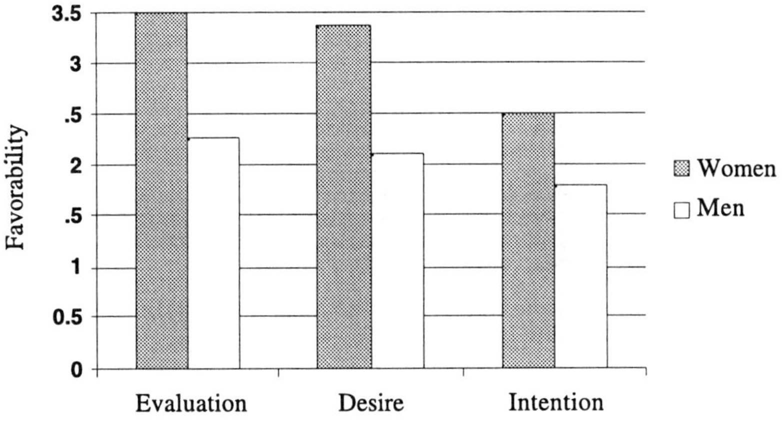

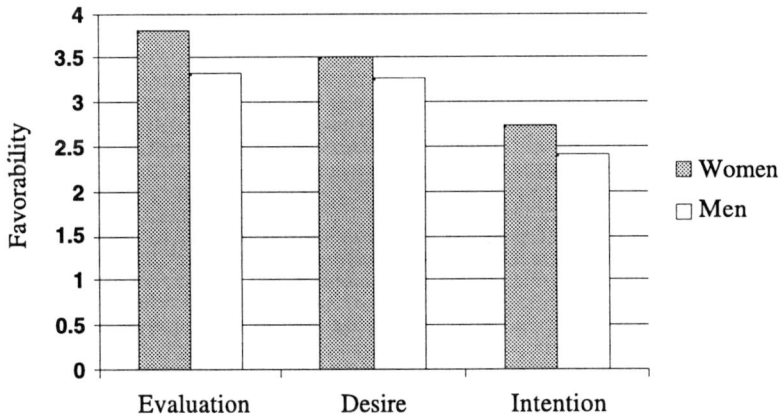

Gender and Consumer Decision Making

Although women were generally more susceptible to the three ads, the greatest differences between men and women were found in the SP condition, in which men were substantially more resistant to social pressure (see Fig. 5-2a). Significant differences between men and women were found in regard to product perception ($t = 5.9$, df-90, $p < .001$), desire to have the product ($t = 7.9$, df-90, $p < .001$), and intention to order the product immediately ($t = 4.38$, df-90, $p < .001$).

In the scarcity condition, women exhibited significantly more desire for the product than men ($t = 3.3$, df-98, $p < .01$). They also tended to be more

FIG. 5-2c. Product favorability with authority appeal among women and men.

FIG. 5-3a. Product favorability with authority appeal among age groups.

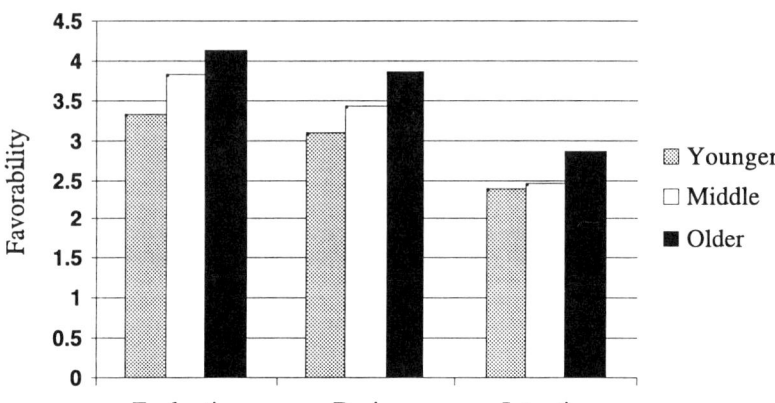

positive than men in product evaluation (t = 1.63, df-98, p < .1), as well as more likely to order the product (t = 1.68, df-98, p < .1; see Fig. 5-2b). No significant differences were found in the AU manipulation (see Fig. 5-2c).

All in all, gender turned out to significantly impact product evaluation, product desirability, and intention to order the product—in that women demonstrated greater compliance than men. This discrepancy does not necessarily reflect greater compliance in general to the three principles by women, but instead may result from the type of product advertised: The self-massage device is a health and beauty product that is more likely to appeal to women. The other possibility, and one that cannot be excluded, is that basic differences between men's and women's responses to social pressure or social proof exist, with women tending to be more vulnerable.

Age and Consumer Decision Making

Although in general the social influence principles did not differentiate strongly among the age groups (the three groups were up to 35, 36–50, over 50), there was one exception.[2] The older respondents were more influenced than others by the authority principle (see Fig. 5-3a). When reading the leaflet that included the doctor's

[2]One of the important assumptions of the age divisions was the differing experience of these three groups of Poles on social, political, and economic dimensions. Namely, the youngest started their adult life and related activity during major economic and political transformations in Poland, whereas the middle-aged *divided* their experiences between the period before these transformations began and the subsequent years, while the experiences of the older were dominated by the period before these transformations.

FIG. 5-3b. Product favorability with social proof appeal among women and men.

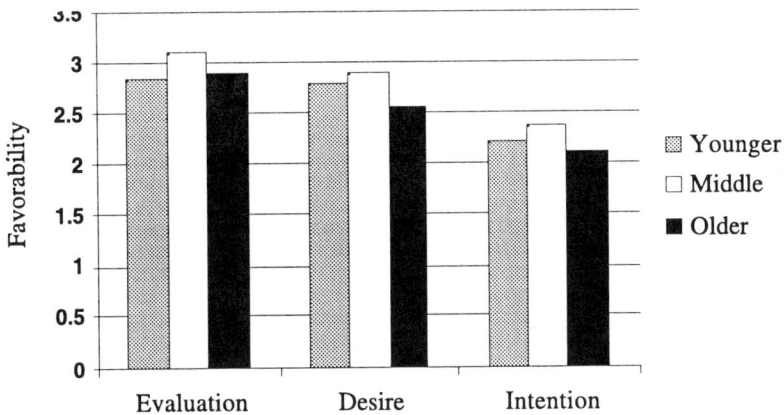

recommendation, they expressed significantly more positive opinions of the product than younger consumers ($t = 2.02$, df-58, $p < .05$). In the AU condition. The older consumers also desired the product more than the younger ones ($t = 2.04$, df-58, $p < .05$); however, no significant differences were found when intentions to order the product were taken into account.

Appealing to *others* (SP) did not significantly differentiate the age groups (see Fig. 5-3b). Similarly, no significant differences were found among age groups in the SC condition. However, in this case, favorability of the product was much higher than for the SP appeal (see Fig. 5-3c). It is interesting that, in the SC condition, only half of the older consumers perceived the product as healthy, whereas such evaluation was expressed by about 75% of the older group in the authority and

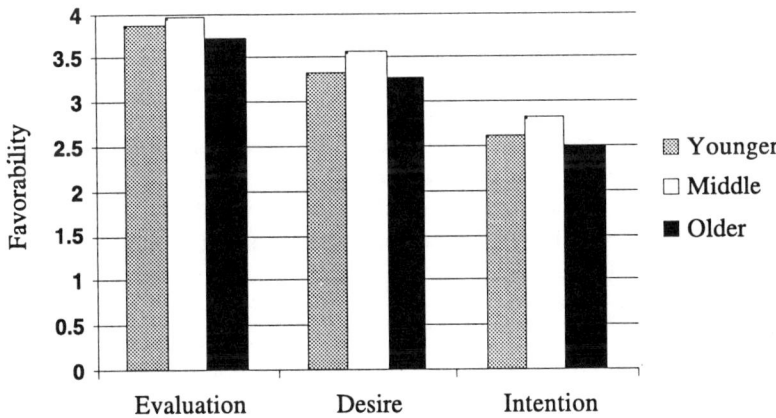

FIG. 5-3c. Product favorability with scarcity appeal among age groups.

FIG. 5-4a. Product favorability with social proof appeal among income groups.

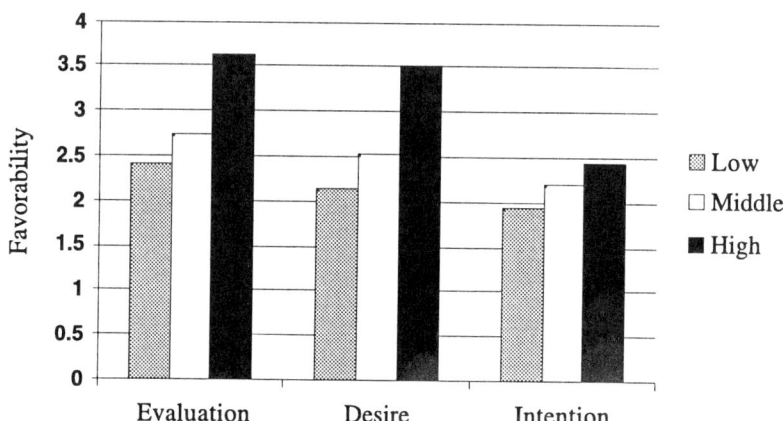

social proof conditions. Such a devaluation of this desirable attribute of the appliance might be interpreted as a defensive reaction of older consumers against the unavailability of a product, which could improve their health.

Income Level and Consumer Decision Making

The greatest differences among income groups in the favorability of the product were found with regard to the social proof principle (see Fig. 5-4a).[3] It appeared that the perception of the high-income consumer group was the most influenced by this principle. They evaluated the product significantly more positively than low-income respondents ($t = 2.41$, df-49, $p < .05$) and somewhat more positively than middle-income consumers ($t = 1.71$, df-63, $p < .1$).

Similarly, only the SP condition clearly differentiated among income groups on the desirability measure (see Fig. 5-4a). That is, consumers with high income expressed a significantly higher desire to buy the product than consumers of low ($t = 2.62$, df-49, $p < .05$) and middle income ($t = 1.96$, df-63, $p < .05$). Perhaps the *others* introduced in the leaflet (people living in Western Europe and America) were more likely to been seen as a relevant reference group by high-income than by middle- or low-income Polish consumers, at least for a luxury like the self-massage device.

[3]Respondents were divided into income groups based on monthly income after taxes per person in the family. Three income groups were as follow: (a) below 350 PLZ per family member; this amount just reaches the so-called *social minimum* in Poland for that time; (b) 350-600 PLZ per family member; and (c) more than 600 PLZ per family member.

FIG. 5-4b. Product favorability with scarcity appeal among income groups.

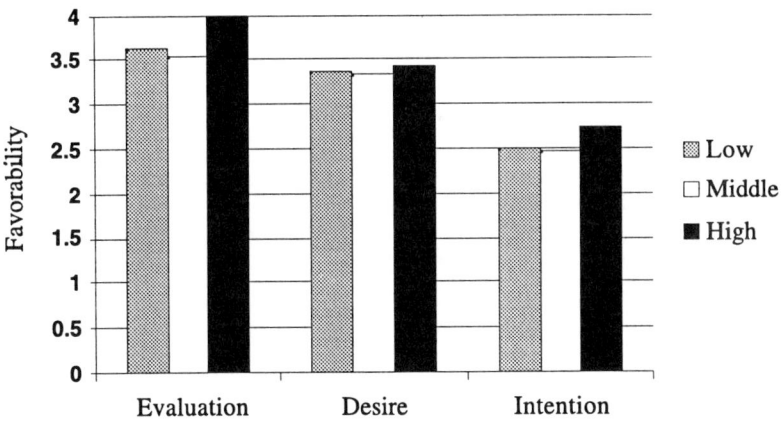

The advertisement based on the scarcity principle provoked a positive product evaluation and level of desirability among all , and no significant differences were found within income groups (see Fig. 5-4b).

Interestingly, the authority-based appeal produced greater desirability for the product among lower income customers, especially in comparison with middle-income group, though the difference was not conventionally significant ($t = 1.69$, df-64, $p < .1$; see Fig. 5-4c). Thus, it seemed to operate in the opposite direction than social proof. Typically, lower income groups include a large portion of the less well educated and, as Hovland, Lumsdaine, and Sheffield (1949)

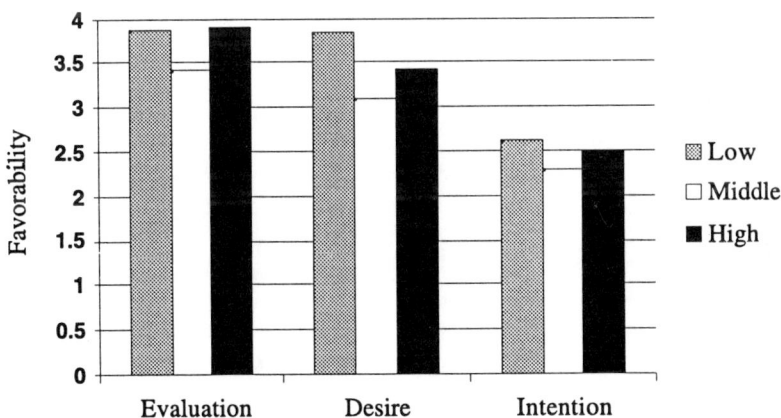

FIG. 5-4c. Product favorability with authority appeal among income groups.

FIG. 5-5a. Product favorability with social proof appeal among LOC groups.

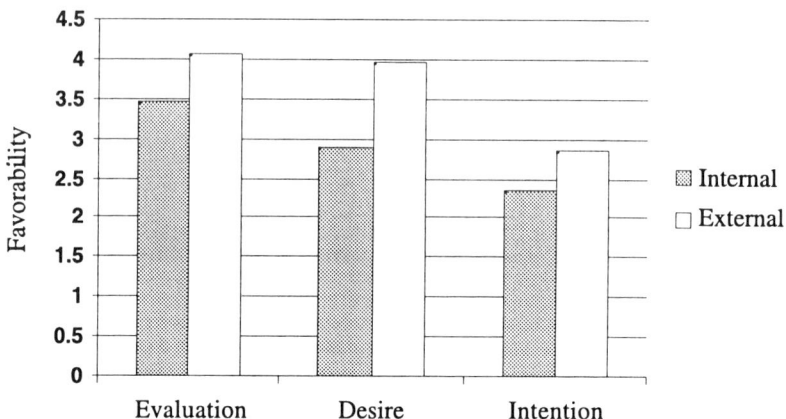

documented a half century ago, they tend to be more vulnerable to one-sided information especially if it comes from a powerful source.

Locus of Control and Consumer Decision Making

The most evident differences between high and low locus of control (LOC) individuals were found when they were induced with the social proof principle (see Fig. 5-5a). Consumers with external LOC evaluated the device much more positively than internal LOC subjects ($t = 3.62$, df-54, $p < .001$). It was also

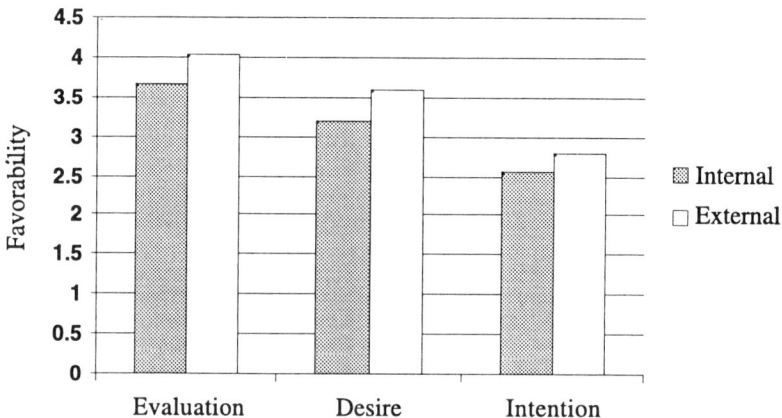

FIG. 5-5b. Product favorability with authority appeal among LOC groups.

FIG. 5-5c. Product favorability with scarcity appeal among LOC groups.

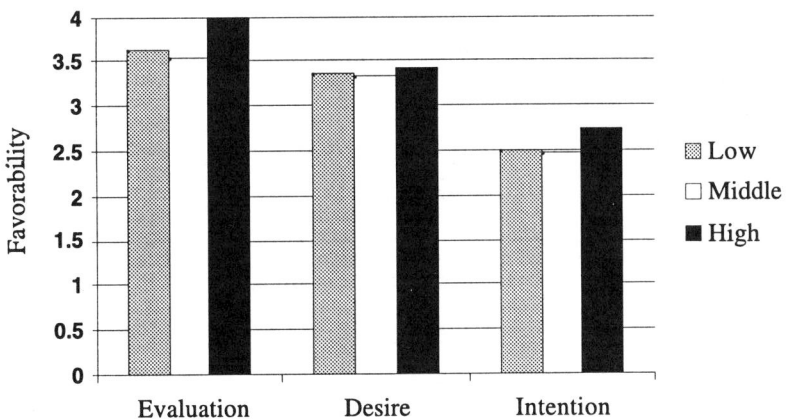

found that external LOC consumers desired the product significantly more than internal LOC individuals when exposed to the social proof principle ($t = 2.92$, df-54, $p < .01$). When exposed to the leaflet with authority appeal, external LOC consumers tended to desire the product more than internal ones ($t = 1.97$, df-54, $p < .1$; see Fig. 5-5b).

In the scarcity condition, no significant differences were found between internal and external LOC consumers in product evaluation or product desirability (see Fig. 5-5c). Therefore, the scarcity principle may be more universal, inducing compliance in both external and internal LOC consumers.

DISCUSSION AND PRACTICAL IMPLICATIONS

Overall, Polish consumers responded in a differentiated way to the compliance-gaining tactics applied in the advertisements. These differences were more evident in the product evaluations than in the consumers' desires and declarations to immediately purchase it.

The social proof tactic appeared to be the least influential when moderating factors were not considered. Therefore, the expectation of high vulnerability to an *others* appeal within the more collectivistically oriented society was not confirmed. It should be noted that social proof was compared with two other social influence principles, and thus no conclusions can be drawn about its efficacy relative to a no influence principle appeal or to appeals that implement the remaining three social influence principles (of commitment/consistency, reciprocity, and liking). This apparent failure of prediction may reflect the way in which social proof was operationalized in this experiment. That is, in a naturalistic setting, the reference group to which the uncertain consumer might look for guidance would probably be a group of similar Poles, rather than individuals in Western European nations and America, as was used in this experiment.

Other cross-cultural research on vulnerability of different cultures and nations to more individualistic or more collectivistic advertising appeals utilized *others* from the same culture as the subjects (e.g., Han & Shavitt, 1994). Perhaps contrary to the opinions of many Poles, Western patterns of consumer behavior may not be easily assimilated in the newly emerging market economies. Moreover, the *others* described in this experiment may not have appeared sufficiently similar to affect the prevalent interdependent self still prevalent among the Polish. As Triandis (1995) pointed out, collectivists tend to create sharper boundaries between ingroups and outgroups, which may result in stronger rejection of outgroups.

In addition, previous findings of a strong social proof effect in Poland contrasted social proof with an incompatible, individualistic principle (commitment/consistency; see Cialdini et al., chap. 2, this volume) and not with authority and scarcity, as was done here. Thus, the current study does not represent a true test of the Cialdini et al. (1997) findings, which demonstrated that social proof was more powerful among collectivists than the commitment/consistency principle. Furthermore, unlike in the Cialdini et al. (1997) study, the level of personal individualism/collectivism was not measured in this study, therefore it is likely that a significant number of individualists were included in its respondent pool. Therefore, the interaction between situational considerations and personal individualism/collectivism was not evaluated by this study.

It is also true that, in the present study, the social proof principle did not affect all consumers in the same way; in fact it provoked the most differentiated responses of the three manipulations. Women and individuals with external LOC or high income were more vulnerable to SP than to the other principles. It appears, then, that the efficacy of appealing to social proof in ads significantly depends on specific target audience features that facilitate or limit its impact.

Overall, the authority manipulation was much more effective than the social proof manipulation. Participants in the AU condition perceived the product in a more positive light, especially in regard to its healthy attributes, when exposed to the expert opinion of the physician. They were also more likely to agree to order it. It can be seen that the respondents placed heavy trust in the doctor's authority, and the fact that he was of foreign origin may have been insignificant. Such high compliance to authority might result from the relatively high level of authoritarianism of many Poles, understood as an evaluative orientation including convictions about the hierarchical organization of social relations and the necessity of submission to authorities (Korzeniowski, 1993). It was also found that—consonant with research from other nations (see Lipsitz, 1965; Meloen et al., 1988)—vulnerability to authority was higher among poor, low-educated men and older persons of both genders.

Of the three principles, the scarcity principle was the most effective across different groups of Polish consumers: It provoked similar and positive responses in both genders, in all three age groups, and among both internal and external LOC individuals. High-income consumers were slightly more persuaded by using this tactic than were middle- and low-income individuals. This almost universal vulnerability of Polish consumers to the scarcity principle may be related to their long-lasting experience with deep shortages in the Polish market in the 1980s (and, periodically throughout the post-World War II era), which led Polish consumers to become more sensitive to any scarcity. The abundance of products in today's market has not erased the tendency to value, desire, and try to obtain items simply because of their possible scarcity. Further support for this interpretation is found in American research, which shows the power of scarcity when compliance is elicited from strangers in non face-to-face interactions (by telephone; Brock, Good, & Brannon, 1989). Brock et al. (1989) found that appealing to scarcity is more effective in inducing compliance than appealing to authority, social proof, and liking, at least in short term, impersonal interactions.

Although the previously mentioned results of Polish and American research might suggest that scarcity is universally effective in gaining compliance, other empirical evidence has demonstrated some limits to its efficacy. For instance, Cody and Seiter (chap. 17, this volume) found that sales clerks were less likely to use the scarcity tactic than other tactics in interactions with customers because it would serve to diminish the store's image by implying that the store is not well stocked.

Thus, successful implementation of the principles of social influence requires —as Cialdini et al. (chap. 2, this volume) similarly concluded—consideration of the specific conditions under which they may be effective. This leads to some suggestions regarding maximizing the effectiveness of the social influence principles when attempting mass-mediated influence via advertisements.

First of all, cultural and national specificity should be taken into account. This is not limited to core cultural values (like individualism/collectivism), but also includes a nation's specific history, which might significantly impact vulnerability to different social influence principles in advertising (e.g., a history of economic shortages).

Second, different compliance-gaining tactics may be best suited to different groups of consumers. As demonstrated in the current research, their efficacy strongly depends on the demographic and psychological characteristics of consumers, such as gender, age, income level, and LOC. Some of these characteristics also turned out to be significant mediators of compliance in other studies described in this volume.

Third, particular caution should be taken when attempting to implement the social proof principle, because its effectiveness seems to depend more heavily on characteristics of the target audience than do scarcity and authority. Relatedly, a reference group of *influential others* should be carefully selected.

Otherwise the results of the applied social pressure might be unpredictable and even opposite to the intended ones.

Finally, the least risky strategy in advertisements seems to be utilization of the scarcity principle, at least for consumers with significant experience with market shortages. This principle of social influence affected respondents in the most universal way. Yet its influence may be waning in Poland because advertisers find it increasingly difficult to convince consumers that a product actually is scarce or unavailable. Typically, scarcity-related messages are expressed in such slogans as "last chance offer," "limited supply," or "limited time only." In conditions in which products are abundant, Poles may no longer believe that true shortages exist. Thus, the real challenge for professional influencers is not whether to employ scarcity, but rather how to effectively use the deeper psychological mechanisms underlying consumers preferences for scarce goods (e.g., the uniqueness motive, competition) in compliance-gaining tactics.

REFERENCES

Aaker, J. L., & Williams, P. (1998). Individualist versus collectivist cultures: How emotional appeals affect attitudes. *Journal of Consumer Research, 25*(3), 241–261.

Alden, D. L., Hoyer, W. D., & Lee, C. (1993). Identifying global and culture-specific dimensions of humor in advertising: A multinational analysis. *Journal of Marketing, 57*(2), 64–75.

Baran, S. J., & Blasko, U. J. (1984). Social perception and the by-products of advertising. *Journal of Communication, 34*(3), 12–20.

Brock, T. C., Good, K. E., & Brannon, L. A. (1989). Relative efficacy of influence tactics: *Effect of scarcity, authority, social proof and liking on the compliance of telephone operators and hotel desk clerks.* Unpublished laboratory report, Ohio State University.

Cialdini, R. B. (1993). *Influence: Science and practice.* New York: HarperCollins.

Cialdini, R. B., Wosinska, W., Barrett, D. W., Butner, J., & Gornik-Durose, M. (1997, August). *Compliance with influence attempts using the principle of social proof and commitment/consistency in two cultures.* Paper presented at the conference "The Practice of Social Influence in Established and Emerging Democracies," Przegorzaly, Poland.

Crowley, A. E., & Hoyer, W. D. (1994). An integrative framework for understanding two-sided persuasion. *Journal of Consumer Research, 20*(4), 561–574.

Drwal, R. (1979). Opracowanie kwestionariusza Delta do pomiaru poczucia kontroli. [Elaboration of Delta-questionnaire for locus of control measurement]. *Studia Psychologiczne, t.XVII/1*, 66–80.

Foxal, G. R., & Goldsmith, R. E. (1988). Personality and consumer research: Another look. Special issue: Developments in consumer research. *Journal of the Market Research Society, 30*(2), 111–125.

Gabennesch, H. (1972). Authoritarianism as world view. *American Journal of Sociology, 77*(5), 857–875.

Gotlieb, J. B., & Sarel, D. (1991). Comparative advertising effectiveness: The role of involvement and source credibility. *Journal of Advertising, 20*(1), 38–45.

Guy, B. S., Rittenburg, T. L., & Hawes, D. K. (1994). Dimensions and characteristics of time perceptions and perspectives among older consumers. *Psychology and Marketing, 11*(1), 35–56.

Han, S., & Shavitt, S. (1994). Persuasion and culture: Advertising appeals in individualistic and collectivistic societies. *Journal of Experimental Social Psychology, 30*, 326–350.

Haugtvedt, C. P., Petty, R. E., & Cacioppo, J. T. (1992). Need for cognition and advertising: Understanding the role of personality variables in consumer behavior. *Journal of Consumer Psychology, 1*(3), 239–260.

Hawkins, B. I., Best, R. J., & Coney, K. A. (1995). *Consumer behavior: Implications for marketing strategies.* Chicago: Irwin.

Hofstede, G. (1983). Dimensions of national cultures in fifty countries and three regions. In J. Deregowski, S. Dzuirawiec, & R. Annis (Eds.), *Explication of cross-cultural psychology* (pp. 335–555). Lisse, The Netherlands: Swets & Zeitlinger.

Hong, J. W., Muderrisoglu, A., & Zinkhan, G. M. (1987). Cultural differences and advertising expression: A comparative content analysis of Japanese and U.S. magazine advertising. *Journal of Advertising, 16*(1), 55–62.

Hovland, C. I., Lumsdaine, A. A., & Sheffield, F. D. (1949). Experiments on mass communication: *Studies in social psychology in World War II* (Vol III). Princeton, NJ.: Princeton University Press.

Korzeniowski, K. (1993). Orientacja demokratyczna vs. autorytarna w spoleczenstwie polskim [Democratic vs. Authoritarian orientation in Polish society]. In J. Reykowski, (Ed.) *Social values and attitudes in system changes* (pp. 129–154). Warszawa: Wyd. Instytutu Psychologii PAN.

Lipsitz, L. (1965). Working class authoritarianism: A re-evaluation. *American Sociological Review, 30*, 103–109.

Maccoby, N., & Alexander, J. (1980). Use of media in lifestyle programs. In P. O. Davidson & S. M. Davidson (Eds.), *Behavioral medicine: changing health lifestyles* (pp. 201–220). New York: Brunner/Mazel.

McCullough, L. S. (1993). A cross-cultural test of the two-part typology of humor. *Perceptual and Motor Skills, 76*(3), 1275–1281.

McDonald, W. J. (1994). Psychological associations with shopping: A moderator variable perspective. *Psychology and Marketing, 11*(6), 549–568.

Melville, D. J., & Cornish, I. M. (1993). Conservatism and gender in the perception of sex-roles in television advertisements. *Perceptual and Motor Skills, 77*(2), 642–643.

Meloen, J. D., Hagendoorn, L., Raaijmakers, Q., & Visser, L. (1988). Authoritarianism and the revival of political racism: Reassessments in the Netherlands of the reliability and validity of the concept of authoritarianism by Adorno et al. *Political Psychology, 9*(3), 413–429.

Miller, J., Slomczynski, K. M., & Schoenberg, R. J. (1981). Assessing comparability of measurement in cross-national research: Authoritarian conservatism in different socio-cultural settings. *Social Psychology Quarterly, 44*(3), 178–191.

O'Guinn, T. C., & Shrum, L. J. (1991, June). *Mass-mediated social reality: The social cognition and ecology of economic norms.* Paper presented at IAREP/SASE Conference, Stockholm, Sweden.

Parekh, H., & Kanekar, S. (1994). The physical attractiveness stereotype in a consumer-related situation. *Journal of Social Psychology, 134*(3), 297–300.

Petty, R. E., & Cacioppo, J. T. (1981). *Attitudes and persuasion: Classic and contemporary approaches.* Dubuque: William C. Brown.

Petty, R. E., Cacioppo, J. T., & Schumann, D. (1983). Central and peripheral routes to advertising effectiveness: The moderating role of involvement. *Journal of Consumer Research, 10*, 135–146.

Phares, E. J. (1976). *Locus of control in personality.* Morristown: General Learning Press.

Reykowski, J. (1994). Collectivism and individualism as dimensions of social change. In U. Kim, H. Triandis, C. Kagitcibasi, S. Choi, & G. Yoon (Eds.), Individualism and collectivism: *Theory, method and applications* (pp. 276–292). Thousand Oaks, CA: Sage.

Roberts, D. F., & Bachen, C. M. (1981). Mass communication effects. *Annual Review of Psychology, 32*, 307–356.

Rotter, J. B. (1966). Generalised expectancies for internal versus external control of reinforcement. *Psychological Monographs, 80*(1) (Whole No. 609).

Shavitt, S., Lowrey, T. M., & Han, S. (1992). Attitude functions in advertising: The interactive role of products and self-monitoring. *Journal of Consumer Psychology, 1*(4), 337–364.

Triandis, H. C. (1995). *Individualism and collectivism.* Boulder, CO: Westview.

Warneryd, K. E. (1988). Social influence on economic behavior. In W. F. Van Raaij, G. M. Van Veldhoven, & K. E. Warneryd (Eds.), *Handbook of economic psychology* (pp. 206–248). Dordrecht: Kluwer.

6

Culture, Norms, and Obligations: Cross-National Differences in Patterns of Interpersonal Norms and Felt Obligations Toward CoWorkers

Michael W. Morris

Joel M. Podolny

Sheira Ariel

Stanford University

ABSTRACT

This chapter reviews theory and evidence on cross-national differences in the dynamics of interpersonal obligation in the workplace. We propose that national culture shapes the normative systems that guide interaction in the workplace, and thereby moderates the salience of different sources of obligation. Drawing on past analyses of culture in terms of norms, we develop hypotheses about the dominant orientation of employee obligation in American, Chinese, German, and Spanish settings. We review evidence from a survey of employees in American, Chinese, German, and Spanish operations of a multinational retail bank. Because the formal structure of the organization is held constant across national operations, but the sourcing of employees is local, these sites provide a natural experiment to test how culture shapes employees' informal interactions and feelings of obligation. Predictions about differences in norms were supported by descriptive evidence from measures of employees' subjective attitudes and relationship patterns. Also, the determinants of employees' obligation differed in ways predicted from these larger normative systems.

Coordinating the efforts of employees in complex organizations relies on influence rather than coercion. Studies of organization and administration have long concluded that success depends on employees feeling obligated to cooperate with one another and their managers (Barnard, 1938). In recent years, as organizations have reduced hierarchies and explicit chains of command, the role of employee obligation in research and popular writing on management has become more prominent than ever (Cohen & Bradford, 1990; Moorman, 1991).

Organizational theorists and researchers have identified several distinct ways in which employees come to feel obligated to contribute by assisting others in the workplace. These analyses of workplace obligation can be understood in relation to more general principles of social influence (see Cialdini, 1993). For instance, a tradition flowing from Weber's (1947) studies of bureaucracy links obligation to employees' perceiving leaders as holding a position within a legitimate system of rules—in short, the principle of *legitimate authority*. A subsequent tradition contends that obligation to leaders reflects an instrumental exchange of information and resources—that is, the principle of *reciprocity* (Blau, 1955). Other traditions emphasize the obligation that employees feel in solidaristic peer relationships and attribute it to the affective rewards of friendship—in short, the principle of *liking* (Roethlisberger & Dickson, 1939). Empirical studies in each of these traditions of organizational research have extensively documented how feelings of interpersonal obligation drive employees to contribute to work organizations.

Although there can be little doubt that employee feelings of obligation arise toward many kinds of coworkers for many different reasons, including authority, reciprocity, and liking, it also stands to reason that not all sources of obligation are equally salient. Because time and energy are limited, there is a conflict between obligations in different directions, and some must be given higher priority than others. Hence, a crucial question is how the dominant source of obligation differs across settings. Unfortunately, however, organizational research has made relatively little effort to identify the moderating conditions that influence the salience of various, alternative sources of obligation. In this chapter, we propose that the salience of different sources of obligation differs as a function of the culturally bound 'normative systems of interpersonal interaction at the workplace. Our work departs from other cross-cultural studies in that we propose norms-existing in subjective attitudes and relationship structures-that allow finer distinctions than those highlighted in traditional arguments about the dichotomy between individualistic and collectivist cultures. We draw our evidence primarily from a recent study of attitudes, relationship patterns, and feelings of obligation among employees in a multinational retail bank (Morris, Podolny, & Ariel, 1997).

PAST APPROACHES TO CULTURE AND SOCIAL BEHAVIOR

Cross-national comparisons provided the inspiration and the evidential basis for some of the most important classical works of theory on social behavior, such as accounts distinguishing the loosely knit fabric of individualistic societies and groups from the more tightly knit social fabrics of many traditional cultural groups (de Tocqueville, 1945 [1848]; Durkheim, (1951)[1897]; Tonnies, 1957 [1887]). Yet as research on social and organizational behavior became institutionalized within the field of psychology, researchers focused on causes of social behavior that were operationalizable in experiments and, consequently, did not focus on historical and cultural factors that shape people's understandings and actions. As a result, the role of culture and, moreover, the role of evidence from non-Western settings became more marginal.

In the last two decades, however, culture has reemerged as a central variable in social and organizational psychology. Researchers have sought to develop precise hypotheses about (a) how cultures differ, and (b) how these differences influence social behavior. With regard to the first question, a milestone in the reemergence of research was Hofstede's (1980) worldwide study of IBM employees. The results of this study show that general attitudes about life and work vary greatly as a function of country, controlling for other variables such as employer, occupation, and income. Countries differed on several dimensions, one of which, labeled *individualism/collectivism*, has been the most influential because (a) it resonated with contrasts drawn in classical social theories, and (b) it revealed that Western Anglophone nations such as the United States, from which social science has drawn the bulk of its data, are extremely individualistic relative to most countries in the world. A large research program comparing individualistic and collectivistic settings has ensued.

A key feature of the individualism/collectivism research program is that cultural differences are documented in terms of respondents' attitudes and values, reflecting a conception of culture in terms of the subjective contents of individuals' heads rather than in terms of objective artifacts that an ethnographer might document (Triandis, 1995). Inventories to measure collectivistic attitudes as an individual difference have been developed and validated (Triandis, McCusker, & Hui, 1990). As with Hofstede's (1980) country-level data, North Americans tend to score closer to the individualist pole than people in almost all other countries, including East Asian, Latin European, and North European settings (Triandis, 1990). In this respect, the findings of subjective culture research comport reasonably well with the ethnographic and historical record: Compared with Western Anglophone societies, there seems to be a greater emphasis on social relations in the Chinese societies of East Asia, in social democratic nations of Northern Europe, in Southern European nations on the Mediterranean, and in most other cultural traditions.

Yet, critics of the unidimensional individualism/collectivism construct have pointed out ways in which it fails to capture differences among non-Western societies. It has been argued that a unitary dimension conflates a number of qualitatively distinct emphases on different kinds of relationships and collectivities (Ho & Chiu, 1994). In recent years, subjective culture researchers have proposed multidimensional models of collectivism to redress these limitations (e.g., Schwartz, 1994; Triandis & Gelfand, 1998). In summary, although subjective culture analyses of collectivism have been enormously influential, the flux and mutability of constructs in this area indicates an incompleteness of this approach.

Research on the second issue of how cultural differences impact social behavior has drawn similarly on the individualism/collectivism construct. In recent years, several prominent theorists have used this single dimension to develop integrated accounts of how culture moderates basic relationships in social psychology (Triandis, 1990) and organizational psychology (Erez & Earley, 1993). A number of studies have focused on an individual's willingness to contribute to others or a group. Earley (1989, 1994) found that participants' level of effort in contributing to a group task was more influenced by individual- versus group-level accountability in North American settings than in Chinese settings. Similarly, the reward a participant allocates to a partner in a joint task depends more on the ingroup versus outgroup status of the other participant in Chinese cultural settings than in North American settings (Leung & Bond, 1984). Also a number of findings suggest that in collectivistic settings, such as Chinese and Latin societies, individuals are more likely to avoid acrimonious conflict in relations with in-group members than are individuals in NORTH American settings (Leung, 1987; Leung et al., 1992).

Similar findings have emerged in research on compliance and persuasion. When behavioral intentions are examined as a function of both individuals' personal preferences and their sense of what others expect them to do, Brazilians display stronger intentions to do what is expected of them, whereas North Americans display a stronger intention to do what they personally desire (Bontempo, Lobel, & Triandis, 1990). In research on the effects of advertisements, studies have found that appeals to consensus or social proof have relatively more impact on East Asian than North American subjects (Aaker & Maheswaran, 1997; Han & Shavitt, 1994). Likewise, research on the effectiveness of compliance tactics has found that tactics based on the principle of social proof are more powerful in collectivistic cultural settings, whereas tactics based on the principle of personal consistency are more powerful in individualistic cultural settings (Cialdini et al., chap. 2, this volume). Results such as these suggest that the individualism/collectivism dimension corresponds to a set of related differences in social behavior. These differences support the notion that, in collectivist settings, more attention is paid to group memberships in guiding one's conduct toward others than in individualistic settings. Hence, there is reason to believe that individualism/collectivism may also be the crucial variable in determining to whom employees feel most obligated in work settings.

Nevertheless, findings from other research programs highlight differences among different collectivistic cultural traditions. One example is research on how collectivists maintain relationships with ingroup others. Research in Latin societies finds that interactions are characterized by outward displays of warm, expressive behavior (Lindsley & Braithwaite, 1996; Sanchez-Burks, Nisbett, & Ybarra, 1998; Triandis, Marin, Lisansky, & Betancourt, 1984). This pattern of emotional expressivity contrasts sharply with that observed in Confucian-influenced East Asian societies. In the Chinese virtue of jen (Hsu, 1985) or the Japanese tradition of amae (Doi, 1962), conflicts are avoided through a passive, harmonizing stance rather than an active, expressive stance. Hence, although the Latin and Confucian traditions both emphasize avoiding overt conflict with ingroup others, the scripted way to avoid conflict diverges sharply in these two collectivistic settings. This is just one of many examples suggesting that, although the unidimensional individualism/collectivism construct serves well to capture differences in social behavior between Western Anglophone settings and most other societies, it also misses other differences. If one wants to capture differences among the rest of these countries, the individualism/collectivism dimension falls short. Because we are interested in such differences, we developed hypotheses in terms of more specific cultural norms. Because this construct of norms has a complicated history in psychology and sociology, it is worth reviewing how our use of the construct relates to previous analyses.

DO WORKPLACE NORMS DIFFER AS A FUNCTION OF NATIONAL CULTURES?

Defining the Norm Construct

Norms have a number of definitions in social science (for a review, see Shaffer, 1983). As an explanatory construct in psychology, norms were embraced by mid-century theories (e.g., Sherif, 1936), were critiqued by later researchers seeking more rigorous empirical evidence (Darley & Latane, 1970), and have resurfaced in recent years (Cialdini, Reno, & Kallgren, 1990). Similarly in sociology, the notion that people are guided by injunctive norms was central in Weber's (1922 [1963]) analyses of Protestant versus Catholic societies in Europe and in Parsons' (1951) descriptions of social systems—only to be critiqued in succeeding sociological movements (for a review, see Morris, Podolny, & Ariel, 1999a).

Let us review Parsons' proposal as a point of departure for presenting our hypotheses. A distinctive emphasis in Parsons' arguments concerned the role of norms as standards to guide interpersonal conduct. Norms allow an individual, *ego*, to navigate interpersonal interactions with other persons, *alters*. Parsons asserted that social interaction requires an organized system because social behavior requires complementarity of actions and understandings. He discussed types of systems in terms of two dilemmas. The first dilemma, termed *universalism versus particularism*, centers on whether ego should act on the basis of general principles that all actors would be expected to use in a given situation, or on the basis of reasons specific to ego and to the web of alters connected to the situation. The second dilemma, termed *achievement versus ascription*, concerns whether to judge alters on the basis of what they do, as determined by their actions and performances, or on the basis of who they are, as defined by their relationship- and group-conferred characteristics. Parsons insisted that these were dilemmas not dimensions and that one dilemma could not be answered in isolation from the other. Hence, he described normative systems in terms of a system of four ideal types and exemplified each with a review of ethnographic and historical observations.

This set of comparative observations, more so than Parsons' theory per se, influenced our work and is worth reviewing. The universalistic-achievement type was exemplified by the United States, where ego's treatment of alter depends on how alter's behavior enhances ego's pursuit of desired achievements. Achievement is the desired end and is pursued by means of any alter available, with little regard to alter's position in relationships and groups. The particularistic-achievement type was exemplified by traditional Chinese society. In an interesting contrast to scholars who have portrayed American and Chinese cultures as cultural antipodes, Parsons argued that the two cultures are similar in their orientation toward achievement. Yet whereas the American norm permits getting ahead by leaving or overturning the social order, the Confucian Chinese norm valorizes mobility within the stable ordering of hierarchical relations. The universalistic-ascriptive type was exemplified by traditional German society. Ego's treatment of alter is not guided by the instrumental calculus of what alter can do for ego, but by the compass of abstractly defined classes, categories, and ranks. These are ascribed characteristics defined universalistically (e.g., alter's membership in bureaucratic, occupational, or social class categories), rather than particularistically relative to ego (e.g., alter's membership in ego's network of friends or relatives). Finally, Spanish culture exemplified the particularistic-ascriptive social system. In this system, an actor's treatment of another is not structured either by instrumental purposes (as in both achievement-oriented systems) or by bureaucratic categories (as in universalistic-ascriptive societies). Rather, treatment of alter is based on the pursuit of affective expressiveness as an end in itself, and it depends on alter's particular relationship to ego.

Parsons' theory of social systems met considerable critique among the subsequent generation of sociologists. Many objected to his assumptions that normative systems are (a) stable, (b) internalized, and (c) shared in a society-wide consensus. Our analysis builds on the work of these subsequent scholars, so these three issues are worth reviewing. First, Parsons assumed that normative systems exist in a stable state of homeostasis or equilibrium, in that there are only a finite number of system types that serve the function of maintaining a degree of order and structure necessary for social interaction. Particularly for scholars witnessing swift changes in social behavior in their own societies, these assumptions have seemed both ill-founded and reactionary, seeming to limit the possibilities for change in social roles and norms. Subsequent scholarship on social norms has generally dropped the assumption that the possible forms of social systems can be captured by a finite typology and instead have limited their ambitions to describing particularly historically bound traditions. Consistent with this, we examine the cultural traditions Parson suggested, but we propose that the norms in these cultures are not four ideal-typical equilibrium, points but rather four of many historically contingent patterns.

A second target has been the Parsonsian assumption that norms exist as internalized tacit value orientations. This makes it difficult to separate evidence for the explanatory construct, the norm, from what it explains, the behavior. Reacting against this style of explanation, sociologists focused on identifying the external constraints and structures that may be producing behavioral patterns (see Granovetter, 1985). In addition to accounts in terms of macrolevel structures, such as economic systems or institutions (Inkeles, 1960; Marx, 1972[1844]), theorists have focused on microlevel structures through linking action to an individual's relationship network (see White et al., 1976). In our work, we do not conceptualize norms as existing entirely as internalized standards, but rather as existing in both the form of subjective attitudes and in the form of crystallized structures of relations. Values lead to relational structures and vice versa; individuals have a degree of agency but direct that agency in ways that create constraining structures (Giddens, 1984). We draw on recent developments in research on individualistic and collectivistic attitudes, which distinguishes the economic and expressive aspects of collectivist values (Triandis & Gelfand, 1998). Yet we integrate these subjective measures with network structuralist measures that also distinguish socioemotional ties to friends from more instrumental exchange or dependence ties (Podolny & Baron, 1997).

Third, Parsons' assumption that norms are organized in a society-wide equilibrium came to be seen as representing an oversocialized view of the individual and an overintegrated view of society (Wrong, 1961). As cross-national research shifted from ethnographic portraits to surveys of representative samples, researchers became increasingly aware of the diversity of social attitudes and norms within societies (Cantril, 1965). Subsequent theorists have argued that norms exist in a more concrete, situation-specific form, as scripts for action (Garfinkel, 1967). Depictions of social norms in recent years portray them as rules that are evoked by and applied to specific domains of life-such as a given workplace-rather than across social domains (Swidler, 1986). Albeit many contemporary anthropologists argue that scholars should seek only to describe local norms in local terms (Geertz, 1975); others have proposed that the localized norms present in all cultures are constructed from a set of elemental models of sociality, such as market pricing, authority ranking, and communal sharing (Fiske, 1991). That is, norms are historically bound and locally constructed, yet they have common elements that allow for meaningful comparison. Building on this notion, we suggest that national culture influences the emphasis of the normative system that develops in a workplace, determining the relative influence of norms from other institutions such as markets, families, and so forth.[1]

Testing for Country Differences in Workplace Norms

We proposed and tested a set of claims about the interpersonal norms for workplace interactions that emerge in similar work settings as a function of cultural traditions. Following Parsons, we focused on the contrast between the individualistic norms in North American settings and the qualitatively different forms of collectivistic norms that emerge in Chinese, German, and Spanish settings. Yet our assumptions in developing these hypotheses differ in ways that reflect the three objections to Parsons reviewed earlier. Given that our proposal concerns ceteris paribus country differences, we studied and framed specific predictions in a multinational consumer bank—an organizational setting where it was possible to hold constant factors other than the cultural context. Two policies of this firm make it particularly appropriate as a site to test our hypotheses. First, employees are hired from the locality in which the bank is situated. This policy of embeddedness allows for local norms of interaction to arise within the workplace although the bank is a North American corporation. Second, there is a global strategy of standardizing organizational structure and products across countries. The formal organization chart and job categories, the physical layout of the bank branches, and the financial services provided and sold are similar across the retail operations in the different countries that we sampled. This policy of maximizing cross-country variation in the human composition of the organization, while minimizing cross-country variation in the formal structure and practical content of work, virtually creates a natural experiment for investigating the effects of cultural norms on workplace behavior.[2]

---

[1]Nor do we assume that norms are constant across workplaces in a society. On the contrary, these systems may vary depending on particular aspects of the social context, such as the organizational structure and the nature of the work. In addition, it is likely that certain norms will prevail in certain kinds of workplaces regardless of the country. For example, authority norms are more likely to prevail in a military organization than in a medical partnership. Nevertheless, we assume that country differences may still exist in the norms that guide workplace interactions when other factors are held constant.

[2]The experiment provides a conservative test of the hypotheses, of course, because cultural differences are diluted by the Citibank organizational culture. If a pattern of predicted cultural differences can be observed in the contrast between employees of Citibank Hong Kong and Citibank Spain, we would expect the same difference to be much sharper in the contrast between two completely local firms.

Within selected areas, all employees above the level of part-time tellers and below the level of area directors were surveyed concerning their subjective attitudes, their network, and their feelings of obligation to each of the alters in their network. Social attitudes were measured with adapted measures of economic and expressive collectivism (Triandis & Gelfand, 1998) and ad hoc scales to measure other attitudes brought to attention by the analysis, such as filial loyalty toward superordinates. Relational patterns were assessed with standard procedures for eliciting egocentric networks (Podolny & Baron, 1997) of friendship relations and dependence relations. The survey first elicited names of alters with whom the respondent communicates at work by prompting for names of those who provide friendship, power/support, as well as other exchanges such as task advice and gossip. The survey then assessed attributes of each mentioned relationship, such as interaction frequency and affective closeness. The survey also assessed properties of each alter, such as their hierarchical rank relative to that of ego and their belonging to the same versus different bank branch. For full detail sabout sampling, procedures, and materials, see Morris, Podolny, and Ariel (1997, 1999b).

To substantiate our proposal that feelings of obligation are differentially produced by culturally bound normative systems, we first needed to illustrate that countries do display differences in their systems of interpersonal interaction norms. To do so, we examined both the subjective attitudes and relationships. In checking our predictions about relational patterns, we attended primarily to the friendship network—the type of relation least constrained by the necessities of work, and hence most likely to reflect employees' norm-based discretion. An outline of the predictions and findings that we now review is presented in Table 6.1. In terms of our argument about culture and obligation, these measures serve as a method check—an assurance that the countries we compare do in fact differ in emphases of the system of norms governing interpersonal interaction in this work organization.

Market Orientation in North American Settings

A feature of North American culture noted by many social observers and critics is the tendency for people to enter or exit social exchanges according to whether it profits their individual achievement goals. The popular conception of *networking* captures how this norm plays out in the context of work organizations-one manages one's portfolio of relations in pursuit of health, wealth, and happiness, interacting with anyone who is useful and necessarily making room for them by discarding old ties that have outlived their instrumental value (Baker, 1993). From de Toqueville (1945) [1848] onwards observers of American individualism have described the relative ease with which instrumental work relations can be established without the prior basis of friendship or family connection. In terms of network analysis, Americans can form

TABLE 6.1
Predictions About Features Distinguishing Workplace Norms in Four
Cultural Settings

Emphasis	Culture
1. *Market*	*North American*
Distinguishing subjective attitudes	Belief in interpersonal competition
Distinguishing relational structures	Short-lived, single-stranded relationships
2. *Familial*	*Chinese*
Distinguishing subjective attitudes	Belief in sacrifice for the group and in filial loyalty
Distinguishing relational structures	Ties to powerful sponsors that involve both resource dependence and affect
3. *Legal-Bureaucratic*	*German*
Distinguishing subjective attitudes	Dislike of interpersonal competition; Low emotional involvement with coworkers
Distinguishing relational structures	Relations bounded by official; Low affective intensity
4. *Affiliative*	*Spanish*
Distinguishing subjective attitudes	High emotional involvement with coworkers
Distinguishing relational structures	Long-lived, affectively close relations

Note. Italics indicate nonsupported predictions.

instrumental exchange ties without a prerequisite base of socioemotional connection. At the same time, individuals are relatively willing to break ties to achieve success. From the time of the expanding frontier onward, the paragon of the successful American has been the person who leaves the group or disrupts the social order. Americans remain relatively willing to reshape their social networks to pursue their professional goals (Bellah et al., 1985). The values that support these actions have been linked to the individualistic Anglo-American economic, legal, and philosophical traditions (see Lukes, 1973). In terms of Fiske's analysis of elemental forms of sociality, we would suggest that the norms that emerge within the American context draw more on rules and expectations associated with market exchange.

What evidence of a distinctive market emphasis in interpersonal norms was seen in our measures of subjective social attitudes? North Americans stand out in their endorsement of economic individualism—the belief in achievement through social competition (e.g., "Competition is the law of nature"). As expected, employees in the North American setting adhere to this value more than do employees in the other three settings. The difference between American and Chinese values was small on items measuring competition in general but more dramatic on items measuring competition within the ingroup (e.g., "Without competition between colleagues, it is not possible to have a good company"). As expected, the evidence from relational structures was that North American employees' relationships are characterized by lower levels of multiplexity and lower duration. These are indirect indicators of the ease with which relations can be entered and exited for instrumental purposes.

Familial Orientation in Chinese Settings

The norms of social interaction in Chinese organizations have been described as familial collectivism (Bond & Hwang, 1986). As in a family, employees make sacrifices for the group. Interestingly, however, this Confucian concern for harmony within the group does not preclude a strong value on achievement through competition (Hsu, 1953). Rather, it allows for achievement through the existing social order by competing as a group. Another pattern of achievement striving should be seen in the cultivation of filial relationships to those in power (Ho, 1976, 1998). Field studies of Chinese organizations have noted the extent to which employees seek to exchange personal loyalty to powerful alters for protection and support (Redding & Wong, 1986). The implications for the structure of relations are suggested by past findings concerning Japanese managers who have also been influenced by Confucian social norms. Compared with American employees, who prefer same-status friends, Japanese employees seek higher status friends (Nakane, 1970; Nakao 1987).

The evidence for this Chinese familial orientation is best described in contrast to that of the American market orientation. With regard to subjective attitudes, Chinese employees were more inclined than Americans to exhibit *economic collectivism* or endorse sacrifice for the group (e.g., "A group of coworkers should stick together even if sacrifices are required"). Also, Chinese employees are most likely to endorse measures of filial loyalty toward superordinates (e.g., "A good manager is more like a parent than a friend"). A tendency toward filial relations as a model for workplace interactions was also evident in our measures of relational structures, in that there was a greater trend for Chinese employees to form socioemotionally close relationships to those higher up in the hierarchy.

Legal-Bureaucratic Orientation in German Settings

Our expectations about the norms of German workplaces were influenced by observations that there remains a distinctive emphasis on formal categories and rules as standards for social behavior (Hall, 1990). Certainly a kind of collectivist solidarity is evident in these observations, yet the relevant collectives are units of the firm and worker's council rather than networks of exchange or friendship radiating outward from each individual (Borneman, 1992). A second point made by many German and non-German observers is that affective expression in workplace relations is somewhat muted or at least slow to develop compared with other countries (e.g., Lewin, 1948). These two features may both derive from an emphasis on rules rather than personal qualities as standards in one's treatment of another person. That is, in a legal-bureaucratic system, ego decides how to act toward a given alter according to alter's formal status, not according to what alter as a specific individual offers ego (as in the market system) or according to the filial relation established between ego and alter (as in the familial system).

Given the prior characterization of German workplace relations as guided by legal-bureaucratic norms, what is the evidence of subjective attitudes that support such an emphasis? We expected that German employees would be characterized by high endorsement of economic collectivism (sharing resources with the ingroup) but not to be very high on economic individualism (achievement through competition) or expressive collectivism (affective involvement with the ingroup). Counter to predictions, results showed that German employees were low in endorsing sacrifice for the ingroup. Perhaps their rule orientation leads them to construe their assistance to coworkers as a duty rather than a favor or sacrifice, and hence subjective attitude measures fail to pick up the economic collectivism.

Fortunately, the relational measures allowed us a second window into norms. First, we expected that informal interaction should be highly aligned with formally required interaction. This was supported by the finding that Germans reported less interaction with friends beyond that officially required than did employees in the other countries. More specifically, we expected that German friendships should be more inclined to stay within the boxes of the organization chart, extending to same unit, same rank alters rather than spanning horizontal and vertical boundaries. Support for these predictions was found, in that German friendships were most likely to be with same-rank employees and most likely to encompass a high fraction of the alters in one's branch. Second, we expected relations to be characterized by lower affective intensity than in other systems. This was also supported.

Affiliative Orientation in Spanish Settings

Anthropologists who have described work relations in the context of Spanish culture have pointed to strong norms of warm sociability toward the peer friendship group (Murphy, 1983). Similarly, as we have reviewed, psychological studies of social behavior in Latin cultures have observed an expectation of warm, friendly behavior among coworkers (Triandis et al., 1984). It is instructive to consider how the implications of an affiliative norm differ from those of the legal-bureaucratic norm. In both systems, actions toward others depends on characteristics rather than performances, yet the relevant characteristics differ. A bureaucratic norm focused on characteristics of the alter as defined by the formal organization, whereas an affiliative norm focuses on characteristics of the alter defined in relation to ego, such as membership in or connections to ego's friendship network. The consequence is that, for German employees it is appropriate to adjust their network of workplace communication as their job title changes, whereas for Spanish employees it violates a norm to change one's pattern of interaction after transfers or promotion.

The expected evidence for an affiliative norm in subjective values was that Spanish employees should stand out as high in expressive collectivism (affective involvement with coworkers) as well as economic collectivism (sharing resources with coworkers). Although they were fairly high on these subjective measures, and significantly higher than North Americans on both, the subjective dimensions do not clearly distinguish the Spanish affiliative emphasis from the Chinese familial emphasis. However, the affiliative norms should be evidenced by distinctive patterns of social relations—in particular, friendships that are high in affective intensity and longevity. The duration of relations should be longer than in other systems because the relations are not delimited instrumental purposes (as in the North American and Chinese systems) or by formal job categories (as in the German system). As expected, we observed that Spanish employees had friendships that were reliably higher in affective closeness than employees in the other three cultural settings. They were also the most extreme in the longevity of friendships.

DO PATTERNS OF EMPLOYEE OBLIGATION DIFFER AS A FUNCTION OF WORKPLACE NORMS?

Now that we have established some support for our proposal about differences between the norms of workplace interaction that emerge in North American, Chinese, German, and Spanish settings, let us consider how social influence is likely to be played out in these settings. Our argument is based on the notion that cultural norms make some sources of social influence more salient and others less salient. To develop specific hypotheses, let us review the major ideas in organizational scholarship about the kinds of social influence involved in creating employees' feelings of obligation toward others in the workplace.

Previously Identified Determinants of Employee Obligation

Scholarship on the obligation felt by employees in work organizations begins with Weber's (1947) study of obligation in a bureaucracy—namely, a German hospital. He concluded that employees' obligation in vertical relations to those in power is not based on a sentimental loyalty to leaders, but rather on a perception of the system, and the formal organizational categories within it, as fair and legitimate.

Subsequent scholars, such as Blau (1955), maintained the emphasis on vertical relations to those in power, but qualified Weber's stylized portrait of deference based on legitimate authority by elucidating the reciprocal exchange basis of obligation. This social exchange account has been elaborated by network theorists who have built on insights of Simmel (1950)—that ego's feelings of obligation toward an alter, depend not only on the direct dyadic relationship to alter but on the triangles formed by their mutual connections to third parties (Coleman, 1988). Hence, an analysis of ego's treatment of alter reflects not only the costs and benefits involved directly with alter, but also those that occur indirectly as a result of third parties (Burt, 1992).

Another tradition has argued that in many organizational contexts the primary obligations lie in horizontal relations to peers rather than in vertical relations to authorities. Roethlisberger and Dickson's (1939) study of workers in a bank wiring room described strong bonds of obligation in cohesive friendship cliques. The primacy of these obligations was evident in the ability of the peer groups to effectively sanction workers who were overly compliant toward superordinates (i.e., *rate busters*).

Although a great deal of research has documented that employees feel obligated in each of these distinct ways, little attention has been given to the factors that moderate the salience of these determinants. One of the only such proposals is Merton's (1969) argument that, when employees' mobility expectations are frustrated, the dominant orientation of obligation shifts from vertical relations with authorities to horizontal relations with friends. Some evidence for this boundary condition has been obtained in North American settings (for a review, see Kanter, 1977).

However, as with most research that has been conducted in Western settings, we cannot be confident that Merton's account applies in other cultural settings. The Merton account presupposes that employees start with a dominant obligation to powerful others that is instrumental, in that it hinges on the fulfillment of mobility aspirations. It also presupposes that employees who once devoted their energies to authorities are welcomed in the friendship cliques of their peers once they decide to switch loyalties. As a matter of fact, we suggest that it may only be in a normative context largely infused by a market orientation that employees have a primary instrumental obligation toward powerful others and, at the same time, can initiate peer relationships involving strong mutual obligations. The market orientation condones any kind of relation that serves ego's current aspirations and also allows easy initiation of relationships. Hence, in a normative system largely shaped on a market model, we would expect employees to feel obligated for a wide variety of reasons. In settings where the normative system is shaped on other models, the dominant source of employee obligation should be more restricted in ways that prevent the mixing of allegiances described by Merton.

Let us examine the dominant sources of obligation expected in the other three normative contexts we have described. The familial emphasis in Chinese workplace norms should create a strong obligation to alters in power relative to ego. These obligations felt in vertical relations are instrumental like those characteristic of a market system, where ego is obligated in exchange for resources that alter can provide. Yet as in familial relations, there should be a consideration of how the dyadic relationship is embedded in a larger network of relationships. Indeed there is a substantial literature on the attention in Chinese commercial settings on the cultivation of connections or *guanxi* as part of a general effort to enrich one's social face or *mianza* (King, 1991). Chinese employees should show a greater sensitivity to the indirect connections to third parties involved in a relationship to an alter. In another difference from the market-oriented American context, we would expect that strong feelings of obligation purely as a function of friendship should be less salient in the familial-oriented Chinese normative system.

Our expectations about the German workplace characterized by a legal-bureaucratic emphasis is that feelings of obligation should occur in both vertical and horizontal relations but for different reasons than in the American market-oriented system. In a normative system largely shaped on a legal-bureaucratic model, obligation should follow the lines of reporting relations and formal categories. Hence, obligation in vertical relations should occur in response to the alter's formal authority rather than the instrumental resources that the alter provides. Obligation in horizontal relations should occur in response to whether formal organizational categories indicate that one should assist this person (i.e., alter is a coworker in the same bank branch) rather than in response to whether the alter is a close friend. In summary, the distinguishing characteristic of this setting should be a comparatively greater tendency for the employees' feelings of obligation to follow the lines of the formal structure of the organization.

Finally, our expectations about the Spanish workplace characterized by an emphasis on affiliative norms were that the strongest feelings of obligation would occur in lateral relations based on the socioemotional connection of friendship. A theme in descriptions of Spanish workplaces is strong obligation to friends and their associates (Gilmore, 1987). Scholars in several disciplines have suggested that, in such a normative system, it is a matter of honor to not withhold a favor from a friend or to not instrumentally do favors for those in power (Alvarez & Cantos, 1994; Murphy, 1983).[3]

We have argued that the dominant pattern of employee obligation should differ as a function of normative orientations. We can summarize our argument in terms of the dominant criterion for ego in whether to feel obligated to help an alter: A market orientation suggests that any kind of reciprocal exchange warrants obligation. In other words, the question implicitly asked of an alter is, "What have you done for me lately?" A familial orientation suggests that the strongest feelings of obligation are filial ties to powerful sponsors, especially those who are also tied to others in power. In other words, the question asked of an alter is, "Do you have power over me or ties to those who do?" A legal-bureaucratic orientation suggests that a salient determinant of obligation should be the formal structure of the organization-reporting relations to authorities and shared work units with peers. The implicit standard guiding conduct toward an alter is, "Am I officially supposed to assist you?" Finally, in the Spanish context, the primary determinant of obligation is loyalty toward friends; the implicit standard guiding feelings of obligation is, "Are you my friend or a friend of my friend?" In summarizing our hypotheses this way, we do not mean to underemphasize the extent to which all employees feel conflict between the pull of conflicting obligations in directing their energies in the workplace. Yet employees ultimately have to resolve this conflict, and we suggest that normative systems give rise to implicit standards that privilege some obligations over others.

Modeling the Determinants of Obligation

To test our hypotheses about the patterns of obligation in each cultural setting, we needed an indicator of ego's feeling of obligation toward each of the alters with whom the respondent interacts in the workplace. As we have described elsewhere, our computerized survey program elicited from respondents the names of all the other persons with whom they communicate at work, including relations that primarily involve an exchange of friendship, those that involve power or support from above, and those that involve informational exchanges such as task advice or gossip. The survey allowed us to probe the respondent for how much obligation is felt toward each of these alters. We

---

[3]Although we know of no previous comparative studies of networks and obligations in the workplace, results from studies of networks and social support are also somewhat consistent with our argument concerning the primacy of obligation to the friendship network in Latin contexts. That is, Hollinger and Haller (1990) found that, in the Latin country in their data (Italy), expectations with regard to friends' obligations were not conditional on the kins' proximity. This differed from the pattern in other countries—that the obligation of friends was inversely related to the proximity of kin.

developed a site-specific measure of the extent of obligation (Alderfer & Brown, 1972) developed after ethnographic observation and interviews with bank branch employees in the United States and Hong Kong. Respondents were asked to imagine a scenario in which the alter asked whether they would volunteer their assistance on a dull task on a busy day. Respondents were asked how likely they would be to volunteer to do this favor for the other person on a rating scale. This served as our dependent measure of felt obligation.

We modeled the primary determinants of felt obligation toward coworkers by predicting the obligation felt toward an alter from characteristics of one's relation to the alter, the network surrounding this relationship, and the position of the alter in the formal structure of the organization. Specifically, we regressed the obligation score on a series of dummy variables tapping the determinants of obligation that we expected might differ in importance from one country to the next. The first two dummy variables indicated, respectively, whether the alter was listed as a source of power/support and whether the alter provides an indirect connection to power (i.e., was judged to have a close relationship with another alter who was listed as a source of power/support). In parallel, the next two dummy variables indicated whether the alter was listed as a source of friendship and whether the alter is an indirect link to one's friends (i.e., was judged to have a close relationship with another alter who was listed as a friend). The remaining dummy variables tapped aspects of the alter's formal position—namely, whether the alter works in the same bank branch and whether the alter is either superordinate or a subordinate in official reporting lines.

To assess that country differences in these coefficients result from differences in how alters are judged rather than from differences in respondents' age, gender, and other characteristics, we used a fixed-effect model, which corrects for the influence of any stable characteristics of respondents. The concern addressed here is this: If employees differ by country in the distribution of age, gender, or other more difficult-to-measure characteristics that affect sensitivity to particular determinants of obligation, regression analyses might reveal differences in the dominant patterns of obligation that result from simple differences in the kinds of respondents across countries, rather than differences in how the same kinds of respondents feel obligated in different types of relationships. The effect of differences due to these unobserved factors are removed by subtracting respondent-specific means from all variables included in the regression. That is, for each respondent, we calculate the mean value for each variable. We then subtract these mean values from all the respondents' observations. The unique effect of the stable but unmeasured characteristics of each individual is the fixed effect from which the method takes its name. The resulting coefficients are those that would be obtained if dummy variables for each respondent had been included in the regression models. Because the respondent variable is confounded with country, one must run separate models on the data from each of the four countries.

The results of our analyses of the predictors of felt obligation among North American, Chinese, German, and Spanish employees reveal some understandable similarities in the causes of obligation, but also reveal differences in the dominant sources of obligation. In Table 6.2, we summarize which variables were found to be major and minor determinants of employee obligation in each of the four countries. The one constant finding across all countries is that employees feel obligated to respond positively more when the request comes from a direct superordinate than when it does not. In a sense, it would be surprising if this pattern did not exist given that the effectiveness of an organization depends on some minimal level of acceptance of hierarchical authority. However, beyond the finding of this basic similarity, there are some important differences across the four countries, and these differences are largely consistent with our expectations based on how workplace interaction norms are shaped by cultural traditions. Let us review findings in the four countries.

Among North American employees, obligation was increased by the direct or indirect provision of power by an alter and also by friendship or the alter's connection to one's friends. There was evidence for both of the exchange relationships posited by Merton (1969): mobility-related exchanges with those in power and socioemotional exchanges with peers. Whereas obligation was affected by these matters of exchange with alters, it was not affected by the formal

TABLE 6.2
Summary of Sources of Obligation Observed In Four Countries

Alter is:	Country			
	US	HK	GR	SP
Powerful	X	X	x	
Linked to powerful others	x	X		
A friend	X		x ·	X
Linked to friends	X			
A same-branch coworker			X	
A superordinate	X	X	X	X

Note. X indicates a strong effect, x a weak effect.

structural variable of whether alter belonged to the same branch. In general, the pattern is consistent with the image of a normative system largely shaped on a market exchange model.

Among employees in Hong Kong, feelings of obligation were primarily felt in relations to superordinates, to those who provide power, and to those who are connected to those who provide power. This is consistent with the notion that a familial norm warrants a focus on vertical relationships to those in power. The finding that Hong Kong employees are additionally sensitive to an alter's position in the network of powerful others is consistent with our other prediction— that a familial norm warrants attention to the interconnectedness of one's alters. These findings suggest the usefulness of network analysis in operationalizing concerns for instrumentally valuable relationships noted in ethnographic studies of Chinese business communities, such as *guanxi* (connections) and *mianza* (the face or standing that a person gains by dint of connections).

In Germany, obligation was driven slightly by direct power and friendship but not by indirect ties. However, the primary determinants of obligation had to do with alter's formal position—namely, whether alter is a member of the same work unit and, of course, whether alter is a direct superordinate. The fact that the formal organizational categories were dominant determinants of obligation in the German setting is consistent with the notion that, to the extent that norms in Germany involve a concern for the collective, it is legally or bureaucratically defined collectives rather than personally defined collectives that are emphasized.

The results in Spain differ from those in the other countries, in that employees did not feel obligated to others as a function of the power provided by the others. Interestingly, the effect of whether the alter was a direct superordinate was as strong as in the other three countries. Yet there was no increase in obligation as a function of whether the other was a source of power in the sense of support or resources that would help advance one's career. Consistent with the apparent absence of instrumental orientation in feelings of obligation was the additional lack of concern for the extent to which alter was connected to others who provided power. Another piece of evidence for the differing importance of loyalty to friends in Spain is this: When a covariate for the affective closeness of relations is included in the model, the effect of friend turns from positive to negative in all the countries except for Spain. This suggests that, in most countries, the obligation to friends is based on socioemotional exchange. When a friendship is no longer close,it no longer earns obligation. In Spain, the mere fact of friendship triggers obligation in addition to the obligation triggered by closeness. This is consistent with the notion that assistance to friends at work is a matter of honor in a normative system with an affiliative orientation, not simply a matter of reciprocal exchange.

In summary, our analysis of what influences an employee to feel obligated to coworkers shows that, in addition to some obvious similarities across cultures-everywhere people are more likely to acquiesce to a request when it comes from their superordinate-there are some dramatic differences that are largely interpretable in terms of culturally varying norms.

THEORETICAL IMPLICATIONS

The research discussed here has several implications for the growing effort to incorporate culture as a variable in studies of social influence and other social behaviors. A first point is the level of abstraction at which culture is conceptualized. As noted at the outset, there has been a tendency to investigate cultural variation in terms of a unidimensional individualism/collectivism dimension. Many researchers have conceptualized North American and Chinese cultures, respectively, as polar opposites on this dimension. Some aspects of culture are captured by this dimension. For example, in our measures of the subjective attitudes typically measured in cross-cultural studies, we observed a greater North American emphasis on individual achievement and a greater Chinese emphasis on sacrifice for the ingroup. However, looking across all of the variables we measured, we do not see a general pattern in which American and Chinese cultures are opposite. We see that their differences notwithstanding, American and Chinese employees have much in common that is not shared with Spanish and German employees. Hence, the individualism/collectivism dimension can take us only so far.

We were able to predict more fine-grained patterns by conceptualizing culture at the more concrete level of interpersonal norms. Our analysis is indebted to Parsons, who also decried the limits of the individualism/collectivism dimension, for his premise of implicit standards guiding interpersonal conduct and for the particular cultures he used to make his case that cultural differences can only be fully understood in terms of norms. Yet this analysis is also indebted to subsequent theorists who refined the construct of norms to refer to standards that are historically bound, that are manifest in relationship structures as well as subjective attitudes, and that are domain-specific. This level of analysis is consistent with new developments in cross-cultural research, in which national culture is conceptualized as having an indirect relationship in shaping behavior. Cultural traditions shape middle-level variables such as the interpersonal norms that prevail in a setting, and these norms are the proximal causes of an individual's behavior (see Lonner & Adamopoulos, 1997).

A second notable feature of the current analysis is the investigation of cultural differences using network structural measures. We submit that measures of relationship structure would greatly enrich the understanding of how social and organizational behavior are influenced by culture, just as they have benefited the understanding of the influence of gender (Ibarra, 1997). Cross-cultural researchers have tended to rely exclusively on people's self-reports of attitudes and values. Many problems with this method have been documented, including individuals' tendency to rate their attitudes and values relative to others in their own society, rather than on an absolute scale (Peng, Nisbett, & Wong, 1997). Hence, there is reason to believe that a shift toward less subjective measures, such as relationship structure, may expose cultural differences that fail to emerge in measures of subjective attitudes.

An example of the benefits of relational measures in describing culture can be seen in the current results. In our results, the standard measures of individualistic and collectivistic attitudes failed to distinguish Germany from Spain. However, a number of related relational measures clearly show the two predicted distinguishing features. In Germany, friendships were more likely to follow the lines of the organizational structure. Also, German employees showed a relative lack of interaction with others that was beyond the level required—interaction that results in other settings for reasons of opportunism, filial loyalty, or loyalty to friends. Finally, German employees reported less affective closeness in work relationships. Although the magnitude of the country differences in the structure of relations is not extreme on some of these variables, these differences are impressive when one remembers that differences have to be created against the current of many factors pushing employees to a standardized pattern of interaction across all countries (i.e., the physical layout of branches, the formal structure of command and control, and design of work tasks are all standardized in this organization across countries).

PRACTICAL IMPLICATIONS

In addition to suggesting new approaches to cross-cultural researchers, the current study also has implications for practical issues faced by multinational organizations and individuals who engage in cross-national business interactions. The key lesson is that employees' feelings of obligation are triggered by different factors in different cultural settings. A first implication is that organizations have to be careful when transferring novel practices and organizational structures from one culture to another. Practices and structures may rely on the psychology of obligation in the source country that are not shared in the destination country.

A second implication is that managers who move across different cultural settings may need to learn to frame requests differently depending on the cultural setting in which they are working. For example, incurring the obligation of employees in Spain may require the development of a socioemotional connection. In Germany, it may be more important to ensure that the request falls within the formal guidelines from which employees take their bearings.

Finally, the cultural differences observed in the current study also suggest particular challenges that managers in different cultures may face in orchestrating the felt obligation of employees into effective collective action. In North America, the market orientation may encourage employees to pursue actions that serve their individual careers rather than serving the organization unless the incentive structure is carefully managed, such that individual and organizational interests are aligned. In Chinese settings, the familial orientation may make it hard for employees to maintain influence when moving between different divisions of an organization; in turn, this may reduce a firm's ability to maintain coordination as it grows large. In German settings, the legal-bureaucratic orientation may make it difficult for managers to request assistance for unforeseen tasks that go beyond formally stipulated duties. In Spanish settings, the affiliative orientation may make it difficult to engage employees with the promise of resources if a manager has no socioemotional connection and is not a direct superordinate.

In conclusion, in our increasingly interconnected world, an understanding of the factors that lead individuals to cooperate—and of similarities and differences across cultures—is of utmost practical importance. Although the current study only concerns the cooperation of employees with coworkers in a bank, the patterns observed may speak to the difficulties experienced in many international organizations, such as the United Nations, in coordinating on matters of global importance.

ACKNOWLEDGMENT

This chapter describes findings presented in a previous empirical report by the authors and touches on theoretical issues covered more explicitly in a previous chapter.

REFERENCES

Aaker, J. L., & Maheswaran, D. (1997). The effect of cultural orientation on persuasion. *Journal of Consumer Research, 24*, 315–328.

Alderfer, C. P., & Brown, D. (1972). Designing an empathic questionnaire for organizational research, *Journal of Applied Psychology, 56*, 456–468.

Alvarez, J. L., & Cantos, C. M. (1994). From escapism to resented conformity: Market economies and modern organizations in Spanish literature. In B. Czarniawska-Joerges & P. G. de Monthoux (Eds.), *Good novels, better management: reading organizational realities* (pp. 175–199). Chur, Switzerland: Harwood.

Baker, W. (1993). *Networking smart: How to build relationships for personal and organizational success.* New York: McGraw-Hill.

Barnard, C. (1938). *The functions of the executive.* Cambridge, MA: Harvard University Press.

Bellah, R. N., Madsen, R., Sullivan, W. M., Swidler, A., & Tipton, S. M. (1985). *Habits of the heart: Individualism and commitment in American Life.* Berkeley, CA: University of California Press.

Blau, P. M. (1955). *The dynamics of bureaucracy: A study of interpersonal relationships in two government agencies.* Chicago: University of Chicago Press.

Bond, M. H., & Hwang, K. K. (1986). The social psychology of Chinese people. In M. H. Bond (Ed.), *The psychology of the Chinese people* (pp. 213–266). Hong Kong: Oxford University Press.

Bontempo, R., Lobel, S., & Triandis, H. (1990). Compliance and value internalization in Brazil and the United States: Effects of allocentrism and anonymity. *Journal of Cross-Cultural Psychology, 21*, 200–213

Borneman, J. (1992). *Belonging in the two Berlins. Kin, state, nation.* London: Cambridge University Press.

Burt, R. (1992). *Structural holes: The social structure of competition.* Cambridge, MA: Harvard University Press.

Cantril, H. (1965). *The pattern of human concerns.* New Brusnwick, NJ: Rutgers University Press.

Cialdini, R. B. (1993). *Influence: The psychology of persuasion.* New York: Morrow.

Cialdini, R. B., Reno, R. R., & Kallgren, C.A. (1990). A focus theory of normative conduct: Recycling the concept of norms to reduce littering in public places. *Journal of Personality and Social Psychology, 58*, 1015–1026.

Cohen, A. R., & Bradford, D. L. (1990). *Influence without authority.* New York: Wiley.

Coleman, J. S. (1988). Social capital and the creation of human capital. *American Journal of Sociology, 94*, S95–S121.

Darley, J. M., & Latane, B. (1970). Norms and normative behavior: Field studies of social interdependence. In J. Macaulay & L. Berkowitz (Eds.), *Altruism and helping behavior* (pp. 83–103). San Diego, CA: Academic Press.

Doi, L. T. (1962). Amae: A key concept for understanding Japanese personality structure. In R. J. Smith & R. K. Beardsley (Eds.), *Japanese culture: Its development and characteristics* (pp. 132–140). Chicago, IL: Aldine.

Durkheim, E. 1951 [1897]. *Suicide.* New York: The Free Press

Earley, P. C. (1989). Social loafing and collectivism: A comparison of the United States and the People's Republic of China. *Administrative Science Quarterly, 34*, 565–581.

Earley, P. C. (1994). *Self or group? Cultural effects of training on self-efficacy and performance.* Irvine, CA: Graduate of Management, Working Paper #OB94004.

Erez, M., & Earley, P. C. (1993). *Culture, self-identity, and work.* New York: Oxford University Press.

Fiske, A. P. (1991). *Structures of social life: The four elementary forms of human relations.* New York: The Free Press.

Garfinkel, H. (1967). Studies in ethnomethodology. Englewood Cliffs, NJ: Prentice-Hall.

Geertz, C. (1975). On the nature of anthropological understanding. *American Scientist, 63*, 47–53.

Giddens, A. (1984). *The constitution of society*. Oxford, England: Polity.

Gilmore, D. D. (1987). Honor, honesty, shame: Male status in contemporary Andalusia. In D. D. Gilmore (Ed.), *Honor and shame and the unity of the Mediterranean* (pp. 90–104). Washington, DC: American Anthropological Association.

Granovetter, M. (1985). Economic action and social structure: The problem of embeddedness. *American Journal of Sociology, 91*(3), 481–510.

Hall, E. T. (1990). *Understanding cultural differences*. Yarmouth, ME: Intercultural Press.

Han, S., & Shavitt, S. (1994). Persuasion and culture: Advertising appeals in individualistic and collectivistic societies. *Journal of Experimental Social Psychology, 30*, 326–350.

Ho, D. Y. F. (1976). On the concept of face. *American Journal of Sociology, 81*, 867–884.

Ho, D. Y. F. (1998). Interpersonal relationships and relationship dominance: An analysis based on methodological relationism. *Asian Journal of Social Psychology, 1*, 1–16.

Ho, D. Y., & Chiu, C. Y. (1994). Component ideas of individualism, collectivism, and social organization: An application in the study of Chinese culture. In M. Kim, H. C. Triandis, C. Kagitcibasi, S. C. Choi, & G. Yoon (Eds.), *Individualism and collectivism: Theory, method, and application* (pp. 90–104). Thousand Oaks, CA: Sage.

Hofstede, G. (1980). *Culture's consequences: International differences in work-related values*. Beverly Hills, CA: Sage.

Hollinger, F., & Haller, M. (1990). Kinship and social networks in modern societies: A cross-cultural comparison among seven nations. *European Sociological Review, 6*, 103–124.

Hsu, F. L. K. (1953). *Americans and Chinese: Two ways of life*. New York: Abelard-Schuman.

Hsu, F. L. K. (1985). The self in cross-cultural perspective. In A. J. Marsella, G. De Vos, & F. L. K. Hsu (Eds.), *Culture and self* (pp. 24–55). New York: Tavistock.

Ibarra, H. (1997). Paving an alternative route: Gender differences in managerial networks. *Social Psychology Quarterly, 60*, 91–102.

Inkeles, A. (1960). Industrial man: The relation of status to experience, perception, and value. *American Journal of Sociology, 66*, 1–31.

Kanter, R. M. (1977). *Men and women of the corporation*. New York: Basic Books.

King, A. Y. C. (1991). Kuan-hsi and network building: A sociological interpretation. *Daedalus, 120*, 63–84.

Leung, K. (1987). Some determinants of reactions to procedural models for conflict resolution: A cross-national study. *Journal of Personality and Social Psychology, 53*, 898–908.

Leung, K., Au, Y. F., Fernandez-Dols, J. M., & Iwawaki, S. (1992). Preference for methods of conflict processing in two collectivist cultures. *International Journal of Psychology, 27*, 195–209.

Leung, K., & Bond, M. H. (1984). The impact of cultural collectivism on reward allocation. *Journal of Personality and Social Psychology, 47*, 793–804.

Lewin, K. (1948). Social-psychological differences between the United States and Germany. In G. W. Lewin (Ed.), *Resolving social conflicts* (pp. 15–35). London: Souvenir.

Lindsley, S. L., & Braithwaite, C. A. (1996). You should "wear a mask": Facework norms in cultural and intercultural conflict in Maquiladoras. *International Journal of Intercultural Relations, 20*(2), 199–225.

Lonner, W. J., & Adamopoulos, J. (1997). Culture as antecedent to behavior. In J. W. Berry, Y. H. Poortinga, & J. Pandey (Eds.), *Handbook of cross-cultural psychology: Volume 1. Theory and method* (pp. 43–83). Boston, MA: Allyn & Bacon.

Lukes, S. (1973). Types of individualism. In P. P. Wiener (Ed.), *Dictionary of the history of ideas: Studies of selected pivotal ideas* (Vol. 2, pp. 594–604). New York: Scribner's.

Marx, K. (1972) [1844]. Economic and philosophical manuscripts of 1844. In R. C. Tucker (Ed.), *The Marx-Engels reader* (pp. 53–103). New York: Norton.

Merton, R. K. (1969). *Social theory and social structure.* New York: The Free Press.

Moorman, R. H. (1991). Relationship between organizational justice and organizational citizenship behaviors: Do fairness perceptions influence employee citizenship? *Journal of Applied Psychology, 76*, 845–855.

Morris, M. W., Podolny, J. M., & Ariel, S. (1997, November). *The ties that bind in different cultures: A cross-national comparison of the determinants of employee obligations to coworkers.* Paper presented at Citibank Behavioral Research Council Conference, New York.

Morris, M. W., Podolny, J. M., & Ariel, S. (1998a). *Culture and normative systems of informal interaction at work: A study of North American, Chinese, German, and Spanish operations of a multinational consumer bank.* Unpublished manuscript, Stanford University, Graduate School of Business.

Morris, M. W., Podolny, J. M., & Ariel, S. (1999a). Missing relations: Incorporating relational constructs into models of culture. In P.C. Earley (Ed.), *New approaches to international differences in organizational behavior.*

Morris, M. W., Podolny, J. M., & Ariel, S. (1999b). *The ties that bind in different cultures: Norms and orientation of obligation among employees in an international organization.* Unpublished manuscript, Stanford Graduate School of Business.

Murphy, M. (1983). Coming of age in Seville. *Journal of Anthropological Research, 39,* 376–392.

Nakane, C. 1970. Japanese society. Berkeley: University of California Press.

Nakao, K. (1987). Analysing sociometric preferences: An example of Japanese and U.S. business groups. *Journal of Social Behavior and Personality, 2,* 523–534.

Parsons, T. (1951). *The social system.* New York: The Free Press.

Peng, K., Nisbett, R. E., & Wong, N. (1997). Validity problems comparing values across cultures and possible solutions. *Psychological Methods, 2*(4), 329–344.

Podolny, J. M, & Baron, J. N. (1997). Resources and relationships: Social networks and mobility in the workplace. *American Sociological Review, 62,* 673–693.

Redding, G., & Wong, G. Y. Y. (1986). The psychology of Chinese organizational behavior. In M. H. Bond (Ed.), *The psychology of the Chinese people* (pp. 213–266). Hong Kong: Oxford University Press.

Roethlisberger, F. J., & Dickson, W. (1939). *Management and the worker.* Cambridge, MA: Harvard University Press.

Sanchez-Burks, J., Nisbett, R. E., & Ybarra, O. (1998). *Relational schemas, cultural styles, and prejudice against outgroups.* Unpublished manuscript, University of Michigan Psychology Department.

Schwartz, S. H. (1994). Beyond individualism/collectivism: New cultural dimensions of values. In U. Kim, H. C. Triandis, and C. Kagitcibasi (Eds.), *Individualism & collectivism: Theory, methods, and application* (pp. 85–119). Thousand Oaks, CA: Sage.

Shaffer, L. S. (1983). Toward Pepitone's vision of a normative social psychology: What is a social norm? *Journal of Mind and Behavior, 4,* 275–294.

Sherif, M. (1936). *The psychology of social norms.* New York: Harper.

Simmel, G. (1950). *The sociology of Georg Simmel (K. H. Wolff., Trans. and Ed.). Glencoe, IL: The Free Press.*

Swidler, A. (1986). Culture in action: Symbols and strategies. *American Sociological Review, 51, 273–286.*

Tonnies, F. 1957 [1887]. *Community and society.* New Brunswick, NJ: Transaction Books.

Toqueville, A. de. 1945 [1848]. *Democracy in America.* New York: Vintage Books.

Triandis, H. C. (1990). Cross-cultural studies of individualism and collectivism. *Nebraska Symposium on Motivation, 1989.* Lincoln, NB: University of Nebraska Press.

Triandis, H. C. (1995). *Individualism and collectivism.* Boulder, CO: Westview.

Triandis, H. C., & Gelfand, M. J. (1998). Converging measurement of horizontal and vertical individualism and collectivism. Journal of Personality and Social Psychology, 74(1), pp. 118–128.

Triandis, H. C., Marin, G., Lisansky, J., & Betancourt, H. (1984). Simpatia as a cultural script of Hispanics. *Journal of Personality and Social Psychology, 47*(6), 1363–1375.

Triandis, H. C., McCusker, C., & Hui, C. H. (1990). Multimethod probes of individualism and collectivism. *Journal of Personality and Social Psychology, 59,* 1006–1020.

Weber, M. (1922) [1963]. *The sociology of religion.* Boston, MA: Beacon.

Weber, M. (1947). *The theory of social and economic organization.* New York: Oxford University Press.

White, H. C., Boorman, S. A., & Breiger, R. L. (1976). Social structure from multiple networks, I. *American Journal of Sociology, 81,* 730–738.

Wrong, D. H. (1961). The oversocialized conception of man in modern sociology. *American Sociological Review, 42,* 32–56.

7

Social Influence Factors in Euro-American and Mexican-American Women's Vulnerability to Misuse of Illicit Substances

Sara E. Gutierres

Arizona State University West

Christina M. Van Puymbroeck

Arizona State University

ABSTRACT

This chapter discusses how the interpersonal influences of family members and romantic partners may differentially affect women's and men's initiation into drug use and their decision to enter drug treatment. The role of culture on Mexican-American women's drug use is described, with specific attention paid to the way in which culture and these interpersonal influences interact to affect these women's drug use and entry into treatment. Finally, structural and interpersonal influence factors that affect women's successful completion of treatment are examined, and suggestions for designing more effective and relevant treatment programs for women are offered.

In the past, drug and alcohol abuse (i.e., substance misuse) was a greater problem among men than women. Unfortunately, this gap is narrowing, and recent surveys report increasing numbers of women with substance misuse problems. Complicating this issue is the stigma attached to substance misuse for women. Women are expected to play a stable role and *be there* for men who stray. Therefore, when women's behavior does not fit with these expectations, they are given little sympathy and are harshly criticized. Because of this and other factors, fewer women than men seek treatment help; for those women who do go into treatment, studies show that women do worse relative to men. Women's rates of entry into treatment, retention in treatment, and successful completion of treatment are significantly lower than rates for men (Blume, 1990; Gutierres & Todd, 1997; Reed, 1985; Stevens, Arbiter, & Glider, 1989).

What are the factors that contribute to women's problematic drug use and subsequent resistance to recovery from drug use? There are social structural influences such as sexism, socioeconomic status (SES), or immigration status, and mass-mediated influences such as films with drug-using protagonists or campaigns for high-fashion designers featuring "heroin chic" images. There are also the interpersonal influences of romantic partners, family members, and peers. This chapter focuses primarily on the social influence factors in interpersonal relationships that have been shown to be related to women's substance misuse and difficulties in drug treatment programs. We also briefly discuss how culture and structural influences, such as proportional representation in groups and gender role socialization, interact with interpersonal influences. The review includes data from our recent study of substance misuse among Arizona drug treatment clients (see Table 7.1 for a

TABLE 7.1
Demographic Description of Respondents in Arizona Study

Variable	Euro-Americans		Mexican-Americans	
	Females ($n=22$)	Males ($n=21$)	Females ($n=20$)	Males ($n=24$)
Mean age (years)	28.9	34.80	31.70	31.0
Range	19–49	22–51	18–46	20–59
Marital status				
Single	36.4%	28.6%	50%	41.7%
Married	27.3%	23.8%	20%	12.5
Separated/divorced	36.4%	47.6%	30%	45.8
Education				
<12 years	36.4%	14.3%	65%	70.8%
High school graduate	22.7%	52.4%	10%	25.0%
Trade school/some college	36.4%	33.4%	25%	4.2%
College graduate	4.5%	—	—	—

Note. Males comparing ethnicity: $X^2 = 16.81, p < .001$.

demographic description of participants). Data were gathered via questionnaires and interviews with female and male Mexican-Americans and Euro-American drug misusers in residential treatment programs in Arizona.

INTERPERSONAL INFLUENCES ON INITIATION OF DRUG

Why do women and men begin to use drugs? Respondents in our Arizona study provided some of the following answers. In general, it was noted that women were more likely than men to refer to family problems, whereas men were more likely than women to mention peer influence or personal responsibility.

Quote from a Mexican-American woman—Oh, my father...who was real abusive. He used to beat us...plus he was an alcoholic–still is. And he also molested me, and he used to beat my Mom in front of us, and I just wanted to block those things out...

Quote from a Euro-American woman—I would have to say that...my Dad was a drug addict and an alcoholic. Being abused mentally and physically by my Dad and wanting to be like him for a long time so he would accept me...

Quote from a Mexican-American man—I believe it was peer pressure. And certain people I hung around with had a lot to do with my addiction. Coming up, being young and all my friends started using drugs before I did. Being the only, like, the only guy out of the group that wasn't using drug or alcohol. You know, considered a church going guy, and I guess the peer pressure really got to me and I just tried something different.

Quote from a Euro-American man—I'd say when I was younger it was just hanging around with my friends, going to parties and stuff, and then secondly my job–I'm a truck driver, so I work long hours, so I took pills and stuff to stay awake.

One explanation for drug use initiation is that when individuals experience stressful events they will select coping strategies that will allow them to tolerate the demands created by these events (Lazarus & Folkman, 1984). Certain strategies, although not necessarily leading to long-term positive outcomes, produce short-term relief. One of these short-term strategies is indulging oneself in a variety of reinforcers, including alcohol and drugs. Some support for this explanation comes from a study with adolescent substance misusers who reported that they used drugs to get away from problems and to relax and relieve tension (Gutierres, Molof, & Ungerleider, 1994). At least two types of stressful events reported by respondents in the Gutierres et al. (1994) study have been found to be more prevalent in the family environments of young women than of young men. These life events are the misuse of drugs or alcohol by family members and childhood abuse.

Family Influences on Women's Drug Use

Several studies have shown that female substance misusers, more than males, come from disrupted and dysfunctional families with histories of drug and alcohol abuse problems (Blume, 1990; Cuskey, Berger, & Densen-Gerber, 1977; Cuskey, Wathey, Richardson, & Densen-Gerber, 1980; Finkelstein & Piedade, 1993; Mumme, 1991). Data from our Arizona study also showed that family substance abuse problems were more prevalent in the homes of female clients than male clients. Female respondents reported a significantly higher mean number of family members with alcohol or drug problems (X = 2.36) than males [X = 1.68; $F(1,134)$ = 12.64, p < .001]. In addition, when asked how many family members had substance abuse problems, a significantly higher percentage of women respondents (40.0%) than men (9.1%) reported multiple family members—that is, mother and father and brothers and sisters—with problems (c^2 = 11.6, p < .001). Substance misuse by family members creates a stressful home environment whereby children seek to escape the disruption through their own use of substances. Moreover, observing family members misusing substances to cope with stress and negative life events provides multiple negative role models for the observers.

There is also growing evidence that substance misusers often have been victims of childhood abuse. The majority of the studies have focused on sexual abuse, for which most victims are women (see Browne & Finkelhor, 1986, for a review). However, some of the studies investigating physical

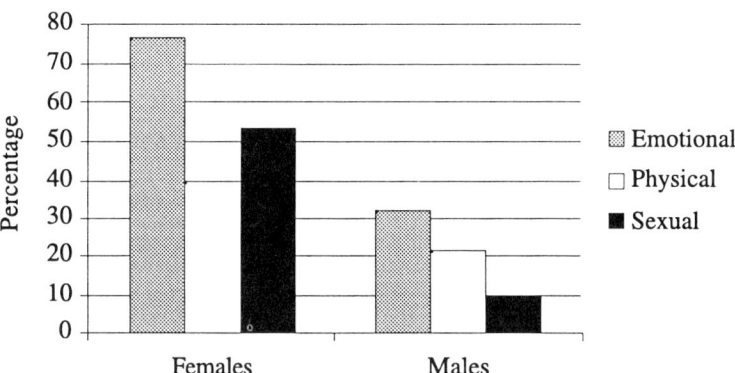

Sexual Abuse χ^2 = 20.80, p < .001
Emotional Abuse χ^2 = 18.36, p < .001
Physical Abuse χ^2 = 6.34, p < .01

FIG. 7.1. Percentage of female and male respondents reporting emotional, physical and sexual abuse in childhood.

abuse and substance misuse have found a higher reported prevalence among women than men of this type of victimization as well (Dembo, Dertke, LaVoie, Borders, Washburn, & Schmeidler, 1987; McClellan, Farabee, & Crouch, 1997). Data from our Arizona study support these findings. Higher percentages of female than male substance misusers reported experiencing childhood emotional, physical, and sexual abuse (see Fig. 7.1).

The long-term effects of sexual and physical abuse include depression (Bagley & Ramsay, 1985; Briere, 1992; Briere & Runtz, 1988; Sedney & Brooks, 1984), anxiety (Briere &Runtz, 1988; Sedney & Brooks, 1984), and low self-esteem (Bagley & Ramsay, 1985; Courtois, 1979; Herman, 1981). Although these negative psychological outcomes do not differ by gender, female victims have been found to be more likely than male victims to seek to alleviate the physiological, behavioral, and cognitive symptoms resulting from the abuse by self-medicating with substances, whereas male victims are more likely than females to engage in aggressive or violent activity (Stewart, 1996; Toray, Coughlin, Vuchinich, & Patricelli, 1991; Van der Kolk & Fisler, 1994; Widom, 1989, 1995).

The experiences that young women have in dysfunctional and often violent homes may lead to the dependency exhibited by women substance misusers reported in several studies (Amaro & Hardy-Fanta, 1995; Marsh & Neely, 1978; Tucker, 1979). As a result, women may be particularly susceptible to attention from men who promise them relief from their psychological distress through the use of alcohol or drugs.

Influence of Male Partners in Female Drug Use

Female respondents in our Arizona study often acknowledged the influence of males in their substance use:

A Mexican-American woman—I met my little girl's father, I started drinking more than I used to, and it got me into this situation that I'm in now...

A Euro-American woman—very young marriage—having just turned 15 and being married to a man who was an alcoholic and addict himself.

In studies examining influences on initiation of drug use, Freeland and Campbell (1973) found that, in mixed-sex couples, the most common direction of influence was an experienced male introducing drugs to an inexperienced female. Other researchers have shown that, for women, the initiation into any drug use, but particularly hard drug use, was usually by a man with whom she was living or emotionally or romantically involved. In contrast, men are rarely influenced by a female partner to use drugs (Amaro & Hardy-Fanta, 1995; Amaro, Zuckerman, & Cabral, 1989; Cooperstock, 1971;

Gutierres, Raymond, & Rhoads, 1979; Hser, Anglin, & McGlothlin, 1987; O'Donnell, Besteman, & Jones, 1967; Rosenbaum, 1981; Waldorf, 1973).

Gender role socialization provides an explanation for why men are influential in women's drug use. As in most societies, women and men in the United States are socialized to behave in gender-specific ways, with many social rewards associated with successful performance and punishments with deviations from these roles. Males are encouraged and rewarded for behaviors related to instrumentality, competitiveness, dominance, lack of emotionality, lack of influenceability, autonomy, and independence. In contrast, appropriate feminine behavior is considered gentle, dependent, quiet, having the ability to express tender feelings, possessing a need for security, being aware of feelings of others, and interdependence (Broverman, Vogel, Broverman, Clarkson, & Rosenkrantz, 1972; Canter & Meyerowitz, 1984; Del Boca & Ashmore, 1980; Rosenkrantz, Vogel, Bee, Broverman, & Broverman, 1968; Ruble, 1983; Smith & Midlarsky, 1985; Spence & Sawin, 1985). Women are expected to need intimate relationships, to follow the male's lead, to respect his knowledge and experience in areas in which she is inexperienced, and to support his ideas and activities. The few studies that have examined the gender role orientation of substance users have found that these women generally have quite traditional feminine attitudes (Cuskey et al., 1977; Marsh & Neely, 1978; Wilsnak, 1973).

Once women are initiated into drug use, their experiences in the male-dominated world of drugs and addiction maintain their vulnerable psychological state. For example, women generally support their addiction either by prostitution or reliance on a drug-dealing male. In these circumstances, they are likely to continue to be victimized through violence from prostitution customers and drug-using partners. Fifty percent of Amaro and Hardy-Fanta's (1995) sample reported experiencing this type of violence. Millstein (1993) suggested that drug-using women live in a subculture that is dominated by males and masculine values and in which they fill secondary and dependent roles. This way of life may continue for many years before women decide to enter treatment. At that decision point, there are several interpersonal influence factors that affect women, but not men. These factors are discussed next.

INTERPERSONAL INFLUENCES ON WOMEN'S DECISION TO ENTER DRUG TREATMENT

The decision to stop using substances and get help for the problem is difficult for anyone who misuses substance. For women, however, these difficulties may be compounded by lack of support from drug-using partners or other family members, and by parenting concerns if the woman is pregnant or a mother to young children.

Lack of Social Support

Previous research has noted that the only consistent predictor of success in treatment (for both genders) is social support from individuals' partners. Tucker (1979) and Eldred and Washington (1976) found that over 70% of successful women and men had the support of their partners in their treatment attempts. Clients who reported that their partners had influenced them to enter treatment remained there significantly longer than those whose partners did not provide encouragement. However, women substance users were much less likely than men to receive the support of their partners or other family members to enter and remain in treatment programs (Kane-Cavaiola & Rullo-Cooney, 1991; Nurco, Wegner, & Stephenson, 1982; Reed, 1985). In fact, in Amaro and Hardy-Fanta's (1995) recent interview study, almost all of the women indicated that their partners expressed strong and persistent opposition to their entering treatment. Considering the primary importance of relationships for women, partner opposition is a major barrier for women entering drug treatment programs (Gilligan, 1982; Jordan, Kaplan, Miller Stiver, & Surrey, 1991).

Pregnancy and Children

In addition to lack of social support, female drug misusers who are pregnant or have children frequently cite the absence of child-care alternatives as a major barrier to entering treatment programs (Nelson-Zlupko et al., 1995). Although drug users are often stereotyped as neglectful and abusive mothers, empirical research contradicts this belief. Zankowski (1987) found that the desire to take care of their children was the most common reason for women leaving treatment prematurely. Eliason, Skinstad, and Gerken (1995) reported that, overall, mothers with dependent children spend less time in treatment than women who are not mothers. Consistent with this finding, women interviewed in our Arizona study cited their children as the most frequently cited reason for a desire to quit drug use. For example:

> A Mexican-American woman —…it concerns me and my children and I would like to change my life and be a human being, to be somebody.

> A Euro-American woman—I think my kids being taken away was very important in helping me deal…with the situation, because I love my kids and I want to be a mother to them.

> A Mexican-American woman—My kids and myself, because I didn't want to go back to prison either, I already wasted too much time in jail and prison…

TABLE 7.2
Percent of Respondents Completing Treatment and Percent
of Respondents With Good Prognoses for Recovery

Variable	Mexican-Americans		Euro-Americans	
	Females (%)	Males (%)	Females (%)	Males (%)
Completed required Number of Days in Treatment[a]	36.4	45.5	70.8	75
Good Prognoses for Recovery[b]	13.6	54.2	18.2	25

[a] X^2 for Mexican-Americans comparing gender = 5.60, $p < .02$.
X^2 for Euro-Americans comparing gender = 3.88, $p < .05$.
[b] X^2 for Mexican-Americans comparing gender = 8.81, $p < .003$.

Few treatment programs offer child-care arrangements, and many women are unable to find or afford alternative care. In addition, women fear that if they enter treatment while their children are put into the care of family members or foster care, they will not be able to get them back. This issue creates a great deal of concern for women contemplating entering drug treatment programs.

For Mexican-American women, culture may interact with the interpersonal influence factors that women in general experience in the initiation and maintenance of substance misuse. These cultural issues are discussed in the following section.

CULTURE AND INTERPERSONAL INFLUENCES ON MEXICAN-AMERICAN WOMEN'S DRUG USE AND DECISION TO ENTER DRUG TREATMENT

Cultural issues, including acculturation, may be particularly important in understanding Mexican-American women's drug misuse. Acculturation is a process that affects individuals who have an *immigrant history* or who have been affected by economic, social, or political changes that force migration and/or adaptation to new cultural conditions. Contact with a new culture is hypothesized to influence substance use through exposure to competing cultural values concerning this behavior, and by increasing psychosocial stress related to changes in values, attitudes, behaviors, and lifestyle induced by the need to adapt to a new cultural environment. Some research has linked acculturation experience to substance misuse for Hispanics (Delgado, 1989; Schinke, Moncher, Palleja, Zayas, & Schilling, 1988).

Although no study has specifically examined the role of gender in the relationship between acculturation and drug misuse, the fact that Mexican-American women have particularly poor outcomes in drug treatment programs suggests that acculturation or other cultural issues might be important. A number of studies have found that, compared with Mexican-American men and Euro-American women, Mexican-American women experienced more extensive criminal involvement, were less likely to be employed when they entered treatment, and had the least positive treatment outcomes (Anglin, Hser, & Booth, 1987; Moore & Mata, 1981). Similarly, the Mexican-American women in our Arizona study had worse prognoses for recovery than Mexican-American men or Euro-American women and men and were less likely than all other groups to complete the required number of days in treatment (see Table 7.2).

The indications that Mexican-American women exhibit more severe problems with substance misuse are in direct contrast to other literature that consistently finds Mexican-American women, compared with Mexican-American men and Euro-American women and men, more likely to abstain from alcohol use or use alcohol in much lower quantities and frequencies than the other groups. This latter finding applies to women in rural and urban communities, to women in Mexico, to recent immigrants, and to second and later generation populations. These distinctions have been linked to traditional cultural expectations of abstinence from substance use for Mexican-American women. When Mexican-American women have violated the abstinence norm, this may prompt a Mexican cultural "abstinence violation effect" (Marlatt & Gordon, 1985), where women decide they may as well continue to use, because the sacred vow of abstinence has already been violated (Castro & Gutierres, 1997). These cultural expectations and values result in substance misuse being highly stigmatized for Mexican-American women. Thus, the resulting shame for engaging in the behavior may serve as a barrier to seeking social support from family and friends and as a barrier to seeking treatment.

STRUCTURAL AND INTERPERSONAL INFLUENCES IN TREATMENT PROGRAMS

Despite the barriers mentioned earlier, some women do enter treatment. For those women who enter treatment, however, the male-dominated drug world they have just left is often replaced by the male-dominated world of drug treatment.

Women are proportionately a minority in most alcohol and drug treatment programs. The overall proportion of women is fairly consistently reported to be about 20%, although male-to-female program ratios vary from 2:1 to as high as a 10:1 ratio. Women in drug treatment state that this gender imbalance is most keenly felt in group therapy sessions, in which there may be only 1 woman in a group of 10 or more members (Woodhouse, 1990).

These skewed gender ratios have effects on both women and men. The research on tokenism and proportional representation in a group suggests that solo status (being the only one or one of a few people of a given gender or ethnicity in a larger group, in which the majority are of a different category membership) produces disproportionate scrutiny, extreme evaluations, and highly stereotyped impressions of the minority on the part of majority members (Kanter, 1977; Taylor, Fiske, Close, Anderson, & Ruderman, 1977). More specifically, Kanter (1977) and Wolman and Frank (1975) found that the presence of a solo woman in otherwise all male work groups was disruptive to group functioning, causing strains for which the solo woman was seen as responsible. The tension was often alleviated by the solo woman taking on or falling into a special role in the group—often a highly gender-typed one, such as *mother* or *seductress*. Some researchers have reported that women are put in similarly gender-stereotyped roles in group therapy sessions at drug treatment programs, playing the role of mother, girlfriend, or wife as females and males attempt to work out their problems in mixed-gender relationships (Cuskey et al., 1977). In addition to the low proportion of female clients, researchers have reported that female representation among staff is lo, and women are more likely than men to experience some form of sexual harassment while in treatment—either by a staff member or another client (Cuskey et al., 1977; Marsh & Simpson, 1986; Sutker, 1981).

Most treatment programs—whether they be inpatient drug free, outpatient drug free, or methadone maintenance—were designed by men for male clients, and their approaches have been informed predominantly by research conducted on male substance-using clients. The Synanon model is the most prevalent model currently in use. This model stresses the necessity of totally breaking down the substance misuser's defenses and denial to build a new, responsible individual. The main method for achieving this is thought to be brutally honest confrontation and harshly condemning the individual's character and behavior; this is usually accomplished in the context of a group therapy setting composed of a small group of drug-using peers (Yablonsky, 1965). Although little empirical evidence exists to support the efficacy of this approach for women or men, at least two studies have specifically found confrontational approaches to be counterproductive with female substance users (Reed, 1985; Zankowski, 1987). Again, gender role socialization offers an explanation for these outcomes. Males are socialized to confront, challenge, and criticize each other in group contexts and are rewarded for performing well in the roles of challenger and challenged. In contrast, women are taught to be cooperative, to be aware of the feelings of others, and to look for others' approval in group contexts, none of which prepares them to participate effectively in this confrontational style.

Given the interpersonal influences on women's drug misuse, the barriers to women entering drug treatment and the lack of sensitivity to women's needs within treatment programs, it is not surprising that women's rates of recovery are lower than men's. The next section discusses ways that treatment programs might improve services for substance-misusing women.

PRACTICAL IMPLICATIONS: IMPROVED TREATMENT PROGRAMS FOR WOMEN

The analysis of social influence factors on women's drug misuse outlined earlier suggests several ways that drug treatment programs may be able to improve services for women.

Separate Treatment Facilities

Because of the imbalanced gender ratios in most coed programs, as well as the gender-specific health and social problems experienced by women, separate treatment facilities should be provided for women and men. These facilities should include services for pregnant drug misusers and women with children. Pregnant drug users are a particularly high-risk group that often avoids treatment because of the stigma attached to drug use while pregnant, and because of the lack of services that allow women to keep and care for their infants after birth. Program components addressing issues of parenting and relationships with children should be incorporated and included along with components that deal with addiction and psychological issues. The treatment programs should also provide services for the children to help them deal with the disrupted family lives they have experienced. The services for children could provide an important prevention function, because children from these families are at high risk for developing substance misuse problems as adolescents and adults.

Treating Victims of Abuse

The high rates of reported childhood abuse from our Arizona sample and other studies suggest that drug programs must include treatment components to address the issue of childhood victimization. Indeed, an important part of training for drug treatment personnel should include the physical and psychological consequences of childhood verbal, physical, and sexual abuse. Program personnel must be aware that many clients have begun to use substances to deal with childhood trauma and that, after a period of abstinence, suppressed memories may return, resulting in anxiety, depression, and an increase in motivation to return to drug use. In addition, there is abundant evidence that children who are abused or exposed to violence in their home environments are more likely to become violent adults (Widom, 1989). Treatment programs could serve as important intervention resources in the cycle of intergenerational violence. They should incorporate parenting skills, anger management, and modification of violent behaviors into client treatment plans.

In addition to childhood victimization, many women have been victims of domestic violence and/or community violence. Some evidence suggests that a history of abuse in childhood predicts greater psychological distress in response to experiences of violence as an adult (Cimino & Dutton, 1991). It is vitally important for drug treatment providers to be aware of these patterns of abuse because they may impair successful recovery from substance misuse. In addition, treatment program personnel should be aware that women do not readily acknowledge victimization as children or adults in intake interviews. This reluctance to reveal information may necessitate multiple inquiries about abuse throughout the treatment process.

The psychological sequelae likely to result from victimization—that is, guilt, self-blame, low self-esteem and feelings of hopelessness and powerlessness—should be addressed in the treatment setting. Although most clinical personnel would acknowledge that increasing one's feelings of self-worth is difficult in the short period of time that individuals are in treatment, there is some evidence that certain self-esteem enhancement strategies can be successful in changing one's self-image (Osborne, 1996). In addition, increasing feelings of self-worth may be an important step in helping clients toward achieving perceptions of self-efficacy (Bandura, 1986). Several empirical studies with substance users have shown a relationship between self-efficacy and positive treatment outcomes (Burling, Reilly, Moltzen, & Ziff, 1989; Castro, Barrington, Walton, & Rawson, 1995; Peele, 1991). Further, female drug misusers' feelings of hopelessness and powerlessness should be addressed with interventions that help clients feel strong and powerful as individuals. A wide range of interventions based on assertiveness/communication training, role playing, coping skills training, cognitive restructuring, self-confirmation and self-nurturing skills, and decision-making training are recommended for helping individuals feel capable and effective (Enns, 1993).

Culturally Relevant Treatment

Given the serious outcomes of substance misuse and difficulties in treatment for Mexican-American women, the treatment centers that serve this ethnic group should consider incorporating cultural components into their programs. As a first step, bilingual female Mexican-American counselors should be hired to work with female Mexican-American clients. The strong familialism value in Mexican-American culture (the central importance of family bonds and obligations) should be acknowledged. If possible, immediate and extended family members should be educated about issues relevant to substance misuse and encouraged to be involved in the recovery process. In addition, in the process of teaching individuals how to use alternative methods to substance use to deal with stressful events, the concept of dignidad could be stressed. In Hispanic cultures, this concept emphasizes the importance of self-respect and self-worth—values that may be threatened by the indignities associated with misuse of substances. Finally, ito be culturally relevant for

Mexican-American women, assertiveness training should have more emphasis on a sense of community and respect for others' experiences and less emphasis on the dominant culture's belief in individualism.

CONCLUSIONS

To improve treatment outcomes for women, treatment providers must address a multitude of structural and interpersonal influences on women's initiation into drug use, maintenance of drug use, and successful recovery from drug misuse. These include victimization from violent families and male partners, insensitivity to issues surrounding care for children, insensitivity to cultural issues, and inadequate and inappropriate treatment services for women. Until these issues are acknowledged and addressed, women drug misusers will continue to exhibit low rates of entry into treatment, high rates of dropout from treatment, and low rates of recovery from drug misuse.

ACKNOWLEDGMENTS

The research reported in this chapter was supported in part by Grant BRSG 2 SO4 RR07112 from the Division of Research Resources, National Institutes of Health; a grant from Arizona State University, West, Scholarship, Research, and Creative Activity Grant Program; a grant from Arizona State University Hispanic Research Center; and a grant from Arizona State University Research Assistant Program.

REFERENCES

Amaro, H., & Hardy-Fanta, C. (1995). Gender relations in addiction and recovery. *Journal of Psychoactive Drugs, 27*, 325–337.

Amaro, H., Zuckerman, B., & Cabral, H. (1989). Drug use among adolescent mothers: A profile of risk. *Pediatrics, 84*, 144–151.

Anglin, M. D., Hser, Y., & Booth, M. W. (1987). Sex differences in addict careers: IV. Treatment. *American Journal of Drug and Alcohol Abuse, 13*, 253–280.

Bagley, C., & Ramsay, R. (1985, February). *Disrupted childhood and vulnerability to sexual assault: Long-term sequels with implications for counseling.* Paper presented at the conference on Counseling the Sexual Abuse Survivor, Winnipeg, Canada.

Bandura, A. (1986). *Social foundations of thought and action: A social cognitive theory.* Englewood Cliffs, NJ: Prentice-Hall.

Blume, S. B. (1990). Chemical dependency in women: Important issues. *American Journal of Drug and Alcohol Abuse, 16,* 297–307.

Briere, J. N. (1992). *Child abuse trauma.* Newbury Park: Sage.

Briere, J. N., & Runtz, M. (1988). Multivariate correlates of childhood psychological and physical maltreatment among university women. *Child Abuse & Neglect, 12,* 331–341.

Broverman, I., Vogel, S. R., Broverman, D. M., Clarkson, F. E., & Rosenkrantz, P. S. (1972). Sex role stereotypes: A current appraisal. *Journal of Social Issues, 23,* 59–78.

Browne, A., & Finkelhor, D. (1986). Impact of child sexual abuse: A review of the research. *Psychological Bulletin, 99,* 66–77.

Burling, T. A., Reilly, P. M., Moltzen, J. O., & Ziff, D. C. (1989). Self-efficacy and relapse among inpatient drug and alcohol abusers: A predictor of outcomes. *Journal of Studies on Alcohol, 50,* 354–360.

Canter, R. J., & Meyerowitz, B. C. (1984). Sex-role stereotypes: Self-reports of behavior. *Sex Roles, 10,* 293–306.

Castro, F. G., Barrington, E. H., Walton, M. A., & Rawson, R. A. (1995). *Indicators of lapse/relapse in stimulant users: A lifestyle perspective.* Unpublished manuscript.

Castro, F. G., & Gutierres, S. E. (1997). Drug and alcohol use among rural Mexican-Americans. In E. B. Robertson, Z. Sloboda, G. M. Boyd, L. Beatty, & N. J. Kozel (Eds.), *Rural substance abuse: State of knowledge and issues* (National Institute on Drug Abuse Research Monograph 168. NIH Pub. No. 97–4177). Washington, DC: U.S. Government Printing Office.

Cimino, J. J., & Dutton, M. A. (1991, August). *Factors influencing the development of PTSD in battered women.* Paper presented at the 99th annual convention of the American Psychological Association, San Francisco, CA

Cooperstock, R. (1971). Sex differences in the use of mood-modifying drugs: An exploratory model. *Health and Social Behavior, 23, 238–244.*

Courtois, C. (1979). The incest experience and its aftermath. *Victimology: An International Journal, 4,* 337–347.

Cuskey, W. R., Berger, L. H., & Densen-Gerber, J. (1977). Issues in the treatment of female addiction: A review and critique of the literature. *Contemporary Drug Problems, 6,* 307–371.

Cuskey, W. R., Wathey, R. B., Richardson, A. H., & Densen-Gerber, J. (1980). Evaluation of a therapeutic community program for female addicts. *Journal of Addictive Health, 1,* 186–203.

Del Boca, F. K., & Ashmore, R. D. (1980). Sex stereotypes and implicit personality theory. II. A trait-inference approach to the assessment of sex stereotypes. *Sex Roles, 6,* 519–535.

Delgado, M. (1989). Treatment and prevention of Hispanic alcoholism. In T.D. Watts & R. Wright (Eds.), *Alcoholism in minority populations* (pp. 77–92). Springfield, IL: Charles C. Thomas.

Dembo, R., Dertke, M., LaVoie, L., Borders, S., Washburn, M., & Schmeidler, J. (1987). Physical abuse, sexual victimization and illicit drug use: A structural analysis among high risk adolescents. *Journal of Adolescence, 10*, 13–33.

Eldred, C. A., & Washington, M. N. (1976). Interpersonal relationships in heroin use by men and women and their role in treatment outcome. *International Journal of the Addictions, 11*, 117–130.

Eliason, M. J., Skinstad, A. H., & Gerken, K. (1995). Substance abuse and motherhood. *Alcoholism Treatment Quarterly, 13*, 81–88.

Enns, C. Z. (1993). Twenty years of feminist counseling and therapy: From naming biases to implementing multifaceted practice. *The Counseling Psychologist, 21*, 3–87.

Finkelstein, N., & Piedade, E. (1993, May–June). The relational-model and the treatment of addicted females. *The Counselor Magazine*, 8–11.

Freeland, J. B., & Campbell, R. S. (1973). The social context of marijuana use. *International Journal of the Addictions, 8*, 317–324.

Gilligan, C. (1982). *In a different voice.* Cambridge, MA: Harvard University Press.

Gutierres, S. E., Molof, M., & Ungerleider, S. (1994). Relationship of "risk" factors to teen substance use: A comparison of abstainers, infrequent users, and frequent users. *International Journal of the Addictions, 29*, 1559–1579.

Gutierres, S. E., Raymond, J. S., & Rhoads, D. L. (1979). *A comparative study of women heroin abusers during and after treatment: Needs and attributions.* Final report to Arizona Department of Health Services-Behavioral Health Services.

Gutierres, S. E., & Todd, M. (1997). The impact of childhood abuse on treatment outcomes of substance users. *Professional Psychology: Research and Practice, 28*, 348–354.

Herman, J. S. (1981). *Father-daughter incest.* Cambridge, MA: Harvard University Press.

Hser, Y., Anglin, M. D., & McGlothlin, W. (1987). Sex differences in addict careers: I. Initiation of use. *American Journal of Drug and Alcohol Abuse, 13*, 33–57.

Jordan, J. V., Kaplan, A. G., Miller, J. B., Stiver, I. P., & Surrey, J. L. (1991). *Women's growth in connection: Writings from the Stone Center.* New York: The Guilford Press.

Kane-Cavaiola, C., & Rullo-Cooney, D. (1991). Addicted women: Their families' effect on treatment outcome. *Journal of Chemical Dependency Treatment, 4*, 111–119.

Kanter, R. M. (1977). Some effects of proportions on group life: Skewed sex ratios and responses to token women. *American Journal of Sociology, 82*, 965–90.

Lazarus, R. S., & Folkman, S. (1984). *Stress, appraisal and coping.* New York: Springer.

Marlatt, G. A., & Gordon, J. (1985). *Relapse prevention: Maintenance strategies in the treatment of addictive behaviors.* New York: Guilford Press.

Marsh, J. C., & Neely, B. (1978). *Women helping women: The woman center evaluation report* (Final Report of NIDA Grant DA01496). Ann Arbor, MI: University of Michigan.

Marsh, K., & Simpson, D. (1986). Sex differences in opiad addiction careers. *American Journal of Drug and Alcohol Abuse, 12,* 309–329.

McClellan, D. S., Farabee, D., & Crouch, B. M. (1997). Early victimization, drug use, and criminality. *Criminal Justice and Behavior, 24*(4), 455–476.

Millstein, R. A. (1993). National Institute on Drug Abuse—Focus on the future: A steadfast commitment to research. In L. Harris (Ed.), *Problems of drug dependence,* 1992 (NIDA Research Monograph 132). Rockville, MD: National Institute on Drug Abuse.

Moore, J. W., & Mata, A. (1981). *Women and heroin in Chicano communities.* Final Report Chicano Pinto Research Project.

Mumme, D. (1991). Aftercare: Its role in primary and secondary recovery of women from alcohol and other drug dependence. *International Journal of the Addictions, 26,* 549–564.

Nelson-Zlupko, L., Kauffman, E., & Dore, M. M.. (1995). Gender differences in drug addiction and treatment: Implications for social work intervention with substance-abusing women. *Social Work, 40,* 45–54.

Nurco, D. N., Wegner, N., & Stephenson, F., (1982). Female narcotic addicts: Changing profiles. *Journal of Addictive Health, 3,* 62–105.

O'Donnell, J. A., Besteman, K. J., & Jones, J. P. (1967). Marital history of narcotics addicts. *International Journal of the Addictions, 2,* 21–38.

Osborne, R. E. (1996). *Self: An eclectic approach.* Boston: Allyn & Bacon.

Peele, S. (1991). What works in addiction treatment and what doesn't: Is the best therapy no therapy? *International Journal of the Addictions, 25,* 1409–1419.

Reed, B. G. (1985). Drug misuse and dependency in women: The meaning and implications of being considered a special population or minority group. *International Journal of the Addictions, 20,* 13–62.

Rosenbaum, M. (1981). When drugs come in the picture, love flies out the window: Women addicts' love relationships. *International Journal of the Addictions, 16,* 1197–1206.

Rosenkrantz, P., Vogel, S. R., Bee, H., Broverman, I. K., & Broverman, D. M. (1968). Sex role stereotypes and self-concepts in college students. *Journal of Consulting and Clinical Psychology, 32,* 287–295.

Ruble, T. L. (1983). Sex stereotypes: Issues of change in the 1970's. *Sex Roles, 9,* 397–402.

Schinke, S. P., Moncher, M. S., Palleja, J., Zayas, L. H., & Schilling, R. F. (1988). Hispanic youth, substance abuse, and stress: Implications for prevention research. *International Journal of the Addictions, 23*, 809–826.

Sedney, M. A., & Brooks, B. (1984). Factors associated with a history of childhood sexual experience in a nonclinical female population. *Journal of the American Academy of Child Psychiatry, 23*, 215–218.

Smith, P. A., & Midlarsky, E. (1985). Empirically derived conceptions of femaleness and maleness: A current view. *Sex Roles, 12*, 313–328.

Spence, J. T., & Sawin, L. L. (1985). Images of masculinity and femininity: A reconceptualization. In V. O'Leary, R. Unger, & B. Wallston (Eds.), *Women, gender and social psychology* (pp. 35–66). Hillsdale, NJ: Lawrence Erlbaum Associates.

Stevens, J., Arbiter, M., & Glider, P. (1989). Women residents: Expanding their role to increase treatment effectiveness in substance abuse programs. *International Journal of the Addictions, 24*, 425–434.

Stewart, S. H. (1996). Alcohol abuse in individuals exposed to trauma: A critical review. *Psychological Bulletin, 120*, 83–112.

Sutker, P.B. (1981). Drug dependent women: an overview of the literature. In G.M. Beschner, B.G. Reed & J. Mondanaro (Eds.), Treatment services for drug dependent women (Vol. 1, pp. 25–51). Rockville, MD: National Institute on Drug Abuse.

Taylor, S. E., Fiske, S. T., Close, M. M., Anderson, C. E., & Ruderman, A .J. (1977). *Solo status as a psychological variable.* Unpublished manuscript.

Toray, T., Coughlin, C., Vuchinich, S., & Patricelli, P. (1991). Gender differences associated with adolescent substance abuse: Comparisons and implications for treatment. *Family Relations, 40*, 338–344.

Tucker, M. B. (1979). A descriptive and comparative analysis of the social support structure of heroin-addicted women. In *Addicted women: Family dynamics, self-perceptions and support systems* (pp. 37–76). Rockville, MD: DHEW, Alcohol, Drug Abuse and Mental Health Administration.

Van der Kolk, B. A., & Fisler, R. E. (1994). Childhood abuse and neglect and loss of self-regulation. *Bulletin of the Menninger Clinic, 58*, 145–168.

Waldorf, D. (1973). *Careers in dope.* Englewood Cliffs, NJ: Prentice-Hall.

Widom, C. S. (1989). Does violence beget violence? A critical examination of the literature. *Psychological Bulletin, 106*, 3–28.

Widom, C. S. (1995). *Victims of childhood sexual abuse: Later criminal consequences* (Research in Brief). Washington, DC: U.S. Department of Justice.

Wilsnak, S. C. (1973). Sex role identity in female alcoholism. *Journal of Abnormal Psychology, 82*, 253–261.

Wolman, C., & Frank, H. (1975). The solo woman in a professional peer group. American Journal of Orthopsychiatry, 45, 164–171.

Woodhouse, L.D. (1990). An exploratory study of the use of life history methods to determine treatment needs for female substance abusers. *Response fo the Victimization of Women and Children, 13*(3), 12–15.

Yablonsky, L. (1965). *The tunnel back: Synanon.* New York: Macmillan.

Zankowski, G. L. (1987). Responsive programming: Meeting the needs of chemically dependent women. *Alcoholism Treatment Quarterly, 4*, 53–65.

Part II: Social Influence and Social Change Across Cultures

Janusz Reykowski
Polish Academy of Science

Overview and Commentary

In his seminal work on social influence, Cialdini (1993) describe the mechanisms by which one person (or persons)—an agent—instigates a specific change in the beliefs, attitudes, or behavior of another person (a target). He presents theory, research, and practical experience that elucidate how it is possible that the agent, without resorting to coercion or outright deception, can make the target think and act in the particular manner expected and desired by the agent. Cialdini's work revealed the multitude of forms of what seems to be one general phenomenon of critical importance for social life: that one human being is a powerful source of influence on another human being.

The effect of influence is some change in an individual—it may be a momentary change in affect, preference, or action tendency. Sometimes it is more than that and produces relatively permanent transformations in a person's psychological makeup, like in cases of changes in beliefs, attitudes, or values as a result of education, psychotherapy, political socialization, and so on. The changes may appear not only in some individuals, but may concern larger groups of people. Given this, one can easily realize that social influence operates not only on the interpersonal but also on the societal level. In the second part of the present volume, social influence on a scale greater than the interpersonal is examined in some detail.

The initial of chapter by Nowak and Vallacher (chap. 8), describes an elegant theoretical model of social change. The authors postulate that, "social influence is the mechanism by which individuals coordinate their opinions, moods, and behaviors." Their model is based on specific assumptions concerning the factors that determine the effectiveness of the influence (strength, immediacy, and number of targets)—assumptions that are well grounded in existing empirical research. These assumptions can be interpreted in formal terms describing the relationship between the main parameters of social influence as a cellular automata model. Such a model can be tested by means of computer simulation.

The main effect of this simulation is a model that characterizes the dynamics of social change. The model both describes and explains social change in terms of underlying psychological factors. The power of the model is illustrated by the fact that it generates clear recommendations concerning the facilitation of social change. These recommendations have been successfully applied to a strategy for combating unemployment among young people in Poland.

A puzzling attribute of the model is its high level of generality. In fact, on the basis of the same assumptions, one can describe processes of a change of nonsocial phenomena, such as in physical or biological systems. One may wonder, what is *social* in the social influence processes described by Nowak and Vallacher? One is prone to suspect that some abstract characteristics of the social influence represent a general law of nature.

An important feature of the Nowak and Vallacher model is that it describes how new ideas initially proposed by a rather small contingent of individuals can be disseminated and eventually adopted by a majority. The authors emphasize the role of *bubbles of the new* in the *sea of the old*. These bubbles of the new—agents of change—must have some characteristics that are described within the framework of the model in formal terms (strength, clustering). One may wonder what the psychological content of these formal characteristics is. Some approximation to the answer to this question contains the chapter by Wojciszke.

Wojciszke's research indicates that a combination of psychological and political factors exists that may facilitate the power of a minority to influence the corresponding majority. The psychological factors described in Wojciszke's chapter are specific characteristics of how humans process political information. First of all, there is the potential misperception of one's power. One manifestation of this misperception is a gross overestimation of the popularity of one's own ideological position: Strangely enough, the minority tends to perceive itself as the majority. In real life, there are many situations in which information about one's minority status is unequivocal and cannot be questioned. Nevertheless, a minority may have such a firm belief that, despite differences in size, it nevertheless possesses some qualities (e.g. moral power) that give it superior strength vis-à-vis the majority. For example, this phenomenon can be observed in every case of a small country or small ethnic group challenging a much greater adversary. Another psychological factor that contributes to the sometimes surprisingly powerful influence of a minority is the radicalism of its view—the members of minority much more often than members of the majority assume extreme positions on attitude dimensions. This means that they are not hesitant to affirm the rightness of their own convictions, a phenomenon that is associated with a tendency described by Wojciszke as the *moralization of an issue*. The end result is that the given ideological controversy is treated as a moral struggle by the minority: the forces of good are fighting against the forces of evil.

This combination of beliefs can arm a minority with effective means of influence on members of the majority who are less certain of their position. The real impact of the minority can be reinforced by certain political arrangements.

For example, in a parliamentary setting, a small party can attain disproportional power due to its location between big players who have to compete for its favors. Strategic political position of a minority, combined with its psychological strength, can make a minority a powerful source of influence.

The model described by Nowak and Vallacher can be regarded as one general frame of reference for studying social change. However, when one wants to study the concrete processes of change, one must be aware that there are some additional mechanisms that should be taken into consideration. One such process is the acculturation of immigrants. Acculturation can be looked on as a process of transformation of the beliefs, attitudes, and behavior patterns of immigrants as a result of social influences originating in the host culture. Truly, it is not a one-way process: Although immigrants are a minority, they exert a reciprocal influence on their hosts.

In the chapter by Klinger and Bierbrauer (chap. 10) on the acculturation of Turkish immigrants in Germany, one specific aspect of the process is examined: immigrants' attitudes toward conflictual situations as an indication of acculturation mode. The authors postulate that there are different patterns of handling conflict in the traditional Turkish society than in German society. Hence, studying attitudes toward conflict can tell us something about the process of acculturation.

The main finding of this study seems to be that acculturation is not a homogenous process. The same persons may manifest different styles of conflict management behavior depending on context and, more specifically, on the source of conflict and the nature of the adversaries. If conflict with a German adversary concerned tangible resources, it was most likely approached in the *German way*, indicating an assimilation mode of acculturation. However, in conflicts over intangible resources and with other Turks, the *Turkish* resolution style was more likely to be employed, indicating separation as an acculturation mode. In other words, in some contexts, the immigrants manifested the more individualistic patterns of behavior characteristic of the host country; in others, they exhibited the more collectivistic characteristics of their traditional culture. The latter one tended to appear if the problem was related to some more basic social identity issues.

These findings have some bearings on the theory of social influence. They suggest that the massive influence a dominant culture may have on an immigrant minority can have different effects on various *psychological levels*. Although it can transform relatively easily the behavioral patterns associated with everyday life, it may have much less impact on the deeper structures of personality. The Nowak and Vallacher model of social change would suggest that forms of the traditional culture may survive for a long period of time if members of the minority are not dispersed but instead form clusters.

Does this suggest that the Nowak and Vallacher model provides a complete account of the facts described by Klinger and Bierbrauer? Apparently not, because their findings suggest that there is a multilevel difference between the old and the new. In other words, another dimension for the description of the data may be needed so that both horizontal (where polarization and clustering are taking place) and vertical (which accounts for different processes at the different levels of personality) processes can be explained.

The foregoing three chapters have considered the social influence process as a mediating factor in a social change. The next chapter by Kopp, Skrabski, and Szedmák (chap. 11) deals with another kind of an issue—some specific concomitants of social change in Hungary. The authors consider the consequences of the postcommunist modernization process for morbidity and mortality in the Hungarian population. At first glance, it is difficult to guess what this topic may have to do with the main theme of the present volume (i.e., with social influence). It turns out that social influence plays a prominent role in the chain of processes that lead to the steady increase in morbidity and mortality rate in Hungary over more than two decades. The authors postulate that there is a specific sequence to the processes initiated by the social transformations taking place in Hungary (which may also characterize many other Central and East European countries): (a) the development of a market economy, (b) the rise in the prevalence of individualistic attitudes such as competitiveness and achievement orientation, and (c) the decrease of social support and increase in depressive symptoms, morbidity, and mortality. It should be noted that in Hungary some elements of a market economy were introduced long before the breakdown of the so-called *communist regime*.

From a psychological point of view, a critical role was played by changes in social relations and in people's mentality that can best be described as the ascent of individualism. In an individualistic society, other people tend to be perceived, first of all, as rivals and as providing standards against which one's achievement is measured. One result of this reorientation is that there are far fewer occasions when others may be drawn on for help and support. This indicates that the structure of the social influence is changing: Others become a powerful source of stress while social networks, which previously offered some protection against stress, are fading away.

This analysis underscores the less obvious facet of the social influence processes as involuntary, automatic mechanisms that can engender greater motivation and stress as well as provide psychological support and help in dealing with the adversities of everyday life. Having this in mind, one can develop some remedial strategies aimed at reducing the level of morbidity, suggesting that to favorably impact morbidity and mortality one has to think about the development of social support networks. Such networks can most likely contribute to the improvement of the psychological conditions of many people while also having positive consequences for their health.

The last chapter deals with still another consequence of major social transformation—namely, change in consumption patterns. Chapter 12, authored by Gornik-Durose, concerns the emerging patterns of consumption among young

Polish adults. Again, this is a large-scale process in which social influence is an important mediating factor. Gornik-Durose's research investigated which material possessions are considered to be valuable for Polish youths and what are the sources of their preferences. Both preferences and their sources were assessed by means of self-report.

Probably the most significant finding of this research is a demonstration of the success of large-scale media campaigns advocating Western patterns of consumption. Namely, it turned out that in Poland, which is still a relatively poor country, a high proportion of the respondents declared that the most important material possessions were clothing and accessories with (world)widely recognized expensive brand labels. One should keep in mind that these preferences were reported just a few years after the sociopolitical changes that opened the Polish market to Western goods and Western advertisements. This fact reveals the powerful influence of models and means of propagation of influence on the young Polish audience.

What makes this influence so powerful? The author tried to find some explanation by asking her subjects about criteria used in making purchasing decisions. She examined internal influences (subject's own opinions, attitudes, etc.), external personal influences (parents, colleagues), and external impersonal influences (advertising, trends in fashion, etc.). The results indicate that the youths were convinced that their preferences originated primarily from internal factors. Apparently they were not particularly aware of the impact of the mass media on their supposedly *private* preferences. The power of the media influence is revealed by the fact that a high proportion of the respondents attach a strong value to brand names. This means that it is not merely the instrumental function of a possession, but its symbolic function that must play a role in the formation of preferences. Of course it is unlikely that the symbolic meaning of brand names originated from within the person. How much personal (or group) experience does one have to have to learn that the products of a given brand are superior to another brand? Such conviction is, most probably a result of exposure to marketing influences channeled through mass media.

Gornik-Durose also tries to compare the relative strengths of the six social influence principles described by Cialdini (1993) and finds that commitment/consistency was the most powerful. She is aware, however, that the validity of her method of assessment is rather questionable. The meaning attached to this principle may simply be an another indication of the power of the media, which use, as a marketing device, persuasive messages exhorting young people *to be yourself.*

The data provided in this chapter seem to illustrate how quickly and efficiently the young people in the newly emerging democracies of Central and Eastern Europe are transformed into Western-style consumers, at least in their outward preferences. These results may indicate that the social influence principles employed by influence professionals in the West are effective not only in the

Western countries, but in non-Western nations as well. As shown in the previous part of this volume, however, the social influence principles are not equally powerful in all cultural settings.

The main theme of the five chapters presented in this part of the volume is social influence as a mechanism of a social change. What are being dealt with here are changes in societal beliefs and values (e.g., attitudes concerning abortion or consumer preferences), dominant behavioral patterns (e.g., strategies of conflict resolution), and forms of social relations (increase in individualism) and their effects on physical health. These changes cannot be accounted for simply as products of intentional and unidirectional processes of social influence. In fact, they come about in the course of the mutual impact of many actors who are hardly aware of their double role as influencers and influencees. Thus, social influence cannot be looked on as a set of gimmicks that can be used by some people to take advantage of others. Rather, the social influence process should be seen as a universal mediating process that plays a significant role in the functioning and change of social systems small and large and as a precondition for the successful completion of almost any social task. It is a psychological equivalent of neurotransmitters—something like serotonin or dopamine that intervenes in coordinating functions of the central nervous system.

Obviously, there are many mechanisms of social influence. Some of these mechanisms are embedded in institutional arrangements such as political organization (e.g., an electoral law that increases the political power of a minority), market economy (that facilitates the development of individualist orientations), norms and customs (that immigrants have to adapt to in the host country), and so on. These can be described as *structural* mechanisms. Another mechanism of influence is the mass media (which are assumed to be responsible for the changes in consumer values). Of course, another important source of change is interpersonal contact. Certainly the various mechanisms of social influence interact with each other. Thus, for example, a change in consumer values is probably an effect not only of mass-mediated messages, but also of their further elaboration in face-to-face contacts between consumers.

There are some basic underlying conditions of influence that determine its power. According to Nowak and Vallacher, they are the strength of the agent of influence, the immediacy of the influence, and the number of targets of influence. Although these conditions are similar for physical, biological, and social phenomena, they can be interpreted in a physical as well as a psychological sense. Hence, psychological strength can be manifested in a variety of forms (e.g., as political or economic power or as authority). Immediacy can be interpreted as psychological distance—in social, physical, temporal, and semantic space (Reykowski, 1984). It should be stressed that there is an important mediating process that determines the effects of these three conditions the interpretation of the meaning of incoming information. Therefore, one can say that, although on some general or abstract level the social influence process is similar to other kinds of influence, social influence does possess some features that are unique for social psychological entities.

This analysis suggests that there are several levels of social influence mechanisms. First, at the basic level, influence has some general characteristics common for any interacting objects—it is in a sense the *physical aspect* of the influence process as described by Nowak and Vallacher. Next, there is a psychological level—some general mechanisms of influence that are more or less universal for human beings. The psychological principles of social influence as defined by Cialdini (1993) seem to have a broad cross-cultural range of applicability. There might exist some others—for example, the mechanisms described by Wojciszke. Third, there is a culturally specific level—the mechanisms of influence that are characteristic of a given cultural context. The role of this context was taken into consideration in the last three chapters where specific phenomena associated with acculturation and social transformation were described.

There is probably a fourth level of the mechanisms of social influence: the unique characteristics of a particular individual. For instance, people who learn about the peculiar sensitivities of their spouses, coworkers, friends, superiors, and so on can develop specific strategies to influence them. One final point should be made in this context. The social influence process cannot be looked on as a mere psychological phenomenon—a process that can be satisfactorily described by referring to what happens within or between individuals. It is also a process that can originate in the larger social environment and have societal-level consequences. In other words, social influence should be analyzed both on the individual and societal levels.

REFERENCES

Cialdini, R. B. (1993). *Influence: Science and practice.* New York: Harper.

Reykowski, J. (1984). Spatial organization of a cognitive system and intrinsic prosocial motivation. In E. Staub, D. Bar-Tal, J. Karylowski, & J. Reykowski (Eds.), Development and maintenance of prosocial behavior (pp. 51–77). New York: Plenum.

Societal Transition: Toward a Dynamical Model of Social Change

Andrzej Nowak

University of Warsaw

Robin R. Vallacher

Florida Atlantic University

ABSTRACT

This chapter describes a dynamic model of social change and presents the results of computer simulations developed to test the assumptions and predictions of this model. The central notion is that social change sometimes occurs rapidly in an abrupt and nonlinear manner. Social influence processes play a pivotal role in promoting such societal phase transitions. These processes and their group- and societal-level consequences are modeled within a cellular automata framework. The validity of the model is tested against empirical data collected during the societal transitions that occurred in Poland in the late 1980s and early 1990s. In addition to capturing the dynamics of social change, the model has important implications for designing programs to facilitate new attitudes and behaviors in society. The model also provides a framework for understanding cross-cultural differences in the dynamics of social influence and societal transition.

Social change has always represented a primary concern in the social sciences. This concern became especially salient in the last decades of the 20th century, as major political transitions occurred worldwide. In Europe, several countries moved from state-controlled to free-market economies—a profound transition that in turn generated a host of significant social and political changes. These transitional phenomena provide a unique opportunity for generating and testing theories of social change. Fortunately, considerable data have been amassed concerning the European experience, and these data provide a rich basis for gaining insight into the underlying nature of social change. It is becoming increasingly apparent that traditional theories of social change based on the experience of stable societies are not well suited to characterize or predict the European experience in particular, or perhaps the nature of rapid social transitions generally. Indeed, the nature of the transitions experienced in the eastern European countries during the 1980s was neither anticipated nor adequately explained by social scientists at the time.

The unanticipated and counterintuitive nature of the European experience calls for a new conceptualization of social change—one that acknowledges the inherent dynamic nature of this process. With this in mind, we suggest that recent developments in mathematics and natural sciences concerning the behavior of systems composed of many interacting elements (cf. Schuster, 1984) provide a viable framework for understanding the dynamics of social change. Of particular relevance are recent applications of nonlinear dynamical systems to social phenomena (see e.g., Battan, Casti, & Johanson, 1987; Nowak & Vallacher, 1998; Vallacher & Nowak, 1994, 1997; Weidlich, 1991). This work has shown that similar principles underlie the nature of change in vastly different types of systems occupying different levels of analysis. Thus, phenomena as distinct as laser pulsation, heart rhythms, weather patterns, and economic trends can be characterized with respect to a common set of invariant principles.

The aim of this chapter is to describe a dynamic model of social change that applies key concepts and principles from the natural sciences to the investigation of change in social groups and societies. The central notion is that rapid social changes occur in a manner that is remarkably similar to phase transitions as described in physics. Metaphorically, *islands of new* form in the *sea of old* in a manner similar to the formation of gas bubbles in a liquid nearing the boiling point. As the transition progresses, those islands or clusters grow, become connected, and begin to encircle the remaining islands of old. During social transitions, then, two distinct realities co-exist-the reality of the old and the reality of the new. Thus, this type of social change is not only rapid, but also abrupt and nonlinear. To explore this perspective, cellular automata models of change are employed. These models are developed in the context of social influence. Basic properties of the change process, and the factors that shape these processes, are investigated. This approach is then generalized to political and economic transitions occurring at the societal level. The validity of the model is tested against empirical data collected during the social transitions that occurred in Poland in the late 1980s and early 1990s.

CELLULAR AUTOMATA MODELS OF SOCIAL INFLUENCE

Although social influence strategies are commonly employed for purposes of manipulation, social influence also plays a crucial role in assembling individuals into groups and societies. Thus, social influence is the mechanism by which individuals coordinate their opinions, moods, evaluations, and behaviors to create larger social entities—from dyads to collectives and entire societies. This process of coordination may take different forms and operates at different levels of social reality. On the group level, social influence consists of multiple feedback loops, where each individual affects and is in turn affected by opinions, beliefs, and attitudes of other group members. Although such bidirectional causality is difficult to capture in traditional models of causal relations, a class of formal models called *cellular automata* is ideally suited for this task.

A Dynamic Model of Social Influence

Although social influence can take a variety of distinct forms, the key feature for present purposes is that the attitudes and beliefs of a single individual are to a large degree dependent on the attitudes and beliefs of other individuals with whom he or she interacts. Social impact theory (Latané, 1981) provides a useful depiction of this interdependency. According to this theory, the amount of impact other people have on an individual's attitudes and beliefs can be characterized in terms of three variables: (a) the number of people influencing or being influenced, (b) the respective strength of these people, and (c) their immediacy to one another. Whether the nature of group influence concerns conformity (e.g., in the Asch paradigm), interest in current events, stagefright, or the likelihood of signing a petition, the influence of a group grows as a power function of the number of people involved, usually with an exponent of approximately .5. This means that the joint effects of a group exerting influence grows as a square root of the number of people in the group. Influence also grows in proportion to the strength of the individuals exerting the influence. Strength represents the potential for influence and refers both to relatively stable individual characteristics (e.g. social status or persuasion skills) and topic-relevant variables (e.g. motivation to persuade others). Finally, influence depends on proximity and appears to decrease as a square of the distance. For example, here is evidence that the probability that two people will discuss matters of mutual importance decreases as a square of the distance between their physical locations (Latané, Liu, Nowak, Bonavento, & Zheng, 1995).

The joint effect of these three factors is said to represent a multiplicative function of strength, immediacy, and number. The reciprocal of this function, in turn, describes how social influence is divided among the individuals in a group. A well-documented example of this idea is the diffusion of respon-sibility in a group, because the influence each group member experiences is inversely related to the number of other group members. Research on bystander intervention, for example, has shown that a person in need is more likely to receive help when there is a single as opposed to multiple witnesses to his or her plight (e.g., Latané & Darley, 1968). Research on social loafing, mean-while, has established that individuals tend to exert less effort on a task when performing as a member of a team than when performing alone (e.g., Latané, Williams, & Harkins, 1979), although there are important exceptions to this phenomenon (e.g., Kerr, 1983).

The Cellular Automata Approach

The empirical evidence for social impact theory can be used to build a dynamic model of social influence in the form of cellular automata. An initial attempt in this regard was developed by Nowak, Szamrej, and Latané (1990). This model assumes that each individual can be characterized by his or her opinion on a topic, persuasive strength, and position in a social space. The distance between two individuals in social space is inversely related to their immediacy vis-a-vis one another. In the original model, individuals were assumed to have one of two opinions on an issue (e.g., either for or against a particular referendum), but in later versions this restriction was relaxed so that many positions were possible on an issue (Nowak, Lewenstein, & Szamrej, 1993). In that cellular automata model, each individual is portrayed as a cell on a two-dimensional grid. Figure 8.1a por-trays the model for the special case in which an individual's opinion or belief can assume one of two states (e.g., for or against a particular position). Each box in Fig. 8.1a corresponds to an individual. The color (light vs. dark grey) of the box denotes the individual's opinion and the height of the box corresponds to the indi-vidual's strength.

The model assumes that each individual assesses how much support each position has by discussing the issue with other group members. The opin-ions of those who are closest and have the greatest strength are given most con-sideration (i.e., are weighted most heavily). An individual's own opinion is also taken into consideration and is weighted most heavily by virtue of immediacy. As a result of this process, each individual adopts the most prevalent opinion. The strength of influence of each opinion is expressed by the following formula:

$$I_i = \left(\sum_{1}^{N} \left(\frac{s_i}{d_{ij}^2} \right)^2 \right)^{1/2}$$

where I_i denotes total influence, s_j corresponds to the strength of each individ-ual, and d_{ij} corresponds to the distance between individuals i and j.

FIG. 8.1a. Cellular automata model of social influence. From *Dynamical Psychology* (p. 226) by A. Nowak and RR. Vallacher, 1998, New York: Guilford. Copyright 1998 by Guilford. Reprinted by permission.

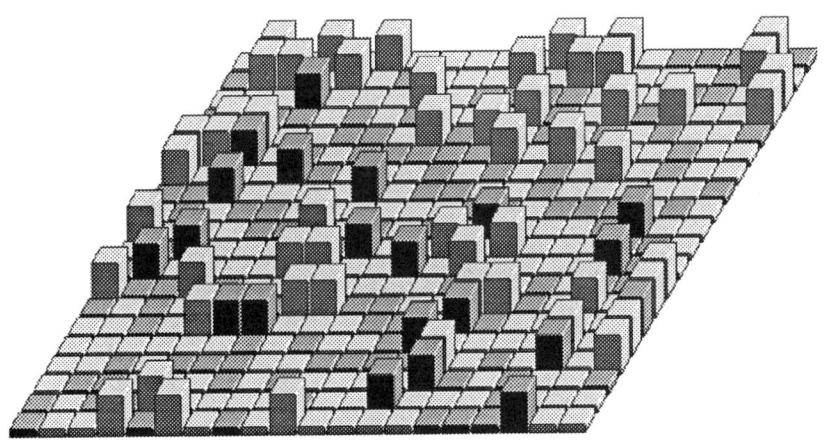

In the simulations, one individual is chosen (usually at random) and influence is calculated for each opinion in the group. If the resultant strength for any opinion is greater than the strength of the individual's current opinion, his or her opinion changes to match the prevailing opinion. This process is performed for each group member. This procedure is repeated until there are no further changes. This typically requires several rounds of simulation, because a person who previously changed his or her position to match his or her neighbors may

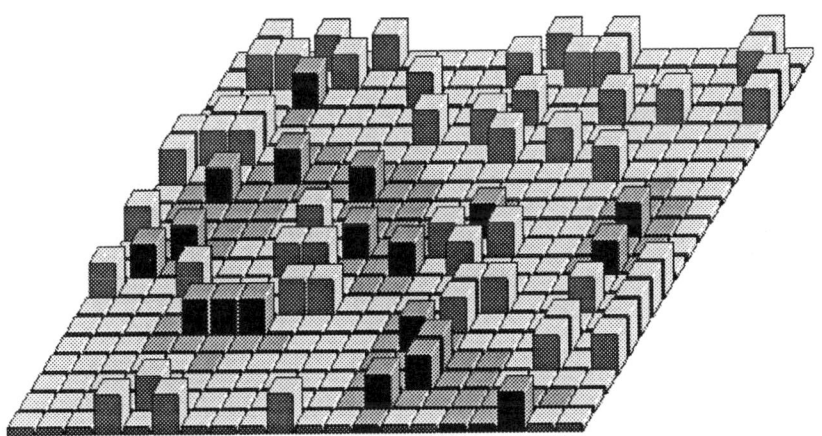

FIG. 8.1b. Typical outcome of social influence processes. From *Dynamical Psychology* (p. 227) by A. Nowak and RR. Vallacher, 1998, New York: Guilford. Copyright 1998 by Guilford. Reprinted by permission.

revert to the original opinion if the neighbors change their opinions. A typical simulation outcome is shown in Fig. 8.1b. In Fig. 8.1a, there is a majority of 60% and a minority of 40%. Figure 8.1b shows the equilibrium reached after six rounds of discussion. Now the majority is 90% and the minority is 10%. Note that the minority opinion survives by the formation of clusters of like-minded people and that these clusters are usually formed around strong individuals. These two outcomes are referred to as polarization and clustering, respectively.

Essential Features of the Model

Polarization and clustering are reminiscent of well-documented social processes. Research on group decision making, for example, has shown that, as a result of group discussion, the average attitude in a group becomes more extreme in the direction of the prevailing attitude in the group (e.g., Moscovici & Zavalloni, 1969; Myers & Lamm, 1976). Noelle-Neumann (1984) observed the same underlying phenomenon in political science, noting that a slight difference in opinion before an election can transform into a landslide by individuals who want to be on the winning side. It is easy to see how polarization develops in the simulation model. In the random initial configuration, the average proportion of neighbors holding a given opinion corresponds to the proportion of this opinion in the group as a whole. The average group member is thus surrounded by more majority than minority members, and this difference results in more minority members converted to the majority opinion than vice versa. Some majority members are nonetheless converted to the minority opinion because they happen to be located in the vicinity of an especially influential minority member or because more minority members happen to be at this particular location.

Clustering is one of the most ubiquitous features of social life. In fact, it is difficult to find a social phenomenon that does not reflect some degree of clustering. For example, there is evidence that attitudes tend to cluster in residential neighborhoods (Festinger, Schachter, & Back, 1950). Clustering has also been observed for farming techniques, political beliefs, social movements, religions, fashions, and a host of other phenomena. In the simulation model, clustering is due to the local nature of influence processes. If opinions are mixed randomly, the sampling of opinions in social interaction provides a reasonably accurate portrait of the distribution of opinions in the larger society. If the opinions are clustered, such an estimation process will yield a highly biased result. The opinions of those located nearby will be weighted the most so that the prevalence of one's own opinion is likely to be highly overestimated. A highly clustered society thus serves to maintain minority opinions, because opinions that are in the minority in global terms form a local majority within a cluster. Even if a minority member is located on the border of a cluster and thus exposed to contrary opinions, his or her opinion may resist change if he or she is relatively strong or flanked by others who are relatively strong.

Computer simulations (Latané & Nowak, 1997) as well as analytical considerations (Lewenstein, Nowak, & Latané, 1993; Nowak, Lewenstein, & Frejlak, 1996) have identified three features that are especially important for the emergence of polarization and clustering: the existence of individual differences in strength, nonlinearity in attitude change, and the local nature of influence dictated by the geometry of social space. Individual differences are important because strong individuals (e.g., leaders) are necessary for the survival of minority clusters. This conclusion is consistent with various findings in sociology and anthropology, which stress the crucial role of leaders in resisting influence within minority cultures. This is because the strength of a leader's influence can outweigh the influence of outgroup (i.e., majority) individuals. Because strong individuals are more likely to withstand majority pressure, over time strength tends to become correlated with opinions. Because weaker individuals are more likely to switch to the majority opinion, on average the remaining minority members are likely to be stronger than those advocating the majority position. This scenario resonates with the observation that individuals advocating minority positions are often more influential than those advocating majority positions (e.g., Moscovici & Zavalloni, 1969).

Computer simulations have revealed that minority groups can survive under majority pressure with three basic configurations of leaders (Nowak et al., 1993, 1996). These configurations are displayed in Fig. 8.2. In the leader and followers configuration (A), a single leader is encircled by a ring of followers. The strong support provided by the leader enables the followers to sustain their opin-

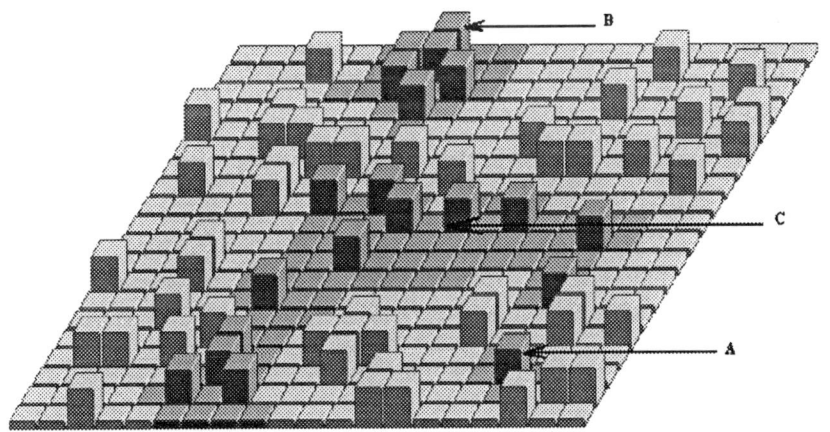

FIG. 8.2. Configurations of social space. From *Dynamical Psychology* (p. 230) by A. Nowak and RR. Vallacher, 1998, New York: Guilford. Copyright 1998 by Guilford. Reprinted by permission.

ion. Because the followers make it easier for the leader to sustain his or her opinion, the leader–follower relationship is symbiotic. In particular, the followers provide additional support to the leader and, more important, they isolate him or her from the direct influence of the majority. In the stronghold configuration (B), several strong individuals form a cluster that is surrounded by weaker group members. This is configuration is more stable than the leader–follower configuration. Even if one of the strong members switches to the majority opinion, the opinions of the other strong members are likely to bring him or her back to the minority position. In the wall configuration (C), the leaders are located near the borders of the cluster, forming a wall that protects weaker group members from the influence of the majority. The wall does not need to be contiguous; just a few leaders can serve as guards at widely separated points and effectively protect the interior of the cluster.

The second important feature is nonlinearity in attitude change. As long as individual changes occur incrementally in proportion to the strength of social influence, the members of a group will invariably move toward uniformity in their opinions (Abelson, 1979)-provided group members are not subjected to influences external to the group. Under these conditions, minority clusters cannot survive. However, the present model assumes a threshold function, such that influences below a certain magnitude of strength have no impact. Above this threshold, changes not only occur, but also converge on the opposing opinion. Thus, opinions are categorical in nature, with individuals holding their opinion and switching dramatically from one category to another rather than incrementally on a dimension of judgment. Computer simulations (Szamrej, Nowak, & Latané, 1992) have shown that nonlinearity in attitude change is indeed critical to the survival of minority clusters. Such a rule implies that attitudes are distributed in a bimodal fashion, in contrast to the normal distribution generated by a linear change rule. Latané and Nowak (1994) have shown that both types of distributions can be observed depending on the importance of the attitude in question. Thus, a normal distribution is typically observed for unimportant (e.g., uninvolving) issues, with intermediate values of the attitude emerging as the most common in the group. Attitudes display a bimodal distribution, however, for important issues, with almost no individuals occupying the intermediate points on the attitude scale. This suggests that minorities have a greater chance of survival if the issue in question is personally important to them.

The third crucial feature of the model concerns the geometry of the interaction space (Nowak, Latané, & Lewenstein, 1994). Interactions among people do not occur randomly, nor does everyone interact equally often with the other group members. Different geometries of social space can be used to approximate different communication patterns. Most of the simulations portray social space as a two-dimensional matrix of n rows and n columns-a reasonable assumption in view of the role of physical proximity in structuring social interactions. Consider first a group in which there is virtually no geometry—in the sense that everyone is equally spaced from everyone else so that each individual interacts equally with all members of the group. In such a group, no minority member is shielded from majority influence, although minority opinion may nonetheless survive for a relatively long time if high value is placed on one's own opinion and individual differences are strongly pronounced (Lewenstein et al., 1993). Because the social space lacks structure, however, minority opinions cannot cluster. Geometry may be said to be lacking as well when the interaction patterns in a group are random. When this is the case, minority opinion rapidly decays and the group converges on the majority position (Lewenstein et al., 1993).

Yet different geometries may be used to portray other types of communication networks (Nowak et al., 1996). For example, one can envision a one-dimensional geometry in which people interact only with neighbors to their left and right. This corresponds to a row of houses along a river or a road. Strong clustering occurs in this case because of well-pronounced local interactions between nearest neighbors, although there is no polarization because individuals on the borders of clusters interact equally often with minority and majority members. Because members cannot encircle members of the minority, they do not have a persuasive advantage. One can also envision a geometry that is hierarchical in nature, such that people are divided into groups, subgroups, and so forth (Lewenstein et al., 1993; Nowak et al., 1996). For example, in a university two individuals in the same research group are close, two individuals from different research groups but the same department are less close, two individuals from two departments within the same college are yet less close, and two individuals from different colleges are furthest apart. The distance between any two individuals in a hierarchical structure depends on the level at which they both belong to a common unit; the higher this level, the greater the distance. When the geometry is hierarchical, the formation of clusters follows this progression in distance. Borders of clusters tend to coincide with subgroups at some level, so that the structure of opinions therefore follows the structure of social interaction. Once formed, clusters are very stable because most of the interactions happen among individuals belonging to the same group.

Crucial Variables for Social Influence

In preparing a computer simulation program, it is necessary to make explicit assumptions concerning the relations among variables in the model. As it happens, however, the results of simulations demonstrate that many variables produce only small quantitative effects, and that only a few variables strongly affect the course of dynamics observed. Three variables in particular play a critical role in group-level social influence processes (Lewenstein et al., 1993; Latané & Nowak, 1997). One of these, referred to as noise, represents the variety of influences external to the group that impact on group members. These influences include such things as personal experiences, communication from people outside the group, and selective exposure to media. In the simulations, the value of noise is added as a random number to the social influence experienced by each person. Without influences from outside the group, minority clusters would exist forever once they reached equilibrium. The introduction of noise, however, can cause a person to adopt a different opinion than the one suggested by social influence. If the noise is relatively small, such changes in opinion happen rarely and the basic scenario of the model is not significantly affected.

When noise is present, attitudes do not stabilize on absolute equilibria because change in the direction opposite to that of social influence is always possible. Well-defined clusters may be formed, however, and these may exist for a long time. With low values of noise, this picture does not change a great deal, even if from time to time some of the weaker minority members change their opinion, because the stronger group members can restore their initial attitude. When random influences are strong, however, social influence within the group plays a correspondingly weaker role so that clusters may lose their stability. This is especially likely if the leaders change their position due to external influences. If the leader is part of a wall protecting a minority cluster, for example, the cluster will start to decay. However, this decay can be terminated if another strong person happens to be on the border and thus in a position to protect the minority members. In this case, the cluster reaches a new equilibrium. In the presence of noise, this scenario may occur several times before a cluster finally vanishes. Because the dynamics here may reflect long periods of relative stability intermixed with rapid decay, this scenario is referred to as staircase dynamics (Lewenstein et al., 1993).

The second factor, self-influence, represents the weight an individual attaches to his or her own opinion relative to the opinions of others. In everyday terms, this variable reflects such psychological states as self-confidence, belief certainty, and strength of conviction. Hence, the stronger the self-influence, the greater the resistance to social influence. Although self-influence is clearly correlated with strength, its absolute value is determined by dividing strength by a constant to represent self-distance. Self-distance reflects the relative importance of one's own opinions relative to others. When an issue is new and confusing, for example, self-distance is relatively high for all group members, because no strong opinion has been formed and members are thus open to external influence. When an issue is familiar and personally important, self-distance takes on a low value, reflecting the general openness to self-influence on the part of all group members. Because self-distance is constant across all members, it represents a variable property that is perfectly correlated with strength.

The value of self-influence relative to the total influence of other group members determines the dynamics of social influence. With low values of self-influence, individuals may switch their opinions several times during the course of a simulation. Decreasing values of self-influence also tend to destabilize clusters and can ultimately promote unification based on the majority opinion. When self-influence is high relative to the combined influence of others, however, there are no dynamics in the absence of noise. Regardless of the strength of self-influence, the introduction of noise may destabilize opinions. Because noise works jointly with social influence, the changes caused by noise will most often be in the direction of majority influence. In this way, a random factor that by itself would not favor any opinion can neutralize the effect of self-influence and enhance the effect of majority opinion. At the same time, however, very high noise values may dilute the effects of social contacts, resulting in random changes in opinion.

The third factor, bias, reflects unequal a priori attractiveness of the various attitude positions. As long as the attitude positions in a group do not differ substantially in their relative desirability, the nature of dynamics are dictated by the level of noise and the magnitude of self-influence. The introduction of bias, however, can qualitatively change the dynamics of opinion formation and change in a group. Especially if a minority opinion is more desirable than the majority opinion, there is strong potential for social change. This scenario is described in detail in the section on the nature of societal transitions.

Implications for Cultural Variation in Social Influence

The variables employed in the simulation model are useful in understanding-and predicting-differences among cultures in the dynamics of social influence. A common theme in cross-cultural comparisons centers on the collectivist versus individualistic dimension (cf. Markus & Kitayama, 1991). In so-called *collectivist* cultures, such as China and Japan, interdependence among individuals is emphasized at the expense of independence so that individuals are readily influenced by the opinions, attitudes, and expectations of others. In so-called *individualistic* cultures, such as the United States, greater emphasis is placed on independence, with individuals maintaining a greater degree of autonomy in their self-concept, attitudes, and lifestyles. This primary cultural difference maps directly on the variable of self-influence in the simulation model. Thus, in a society that values independence in decision making and judgment, the magnitude of self-influence is correspondingly strong—operating at the expense of the social context (i.e., the opinions of others). In this regard, computer simulations have revealed that, as self-influence increases in magnitude, the number of individuals changing their position on a given issue decreases, there is less polarization and clustering, and the average cluster is smaller in size (Latané & Nowak, 1997; Lewenstein et al., 1993).

Societies also vary in their relative stability. In less modernized societies, which are predominantly agrarian and rural as opposed to industrial in nature, the social context for individuals is relatively stable and enduring over time. In relatively modernized (i.e., industrial) societies, in contrast, there is considerably more social mobility (e.g., travel, permanent relocation) and greater frequency of communication over large distances (e.g., by means of phone, FAX, and e-mail). This disturbs the stability of social influence exerted on an individual by his or her social context. At different times, then, the individual is exposed to a broad range of opinions that go beyond the immediate social context. This feature of relatively modernized society can be represented in the model as noise, which reflects the sum of influences not accounted for by local influence. The greater the magnitude of noise, then, the weaker the role played by an individual's local context. Indeed, the opinions of someone in a different part of the country may well have a greater impact on one's opinions than will the opinions of one's immediate neighbors. This is clearly not the case in a stable society, where everyone is exposed to the same local contacts throughout much of his or her life.

Computer simulations of the model have shown that there is a nonlinear relationship between noise and the distribution of opinions in a society (Latané & Nowak, 1997; Lewenstein et al., 1993). Small values of noise tend to destabilize weak clusters (e.g., Nowak, Vallacher, Tesser, & Borkowski, in press). Because weak clusters tend to be small, a low level of noise increases the average size of clusters in the society, which in turn is reflected in higher overall clustering and polarization. In contrast, somewhat higher values of noise can destabilize all minority clusters and in this way promote unification of opinions in the society. At very high levels of noise, however, individuals are likely to adopt opinions that are independent of their immediate social context. This disrupts clusters while preventing unification of opinions in the society. In essence, individuals switch their opinions in a more-or-less random fashion. In a stable society characterized by low levels of noise, then, one might expect a stable pattern of relatively small clusters, whereas in a somewhat less stable society characterized by moderate levels of noise, one might expect larger clusters and greater polarization of opinions. With further decreases in societal stability, meanwhile, one might expect a breakdown in minority opinion clusters and a tendency toward unification in opinion. Finally, in a highly modernized and unstable society, the pattern of opinions will be largely independent of the pattern of social ties, demonstrating instead the influence of other factors (e.g., selective exposure to media, contact with other cultures).

Cultures also differ in their preferences and values regarding everything from clothing to cosmology. This feature is represented as bias in the simulation model. If a new idea resonates well with a culture's predominant preferences and values, it will take relatively less social influence for it to take hold in the society. By the same token, an idea that runs counter to cultural beliefs and values is likely to be resisted even if it is supported by considerable influence. Communist ideology, for example, was never truly accepted in Poland despite the considerable level of influence exerted by the government because communist values ran counter to strong Polish traditions of independence and Catholicism. The degree of correspondence between a particular position and a culture's values can be characterized by the amount of bias in the simulation model. Bias and its role in social influence are discussed in greater detail in the following section.

It is reasonable to suggest that different combinations of these variables-self-influence, noise, and bias-are represented in (and to some extent, define) different cultures. Thus two industrialized societies may both have high levels of self-influence (e.g., an individualistic rather than collectivist orientation), but they may differ considerably in their respective levels of noise (e.g., selective exposure to mass communication) or their bias toward various positions (e.g., religious beliefs). Because each of these variables plays a unique role in social influence, the interaction among them is likely to be decisive in shaping the predominant form of influence characterizing a particular society. Although different cultures may be highly distinctive with respect to social influence processes, it is conceivable that such variation can be traced, in part, to the specific blend of the variables in the simulation model. The exploration of this possibility represents an important avenue for future research.

THE NATURE OF SOCIETAL TRANSITIONS

During a societal transition, there is typically a marked shift in public opinion. An opinion that was held by a minority of citizens suddenly becomes prevalent in the society. As demonstrated in the simulation model, minority opinion can survive if it can create coherent clusters. However, for a society to undergo transition, the minority opinion has to do more than survive-it has to supplant the majority opinion. This is difficult if the minority opinion does not have an advantage in its appeal relative to the majority opinion. In the real world, however, different opinions are rarely equally attractive to members of society. Some attitudes are more compatible with the society's value system, more advantageous in some way, or simply more prominent because of mass media influence or other external factors. We can represent the joint effect of all such factors in the simulation model by introducing bias into the rule describing changes in opinions. This is done by adding a constant to favor one of the positions, which acts in addition to the effects of social interaction. If external sources (i.e., bias) assume a very high value, they can even overwhelm the effects of social interactions. In practice, however, the effects of social interaction and bias are both likely to be observed.

Nowak et al. (1993) tested these ideas in simulations based on cellular automata models of social influence, similar to those described earlier. Figure 8.3 illustrates the typical course of social influence processes when there is a bias favoring the minority position. Panel A shows a starting configuration of 10% minority randomly distributed in the population. The minority opinion would not be able to survive in this configuration without the presence of bias because its

FIG. 8.3. The growth of minority opinion in society. From *Dynamical Psychology* (p. 266) by A. Nowak and R. R. Vallacher, 1998, New York: Guilford. Copyright 1998 by Guilford. Reprinted by permission.

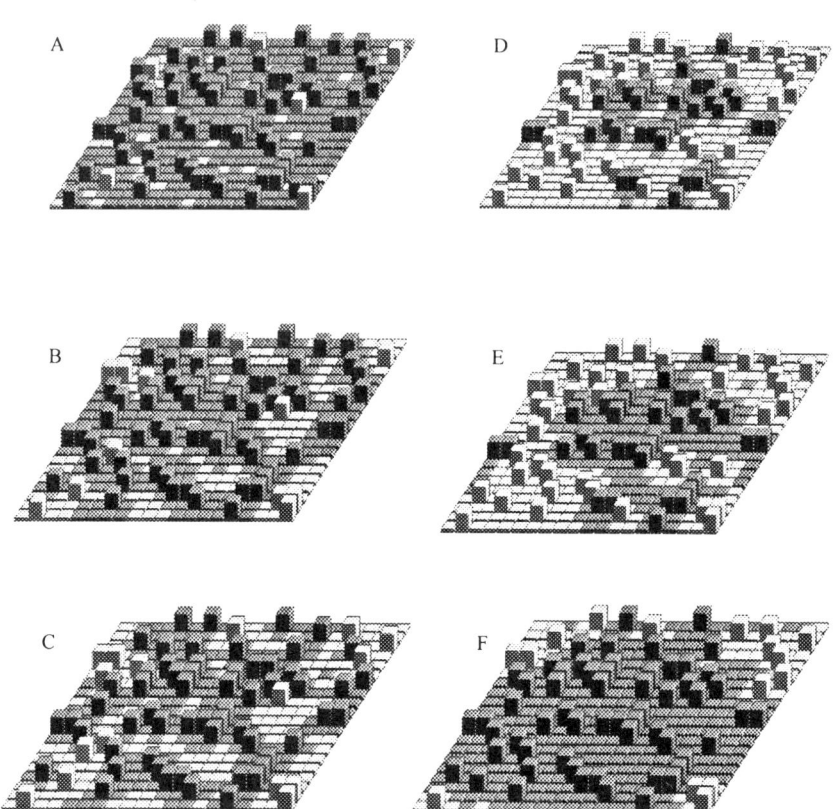

low frequency in the population makes it hard for its advocates to find like-minded people with whom they can cluster. Because of bias, however, the minority opinion is able to grow, as indicated in Panel B. Note that the new opinion forms clusters around the original seeds of the new opinion. As Panel C shows, the clusters of new continue to grow and begin to connect with one another. When the clusters of the initial minority become fully connected, the initial majority is reduced to islands. Finally, a new equilibrium is reached, although clusters of the old opinion still exist, well entrenched in the sea of new (Panel D).

It might appear from Panel D that the transition is complete and irreversible, because the initial majority has been reduced to 20%. Just such a scenario was observed in the late 1980s and early 1990s in former East bloc countries, where all the referendums and elections were won decisively by anticommunist parties. In Poland, for example, not a single communist candidate was elected to Parliament in its first free elections. Note, however, that the strongest and best-interconnected members of the initial majority managed to survive the pressure of the new. As Panel D illustrates, these individuals now exist in strongholds. This suggests that when bias is withdrawn, a new equilibrium should be reached that favors the initial majority opinion. This scenario, illustrated in Panel E, is likely when people experience the costs of the transformation that has occurred. The old opinion shows a rebound, growing to 50% (Panel E). Finally, Panel F shows a reversal of bias, corresponding to sentiments favoring the old opinions. This causes the new opinion to be reduced to 20%. Although it took about 40 simulation steps with the bias favoring the new opinion for the new opinion to prevail, it took only 5 simulation steps for the old opinion to rebound. Although the new is greatly reduced in numbers, it can survive the pressure of the majority because it now exists in strongholds. Hence, when social sentiments change once again, it is easy for the new to launch an offensive from these strongholds.

This scenario predicts swings in public opinion during societal transition. In a transitional society, there may be well-defined strongholds for both the old and the new. The rest of the society can switch between these two options depending on the momentary bias favoring one over the other. This explains why, in almost all European countries of the old socialist camp, postcommunist parties suffered a humiliating defeat but were often able to win the next election. People who were prominent (i.e., strongest) during the communist era tended to form networks that provided strongholds for their opinions. By the same reasoning, however, a societal transition may become irreversible if preferences for the new are positively correlated with strength. This may occur, for example, when economic factors are compatible with the new. Joining the new economy, for example, may provide personal economic benefits. In this case, the social context acts to inhibit rather than encourage a return to the initial majority opinion.

FACILITATING SOCIAL CHANGE: PRACTICAL IMPLICATIONS

Beyond describing the general features of societal transition, this model provides insight into the means by which social change may be facilitated. The basic idea is that successful social intervention should take into account naturally occurring processes, selectively reinforcing those that are desired and inhibiting those that are not desired, rather than imposing a new agenda in a way that runs contrary to natural mechanisms. Rapid social changes in a society occur as growing bubbles or islands of the new that expand and become connected. Social intervention should thus capitalize on this natural process. Several practical implications follow from this idea. First, influence attempts should be highly targeted. Individuals within clusters have already made their changes and are likely to remain with the new because of the social support they receive from others within the cluster. Individuals far from a cluster are unlikely to sustain a change even if they make one because they lack appropriate social contact and support. The most effective strategy is to concentrate one's efforts on the borders of clusters.

Second, special attention should be given to the strongest individuals (i.e., the leaders). The same amount of resources available for influence may be divided in different ways. One can divide the resources equally among all the members regardless of their relative strength. The same resources can be used to convert the highest number of people by concentrating on the weakest members, each of whom requires relatively little before change occurs. An alternative strategy is to concentrate instead on a small number of the strongest individuals, each of whom requires considerable amount of resources to change. Recent work within the simulation model (Nowak & Lewenstein, 1998) independently varied the total amount of available resources and the means by which the resources were divided among group members. Preliminary results indicate that, regardless of the total amount of resources available, in the long run the greatest change was achieved by concentrating on the strongest individuals, whereas the least change was achieved by concentrating on the weakest individuals. Even when many weak members were influenced to change, the change was short lived because of the influence they received from the unchanged stronger members around them. Changing the strongest members, although highly resource intensive, had an effect that became amplified over time. This is because the leaders became agents of change, influencing the opinions of those with whom they interacted.

The third practical implication concerns the structure of contacts in the larger group or society. Both analytical considerations (Lewenstein et al., 1993) and computer simulations (Nowak et al., 1996) indicate that the stability of a cluster is exponentially related to its size. Creating connections between minority individuals or between small minority clusters thus strongly increases the likelihood that minority opinion will survive. This idea was recently confirmed in a computer simulation (Krzymowski, 1998). In practice, creating social ties and channels of communication between members and clusters that advocate a minority position allows this position to resist majority influence and potentially to become established as a majority position.

This model may prove useful in generating strategies for different types of social interventions, including the facilitation of political change, programs to combat social problems, management of organizational change, and marketing of consumer preference. In general, one would start by identifying leaders in a social network. Thus, one would target a subgroup of interconnected high-status group members who are relatively open to the new position. When these individuals adopt the new position, resources can then be reallocated to other members in their social network (e.g., family members, friends) to create a cluster of interconnected individuals who provide support for one another. The resultant cluster can then be connected with other clusters that have received similar interventions (e.g., common meetings, sporting events, social occasions). If the interconnected groups reach a critical mass so that the movement can sustain itself, resources can be gradually withdrawn and reallocated to other social networks. One can test the effectiveness of specific variants on this general scenario with computer simulations before actually committing resources to intervention.

This general approach was employed to design a large-scale social program for unemployed young people in Poland (Nowak et al., 1993). One of the major costs of social change in the Polish example was structural unemployment. In areas where large government-run factories became ineffective and were thus dissolved during the transition, unemployment was the inevitable result. Young people were most strongly affected because in these regions they could not launch a career. As a result, they were less likely to leave home, experienced a loss of social contact because they were neither in school or employed, and, after several months, demonstrated signs of apathy and ceased looking for jobs. These people also became vulnerable to various forms of social pathology, especially excessive drinking of alcohol.

A task force was created by the Polish Psychological Association to intervene in these regions of structural unemployment. Preliminary findings by the task force indicated that the basic problem associated with the unemployed youth was lack of meaningful activity. To address this problem, a training program was designed in which individuals from the affected regions traveled to Warsaw to undergo training. The program involved helping individuals develop their own agenda of meaningful activity, in the form of hobbies, job searches, and so forth. This intervention introduced profound changes for the individuals during the period of training. However, when these people were visited 2 months later in their home regions, virtually all the effects of the intervention had dissipated. In effect, the individuals were reabsorbed by their respective social contexts. This made clear that effective social intervention must change areas of social networks rather than simply change the individuals outside of their social networks.

Consequently, practical experience in conjunction with computer simulations were used to design a program to change areas of social networks as opposed to individuals. The key feature of this coordinated effort was the inclusion of people from the same area in the training program. In this way, a bubble of new was created in which group members provided a supportive social context for one another. The general aim of each group was to foster and reinforce any productive activity spontaneously generated by group members. Group agendas varied a great deal, including establishing an amateur theater, establishing commercial enterprises (e.g., a coffee shop), and finding jobs outside the region. All the members of the task force participated in a workshop devoted to computer simulations of social change. In this workshop, they explored different scenarios of social influence that were simulated on a computer to provide insight into the role of local interactions in promoting change.

The simulation work indicated the importance of leaders for the survival of the bubbles of *new*, suggesting that the initial efforts should be targeted at the most influential individuals in a given group provided they were ready to accept the idea of engaging in meaningful activity. In the initial recruitment process, the first meeting was strongly advertised in a single town rather than throughout the region. This meeting consisted of two parts. The first part of the meeting was devoted to arguments in favor of the program. Opposing arguments were then presented that focused on the various costs associated with the program, so as to exert influence that would discourage participation in the program. Thus, although the first influence attempt was intended to recruit as many people as possible to join the program, the goal of the second attempt was to eliminate those who were not strong enough to withstand influence opposing the program. The second part of the meeting, consisting of those individuals who resisted the negative social influence in the first part, was devoted to establishing organization in the group.

To create a coherent cluster of strong and willing individuals, specific elements were introduced into the program designed to encourage social contacts between group members outside of the formal group gatherings. Because the stability of a minority cluster grows exponentially with the size of the cluster (Lewenstein et al., 1993), a social worker was assigned to each group initially to provide support for the group's agenda. This support was gradually withdrawn as the group gathered new members and became correspondingly stronger. After the clusters achieved sufficient coherence in this manner, the program shifted its emphasis to the creation of links among these bubbles (clusters) of *new*, so that the bubbles would provide support for one another. This was done by arranging periodic meetings of the leaders from each cluster and assisting them in establishing regional structure for communication.

Approximately 1,000 people were included in the program as an experimental group; the control group consisted of approximately 600 people on a waiting list to enter the program. Those in the experimental group found jobs far more frequently than those in the control group. In addition, results from a battery of psychological tests administered at the beginning and the end of the program revealed that indexes of psychological well-being remained stable or improved for those in the experimental group, but decreased dramatically for those in the control group. Overall, there is good reason to suggest that this mode of intervention did in fact facilitate significant social change.

In summary, although it may be desirable to facilitate of social change on a global level, the process of change in a transitional society occurs in an uneven manner, with local environments most susceptible to intervention strategies. Agents of change should thus concentrate their effects on pockets of society containing preferences for the new agenda. This in effect creates seeds that may grow to form clusters. If these clusters develop connections with each other, there is a chance that the new agenda will overcome the old. This perspective suggests that the future may often co-exist with the present. Some elements of the diversity that surrounds us may in fact be harbingers of future global states of the system. However, it may be very difficult to say at present

which local clusters provide a window on the future and which are simply aber-
rations that will pass without leaving any traces.

SUMMARY AND CONCLUSIONS

Many specific mechanisms of social influence have been shown to operate at
the level of individuals (cf. Cialdini, 1988). Regardless of the specific means
by which influence is exerted on individuals, the social context plays an important role in determining whether such influence will result in change and an
even more important role in determining whether any resultant changes will
persist in the face of subsequent opposing influences. Such factors as distribution of leaders, size of the group with a particular position, structure of communication networks, timing of intervention, and importance of the issue in
question should be taken into account when trying to induce change in groups
or societies. In general, social influence attempts are likely to be most effective
when they follow the natural course of social change as it occurs in social interactions. It is possible for a minority to induce social change if the minority con-
centrates first on creating bubbles of *new* and then expanding them, rather than
trying to induce global change.

The computer simulation approach has already provided some important insights into how best to facilitate social change. Many issues remain unresolved, however, and await further simulation as well as empirical work. For
example, if the strongest minority leaders can travel, what route would be most
effective for purposes of inducing social change? Should they try to expand the
borders of strongholds or should they create new passages between existing
strongholds? If a communication structure can be shaped, what is the best structure for maintaining minority position? What is the best structure for expansion?
How should the communication structure change to enable the survival of minority clusters in the beginning and to provide for expansion after such clusters have
achieved coherence? Perhaps of greatest importance, however, will be efforts
devoted to bridging the gap between abstract theoretical models suggested by
computer simulations and concrete strategies of social influence.

In a more general sense, computer simulations are ideally suited for
exploring the group-level consequences of influences occurring at the level of
individual social interactions (see e.g., Messick & Liebrand, 1995; Liebrand,
Nowak, & Hegselmann, 1998, Nowak & Vallacher, 1998). From this perspective,
the mechanisms of individual influence hold potential for generating important
insights into the macrolevel properties of social groups and even entire societies.
Thus, the ideas described in this chapter have clear potential for integrating theories built at different levels of social reality. Clearly, social influence provides
the glue for creating social fabric from the strands provided by individuals, and
thus occupies center stage in any attempt to unite an admittedly fragmented field.

ACKNOWLEDEMENTS

Preparation of this chapter was supported in part by NSF Grant SBR 95-11657 and the Polish Committee for Scientific Research (Grant 1H01F07310).

REFERENCES

Abelson, R. P. (1979). Social clusters and opinion clusters. In P. W. Holland & S. Leinhardt (Eds.), *Perspectives in social network research* (pp. 239–256). New York: Academic Press.

Batten, D., Casti, J., & Johanson, B. (Eds). (1987). *Lecture notes in economics and mathematical systems: Vol. 293. Economic evolution and structural adjustment.* Berlin: Springer.

Cialdini, R. B. (1988). *Influence: Science and practice* (2nd ed.). New York: HarperCollins.

Festinger, L., Schachter, S., & Back, K. (1950). *Social pressures in informal groups.* Stanford, CA: Stanford University Press.

Kerr, N. L. (1983). Motivation losses in small groups: A social dilemma analysis. *Journal of Personality and Social Psychology, 45,* 819–828.

Krzymowski, A. (1998). *Factors that hinder diversity of opinions in social groups.* Unpublished manuscript.

Latané, B. (1981). The psychology of social impact. *American Psychologist, 36,* 343–356.

Latané, B., & Darley, J. M. (1968). Group inhibition of bystander intervention in emergencies. *Journal of Personality and Social Psychology, 10,* 215–221.

Latané, B., Liu, J., Nowak, A., Bonavento, M., & Zheng, L. (1995). Distance matters: Physical space and social influence. *Personality and Social Psychology Bulletin, 21,* 795–805.

Latané, B., & Nowak, A. (1994). Attitudes as catastrophes: From dimensions to categories with increasing involvement. In R. R. Vallacher & A. Nowak (Eds.), *Dynamical systems in social psychology* (pp. 219–249). San Diego: Academic Press.

Latané, B., & Nowak, A. (1997). The causes of polarization and clustering in social groups. *Progress in Communication Sciences, 13,* 43–75.

Latané, B., Williams, K., & Harkins, S. (1979). Many hands make light the work: The causes and consequences of social loafing. *Journal of Personality and Social Psychology, 37,* 823–832.

Lewenstein, M., Nowak, A., & Latané, B. (1993). Statistical mechanics of social impact. *Physics Review A, 45,* 703–716.

Liebrand, V. B. G., Nowak A., & Hegselmann R. (1998). *Computer modelling of social processes.* London: Sage.

Markus, H. R., & Kitayama, S. (1991). Culture and the self: Implications for cognition, emotion, and action. *Psychological Review, 98*, 224–253.

Messick, D. M., & Liebrand, V. B. G. (1995). Individual heuristics and the dynamics of cooperation in large groups. *Psychological Review, 102*, 131–147.

Moscovici, S., & Zavalloni, M. (1969). The group as a polarizer of attitudes. *Journal of Personality and Social Psychology, 12*, 124–135.

Myers, D. G., & Lamm, H. (1976). The group polarization phenomenon. *Psychological Bulletin, 83*, 602–627.

Noelle-Neumann, E. (1984). *The spiral of silence: Public opinion-our social skin.* Chicago: University of Chicago Press.

Nowak, A., Latané, B., & Lewenstein, M. (1994). Social dilemmas exist in space. In U. Schulz, W. Albers, & U. Mueller (Eds.), *Social dilemmas and cooperation* (pp. 114–131). Heidelberg: Springer-Verlag.

Nowak, A., & Lewenstein, M. (1998). *Selective concentration of bias in social influence models.* Unpublished simulation data.

Nowak, A., Lewenstein, M., & Frejlak, P. (1996). Dynamics of public opinion and social change. In R. Hegselman & H. O. Pietgen (Eds.), *Modeling social dynamics: Order, chaos, and complexity* (pp. 54–78). Vienna: Helbin.

Nowak, A., Lewenstein, M., & Szamrej, J. (1993). Social transitions occur through bubbles. *Scientific American* (Polish version), *12*, 16–25.

Nowak, A., Szamrej, J., & Latané, B. (1990). From private attitude to public opinion: A dynamic theory of social impact. *Psychological Review, 97*, 362–376.

Nowak, A., & Vallacher, R.R. (1998). *Dynamical social psychology.* New York: Guilford.

Nowak, A., Vallacher, R. R., Tesser, A., & Borkowski, W. (in press). Society of self: The emergence of collective properties in self-structure. *Psychological Review.*

Schuster, H. G. (1984). *Deterministic chaos.* Vienna: Physik Verlag.

Szamrej, J., Nowak, A., & Latané, B. (1992). Self-organizing structures in society: Visual display of dynamic social processes. *25th International Congress of Psychology.* Brussels, Belgium.

Vallacher, R. R., & Nowak, A. (Eds.). (1994). *Dynamical systems in social psychology.* San Diego: Academic Press.

Vallacher, R. R., & Nowak, A. (1997). The emergence of dynamical social psychology. *Psychological Inquiry, 8*, 73–99.

Weidlich, W. (1991). Physics and social science: The approach of synergetics. *Physics Reports, 204*, 1–163.

9

The Consequences of Being an Influential Minority in the Context of Social Controversies in the Emerging Polish Democracy

Bogdan Wojciszke

Graduate School of Social Psychology

Warsaw

ABSTRACT

Individuals selected via a representative national Polish sample (N = 1,050) were surveyed for their positions on and construal of four attitudinal controversies (abortion, decommunization, privatization of industry, and rising pensions). It was hypothesized that attitudinal minorities would report stronger convictions than attitudinal majorities and that they would do this to survive and become and remain socially influential. Based on this notion, it was predicted and found that attitudinal minorities bolstered their own position by inflating their subjective belief in its validity, overestimating the number of others who shared their stance, and perceiving their stance as morally superior to alternative attitudinal positions. These ways of attitude bolstering were intercorrelated (constituting the so-called militant minority syndrome*), but each of them was independently related to the actual frequency of an attitudinal standing. The findings were applied to an analysis of social influence processes on the societal level in the emerging Polish democracy. Because there are more opportunities for militant opinion groups to acquire positions of power in emerging than in established democracies, they are able to become overly influential and impose their minority views on the majority, such as by changing laws to reflect their positions. Practical considerations for dealing with confident minorities are suggested.*

Social controversies refer by definition to issues on which a society is divided. Frequently the dispersion of opinions is unequal, with a majority of society taking one position and minorities taking other positions. In such a situation, the majority is often able to superimpose its own opinion on minorities using purely democratic procedures (e.g., voting). Nevertheless, the basic tenet of modern democracy is that the majority should refrain from forcing its position on minorities and, instead, compromise in such a way that would take into account minority standings on the issue. For the sake of the common good and to facilitate smooth functioning in a democratic society, both majorities and minorities should—the prescription goes—step down from their preferred ideals in favor of a compromising position. To attain such a compromise, different attitudinal groups would need to engage in mutual influence processes—recognizing what is the actual dispersion of opinions and which social group believes in what, trying to shift opinions of another group, accommodating their opinions, and so on. This suggests that social influence may and should be studied as a phenomenon originating in the dynamics of social structure, in addition to being understood in terms of mass-mediated influence (the perspective reflected in the chapters constituting Part II of the present volume) and interpersonal influence (the chapters in Part III).

The present chapter attempts to study social influence from the structural perspective because, quite frequently, neither the majority nor the minority engages in the constructive or integrative mutual influences that seem to be necessary for the efficient functioning of a democratic society. This may be especially true for the emerging democracies in Eastern Europe, which lack experience in integrative management of conflict of values and opinions. We explore the possibility that the specific position of opinion minorities can make them more uncompromising than majorities and that the former may construe opinion conflicts in such a way that they become militant minorities and, in some situations, may pose a real threat to democracy.

THE PURPOSE AND METHOD OF THE PRESENT RESEARCH

The present work deals with the issue of how the specific position of attitudinal minorities shapes the way in which they construe an attitudinal controversy. The terms *majority* and *minority* refer here not to actual social groups, but rather to categorizations based on the similarity of attitudes. In this sense, a prolife attitude is a minority view in the Polish population because most Poles tend to be prochoice or occupy a middle-of-the-road position on this issue.[1]

---

[1] Although it may appear striking to a non-Polish native that, in a society in which 90% of the citizens are Catholic, the majority is not prolife, it is perhaps more comprehensible in light of five decades of legalized abortion under communist rule.

Generally speaking, we hypothesize that, due to the relatively lower prevalence of their views, people holding minority opinions are confronted much more often by opposing views than are individuals in the majority. The validity of minority opinions is thus threatened more frequently than that of majority views. Therefore, to maintain their opinions and/or influence people of differing opinions, the attitudinal minority members tend to hold relatively more extreme beliefs, thereby bolstering their attitudes in at least three ways:

1. By inflating their subjective belief in the validity of their own attitudes;
2. By overestimating social support for their attitudes; and
3. By perceiving their attitude as morally superior to all alternative views.

Although such attitude bolstering may also be found among majority members, it is expected to be stronger in attitudinal minorities. Together, these three ways of attitude bolstering constitute the militant minority syndrome, on which this chapter is focused.

Attitudinal minorities–majorities were ascertained at the population (nation) level with respect to four highly controversial issues in contemporary Poland. These were abortion, decommunization, privatization (most Polish big and medium size industry is still state-owned), and rising pensions for retired persons (at the expense of tax payers). Because this was a representative sample, it was possible to estimate which of the three possible attitudinal standings (pro vs. moderate vs. anti) on each issue constituted a minority or majority stance in the Polish population, and to estimate the size of each attitudinal group. In addition to measuring the participants' own attitudes, the survey included several questions probing the way in which they construed these attitudinal controversies.

A representative national sample of Polish adults ($N = 1,050$) was selected and surveyed in November 1994 by *Pracownia Badan Spolecznych*, a private opinion poll firm (which made the most accurate predictions in the latest parliamentary elections in Poland). The sample structure was virtually identical to that of the Polish population as described in the official governmental statistics in terms of gender, age, education, and place of living (village vs. town vs. city). The participants ranged in age from 18 to 89 years, with the median age of 41 years. The sample was approximately evenly divided between males and females.

After receiving a brief reminder about the major opposing views on each issue in question, participants were asked several questions about these issues. For example, for the abortion issue, the questions read as follows:

Reminder: In recent years, there has been a hot dispute in Poland about abortion— between those who would like to forbid abortion entirely and those who would like abortion to be legally permitted.

Question 1. Do you think that one side in this controversy is better than the other—that is, that people on one side are decent and moral to a higher extent than people on other side? (answer options: Yes, No, It's hard to say)

Question 2. Please distribute 100 points (percents) of *rightness* among those who (a) oppose abortion, (b) represent some middle-of-the-way solution, and (c) are prochoice (field researchers were instructed to ensure that the points summed up to 100).

Question 3. In your opinion, how should this controversy be resolved? (Answer options: Abortion should be totally forbidden; Some middle-of-the-way solution should be found; or Each individual should be given freedom of choice on this matter).

Question 4. What percentage of adult Poles shares your opinion on this issue?

The answer to Question 3 served two functions. First, it identified a subject's own attitudinal position on the issue in question (pro, moderate, or anti). Second, it served as an estimate of the attitude frequency in the population, because the sample was representative for Polish adults. This estimate is referred to as the *attitudinal group size* or the *actual consensus* measure. Answers to Question 4 yielded a measure of *assumed consensus* (i.e., a subjective belief in the prevalence of the respondent's attitude in the population). For each subject and on each issue separately, the appropriate actual consensus was subtracted from the assumed one, yielding the *consensus overestimation* measure.

Answers to Question 2 yielded estimates of the extent to which respondents assessed the *rightness* of their own versus opposing views; they provided us with a measure of the subjective *self-validity* of the subject's attitudinal position. Question 1 yielded an estimate of *conflict moralization*—that is, the tendency to perceive people taking one position (presumably the subject's own) as morally superior to people who hold opposing views.

Some of the answers were averaged over the four issues to obtain individual-level estimates of the analyzed variables. For example, the attitudinal group size was a group-level measure of an attitude frequency because it was basically a characteristic of an attitudinal group rather than of an individual. However, each individual could occupy a minority, moderate, or majority position on each issue, and each position could be scored for its frequency in the population. Averaging these scores over the four issues allowed us to obtain an estimate of the individual's *majority status*—that is, the tendency to assume a majority position on the issues surveyed. The consensus overestimation and self-validity measures were similarly averaged over the issues (for each subject separately), yielding individual-level estimates of those variables. Answers to the questions about conflict moralization (Question 1) were scored for each individual ($0 = No$, $1 = Unsure$, $2 = Yes$) and summed up, yielding an individual-level estimate of conflict moralization.

COGNITIVE CORRELATES OF HOLDING
MINORITY VIEWS

As already mentioned, our main assumption was that minorities tend to con-strue attitudinal issues in a more uncompromising way than attitudinal majorities. There are at least two mechanisms leading attitudinal minorities to hold more extreme opinions than those of majorities: selective shrinking by attrition and attitude bolstering.

Selective shrinking by attrition is a product of the mutual influences of majorities and minorities. Because the majority is larger and the strength of social impact increases with the number of its sources until a certain level is reached (Latané, 1981), a relatively higher number of minority than majority members yield to pressure exerted by the opposing group and change their opinions accordingly. In the course of repeated interactions between majority and minority members, the minority probably decreases by the attrition of those who have been most ambivalent in their convictions. Computer simulations of interactive, reciprocal, and recursive social influ-ence attempts suggest that differentiation in attitude strength and accumula-tion of strong attitudes in minorities are prerequisites for a minority's sur-vival (Nowak, Szamrej, & Latané, 1990). If not for this factor (and for spa-tial clustering of those who share similar opinions), minorities would simply melt away in the *ocean of the majority*, which is rarely the case, especially for highly important attitudes (Latané & Nowak, 1993). Shrinking by attri-tion leads to a higher incidence of strong convictions among minority than majority members (the latter may afford relatively weaker convictions due to support received from the numerous other majority members).

The mechanism of *attitude bolstering*, which also leads to relatively stronger convictions among a minority members, may be inferred from Moscovici's (1976, 1985) theorizing and findings on the dynamics of minor-ity influence. To be efficient in its influence attempts, the minority should show a consistent behavioral style—repeatedly and steadily presenting its alternative view to the majority, expressing certainty and confidence in this view, signaling that it will not compromise under any circumstances, and that it is the majority who should shift its opinion. The consistent behavioral style is an important factor that increases the influence of minorities, as demon-strated by a recent meta-analysis of numerous studies (Wood, Lundgren, Ouellette, Busceme, & Blackstone, 1994). It seems logical to assume that, to produce such a style of discourse, a minority needs strong confidence in its beliefs: It takes a true believer to persistently express an unpopular view despite the reluctance, hostility, or rejection on the part of the majority. Therefore, attitudinal minorities should show a stronger conviction in their beliefs than attitudinal majorities, and this effect should increase as the size of the minority decreases. As stated earlier, we hypothesized that minorities can bolster their own attitudes in at least three ways: (a) by overestimating the amount of social support for their attitudinal positions, (b) by increasing the subjective validity of their convictions, and (c) by believing in the moral superiority of their own views.

Overestimating the Amount of Social Support for One's Attitudinal Position

Most fierce controversies, like abortion or capital punishment, have to do with values or preferences rather than facts. In effect, there is no objective or physical reality-based test for the most important, value-laden beliefs. To check the validity of their attitudes or beliefs, people often seek social proof (Cialdini, 1993) for their own attitudes or beliefs by examining the opinions of relevant others. Because the belief in the amount of social support for an opinion depends on the attitude holder's own construal of the situation, a simple way to bolster the validity of one's opinions is to perceive them as widely shared by others. This tendency is directly suggested by the false consensus effect—the erroneous tendency to assume that our opinions and behavioral choices are shared by many more others than is really the case (Ross, Greene, & House, 1977). The false consensus effect is a robust phenomenon found in over 100 studies (cf. Marks & Miller, 1987; Mullen et al., 1985).

   Our hypothesis was that attitudinal minorities overestimate the social consensus for their attitudes to a higher degree than majorities and that this difference increases with an increase in the disproportion between the minority and majority size. This hypothesis received solid initial support from Mullen and

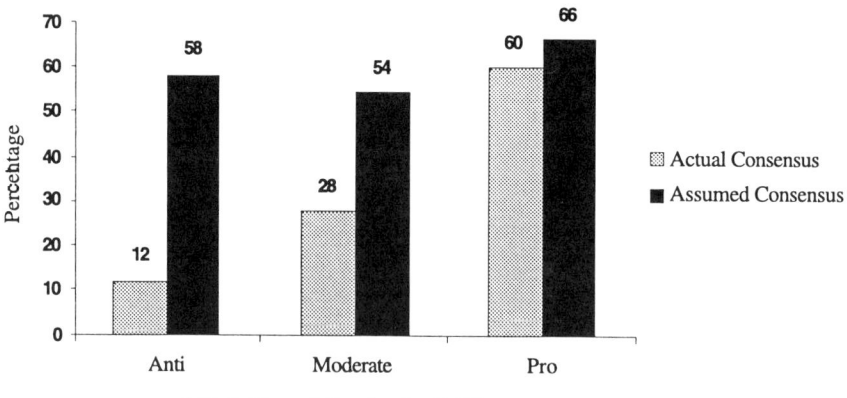

FIG. 9.1. Actual and assumed consensus in attitudes toward abortion on demand (Polish national sample, $N = 1,050$).

TABLE 9.1
Actual and Assumed Consensus on Four Issues as a
Function of Own Attitude Frequency

Issue/Variable	Own Attitude			F^a (attitude)	eta squared[b]	F^c (linearity)
	Anti	Mod	Pro			
Abortion						
N	128	287	629			
Actual consensus	12.2	27.5	60.1			
Assumed consensus	57.5	54.3	65.8	48.86***	.086	66.26***
Consensus overestimation	45.3	26.8	5.7	356,00***	.406	711.01***
Decommunization						
N	270	493	275			
Actual consensus	26.0	47.8	26.2			
Assumed consensus	55.6	51.8	58.2	12.64***	.024	12.01***
Consensus overestimation	16.5	4.0	17.8	304.10***	.370	459.16***
Privatization						
N	131	553	327			
Actual consensus	13.4	54.9	31.7			
Assumed consensus	57.4	51.3	50.2	9.22***	.018	6.82**
Consensus overestimation	44.0	-3.6	18.5	510.26***	.503	1018.60***
Pensions						
N	67	705	246			
Actual consensus	6.7	69.6	23.7			
Assumed consensus	51.4	51.5	51.8	2.52*	.005	3.97*
Consensus overestimation	44.3	-17.8	30.8	1004.31***	.664	129.30***

Note. F^a = the Own attitude main effect; eta squared[b] = size of the Own attitude main effect; F^c = linearity of the Own attitude main effect when attitude groups are ordered according to their size. * $p < .05.$** $p < .01.$*** $p < .001.$

Hu's (1988) meta-analysis of 12 studies, although all those studies dichotomized attitudes (pro and anti positions only), and none of them used a sample that was representative of the studied population. Both of these features may be seen as a drawback in the present context (attitudinal minorities—majorities on the society level) because the majority in a society tends to assume a moderate, middle-of-the-road position on numerous issues; when overestimation of consensus is discussed, the question of actual consensus estimates arises. This problem may be resolved satisfactorily by studying a representative sample that enables a reliable estimation of the actual prevalence of the various positions on the attitude in the population under investigation.

Therefore, as mentioned previously, we surveyed a national sample of Polish adults and estimated the actual dispersions of attitudes toward four controversial issues: abortion, decommunization, privatization, and rising pensions. A subject could choose one of three positions on each issues (pro, moderate, and con). As seen in Fig. 9.1 and Table 9.1, the positions varied greatly in frequency on each issue. Additionally, the respondents were asked to make an estimate of the proportion of Poles sharing their own position. These latter estimates varied to a much lesser degree because each of the groups believed their attitude to be shared by a majority of the population, the actual attitudinal frequency notwithstanding.

However, this does not reflect a comparable universality in erroneous consensus overestimation. When measured as a difference between the assumed and actual percentage of people sharing an attitude, this overestimation only emerged in the attitudinal minorities. The overestimation was substantial in each of the minority groups, whereas it was small, nonexistent, or even inverted in the majority groups (see Table 9.1). The average overestimation (over four issues) amounted to 38% for minorities, but was only -3% for majorities. The influence of the subject's own attitudinal position on the consensus overestimation was very large, as evidenced by eta squared coefficients varying from .370 to .664, depending on the issue. Moreover, when tests of linearity of the attitudinal group size were performed with the groups ordered according to their size, the linearity Fs appeared not only significant, but of at least a three-digit value for each of the issues (see Table 9.1). Finally, when a linear Pearson correlation between the attitudinal group size and the consensus overestimation was computed on all 12 (4 issues x 3 attitudes) attitudinal groups, it reached the nearly perfect value of -.97.

In summary, the actual attitude frequency (or attitudinal group size) played a decisive role in determining consensus overestimation, and only attitudinal minorities bolstered their attitudes by overestimating the amount of actual social support for their own attitudes.

Increasing the Subjective Validity of One's Attitude

An attitude may also be bolstered in another simple way—that is, by increasing its subjective self-validity (i.e., intensifying the belief in the actual correctness of one's own attitude and in the incorrectness of the opposing views). In the case of such issues as abortion, which are value-laden but nonfactual, the attitude holders constitute the main source of self-validity estimates, and they also increase these estimates when necessary. This is possible despite the existence of discrepant views in the population and without losing their belief in the objectivity of their own judgments because people tend to assume a lay philosophy of naive realism when they construe conflicting positions (Ross & Ward, 1995). This implicit philosophy assumes that "I (a social perceiver) do see things as they really are and so do other rational people, thereby sharing my opinion." If they do not, it is because they do not have access to the right information, they do not care for drawing rational conclusions, or they are plainly biased in their opinions by self-interest or some personal flaws. Such a philosophy results in overestimating the us–them differences in construal of a controversy (e.g., Robinson, Keltner, Ward, & Ross, 1995), which should lead to an increased discrepancy in validity ascribed to the conflicting positions. Our hypothesis, then, was that attitudinal minorities, as compared with majorities, believed to a higher degree in the validity of their attitudes and that this difference increased with an increase in the disproportion between the minority and majority size.

To test this hypothesis, we asked our respondents to distribute 100% of rightness among the three attitudinal positions on each of the four issues. Separate analyses were performed on these distributions for each issue. The validity judgments of each attitudinal position depended, of course, on the subjects' own attitude, as evidenced by the strong Own attitude x Target attitude interactions presented in Table 9.2 (F^a values). On average, a person's own position was perceived as more valid than the alternative, as illustrated by within-column differences between the italicized and nonitalicized means in each panel of Table 9.2. However, an inspection of these means shows that the strength of this tendency varied greatly among the attitudinal groups as a function of two variables. One variable was attitude frequency: As predicted by our hypothesis, minority members bolstered their convictions by increasing their belief in their validity. The second was a person's attitude extremity: Individuals who occupied either the pro or con position believed in the validity of their attitudes to a higher extent than people who occupied a moderate position. This finding was probably because the latter were less involved in their attitudes than were the former (as shown by numerous researchers, beginning with the classical studies by Sherif, Sherif, & Nebergall, 1965; see also Johnson & Eagly, 1989, for a review).

To test the impact of these two influences, we performed two analyses of variance (ANOVAs for each issue separately) on the self-validity judgments as a function of the person's attitude. In the first analysis, the attitudinal groups were ordered according to their size and, therefore, the estimates of linearity of the own attitude main effect (Fc values of Table 9.2) could serve

TABLE 9.2
Belief in Different Attitudinal Positions Being Right
as a Function of Own Attitude

Issue/ Target Attitude	Own Attitude			F^a (interaction)	F^b (group size)	F^c (linearity)	F^d (nonlinearity)
	Anti	Mod.	Pro				
Abortion				54.49***	69.06***	20.11***	118.00***
N	128	287	629				
Anti	75.00	35.72	26.81				
Moderate	12.01	35.84	24.80				
Pro	12.98	28.43	48.39				
Decommunization				83.95***	60.00***	74.78***	114.60***
N	270	493	275				
Anti	55.47	30.99	21.96				
Moderate	22.23	38.80	16.43				
Pro	22.29	30.21	61.61				
Privatization				81.22***	73.69***	135.83***	143.67***
N	131	553	327				
Anti	59.42	32.98	24.89				
Moderate	19.59	35.71	20.59				
Pro	20.99	31.31	54.52				
Pensions				36.29***	37.19***	38.37***	28.91***
N	67	705	246				
Anti	45.43	26.67	21.32				
Moderate	25.22	39.84	21.06				
Pro	29.35	33.49	57.62				

Note. The italicized values refer to the self-validity estimates.

F^a = Own attitude x Target attitude interaction; this test was performed on the estimates of rightness of all three target attitudes within a panel; the remaining tests were performed on the estimates of the subject's own group rightness only.

F^b = main effect of the Own attitude.

F^c = linearity of the Own attitude main effect when groups are ordered according to their size.

F^d = deviation from linearity of the Own attitude main effect when groups are ordered in the anti/middle/pro sequence.

* $p < .05$. ** $p < .01$. *** $p < .001$.

as tests of the group size influences. In the second analysis, the attitudinal groups were ordered according to the pro-moderate-con sequence, and the estimates of deviations from linearity of the own attitude main effect (Fd values of Table 9.2) could serve as tests of the attitude extremity influences.

As can be seen in Table 9.2, both influences appeared highly significant for each of the four issues: The belief in validity of one's own position was a function of both the extremity and frequency of the position held. In effect, the highest self-validity judgments emerged for each issue in an attitudinal group that was both extreme and in the minority position (antiabortion, prodecommunization, antiprivatization, and antipension). The antiabortionists yielded the highest self-validity estimates: One third of this group entirely monopolized the validity of their own position, ascribing themselves all 100% of the rightness"(whereas only 11% of the prochoice group showed a similar tendency). This is probably due to the fact that anti-abortionists also showed the highest tendency to moralize the conflict (as many as 72%, but only 27% of prochoice participants did so), and conflict moralization was negatively related to attitude frequency, as discussed later.

Altogether, the tendency to inflate estimates of one's own attitude validity was negatively correlated with the actual frequency of this attitude (r = -.59). Moreover, only the minorities seriously inflated these estimates, ascribing 59% of rightness to themselves on the (cross-issue) average, whereas the majorities perceived their standings in a somewhat less enthusiastic way (ascribing 41% of rightness to themselves).

Moral Superiority of One's Attitude

The third way in which attitudinal minorities may strengthen their views is to see them as morally superior to majority views. This issue moralization hypothesis seems to be highly plausible for heavily value-laden issues studied in the present survey. Therefore, we predicted that attitudinal minorities would believe in the moral superiority of their own positions to a higher degree than would majorities.

To test this hypothesis, we asked our respondents whether they thought "one side of the controversy to be better than the other, and that people on one side are decent and moral to a higher extent than people on the other side." The "yes" response served as an index of issue moralization. As in the case of the previously discussed self-validity estimates, issue moralization depended on a person's attitude extremity, with participants holding extreme pro or con views, yielding a higher number of "yes" responses to this question (35% on the average) than participants holding a moderate position (10%). The attitudinal group size also influenced the issue moralization: Of those who held the minority views, 38% saw one side as morally better than others, whereas only 21% of majority members did so. As predicted, issue moralization correlated with the

TABLE 9.3
Correlations Among Attitude Frequency (Group Size or the Majority Status),
Consensus Overestimation, Belief in Self-Validity, and Conflict Moralization

Variable	1	2	3	4
1. Attitude frequency	—	-.97***	-.59*	-.41a
2. Consensus overestimation	-.62***	—	.67**	.49a
3. Self-validity	-.27***	.32***	—	.77**
4. Issue moralization	-.21***	.20***	.18***	—

Note. Group-level correlations are presented above diagonal; individual-level correlations are presented below diagonal. Group-level correlations (Pearson's *r*s, one-tailed) estimated on the attitudinal group (N = 12) means. Individual-level correlations (Pearson's rs) estimated on the within-subject averages over the four issues surveyed (N = 1,050). [a] $p < .10$. * $p < .05$. ** $p < .01$. *** $p < .001$.

attitude frequency or, in other words, the attitudinal group size ($r = -.41$).

THE MILITANT MINORITY SYNDROME

Attitudinal minorities demonstrated all three predicted ways to bolster their threatened attitudes: They inflated validity estimates of their own position (frequently attributing all of the rightness to themselves, whereas majorities perceived their position as only slightly more right than other positions), they overestimated the consensus of their attitudes (frequently by as much as 40%, whereas majorities sometimes underestimated the consensus), and they perceived fellow minority members as superior to those who held alternative views. Because these three tendencies are positively related to each other (see Table 9.3), a question arises as to whether their correlations with attitude frequency are not spurious. Partial correlation analyses performed on the individual-level correlations showed, however, that each of the three tendencies remained significantly correlated with attitude frequency even when the remaining two had been partialed out.

Intercorrelations among the three ways of attitude bolstering suggest the interesting possibility that they constitute a pattern that may be called the militant minority syndrome. This syndrome may be threatening to democracy because it prevents opinionated minorities from accepting compromises with the majority, because such compromises tend to be seen as "making deals with the devil." Consensus and self-validity overestimation is detrimental to conflict resolution, because it leads to the erroneous expectation that the conflict may be resolved without compromise, by the sheer volume of rightness and apparent popularity of the views cherished by minority members. Finally, the issue moralization is also detrimental because it leads to transference of the conflict to a higher level or broadening its scope (Deutsch, 1973, 1994). Having categorized one of the sides as morally superior to the other, people tend to believe that it is not merely a single, isolated issue that is at stake (like abortion or privatization), but rather that the controversy represents the basic struggle between good and evil. Such inflated perceptions of the conflict size or importance result in adopting more rigid and uncompromising positions (Pruitt & Rubin, 1986). For militant minorities, then, any deal with adversaries seems to be not only morally wrong, but also unnecessary, because their own view is seen as absolutely right and shared by most people.

PRACTICAL IMPLICATIONS ON THE SOCIETY LEVEL: THE CASE OF EMERGING DEMOCRACIES

Militant minorities probably exist in every social system liberal enough to allow the voicing of values discrepant with those of the majority or its rulers. This is well illustrated by the stable existence of splinter political groups both to the far right and far left of the mainstream in mature democracies. This can be evidenced by such events as shootings of pro-choice doctors by fierce antiabortionists in the United States; sometimes extreme and illustrious protests of students, Greens, and gays in Western Europe; and so on. The militant minority phenomenon seems to be universal and is certainly found in many, many cultures. Still it is likely to be particularly dangerous for the young democracies emerging in Europe after the collapse of communism. The reason for this threat lies in the existence of important differences in the sociopolitical structures and corresponding social influence processes between the seasoned democracies of the Western world and the young democracies emerging from the ashes of communism. In a well-established democracy, militant minorities tend to be peripheral formations in the political system that can change mainstream views only in a slow and gradual way. In young democracies, however, with their unstable and kaleidoscopic alliances of small political parties, some militant minorities may easily assume a position of legislative or executive power. Although such a position is typically held only temporarily, it may enable minorities to impose their unpopular views on the entire society.

This is exactly what happened in Poland with the abortion law. A few months after the survey reported in this chapter was conducted, a relatively small political party succeeded in introducing heavily restrictive antiabortion laws clearly against the opinion of a sizable majority of Poles (as shown in our study and in other surveys). Both the Polish parliament and a committee working on the new abortion law were locally dominated by fierce antiabortionists who passed the law without any consideration of the prochoice views that were much more prevalent in the society as a whole. This successful minority party lost the next round of parliamentary elections, but the abortion law it introduced survived and even today remains in place. Moreover, the prolife minority also appeared influential in changing the views of the general population of Poles. When the queries referring to abortion were repeated in a similar national survey 4 years later (in December 1998), a clear prolife shift in opinion emerged: Whereas the percentage of antiabortionists increased to 17% (from 12.2% four years earlier), the percentage of those who would allow abortion on demand decreased to 45.5% (from 60.2%). This change is statistically significant [$\chi^2(2) = 45.41$, $p <$ .0001], although modest in size (Cramer's $V = 0.15$). It is likely that the change in the law served as a vehicle for changing the opinion of many citizens.

Hence, the prolife minority appeared not only extreme in its opinions (to a much higher degree than the prochoice majority), but also successful in imposing its views on the majority and changing the views of society. Of course, because of its correlational nature, the present data do not prove that it was attitudinal extremity that made the prolife minority successful. However, the abortion law currently in effect in Poland represents the minority view. Although the minority is a bit larger than before, it embraces only about 17% of the society, and the question arises whether anything can be done to prevent the imposition of minority views on the majority in an emerging democracy. One remedy is related to some apparent antecedents of the militant minority syndrome in the political life of young democracies.

One of the illusions inadvertently created by the communistic system was an illusion of unanimity. The suppression of free speech was as universal as the pressure to express in public only *officially approved* views—meaning opinions that were at least ostensibly procommunist, but were typically, in fact, simply opportunistic (i.e., consistent with the current party's line, which used to change considerably over time and occasions). This led to great confusion about who truly believed in what and to an implicit assumption that, if only people were allowed to express their true opinions, all would do this in the same voice ("as me," of course). This assumption seemed to be well entrenched, in part, because it could not be tested or disconfirmed on a societal level. Actually the abolition of censorship led immediately to public voicing of opinions as differentiated as were the interests and values of various social groups. Discovering this actual opinion differentiation proved to be a mental shock for many, and numerous groups still cannot accept the inevitability of opinion diversity and conflict. Even if they recognize the conflict, they tend to assume that only a tiny minority holds an opinion different from their own (although actually the opposite is frequently true).

One of the most promising practical remedies to the problem presented by overly powerful minorities is the practice of free speech on the societal level.

Freedom of speech ensures continuous exposure to the diversity of opinions on controversial social issues. Exposure to diversity results in recognition of the existence of various views and their respective rationales, or at least it can make people familiar with the basic fact that others differ in their values and that it is unnecessary to exclude persons or groups of different values from the *we* category. Once achieved, freedom of speech tends to be dismissed by the public as something obvious, thereby less important and sometimes even irritating or obnoxious. The present line of thinking provides another argument as to why freedom of speech, with its explicit cultivation of diversity, is an absolute prerequisite for the functioning of a democratic society.

ACKNOWELDGMENTS

This research was supported by KBN (Komitet Badan Naukowych) grants PB 0178/P1/93/05 and PB 0604/H01/97/13.

REFERENCES

Cialdini, R. B. (1993). *Influence: Science and practice* (3rd ed.). New York: HarperCollins.

Deutsch, M. (1973). *The resolution of conflict: Constructive and destructive processes*. New Haven, CT: Yale University Press.

Deutsch, M. (1994). Constructive conflict resolution: Principles, training, and research. *Journal of Social Issues, 50*, 13–32.

Johnson, B. T., & Eagly, A. H. (1989). Effects of involvement on persuasion: A meta-analysis. *Psychological Bulletin, 106*, 290–314.

Latané, B. (1981). The psychology of social impact. *American Psychologist, 36*, 343–356.

Latané, B., & Nowak, A. (1993). Attitudes as catastrophes: From dimensions to categories with increasing involvement. In R. Vallacher & A. Nowak (Eds.), *Dynamical systems in social psychology* (pp. 219–249). New York: Academic Press.

Marks, G., & Miller, N. (1987). Ten years of research on the false-consensus effect: An empirical and theoretical review. *Psychological Bulletin, 102*, 72–90.

Moscovici, S. (1976). *Social influence and social change*. London: Academic Press.

Moscovici, S. (1985). Social influence and conformity. In G. Lindzey & E. Aronson (Eds.), *The handbook of social psychology* (Vol. 2, 3rd ed., pp. 347–412). New York: Random House.

Mullen, B., Atkins, J. L., Champion D. S., Edwards, C., Hardy, D., Story, J. E., &

Vanderklok, M. (1985). The false consensus effect: A meta-analysis of 155 hypothesis tests. *Journal of Experimental Social Psychology, 21*, 262–283.

Mullen, B., & Hu, L. (1988). Social projection as a function of cognitive mechanisms: Two meta-analytic integrations. *British Journal of Social Psychology, 27*, 333–356.

Nowak, A., Szamrej, J., & Latané, B. (1990). From private attitude to public opinion: A dynamic theory of social impact. *Psychological Review, 97*, 367–376.

Pruitt, D. G., & Rubin, J. Z. (1986). *Social conflict.* New York: Random House.

Robinson, R. J., Keltner, D., Ward, A., & Ross, L. (1995). Actual versus assumed differences in construal: "Naive realism" in intergroup perception and conflict. *Journal of Personality and Social Psychology, 68*, 404–417.

Ross, L., Greene, D., & House, D. P. (1977). The false consensus effect: An egocentric bias in social perception and attribution processes. *Journal of Experimental Social Psychology, 13*, 279–301.

Ross, L., & Ward, A. (1995). Psychological barriers to dispute resolution. *Advances in Experimental Social Psychology, 27*, 255–304.

Sherif, C. W., Sherif, M., & Nebergall, R. E. (1965). *Attitude and attitude change: The social judgment-involvement approach.* Philadelphia: Saunders.

Wood, W., Lundgren, S., Ouellette, J. A., Busceme, S., & Blackstone, T. (1994). Minority influence: A meta-analytic review of social influence processes. *Psychological Bulletin, 115*, 323–345.

10

Acculturation and Conflict Regulation of Turkish Immigrants in Germany: A Social Influence Perspective

Edgar W. Klinger
Günter Bierbrauer
Universität Osnabrück
Germany

ABSTRACT

Acculturation is the process whereby individuals and groups with different cultural backgrounds come into firsthand contact and influence each other. Both structural and interpersonal factors are likely to influence the acculturation process of immigrants. Based on Berry's (1990) acculturation model, four styles of conflict behavior or conflict regulation preferences were suggested: assimilation, integration, separation, and marginalization. In this study, acculturating Turks living in Germany were confronted with typical conflict scenarios and asked how they would handle the conflict described. When conflict behaviors were categorized in terms of the described acculturation modes, almost half of the conflicts were handled in an integration type mode, combining elements of heritage culture and host culture. Conflict regulation preferences also varied along structural factors—namely, type of social relationship and nature of conflict resource. Because general acculturation preferences did not predict corresponding social behaviors or conflict regulation preferences, the assumption of the unidirectional nature of generalized acculturation preferences was questioned. As an extension, a social influence approach based on Ajzen's (1989) theory of planned behavior was suggested that takes into account both structural and interpersonal contextual conditions that may have an impact on the attitudes and behavior of acculturating groups. The chapter ends with some practical implications regarding conflict resolution in ethno-plural societies.

How immigrants accommodate to and are accommodated by their host society is a persistent question in most multiethnic societies with experience with large-scale immigration. Immigrants are newcomers to an established culture. They bring with them values and behaviors that are different than those of their host culture. These immigrants are typically required to interpret, accept, or reject the dominant values and practices of their new environment (Berry, 1990; Bierbrauer & Pedersen, 1996). Although the dominant society will also undergo changes due to the presence of minorities, most changes occur in the minority culture. The process of mutual influence, whereby individuals and groups with distinct cultural backgrounds come into contact with each other, has been termed acculturation (Herskovitz, 1938; Redfield, Linton, & Herskovitz, 1936). Thus, *acculturation* can be conceptualized as the intervening process that links both the influence of the immigrant's heritage culture and the culture of the dominant society.

The way immigrants deal with conflicts is of particular relevance for both society at large and minority groups. Although research on the cross-cultural style of conflict regulation has gained increased attention within cross-cultural psychology (e.g., Smith & Bond, 1998), this literature suffers from two limitations. According to Ting-Toomey et al. (1991), one limitation is the lack of theoretical understanding of the relationship between cultural variability and conflict style. The second limitation concerns the lack of understanding regarding how the conflict styles of immigrants are influenced and changed during the process of acculturation.

This chapter has three objectives. First, because Turkish immigrants in Germany form the target group of the study to be presented, a brief outline of Germany's historic reluctance toward immigration (Martin, 1994) is provided. Second, data from the authors' study are presented so as to understand how the conflict styles of Turkish immigrants can be related to mode of acculturation. Third, the process of acculturation is conceptualized from a social influence perspective. Within this framework, acculturation preferences are conceived as being influenced by normative, attitudinal, and behavioral variables.

GERMANY AS AN IMMIGRATION COUNTRY

Unlike most other Western nations, Germany's past has not included large-scale immigration from Third World countries. However, according to the

United Nations (1994) "Germany has been the country in the world with the largest number of immigrants in recent years. It had an annual average of almost 1.4 million for 1992 and 1993, compared with an annual average of 800,000 in the US" (p. 1). Immigration of nonethnic Germans started in the 1960s when guest workers, mostly from southern European countries and Turkey, were attracted to Germany.

Many of the foreigners who immigrated during the periods of economic boom still live in Germany today. In 1994, some 50% of the foreign nationals had been in Germany for at least 10 years (Statistisches Bundesamt, 1998). Some 7.37 million foreign nationals from all over the world were living in Germany in 1997 (9% of total population; Statistisches Bundesamt, 1998). As a result, Germany has been transformed into a multiethnic society.

Turks have formed by far the largest group of foreigners living in Germany since the early 1970s (Jamin, 1998; Meis, 1993). In 1997, 2.1 million Turks were residing in Germany, comprising almost one third of the total German foreign population. This portion has not varied considerably in the last 25 years. With the exception of the year 1967 and short intervals in the 1970s (1975–1976) and 1980s (1982–1985), the net migration balance of Turkish nationals has been positive, reaching maximum levels in 1970/1971 and 1980 (Statistisches Bundesamt, 1998). Family reunification was the main reason for this development. In 1997, 60% of the Turkish nationals were 30 years of age or younger. and 53% had been living in Germany for more than 14 years.

MODES OF ACCULTURATION

When immigrants enter a new society, they are typically faced with dramatic differences in, language, culture, food, institutions, and religion. This implies that they have to adapt to a certain degree to the dominant culture of their host society. Acculturation can be conceived as an interactive process that results from the influences of both the heritage culture of the immigrant and the culture of the host society. Based on this reasoning, Berry developed a categorization system with four alternative ways in which minority members can relate to their dominant society. The categorization reflects two underlying issues. The first issue refers to the degree to which minority members wish to keep their heritage culture as their primary expressive orientation. The second issue refers to the extent to which minority members wish to establish and express positive relationships with the dominant host society. Berry (1990) dichotomized the possible levels of cultural maintenance and adaptation and distinguished four modes of acculturation: (a) *Assimilation* expresses the wish to join the dominant society, adapt to its cultural values and behavioral norms, and relinquish the heritage culture completely; (b) *integration* means the desire to maintain close contact with the heritage culture and to establish a similarly close contact with the dominant culture;

(c) *separation* describes adherence to the heritage culture and total or near total avoidance of contact with the dominant culture; (d) *marginalization* means maintenance of loose contact with both the heritage culture and the dominant culture. Marginalization can be actively sought by an immigrant (withdrawal) or it can be something that happens to an immigrant due to the activities of the dominant society's members (exclusion).

Given the multitude of influences and demands posed by the dominant society, one can question the assumption about whether the process of acculturation is unidirectional in the sense that it proceeds in the same direction for all spheres of life. Thus, for example, an immigrant may very well assimilate in his or her professional life, whereas in the family sphere he or she may practice a greater separation from the host culture and place heavier emphasis on the heritage culture. A more elaborated view of adaptation was suggested by Gordon (1964), who distinguished seven modes of assimilation: cultural, structural, marital, identificational, attitude receptional (prejudice), behavioral receptional (discrimination), and civic. These distinctions allow for a better understanding of the dynamic of acculturation because not all spheres of life are likely to be influenced to the same degree in the same direction. A number of empirical studies do indeed show that different domains of life are subject to diverse types of influence by host and heritage cultures (Berry, Kim, Power, Young, & Bujaki, 1989; Hazuda, Stern & Haffner, 1988; Mendoza, 1989; Rogler, Cortes, & Malgady, 1991). For instance, Meis (1993) reported that about one third of immigrant Turks prefer to live in neighborhoods with both Germans and immigrants of similar cultural heritage. In contrast, immigrant Turks prefer a separation-type mode with respect to the use of news media and religious customs. Özcan (1995) reported a strong tendency by Turkish immigrants to adhere to familiar religious customs and continue to consume media of Turkish origin and language.

From a more theoretical perspective, Taylor (1991), in his analysis of assimilation and multiculturalism, strongly questioned whether a particular acculturation mode is unidirectional in the sense that it influences all domains of life in a similar fashion. He contended that acculturation may operate in different ways in different domains of life. For instance, within the interpersonal or language domain, assimilation may not prevail to the same extent as in the economic domain. Others have even argued that the more fundamental and instrumental aspects of the heritage culture are lost to assimilation (Heckmann, 1992; Laroche, Kim, & Hui, 1997). Any remaining features are considered a nostalgic allegiance to the heritage culture expressed through symbols (Gans, 1979). To come to a better understanding of the process of acculturation and its societal effects, Taylor (1991) called for a systematic analysis of the motivations and social forces underlying the desire for the maintenance of the heritage culture or the desire to develop other modes of relating to the dominant culture.

ACCULTURATION AND CONFLICT BEHAVIOR OF IMMIGRANT TURKS IN GERMANY: RESULTS OF AN EMPIRICAL STUDY

Within the context of a larger research project on conflict in an ethnoplural society, a study was carried out to aid our understanding of how acculturation influences the way Turkish immigrants handle their conflicts. As is the case with Turkish immigrants (Bierbrauer, 1994), most immigrants migrate from collectivistically oriented cultures to individualistically oriented Western cultures. Therefore, it seems inevitable that diverging cultural values, attitudes, and expectations will cause interpersonal conflicts between immigrants and members of the dominant society. Consequently, the role of intercultural conflict management becomes increasingly important in ethnoplural societies. A basic understanding of how culture and cross-cultural contact shape conflict behavior is necessary for effective management or resolution of intercultural conflicts. This study examines how male immigrant Turks residing in Germany handle conflicts in typical social situations, and seeks to find out whether dispute preferences are systematically related to acculturation modes. Thus, the study provides a conceptual link between the influence of the heritage culture and the culture of the dominant society on the one hand and the conflict behavior of acculturating Turks on the other.

An examination of conflicts between individuals with different cultural backgrounds has to take the participants' perception of the conflict into account (Deutsch, 1973; Ross & Ward, 1996). Ting-Toomey (1985) noted that, "conflict is a situational as well as a cultural dependent construct" (p.83). Individual conflict orientation combines context-specific assumptions regarding the appropriate behavioral strategy to be employed when achieving a certain goal. Thus, the notion of conflict style refers to every single behavioral strategy within a conflict setting that can be differentiated from strategy alternatives.

Implicit in most anthropological work on culture and conflict is the assumption that conflict management style depends on cultural values and goals. These are in turn shaped by the social needs of the cultures in question (Felstiner, 1974; Gluckman, 1969; Nader, 1969; Nader & Todd, 1978). Thus, culture can be conceived as a social context with implicit or explicit rules that guide conflict style. For instance, cultures that rely heavily on long-term interpersonal relationships value interpersonal harmony and therefore prefer compromise oriented procedures that are not likely to destroy such relationships. In an investigation of conflict regulation in a Turkish village, Starr (1978) observed that villagers refrain from open disputes when the reputation of the opponent is likely to become the focus of public gossip. Instead, the assistance of mediators is called on to preserve long-term relationships. In contrast, people from cultures that place greater emphasis on variable and short-term transactions are thought to be more likely to employ conflict-handling procedures that can guide stranger-to-stranger relationships (Bierbrauer, 1994). Potential damage to personal relationships is less of a problem in these cultures (Hamilton & Sanders, 1988; Kim, 1994).

Thus, cultural differences in conflict orientation may either aggravate or perhaps mitigate conflict intensity in situations where individuals with differing cultural orientations come into firsthand contact. This is a typical situation faced by acculturating immigrants, in which their hitherto preferred conflict styles may no longer be acceptable or functional in their new cultural setting.

As mentioned earlier, each mode of acculturation expresses different degrees of relating to the dominant culture. Therefore, it can be expected that the way immigrants handle interpersonal conflicts should also be influenced by acculturation mode and conflict-specific context or structural factors, such as conflict domain and type of conflict. *Conflict domain* refers to disputes over family matters or conflicts with neighbors. *Type of conflict* refers more generally to (a) disputes emerging from different patterns of social relationships (i.e., ingroup vs. outgroup conflicts), and (b) conflicts over various types of resources (i.e., tangible vs. intangible resources).

Relatively little, if any, research has been conducted to date relating acculturation processes to immigrant conflict styles. Based on the literature of acculturation and the writings of Augsburger (1992), Bierbrauer (1994), Ting-Toomey (1985), and Triandis (1994) on cross-cultural conflict behavior, the following framework was developed that relates patterns of conflict style to a particular mode of acculturation:

Assimilation   Confrontational, direct one-to-one negotiation style; factual-inductive pattern of communication; use of analytic and linear logic in argumentation; instrumental function of conflict.

Separation   Nonconfrontational, indirect triangular negotiation style; methods are less likely to destroy social relationships; use of holistic, spiral thinking supplemented by metaphors and similes; expressive function of conflict.

Integration   Combined elements of assimilation- and separation-type conflict styles that deal with negotiation style, patterns of communication, and logic.Marginalization Irritation and avoidance of conflict; misperception or misinterpretation of conflict.

The study to be reported addresses the following issues: How do the conflict behavior preferences of immigrant Turks vary across different social domains (e.g., family matters or money issues in terms of acculturation mode)? More generally, how is type of conflict (social relationship disputes or disputes over resources) related to acculturation mode? For the present study, the frequencies of conflict style preferences among immigrant Turks living in Germany across seven conflict domains were recorded. Conflict resources and type of social relationship presented in the conflict scenarios were varied systematically, and the respondents were asked to describe how they would have handled each of the seven conflicts presented.

Sample. One hundred and one immigrant Turks participated in this study. Approximately half of them were first-generation immigrants who came to Germany as so-called *guest workers.* The other half were either born in Germany as children of immigrant Turks or have lived in Germany since early childhood. The age of the first-generation respondents averaged 48.0 years. They had lived in Germany for 21.8 years on average. The second-generation respondents were 21.6 years of age on average. Respondents were contacted by two Turkish interviewers, and interviews were conducted on an individual basis. first-generation immigrants were interviewed in Turkish, second-generation immigrants in German.

Conflict Scenarios. The conflict scenarios employed in the present research were drawn from a collection of conflict situations reported by immigrant Turks in surveys or originated through group discussions with Turks. The vignettes involved either two immigrant opponents of similar heritage culture or an immigrant Turk and a German or an individual representing a German authority. In addition, the conflicts depicted arose from incompatible perceptions or demands regarding tangible or intangible resources (see appendix). Although the presentation of prestructured conflict scenarios might interfere with the conflict style preferences to be investigated (Graziano, Jensen-Campbell, & Hair, 1996), this procedure was nevertheless used because it allowed an optimal variation of the two conflict dimensions. After each conflict scenario had been read to the respondents, they were asked to indicate their prospective conflict behavior. Each participant responded to all seven scenarios. Answers were coded independently by three researchers, and only consistently coded data were included in the final analysis.

Data Analysis. Frequency of preferences showed that integration mode conflict styles were reported by some 50% of the respondents across all conflict scenarios. Thus, acculturating Turks predominantly preferred a combination of heritage culture and dominant culture elements of conflict behavior when dealing with a dispute, irrespective of conflict resource or the social relationship with the opponent. Comparisons of conflict style preferences revealed no significant differences between immigrant generations. In addition, there were significant variations in the frequencies of conflict style preferences with regard to conflict resource. Separation mode conflict style was preferred significantly more often when intangible resources were at stake. In contrast, assimilation mode conflict style was more frequently preferred in the case of tangible resources. Furthermore, a marginalization mode conflict style was preferred for tangible resources in some 15% of all answers, whereas this conflict style was rarely mentioned in conflicts over intangible resources.

Conflict style preferences were also influenced by the type of social relationships with opponents. Immigrant Turks tended to prefer a separation mode conflict style over an assimilation mode conflict style when facing an opponent from their own ethnic group. In conflicts with Germans, however, preferences for assimilation mode and marginalization mode conflict styles were reported more frequently, whereas only a few immigrant Turks preferred conflict behavior corresponding to the separation mode.

The data in this study suggest that conflict behavior of immigrant Turks varies along conflict domain and conflict type. This result casts doubt on the assumption that the process of acculturation is unidirectional in the sense that it influences all conflict behavior in a similar direction. Moreover, when the Turks were asked about their preferred acculturation mode without reference to any social context, the majority favored integration (70%). Taken alone, these measures are problematic because the integration mode was the obvious choice for acculturating immigrants. When the four acculturation modes reported by the immigrants were employed to predict conflict behavior, no systematic relationship was found.

Thus, acculturating Turks are sensitive to conflict context factors when they handle disputes. Type of conflict resource and social relationship factors do matter. In conflicts over tangible resources, immigrant Turks prefer a solution in a *German way* (i.e., in line with assimilation mode conflict style rather than along the separation mode). In conflicts over intangible resources, however, immigrant Turks more often resort to a style of conflict management that reflects the traditions of their heritage culture. This suggests that symbolic conflicts (e.g., conflicts in which family prestige is at stake) are more likely handled in a traditional *Turkish way*. Symbolic conflicts are more directly linked to the cultural identity of those involved in the conflict (Taylor, 1991). Moreover, a significant number of conflicts among Turks are also handled in the traditional Turkish way.

In summary, one can say that, with respect to conflict behavior, acculturation cannot be seen as a unidirectional phenomenon. Instead it must be concluded that factors specific to the conflict context play a major role in determining the acculturation mode. In general, however, the most preferred mode among immigrant Turks is a conflict style that combines elements of conflict behavior from both heritage and host cultures. This means that the majority of Turkish immigrants in Germany are flexible in their handling of disputes. They prefer to act in ways that do not reflect any one single culture and that are employed irrespective of both conflict resource and the opponent's cultural orientation. Moreover, it seems that generalized acculturation preferences cannot accurately predict actual acculturation in a specific domain of life and context. Thus, serious doubts must be raised concerning the explanatory or even predictive value of data based on general attitudes toward immigrants' preferred acculturation modes called for by Taylor (1991).

ACCULTURATION: A SOCIAL
INFLUENCE PERSPECTIVE

Immigrants setting up a new life in another country are confronted with a great deal of social information and a multitude of expectations that may be different from the kinds of influences they were exposed to in their native culture. Briefly, two sources of influences can be distinguished within the framework of acculturation: (a) Structural influences resulting, for example, from the clash of cultural norms, changes in social status, and—as examined in this paper—type of social relationship and nature of conflict resource; and (b) interpersonal influences produced by, for instance, the preferred acculturation modes and conflict orientations of ingroup members.

It is of interest to see how individuals from different cultures respond to and change under the various sources of social influence. In his model of acculturation, Berry (1990) distinguished acculturation on the group level (ecological, cultural, social, and institutional) from psychological acculturation on the individual level. The latter refers to psychological changes in identity, values, attitudes, and behaviors. Thus, it refers to the changes an individual experiences as a result of being in contact with other cultures and participating in the process that one's ethnic culture is undergoing (Graves, 1967).

One starting point in understanding acculturation in terms of social influence processes is to examine how a person's self or identity - created in part by contact with a new culture - is transformed by his or her new social environment and new social relationships. Implicit in cross-cultural research on the self is the assumption that people develop different identities during the process of acculturation and therefore respond in different way to various social influences. If we assume that a person's identity or self is shaped by his or her social environment (Markus & Kitayama, 1991), we have to focus on the ways social relationships, values, and norms vary across cultures.

Different conceptions of self or identity have been advanced in cross-cultural psychology. Perhaps the most prominent dimensions dealing with cultural variations are (a) individualism versus collectivism (Triandis, 1994), and (b) independent versus interdependent self (Markus & Kitayama, 1991). In both conceptualizations, the self is viewed as being strongly influenced by cultural norms and values. Reciprocally, social relationships are influenced and maintained by an individual's definition of self. For instance, a person who defines his or her identity in terms of close social relationships, such as family or local community, will most likely conform to their influences. Conversely, the behavior of a person who feels free from tight social control will be less influenced by the social values and norms of her or his immediate social environment (Bierbrauer, 1994). In collectivistically oriented cultures, such as those of Asia, Africa and Latin America, identity is defined more in relation to others, whereas in individualistically oriented cultures, such as many of those of North America and Western Europe, identity is construed as relatively independent from others (Triandis, 1994).

Because today's international migration can be characterized by a movement of people from mostly collectivistically oriented cultures to individualistically oriented cultures, a number of additional cultural features vary along with the prior distinction. Whereas the distinction between ingroups and outgroups is relatively unimportant in individualistically oriented cultures, in which values such as autonomy, achievement orientation, and self-sufficiency are of great importance, collectivistically oriented cultures are characterized by behavior toward ingroup members differing at times markedly from behavior toward outgroup members (Triandis, 1994). Further, the general orientation toward social relatedness, such as group harmony and solidarity, is emphasized more in collectivistically oriented cultures (Leung, 1987; Triandis, 1994).

As a result of cultural contact, social influences that are involved in the acculturation process transform an individual so that his or her cultural features are no longer identical to those existing prior to the first contact. Theoretically and empirically speaking, this process of change due to social influence is not well understood. Moreover, there is a lack of longitudinal research that focuses on the antecedent factors that impact acculturation attitudes and consequent behaviors.

It seems, however, that Ajzen and Fishbein's (1980) theory of reasoned action and Ajzen's (1989) theory of planned behavior may be helpful in explaining the dynamics of structural influences involved in the process of acculturation. Both theories assume that a person's behavior can be predicted from behavioral intentions. Intentions are assumed to capture the motivational factors that impact a behavior and to be indicative of how hard people are willing to try or how much effort they are planning to exert. For instance, if immigrants say they want to become part of the new society, then they are more likely to assimilate than those who do not intend to do so.

Within the framework of the theory of planned behavior, three conceptually distinct factors determine intentions. The first is the person's attitude toward the behavior, which refers to the degree to which the person has a positive or negative evaluation of the behavior in question ("Is it good for me to become like a German?"). The second predictor is termed a *social norm* and refers to the perceived social pressure to perform the behavior ("What will the others in my family think if I adopt a German lifestyle?"). The third antecedent is the degree of perceived behavioral control and refers to the extent to which a person believes it is easy or difficult to perform the behavior in question ("It will be rather difficult for me to speak German fluently"). According to Ajzen (1989), the belief in behavioral control reflects past experiences as well as anticipated obstacles.

The theory further explicates the antecedents of attitudes, subjective norms, and perceived behavioral control. It is posited that the antecedents are

FIG. 10.1. Antecedents of acculturation preferences from a social influence perspective: An application of the theory of planned behavior (adapted from Ajzen, 1989).

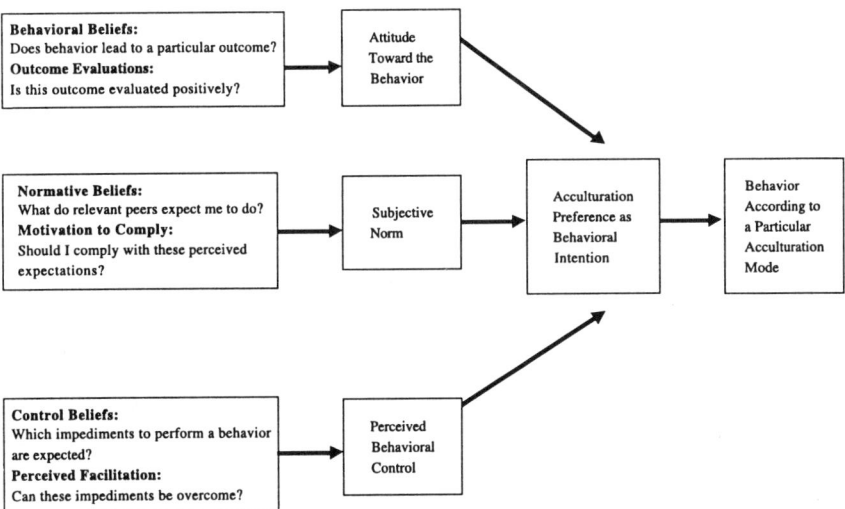

a function of salient interpersonal influence factors originating from beliefs that are relevant for the behavior in question. Three kinds of corresponding beliefs are postulated: (a) behavioral beliefs, which are assumed to influence attitudes toward behavior; (b) normative beliefs, which are the underlying determinants of subjective norms; and (c) control beliefs, which refer to perceptions of behavioral control. An estimate of the strength or weight of each belief component can be calculated using the expectancy-value model. For instance, an estimate of attitude strength is obtained by multiplying belief strength with outcome evaluation. Normative beliefs are related to the likelihood that important referent individuals or groups approve or disapprove of the behavior in question; their strength is obtained by multiplying the person's motivation to comply by the referent in question. They reflect social influences from both individuals and groups of ingroup members and members of host society. Finally, perceived control beliefs refer to the resources and opportunities that persons think they possess. The fewer obstacles they anticipate, the greater should be their perceived control over behavior. InTo obtain the weight of this component, each control belief is multiplied by the perceived facilitating or inhibiting effect of the resource opportunity in question (see Fig. 10.1).

This model can be applied to cross-cultural research because it allows a specification of the weights associated with each factor or component and their separate influence on acculturation preferences and eventually on corresponding behaviors. Specifically, the model can be employed to predict which interpersonal factors are most influential in determining acculturation preferences across social domains. With respect to conflict handling, for instance, the attitudinal factor may be a function of (a) the range of outcomes associated with particular acculturation mode conflict styles in different conflict contexts, (b) the role a particular conflict behavior plays and the expected degree of success in reaching these outcomes, and (c) the evaluations of these outcomes. The normative factor may be influenced across conflict contexts by (a) the type of relevant reference groups, (b) the normative expectations of the respective reference groups held by the immigrant concerning his or her behavior, and (c) the motivation to comply with these expectations in a specific situation. Finally, an immigrant may expect various impediments concerning the behavior in question across a variety of conflict domains, and she or he may also generate different expectations as to whether these obstacles can be overcome.

Hitherto this model has not been employed to predict acculturation preferences. Based on the prior reasoning, two examples could perhaps illustrate the explanatory and predictive power of the model of planned behavior within the context of a social influence perspective. Consider an immigrant whose cultural background can be characterized as collectivistically oriented being involved in a conflict with either a German or an ingroup member. If the immigrant is engaged in a dispute with a member of his or her ingroup, he or she may face a strong normative pressure from his or her peers to handle the conflict in a nonconfrontational way, with perhaps a mediator involved. In a study with Turkish and German respondents, Bierbrauer (1994) observed that the collectivistically oriented respondents favored informal modes of conflict regulations, whereas the individualistically oriented German respondents preferred courtlike formal procedures. Moreover, collectivistically oriented respondents tend to conform to traditional norms and authorities to a significantly higher degree than the German respondents. Therefore, we can conclude that the Turkish immigrant will most likely handle the dispute in a separation type mode.

However, a Turkish immigrant is engaged in a conflict with a German, for example, on business-type issues, she or he may resort to an assimilation or perhaps integration type mode of dispute regulation because there may be less pressure from her or his peers to handle the conflict according to Turkish values and because it seems unlikely that a German would agree to handle the conflict informally (Bierbrauer, 1994).

The model of planned behavior not only permits study of how different culture groups respond to various sources of social influence, but it may also be employed in longitudinal research to observe how acculturating individuals respond to changes over time. For instance, in a study involving Korean students, Bierbrauer et al. (1994) observed that their attitudes toward the practices and norms of their heritage culture became less positive the longer they stayed in Germany.

DISCUSSION AND PRACTICAL IMPLICATIONS

An acculturation approach has been suggested here to study the conflict regulation patterns of immigrant Turks living in Germany. Overall, the data indicate that the process of acculturation is uneven and does not influence conflict regulation preferences in a uniform manner. Structural and interpersonal influences intervene and determine the type of conflict regulation mode. Nevertheless, almost half the conflicts were handled in the integration type mode—that is, Turks acculturating in Germany used a combination of heritage culture and dominant culture elements to regulate disputes irrespective of conflict resource or social relationship with the opponent. For a sizable proportion of conflicts, however, conflict resource and opponent seem to matter. If there are conflicts over tangible resources, it is likely that they are handled in the German (assimilation) way. For conflicts over intangible resources, however, Turks also resort to the traditional Turkish (separation) way of regulating conflicts. This suggests that intangible or symbolic conflicts, such as family disputes, are likely to be handled in the traditional way because these types of conflicts are perhaps more directly linked to their cultural identity. Similarly, a significant proportion of conflicts with fellow Turks are regulated according to the separation mode.

Taken together, there is no need for alarm in the sense that acculturating Turks in Germany fail to adjust to their host society. The majority seem to possess sufficient skills and are flexible enough to respond adequately to the demands of their host society. However, there may be some concern when conflicts over intangible or symbolic resources or conflicts with other Turks are at stake. In these cases, acculturating Turks may resort to a separation mode style of conflict behavior, which may give rise to misgivings in their host culture.

The fact that general attitudes toward acculturation preferences do not reflect corresponding behavior and conflict regulation preferences raises some doubts about the assumption of the unidirectional nature of acculturation processes. As an alternative, a social influence approach has been suggested that takes into account a host of contextual conditions that may influence an individual's attitude and behavior. A social influence perspective based on the theory of planned behavior has been suggested that provides a structure of possible antecedents that impact the acculturation process. Because the model allows a distinction between motivational and social antecedent factors, it may be of considerable diagnostic relevance for both cross-sectional and longitudinal studies.

The findings of this study may have practical implications as well. Knowledge of conflict regulation preferences of immigrants may have great relevance for social and policy planning in ethnoplural societies. Interpersonal disputes among immigrants and conflicts between them and the dominant society may threaten the whole social fabric. To reduce their mutual discomfort, members of both the dominant society and the immigrant groups may find it useful to know the particular ways each group traditionally handles its disputes. Under such circumstances, profound knowledge and skills for the management of intercultural conflicts become increasingly important. Moreover, institutions such as the administrative and legal systems should be more flexible to more adequately respond to different patterns of conflicts prevalent in ethnoplural societies. Perhaps immigrant countries like Germany should establish conflict resolution forums outside the legal arena that enable immigrants to regulate their disputes in agreement with conflict management procedures they prefer and according to the law in force, of course. As we gain more insight into the importance of various normative influence factors on the behavior of acculturating groups, we will be able to better understand the theoretical implications and practical consequences that influence the attitudes and conflict behaviors of acculturating groups.

ACKNOWLEDGMENTS

This research was supported by a grant provided by the Projektverbund Friedens und Konfliktforschung in Niedersachsen. We are grateful to the editors of this volume and to Jostein Rise for their feedback on an earlier version of this article.

REFERENCES

Ajzen, I. (1989). Attitude structure and behavior. In A. R. Pratkanis, S. J. Breckler, & A. G. Greenwald (Eds.), *Attitude structure and function* (pp. 241–274). Hillsdale, NJ: Lawrence Erlbaum Associates.

Ajzen, I., & Fishbein, M. (1980). *Understanding attitudes and predicting social behavior.* Englewood Cliffs, NJ: Prentice-Hall.

Augsburger, D. W. (1992). *Conflict mediation across cultures.* Louisville: Westminster/John Knox.

Berry, J. W. (1990). Psychology of acculturation. Understanding individuals moving between cultures. In R. W. Brislin (Ed.), *Applied cross-cultural psychology* (pp. 232–253). Newbury Park: Sage.

Berry, J. W., Kim, U., Power, S., Young, M., & Bujaki, M. (1989). Acculturation attitudes in plural societies. *Applied Psychology: An International Review, 38,* 185–206.

Bierbrauer, G. (1994). Toward an understanding of legal culture: Variations in individualism and collectivism between Kurds, Lebanese, and Germans. *Law & Society Review, 28,* 243–264.

Bierbrauer, G., & Pedersen, P. (1996). Culture and migration. In G. R. Semin & K. Fiedler (Eds.), *Applied social psychology* (pp. 399–422). London: Sage.

Deutsch, M. (1973). *The resolution of conflict. Constructive and destructive processes.* New Haven, CT: Yale University Press.

Felstiner, W. L. F. (1974). Influences of social organizations on dispute processing. *Law & Society Review, 9,* 63–94.

Gans, H. (1979). Symbolic ethnicity: The future of ethnic groups and culture in America. *Ethnic and Racial Studies, 2,* 1–20.

Gluckman, M. (1969). *Ideas and procedures in African customary law.* London: Oxford University Press for the International African Institute.

Gordon, M. M. (1964). *Assimilation in American life.* New York: Oxford University Press.

Graves, T.–D. (1967). Acculturation in a tri-ethnic community. *Journal of Anthropology, 23,* 337–350.

Graziano, W. G., Jensen-Campbell, L. A., & Hair, E. C. (1996). Perceiving interpersonal conflict and reacting to it: The case for agreeableness. *Journal of Personality and Social Psychology, 70,* 820–835.

Hamilton V. L., & Sanders, J. (1988). Punishment and the individual in the United States and Japan. *Law & Society Review, 22,* 301–328.

Hazuda, H. P., Stern, M. P., & Haffner, S. M. (1988). Acculturation and assimilation among Mexican Americans: Scales and population-based data. *Social Science Quarterly, 69,* 687–706.

Heckmann, F. (1992). *Ethnische Minderheiten, Volk und Nation* [Ethnic minorities, people, and nation]. Stuttgart: Enke.

Herskovitz, M. J. (1938). *Acculturation. The study of culture contact.* New York: Augustin.

Jamin, M. (1998). Die deutsche Anwerbung: Organisation und Größenordnung [The German labor recruitment: Organization and numbers]. In A. Eryilmaz & M. Jamin (Eds.), *Fremde Heimat. Eine Geschichte der Einwanderung aus der Türkei* (pp. 149–170). Essen: Klartext-Verlag.

Kim, U. (1994). Individualism and collectivism: Conceptual clarification and elaboration. In U. Kim, H. C. Triandis, C. Kagitcibasi, S. C. Choi, & G. Yoon (Eds.), *Individualism and collectivism. Theory, method, and applications* (pp. 19–51). Thousand Oaks, CA: Sage.

Laroche, M., Kim, C., & Hui, M. K. (1997). A comparative investigation of dimensional structures of acculturation for Italian Canadians and Greek Canadians. *Journal of Social Psychology, 137,* 317–331.

Leung, K. (1987). Some determinants of reactions to procedural models for conflict resolution: A cross-national study. *Journal of Personality and Social Psychology, 53,* 898–908.

Markus, H., & Kitayama, S. (1991). Culture and the self: Implications for cognition, emotion, and motivation. *Psychological Review, 98,* 224–253.

Martin, P. L. (1994). Germany: Reluctant land of immigration. In: W. A. Cornelius, P. L. Martin, & J. F. Hollifield (Eds.), *Controlling immigration: A global perspective* (pp. 189–227). Stanford: Stanford University Press.

Meis, N. (1993). *Aspekte struktureller und differenzieller Mobilität von Ausländern in der Bundesrepublik Deutschland* [Aspects of structural mobility of foreigners in the Federal Republic of Germany]. Wiesbaden: Bundesinstitut für Bevölkerungsforschung.

Mendoza, R. H. (1989). An empirical scale to measure type and degree of acculturation in Mexican-American adolescents and adults. *Journal of Cross-Cultural Psychology, 20*, 372–385.

Nader, L. (Ed.). (1969). *Law in culture and society.* Chicago: Aldine.

Nader, L., & Todd, H. F. (1978). *The disputing process. Law in ten societies.* New York: Columbia University Press.

Özcan, E. (1995). Die türkische Minderheit [The Turkish minority]. In C. Schmalz-Jacobsen & G. Hansen (Eds.), *Ethnische Minderheiten in der Bundesrepublik Deutschland. Ein Lexikon* (pp. 511 – 528). München: Verlag C.H. Beck.

Redfield, R., Linton, R., & Herskovitz, M. J. (1936). Memorandum on the study of acculturation. *American Psychologist, 38*, 149–152.

Rogler, L. H., Cortes, D. E., & Malgady, R. G. (1991). Acculturation and mental health status among Hispanics. *American Psychologist, 46*, 585–597.

Ross, L., & Ward, A. (1996). Naive realism in everyday life: Implications for social conflict and misunderstanding. In E. S. Reed, E. Turiel, & T. Brown (Eds.), *Values and knowledge* (pp. 103–135). Mahwah, NJ: Lawrence Erlbaum Associates.

Smith, P. B., & Bond, M. H. (1998). *Social psychology across culture* (2nd ed.). London: Prentice-Hall.

Starr, J. (1978). *Dispute and settlement in rural Turkey.* Leiden: E.J. Brill.

Statistisches Bundesamt (1998). *Statistisches Jahrbuch 1998.* Wiesbaden Statistisches Bundesamt.

Taylor, D. M. (1991). The social psychology of social and cultural diversity: Issues of assimilation and multiculturalism. In A. G. Reynolds (Ed.), *Bilingualism, multiculturalism, and second language learning* (pp. 1–19). Hillsdale, NJ: Lawrence Erlbaum Associates.

Ting-Toomey, S. (1985). Toward a theory of conflict and culture. In W. Gudykunst, L. Stewart, & S. Ting-Toomey (Eds.), *Communication, culture, and organizational processes* (pp. 71–86). Beverly Hills: Sage.

Ting-Toomey, S., Gao, G., Trubisky, P., Yang, Z., Kim, H. S., Lin, S.-L., & Nishida, T. (1991). Culture, face maintenance, and styles of handling interpersonal conflict: A study in five cultures. *The International Journal of Conflict Management, 2*, 275–296.

Triandis, H. C. (1994). *Culture and social behavior.* New York: McGraw-Hill.

United Nations. (1994). *International Migration Bulletin, 4*(1).

APPENDIX: SAMPLE SCENARIO USED IN THE STUDY

The Neighbor's Automobile

The German neighbor of the Yilmaz family claims that their kids have scratched his automobile. Mr. Yilmaz happens to know, however, that besides his own kids their were also the kids of German neighbors playing there and so it is not just his own children who are responsible for the scratches to the automobile. The German neighbor threatens to complain to the landlord, or even go to the police, if Mr. Yilmaz does not pay the repair costs for the automobile.

What do you think Mr. Yilmaz will do?

Have you ever experienced a similar situation?

YES ( )   NO ( )

2. If YES, what did you do in this situation?
   (please describe briefly)

3. If NO, how would you handle such a situation?
   (please describe briefly)

Socioeconomic Influences on Depression and Morbidity in the Hungarian Population in the Context of PostCommunist Modernization

Mária Kopp

Árpád Skrabski

Sándor Szedmák

Semmelweis University of Medicine

Budapest

ABSTRACT

Cross-cultural studies have shown that in developed countries socioeconomic conditions strongly influence the psychological and physical health of the public. In this study, depressive symptomatology and self-rated morbidity in the Hungarian population were analyzed from the perspective of structural influences represented by several socioeconomic factors that create social change. A significant polarization in psychosocial and physical health status was discovered, with extremely poor health and high depression scores among persons who could not successfully cope with their environment during the period of postcommunist transition. Hierarchical loglinear analysis showed that depressive symptom severity mediates between relative socioeconomic deprivation and higher morbidity rates. Depressive symptomatology is influenced by the hostility, attitude toward achievement, low perceived social support, and low perceived control in the workplace. A vicious circle might be hypothesized to exist between socially deprived conditions and depressive symptomatology, which together strongly impacted physical health. Prevention researchers and practitioners should take these findings into consideration when developing strategies to prevent and ameliorate problems in physical health.

CULTURE AND SOCIOECONOMIC INFLUENCES ON PHYSICAL AND MENTAL HEALTH

Perhaps the most important public health finding over the last decade has been that socioeconomic influences constitute a major health risk factor in the developed countries. When the mortality and morbidity figures are corrected for traditional risk factors like smoking, obesity, and lack of exercise, it has been shown that socioeconomic deprivation is a much greater risk factor (Marmot et al., 1987; Slater et al., 1985; Wiley & Comacho, 1986). Although at the individual level a person's attitudes and values toward his or her health are strongly determined by interpersonal and mass-mediated influences, at the population level the health status of the population is most closely related to the societal structure (their relative socioeconomic status within their society). For example, in Britain, the typical skilled or unskilled worker who did not attend college will die several years younger than a college graduate even if the laborer does not smoke or

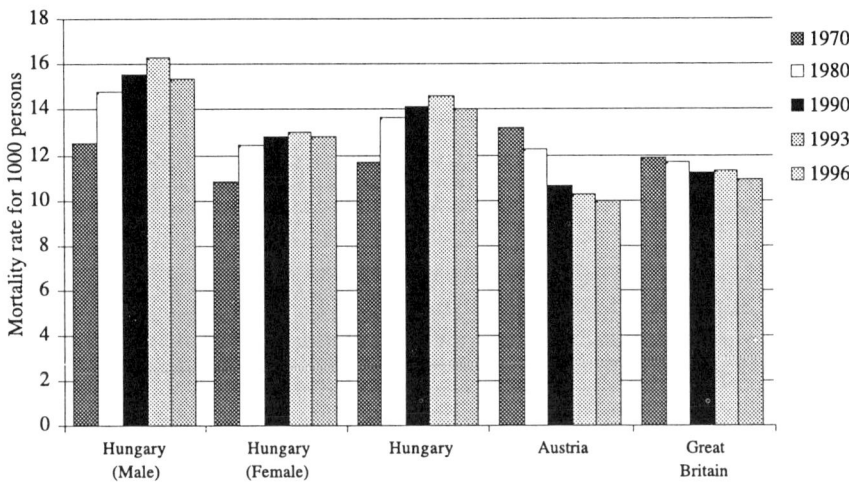

FIG. 11.1. Mortality rates per 1,000 persons between 1970 and 1996.

drink more than the graduate. This chapter examines the role of societal structure on physical health in Hungary as mediated by psychological influences.

Recent trends in the health status of residents in the Central-Eastern-European (CEE) countries are alarming. Up to the end of the 1970s, the mortality rates in the CEE countries, including Hungary, were more favorable than the British and Austrian adult mortality rates. However, whereas in Western Europe the life expectancy rose continuously in the following decades, in the CEE countries this tendency reversed. In particular, by 1990, the Hungarian adult mortality rate was the highest in Europe (Fig. 11.1). This deterioration cannot be ascribed to deficiencies in health care because during these same years there was a significant decrease in infant mortality rate, along with improvements in other dimensions of health care. Nor, through 1990, was this reversal due to a declining standard of living: Between 1970 and 1988, the Hungarian GDP rose by more than 200 %, and in 1988 the economic status of the lowest socioeconomic strata in Hungary was even better than in 1970.

Since 1970, social and economic polarization in Hungary and other CEE countries has gradually intensified. Whereas a large part of the population lived at approximately the same low economic level in 1970, by the end of the 1980s, a large portion of society had achieved a higher socioeconomic level, including owning one or more cars, private property, and receiving a substantially higher income. The mortality difference between manual laborers and nonmanual laborers, which was virtually nonexistent in the 1960s, significantly widened through the 1980s. The gap widened primarily because the mortality of manual laborers increased during this period, whereas the mortality of nonmanual laborers increased less steeply. Inequalities in mortality among women were also minimal in the 1960s and were exacerbated through the 1980s, although their inequalities were less extreme than those among men (Towsend et al., 1992). The purpose of our studies was to uncover the mechanisms that could explain the powerful influence of socioeconomic changes, produced by structural changes, on health in Hungary. Because modern societies often strive to provide their citizens with satisfactory nutrition, housing, and medical care, understanding how socioeconomic status (SES) serves as such an enormous risk factor for health is of vital importance.

Several cross-cultural studies were conducted to analyze the similarities and differences of socioeconomic influences on health among different nations. Marmot et al. (1987, 1989, 1991) showed that among British civil servants there was a strong negative relationship between and mortality rates and the incidence of cardiovascular diseases, angina, ECG-demonstrable ischaemia, and noninfectious respiratory diseases.

Whereas overall health conditions in developing countries are proportional to gross national income, in the technologically advanced (OECD) countries, the larger the income and wealth gaps within the nation, the higher the death rate (Wilkinson, 1994, 1996a, 1996b). Kaplan et al. (1996) compared the states in the United States along similar lines and found comparable findings. The higher the difference between rich and poor in a state, the higher the morbidity and mortality rates. In other words, it is not the absolute level of wealth that serves as the best indicator of a given population's health prospects, but economic differences within that population. For example, Kaplan et al. found the widest income gaps in Louisiana and Mississippi, where the death rates were 9.6 per 1000 people, and the narrowest in New Hampshire and Utah, where the death rates were 7.8 and 7.1, respectively. (In Hungary in 1995 the corresponding figure was 14.2.) Socioeconomic inequality within states is associated not only with worsened health conditions, but also with higher unemployment, higher murder and crime rates, a higher level of disability, a high rate of low birthweight babies, a low proportion of people with higher education, and low per capita funding for education.

In recent years, leading researchers in health psychology have increasingly attended to the mediation of relative deprivation by subjective factors, psychological and social influences, and cultural factors (Kaplan, 1995; Kawachi & Kennedy, 1997; Kawachi, Kennedy, Lochner, & Prothwow-Stith, 1997). Analysis of Japanese health indicators has shown that close societal relationships and high social cohesion are major health protection factors independent from low cholesterol levels, especially as they impact cardiovascular mortality (Marmot & Syme, 1976). Similar differences have been observed in other traditional cultures, such as the low coronary disease rates among Italians and Greeks, which can partially be explained by the experience of social cohesion and identity derived from the group (Keys, 1970).

The foregoing studies suggest that cultural and social identity, along with high social cohesion, are among the most important health protection factors in modern societies (Kawachi et al. 1997). It appears that in these societies, wealthier people are prepared to make sacrifices for the community, and the disadvantaged do not feel that they have been completely left to themselves in a hostile world. According to Fukuyama (1995), trust in each other, esteem for shared values, and acceptance and interiorization of cultural and social identity results in a high level of social cohesion in Japanese society, which is the foundation not only of health but of economic wealth and prosperity. Clearly the Japanese experience stems from cultural roots that are widely divergent from those of Europeans, but useful lessons could be gained from Italian or Greek cultures, which lie closer to the CEE countries.

Wilkinson (1996a, 1996b, 1996c) drew attention to the powerful negative influence of social disadvantage on health through a study of statistics of developed countries. He considered social cohesion to be the most important factor contributing to differences in health status among nations. For a lower level British civil servant, for example, it is not his relative poverty is the cause of his bad health: Even during German bombing in World War II, the death rates of Londoners greatly improved despite difficult living circumstances. The weakening of social cohesion is a significant factor in the emergence of large social differences and in the associated deterioration in health. Putnam, Leonardi, and Nanetti (1993) analyzed the efficiency of local government departments in Italy and arrived at findings similar to Wilkinson's: In provinces where there was a lower level of inequality, community life was stronger and all quality-of-life indicators were better.

PSYCHOSOCIAL INFLUENCES ON THE PHYSICAL AND MENTAL HEALTH STATUS OF THE HUNGARIAN POPULATION IN THE CONTEXT OF POST COMMUNIST MODERNIZATION

In Hungary in 1983, 1988, and 1994–1995, the current authors conducted national representative surveys to collect data on psychosocial influences on physical and mental health (Kopp, 1990; Kopp & Skrabski, 1996; Kopp, Skrabski, & Magyar, 1987; Kopp, Skrabski, & Szedmak, 1995, 1998a, 1998b; Skrabski & Kopp, 1989). We hypothesized that physical and mental health are strongly interrelated, and that psychosocial characteristics—such as depression, hostility, purposes in life, ways of coping, dysfunctional attitudes, and social support—are strongly influenced by socioeconomic factors. Our purpose, then, was to deepen earlier findings regarding the impact of social structure on health.

We interviewed 21,000 people in 1988 and 19,000 in 1994–1995 for approximately 1.5 to 2 hours in their homes. The sample was representative of the 16 years of age and older Hungarian population in terms of age, gender and place of residence (Kopp et al 1995, 1998a, 1998b). The 1988 questionnaire contained 107 items on SES and lifestyle, 148 questions on needs, and 209 questions on physical and mental health conditions and related background factors. The 1994 survey questionnaire was identical to the 1988 survey. Based on observations from the earlier survey administrations, new questions were added to the 1995 regarding new phenomena emerging from changes in society, such as unemployment. The variables analyzed for the present purposes were:

Independent Variables
- Socioeconomic characteristics: father's employment (manager to unskilled worker), employment status, level of education, personal income, housing situation (below standard to luxury), and access to car and property ownership (separate summer residence)

Mediating Variables
- Shortened Beck Depression Inventory (BDI; Beck & Beck 1972; Kopp et al., 1995, 1998a, 1998b)
- Self-Rated Morbidity (Kopp et al., 1995, 1998)

Corresponding to each of the 26 illness listed in the Yearbook of the Ministry of Welfare (1990), the authors added two questions: "Have you been treated for this disease at any time during your life? If yes, how many days were you sick because of the disease in the past year?" The total number of sick days in the preceding year for each individual was calculated by adding up the numbers of days due to individual diseases. (Idler & Benyamini, 1997)

- Self-Rated Disability Questionnaire (Kopp et al., 1998b; Skrabski & Kopp, 1989)
- Shortened Purpose in Life (PL) Questionnaire (Crumbaugh & Maholick, 1964; Kopp & Skrabski, 1996, Kopp et. al., 1998b)
- Shortened Dysfunctional Attitude Scale (DAS; Kopp & Skrabski, 1996, Kopp et al., 1998b; Weisman & Beck, 1979)
- Shortened Hostility Questionnaire (H; Barefoot, Dahlstrom, & Williams, 1983; Cook & Medley, 1954; Kawachi et al., 1997; Kopp & Skrabski, 1996, Kopp et al., 1998b)
- Shortened Ways of Coping questionnaire (C; Folkman & Lazarus, 1980; Kopp & Skrabski, 1996, Kopp et al., 1998b)
- Social Support Questionnaire (SS; Caldwell, Pearson & Chin 1987; Kopp & Skrabski, 1996, Kopp et al., 1998b)
- Shortened Vital Exhaustion Questionnaire (VE; Appels & Mulder, 1988; Kopp et al., 1998b)

Dependent Variable
- Number of sick days
- Self-rated morbidity

RESULTS

Structural Influences on Depressive Symptomatology

In 1988, 24.3% of the Hungarian 16 and older population complained of depressive symptoms. Mildly depressive symptoms were reported by 16.8% of the respondents, moderate depressive symptoms were reported by 4.6%, and 2.9% indicated symptoms of severe depression. In a span of 6 years, the prevalence of depressive symptoms, especially of severe depressive symptoms, grew substantially. In 1994–1995, 30.5% of respondents reported depressive symptoms: 17% were mild, 6.4% were moderate, and 7.1% were severe depressive symptoms.

Low level of education had become the main determining factor in the frequency and severity of depressive symptoms by 1995. In 1995, the percentage of those with less than 8 years of education who suffered from depressive symptomatology was 51.9%, and for 16.7% the symptoms were severe. Surprisingly, the group average of those with low educational level rose above the depression threshold (score above 10). Among college or university graduates, the corresponding numbers were 18.7% and 3.0%, respectively.

Log-linear regression analysis was used to examine the factors impacting depression, which was treated as a dependent measure for this analysis (although we believe it to be a mediating factor). The depressive syndrome can be regarded as mathematically identical to the lack of goals in life, which involves emptiness, boredom, and the loss of the ability to plan in the long term. Other factors contributing to depressive symptomatology were a hostile attitude and lack of trust (i.e., agreement with the statement that it is safest not to trust anybody and that people are generally dishonest and selfish and they only want to take advantage of others). According to Kawachi et al. (1997) and Kawachi and Kennedy (1997), the amount of trust in a society is the best measure of its social capital. In contemporary Hungary, the prevailing feeling of distrust is the result of negative trends at the level of social structure, and the most important remedial action would be to reverse the process of self-destruction.

A multidimensional scaling model was used to investigate the relationships among depressive symptoms, hostility, and dysfunctional attitudes. The data suggest that the depressive symptoms compose a cluster that also includes the hostility questionnaire's question regarding envy: "If I hear of the successes of a good friend, I feel as if I have suffered a failure." This response to this envy question appears to reflect a truly individualistic orientation because it emphasizes competitive striving (Triandis, 1995)—an orientation that fundamentally undermines Hungary's social cohesion. This signals a shift in values that follows the transition to a market-based economy and an undermining of social cohesion.

The cynicism items of Hostility, although related to depression, make up a separate cluster. Additionally, the dysfunctional traits of an extreme demand to be loved, an extreme demand for recognition, and an extreme demand for achievement also lie close to depression. Whenever these attitudes are held to an intensity out of proportion to opportunities and abilities, they are deleterious to mental health. Lack of perceived control or influence at work is also an important background factor for depressive symptomatology. Among social support variables, low perceived support from one's spouse, friends, and parents demonstrated the highest correlations with depressive symptomatology.

The most striking psychosocial changes between 1988 and 1995 manifested themselves in the extreme decrease in perceived control and influence at work and the enormous decrease in perceived social support. Consistent with this, perceived social support from coworkers decreased by almost 60%, and perceived support from friends, relatives, and parents also decreased considerably. It is noteworthy that there was no change in perceived support from spouses and children. Overall, however, there was marked movement toward individualism and a concomitant loosening of social bonds, resulting in a deterioration in mental health as evidenced by the increase in depression.

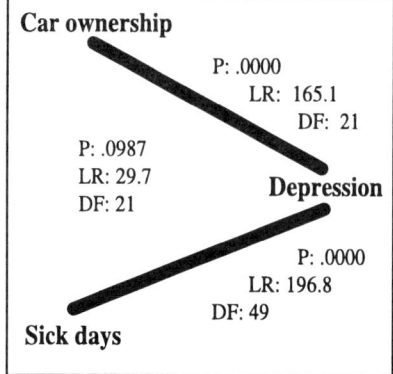

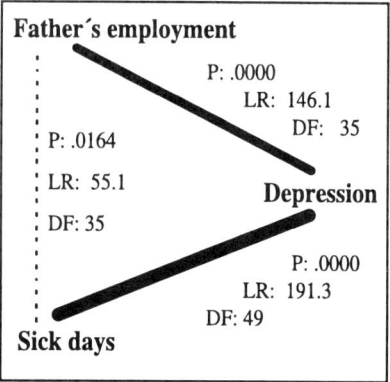

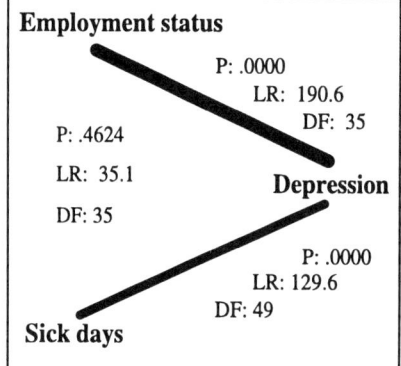

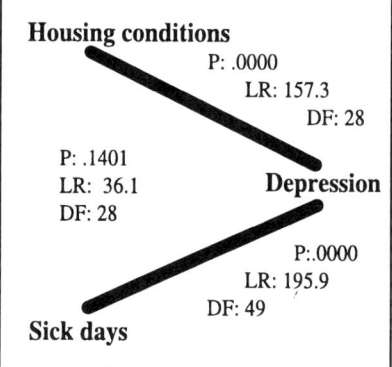

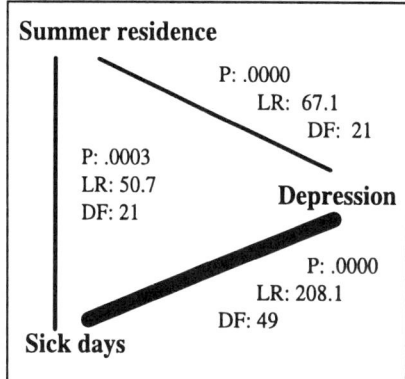

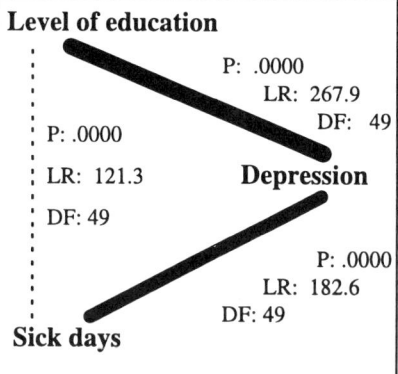

FIG. 11.2. Relationships among socioeconomic characteristics, sick days, and severity of depression for women, controlled by age, in 1995 in Hungary. ($n =$ 6,483).

(LR = likelihood ration, DF = degrees of freedom, P= probability. The thickness of the connecting lines is proportional to the strength of the direct relationship.)

Socioeconomic Influences on Self-Rated Morbidity

In addition to demonstrating the connection between socioeconomic change and depression, our data show that a worsened socioeconomic situation is also associated with higher morbidity rates. As mentioned earlier, morbidity rates were derived from self-reported sick days over the previous year. According to recent studies, self-rated health and morbidity estimates are reliable predictors of health risks, and differences in self-rated health are associated with differences in morbidity between Eastern and Western Europe (Bjorner et al., 1996; Carlson, 1998). According to a review of 27 community studies, self-rated health is an independent predictor of mortality (Idler & Benyamini, 1997).

Multivariate analysis demonstrated that it was not the relatively worse socioeconomic situation that produces higher morbidity rates, but only does so when it is mediated by depressive symptomatology. Therefore, it is not an objectively difficult SES itself that is the most significant health risk factor, but the subjective experience of relative disadvantage. If a person is economically disadvantaged and feels economically disadvantaged (e.g., thinks that he or she cannot properly provide for his or her family), then a deterioration of both mental and physical health is likely to result.

Figures 11.2 and 11.3 depict our log-linear analysis of our data regarding the mutual interactions among the socioeconomic situation, severity of depressive symptomatology and number of sick days in 1995 in the Hungarian population, separately for women and men. The data are corrected for age. The thickness of the connecting line is proportional to the strength of the direct relationship between two variables. In all cases, the relationship between a given socioeconomic factor and the number of sick days is far stronger when mediated by depression. Among women, these factors are, in order of the significance of the mediating role of depression: level of education, employment situation, car ownership, father's employment, and housing conditions (Fig. 11.2). Among men, the severity of depressive symptomatology is most closely connected with low employment status, but no access to a car is almost as important, followed by low level of education, father's employment, and housing conditions (Fig. 11.3).

Interestingly, among women of active age, the role of depression as a mediator between SES and number of sick days becomes much more significant from 1988 to 1995. Whereas in 1988 it was only the general family situation indicators that significantly influenced the depressive state of women (Kopp et al., 1995), by 1995 women's own employment and level of education had become much more important. Overall, these gender differences might explain the fact that the deterioration of health was more severe among men during the last decades.

DISCUSSION

Our data show that there is a strong relationship between socioeconomic disadvantage and physical health that is largely mediated by depressive symptomatology. A self-destructive cycle can be envisaged between the relatively worse socioeconomic situation and depressive symptomatology, which together have a major causal role underlying higher morbidity and mortality rates. It is not the poor socioeconomic situation itself, but rather the subjective evaluation of the relative disadvantage that is the most significant factor. As has been discussed, in the 1970s, when the gap between the rich and the poor was narrow, Hungarian health statistics were significantly better than those of other European countries. Amid rapid socioeconomic changes, those left at the lower tiers see this growing relative deprivation and regard their future as hopeless, experience a perceived, permanent loss of control, and feel helpless. These subjective factors are the main background variables in the development of depressive symptomatology, which has become increasingly common in Hungary in recent decades.

There are many possible explanations for the impact of depressive symptomatology on morbidity rates. First, depression affects perceived state of health and can lead to disability even without organic illness. Second, depression has a close relationship with self-destructive behaviors, such as smoking, alcohol consumption, and suicidal behavior.

Third, people suffering from long-term mood disorders such as depression are more vulnerable to various diseases and are less able to improve their social situation, so that they easily fall into a vicious cycle. In recent decades, depression, *vital exhaustion*, and hopelessness, have been identified as important and independent background factors for coronary disease (Appels, 1983; Everson et al., 1996; Falger & Appels, 1982; Frasure-Smith, Lesperance, (Talajic, 1995; Kopp et al., 1998b; Pratt et al., 1996). Learned helplessness (Seligman, 1975) is widely regarded as a useful model for understanding factors underlying depression. In addition, it is associated with decreased immunological activity, accelerated tumor growth (Sklar & Anisman, 1979), and vulnerability to various infections, each of which open the avenues for death.

PRACTICAL IMPLICATIONS

The major (and obvious) practical implication that may be drawn from our research is the need to intervene at the level of depression and its antecedents to positively impact morbidity and mortality. Attempting to alter the increasing socioeconomic stratification requires political decisions and long-lasting economic change. Health-promoting actions must target the psychological

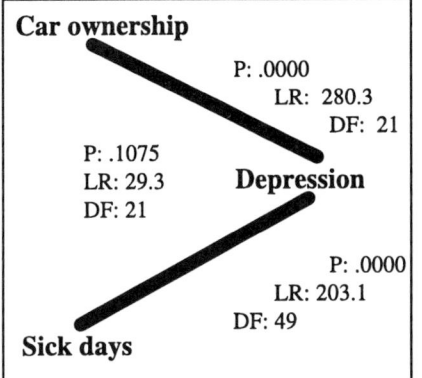

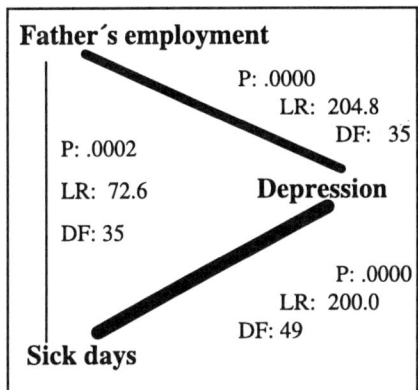

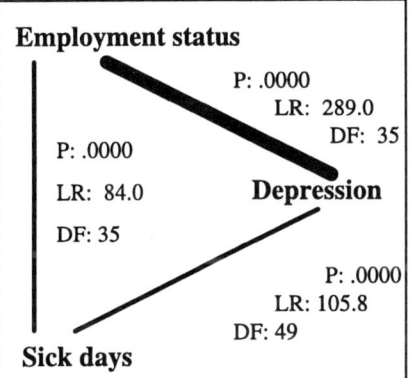

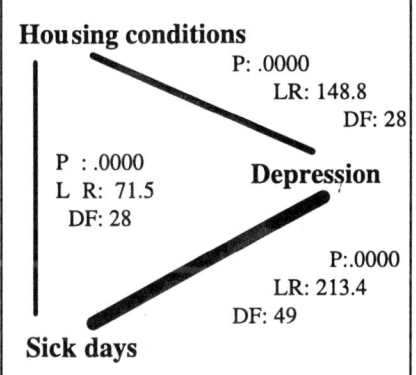

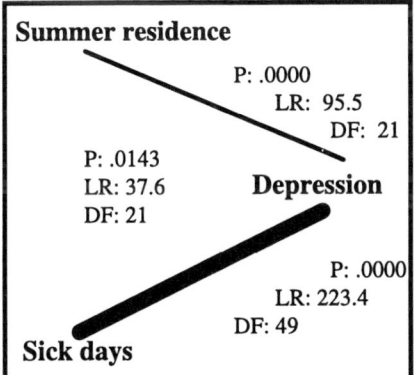

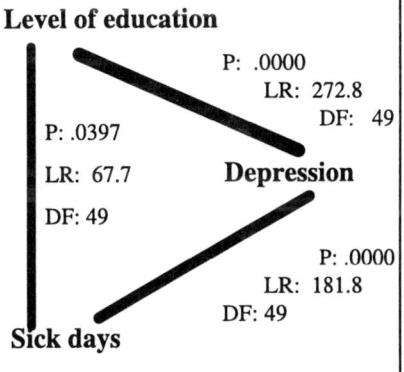

FIG. 11.3. Relationships among socioeconomic characteristics, sick days, and severity of depression for men, controlled by age, in 1995 in Hungary ($n = 5450$). (LR = likelihood ration, DF = degrees of freedom, P= probability. The thickness of the connecting lines is proportional to the strength of the direct relationship.)

consequences of this stratification. There are several courses of action that, if successful in preventing or ameliorating depression, can lead to improvements in the physical well-being of the Hungarian population.

First, increase awareness in the medical, psychological, and psychiatric communities of the connections between psychological and physical health. Although these connections may be widely accepted in the United States and Western Europe, they are not as well known in the eastern nations. Second, mobilize resources to minimize the antecedents to depression that have resulted from the socioeconomic disruptions caused by the large-scale structural changes in Hungary in recent years, such as perceived loss of control, feelings of helplessness, and loss of social support. These interventions could, it seems, occur at both the micro- or community level and the macro- or societal level through specific programs and policies to encourage and support these programs.

ACKNOWLEDGMENTS

This study was supported by the OTKA T-016486 and T-013423 research grants of the National Research Fund and by UNDP/HUN/97/003/A/01/99.

REFERENCES

Appels, A. (1983). The year before myocardial infarction. In   T. M. H. Dembroski, Smidt, (G. Blumchen, (Eds.), *Biobehavioural bases of coronary heart disease* (pp. 135–146). Karger; Basel.

Appels, A., & Mulder, P. (1988). Excess fatigue as a precursor of myocardial infarction. *European Heart Journal, 9*, 758–764.

Barefoot, J. C., Dahlstrom, W. G., Williams, R. B. (1983). Hostility, CHD incidence, and total mortality: A 25-year follow-up study of 255 physicians. *Psychosomatic Medicine, 45*, 59–63.

Beck, A. T., (Beck, R. W. (1972). Shortened Version of BDI. *Postgraduate Medicine, 52*, 81–85.

Bjorner, J. B., Kristensen, T. S., Orth-Gomer, K., Tibblin G., Sullivan, M., (Westerholm, P. (1996). *Self-rated health as a useful concept in research, prevention and clinical medicine.* Stockholm: Swedish Council for Planning and Coordination of Research.

Caldwell, R. A., Pearson, J. L., Chin, R. J. (1987). Stress moderating effects: Social support in the context of gender and locus of control. *Personality and Social Psychology Bulletin, 13*, 5–17.

Carlson, P. (1998). Self-perceived health in East and West Europe: Another European health divide. *Social Sciences and Medicine, 46*, 1355–1366.

Cook, W., (Medley, D. (1954). Proposed hostility and pharisaic- virtue scales for MMPI. *Journal of Applied Psychology, 38,* 414–418.

Crumbaugh, J. C., (Maholick, L. T. (1964). An experimental study in existentialism: The psychosomatic approach to Frankl's concept of noogenic neurosis. *Journal of Clinical Psychology, 20,* 200–207.

Everson, S. A., Goldberg, D. E., Kaplan, G. A., Cohen, R. D., Pukkala, E., Tuomilehto, J., (Salonen, J. T. (1996). Hopelessness and Risk of Mortality and Incidence of Myocardial Infarction and Cancer. *Psychosomatic Medicine, 58,* 113–121.

Falger, P., (Appels, A. (1982). Psychological risk factors over the life course of myocardial infarction patients. *Advances in Cardiology, 29,* 132–139.

Folkman, S., (Lazarus, R. S. (1980). An analysis of coping in a middle-aged community sample. *Journal of Health and Social Behavior, 21,* 219–239.

Frasure-Smith, N., Lesperance, F., (Talajic, M. (1995). Depression and 18 month prognosis after myocardial infarction. *Circulation, 91,* 999–1005.

Fukuyama, F. (1995). *Trust, the social virtues and the creation of prosperity.* New York: The Free Press.

Idler, E. L., (Benyamini Y. (1997). Self-rated health and mortality: A review of twenty-seven community studies. *Journal of Health and Social Behavior, 38,* 21–37.

Kaplan, G. A. (1995). Where do shared pathways lead? *Psychosomatic Medicine, 57,* 208–212.

Kaplan, G. A., Pamuk, E. R., Lynch, J. W., Cohen, R. D., (Balfour, J. L. (1996). Inequality in income and mortality in the United States: Analysis of mortality and potential pathways. *British Medical Journal, 312,* 999–1003.

Kawachi, I., (Kennedy, B. P. (1997). Health and social cohesion: Why care about income inequality. *British Medical Journal, 314,* 1037–1040.

Kawachi, I., Kennedy, B. P., Lochner, K., (Prothwow-Stith, D. (1997). Social capital, income inequality, and mortality. *American Journal of Public Health, 87,* (9) 1491–1498.

Keys, A. (1970). Coronary heart disease in seven countries. *Circulation, 41,* 42 (Suppl. 1).

Kopp, M. (1990). Anxiety, freedom and democracy. *Behavioural Psychotherapy, 18,* 193–206.

Kopp, M., Skrabski, Á. (1989). What does the legacy of Hans Selye and Franz Alexander mean today? (The psychophysiological approach in medical practice). *International Journal of Psychophysiology, 8,* 99–105.

Kopp, M. S., Skrabski, Á. (1996). Behavioural sciences applied to a changing society. Budapest: Biblioteca Septem Artium Liberalium.

Kopp, M. S., Skrabski, Á., Magyar, I. (1987). Neurotics at risk and suicidal behaviour in the Hungarian population. *Acta Psychiatrica Scandinavica, 76,* 406–413.

Kopp, M., Skrabski, Á., Szedmák, S. (1995). Socioeconomic factors, severity of depressive symptomatology, and sickness absence rate in the Hungarian population. *Journal of Psychosomatic Research, 39*, 1019–1029.

Kopp, M. S., Skrabski, Á., Szedmák, S. (1998a). Socioeconomic differences and psychosocial aspects of stress in a changing society. *Annals of the New York Academy of Science, 851*, 538–543.

Kopp, M. S., Skrabski, Á., Szedmák, S. (1998b). Depressive symptomatology and vital exhaustion are differentially related to behavioural risk factors for coronary artery disease. *Psychosomatic Medicine, 60*, 752–758.

Marmot, M. G., Smith, G. D. (1989). Why are the Japanese living longer? *British Medical Journal, 299*, 1547–1551.

Marmot, M. G., Kogevinas, M., Elston, M. A. (1987). Social/ economic status and disease. *Annual Review of Public Health, 8*, 111–135.

Marmot, M. G., Syme S. L. (1976). Acculturation and coronary heart disease in Japanese-Americans. *American Journal of Epidemiology, 104*, 225–247.

Marmot, M. G., White, I., Brunner, E., Feeney, A. (1991). Health inequalities among British servants: The Whitehall II study. *Lancet, 337*, 1387–1393.

Pratt, L. A., Ford, D. E., Crum, R. M., Armenian, H. K., Gallo, J. J., (Eaton, W. W. (1996). Depression, psychotropic medication and risk of myocardial infarction: Prospective data from the Baltimore ECA follow-up. *Circulation, 94*, 3123–3129.

Putnam, R. D., Leonardi, R., (Nanetti, R. Y. (1993). *Making democracy work: Civic traditions in modern Italy*. Princeton, NJ: Princeton University Press.

Seligman, M. E. P. (1975). *Helplessness: On depression, development, and death. San Francisco: Freeman.*

Sklar, L., Anisman, H. (1979). Stress and coping factors influence tumour growth. *Science, 205*, 513–515.

Skrabski, Á., Kopp, M. S. (1989). Needs, decrease of ability to work and disorders of *social adaptation. Research Review of Hungarian Social Sciences*, 71–88.

Skrabski, Á. (Ed.). (1990). *Yearbook of ministry of welfare*. Budapest: Hungarian Ministry of Welfare.

Slater, C. H., Lorimer, R. J., Larison, D. R. (1985). The independent contribution of socioeconomic status and health practices to health status. *Preventive Medicine, 14*, 372–373.

Statistical Yearbook. (1996). Central Statistical Office, Budapest.

Towsend, P., Davidson, N., (Whitehead, M. (Eds.). (1992). Inequalities in health: The Black Report. London: Penguin.

Triandis, H. C. (1995). *Individualism and collectivism.* Boulder, CO: Westview.

Weisman, A. N., (Beck, A. T. (1979). *The dysfunctional attitude scale.* Unpublished master's thesis, University of Pennsylvania, Philadelphia.

Wiley, J. A., Comacho, T. C. (1986). Life-style and future health: Evidence from the Alameda County study. *Preventive Medicine 9*,1–21.

Wilkinson, R. G. (1994). The epidemiological transition: From material scarcity to social disadvantage? *Daedalus, 123*(4), 61–77.

Wilkinson, R. G. (1996a). Income distribution and life expectancy. *British Medical, 304*(18), 165–168.

Wilkinson, R. G. (1996b). How can secular improvements in life expectancy be explained? In D. Blane, E. Brunner, & R. G. Wilkinson (Eds.), *Health and social organization* (pp. 109–124). New York: Routledge.

Wilkinson, R. G. (1996c). Health and civic society in Eastern Europe before 1989. In C. Hertzman (Ed.), *Environmental and non-environmental determinants of the east—west life expectancy gap* (pp. 51–66). Amsterdam: Kluwer.

Mass-Mediated Influences on Patterns of Consumption in Polish Youth

Malgorzata Górnik-Durose

University of Silesia

ABSTRACT

The instrumental and symbolic meanings of personal possessions for Polish teenagers were examined. Similarly to teenagers in Western countries, Polish teens' consumption preferences were largely derivative of the utilitarian, hedonistic, self-expressive, and status-related aspects of available goods. The interpersonal and mass-mediated social influences that shape these preferences were also examined. Mass-mediated influences turned out to play an especially important role, decreasing the impact of the personal opinions of significant others. Three of Cialdini's (1993) six principles of social influence were particularly important: commitment/consistency, attractiveness/liking, and authority. The results are discussed in terms of the overwhelming power of the mass media and advertising in creating the cultural meaning system for material goods and in engendering adolescents' perceptions of themselves and their social environments.

PATTERNS OF CONSUMPTION IN THE CONTEXT OF THE MEANING OF MATERIAL POSSESSIONS

When asked why they want to possess various material goods, people typically answer that they need or like them. The *need*, in this context, means that people perceive material things as tools enabling them to actualize their goals and make their everyday activities easier. In this way, people emphasize the utilitarian aspect of possessions. The second explanation often provided—that people simply like their possessions—reflects the hedonistic value of commodities. In both cases, people see these things in terms of their instrumental function. However, most people tend to neglect the symbolic meanings of things, which situate their owners inside a multifarious network of interpersonal relations.

There is a generally accepted distinction between the instrumental and symbolic functions of possessions (Csikszentmihalyi & Rochberg-Halton, 1981; Dittmar, 1992; Kilbourne, 1991; Prentice, 1987). Things in their instrumental function are used to affect and control the external world and serve as special tools for self-enrichment and self-actualization. As Kilbourne (1991) noted, to fulfill their instrumental role, things have to provide functional satisfaction as determined by the cultural standard. This means that culture, influenced by its level of technological development, defines the minimal comfort and convenience provided by commodities that are acceptable.

When the domain of product definition extends beyond use value, the symbolic function of material possessions becomes evident. Csikszentmihalyi and Rochberg-Halton (1981) stressed the fact that material possessions play a significant role in the process of the creation and expression of individual identity, on the one hand, and the social self, on the other. Thus, people use things to express the uniqueness of their personality, preferences, and values (Dittmar, 1992). Furthermore, material possessions allow people to extend their selves beyond the boundaries of their bodies (Belk, 1988) and even, in the case where acquired wealth is an expression of a desire for *secular immortality* (Hirschman, 1990), beyond their individual lifetimes. Material things reflect an individual's personal history and achievements as well as his or her significant relationships with other people (Csikszentmihalyi & Rochberg-Halton, 1981; Kamptner, 1995). Possessions also play an important role in solving deprivation problems because they serve a compensatory function: They may satisfy the desire for control (Beggan, 1991) and may facilitate the self-completion process (Wicklund & Gollwitzer, 1982).

As Dittmar (1992) argued, certain kinds of material possessions act as particular markers of gender, social class, and/or status, whereas other kinds connote political and/or religious affiliation, profession, or a stage in the lifecycle. Bell, Holbrook, and Solomon (1991) described this function in terms of extrinsic motivation (i.e., in which possessing certain things serves as means for other ends, such as making a desired impression on others).

The fulfillment of symbolic functions by commodities is possible only if people use and understand the specific code or language of material goods (Leiss, Kline, & Jhally, 1990; McCracken, 1986). This unwritten code enables nonverbal communication about one's individual and social characteristics with others via one's possessions. According to the social constructionist perspective, this code is part of a system of rules, beliefs, and understandings shared with other people within a cultural context, which have been transmitted, transformed, and reproduced inside a certain social structure in a reciprocal and circular process (Gergen, 1985). As McCracken (1986) claimed, mass media and advertising are powerful forces that create and transform these rules and standards as they relate to the possession and usage of material things. Media not only influence people to obtain certain products, but also provide a sufficient explanation why—from cultural point of view—possessing these products is *necessary*.

People's possessions, their income, and individual ways of resource management, including earning, saving, and spending money, create specific patterns of consumption. At the psychological level of consumer behavior, patterns of consumption emerge from particular understandings of the meaning of personal possessions by consumers and their ability to take part in the communication process within society using goods as communicators of personal qualities and social position.

PATTERNS OF CONSUMPTION AMONG POLISH TEENAGERS

Although a number of studies have examined the meaning of possessions and patterns of consumption among American (Csikszentmihalyi & Rochberg-Halton, 1981; Kamptner, 1995) and British (Dittmar, 1992; Lunt & Livingstone, 1992) consumers, little research has dealt with non-western cultures. One notable exception is research by Wallendorf and Arnould (1988), which studied the possessions of rural Africans. The possessions listed by these African women as important tended to be connected with marriage and domestic activities, whereas religious and magical items as well as tools and livestock were reported as important to men. The functional and personal meanings of goods dominant in Western cultures were replaced by the magical, spiritual, and aesthetic values of goods, convertibility to cash, and prestige in the African sample.

The present research concentrated on the meaning of material goods and patterns of consumption among young people in Poland—a culture whose members have been recently experiencing a rapid socioeconomic transition toward a market economy and Western consumer patterns. This transformation has exposed these youths to at least partially discordant social values and lifestyles. Although a strong tendency seems to exist among Poles to conform to Western values and the Western lifestyle, the contrasting influences of a completely different historical experience and ethical background, formed by Catholicism rather than Protestantism and relatively lengthy exposure to socialistic norms and values, persist (Dolinski, 1995). These complex facts determining the character of the Polish nation equally impact adults and the young population whose conscious participation in social life began after 1989, when the political and economic transformation was initiated. Their expectations and understandings of the value and meaning of material possessions have been formed within the context of an unstable, developing, and mutating social reference system. Both the mass media and advertising play significant roles in the instability and evolution of this reference system. The latter is, in fact, a relatively new phenomenon for the Polish population.

The primary purpose of the present study followed directly from Csikszentmihalyi and Rochberg-Halton's (1981) inquiry about the special meaning and importance things have for people: What material possessions are considered to be valuable for young Polish adults? No a priori hypotheses were formed, because this was largely an exploratory study.

The subjects in this study were 240 (120 female, 120 male) 18 year-old students from vocational ($n = 120$) and high ($n = 120$) schools in two different regions of Poland. One region was a large industrial urban area in Silesia ($n = 120$), the other was an agricultural, economically underdeveloped area in the central part of Poland ($n = 120$).

More than 40% of the things reported as important by these subjects were clothing and accessories, often with worldwide recognized and expensive brand labels. These types of things constituted 57.2% of the things listed by females. Males also listed such items as trendy jackets, trousers, and shoes (constituting 17% of the possessions they valued).

The next most important items in the ranking were electronic equipment (stereo, TV, video, etc.) and photo cameras (about 18% of the goods listed by all subjects). Subjects from all subgroups almost equally often reported these goods as having personal meaning and value for them. Cars and motorbikes appeared to be important for young males from all groups, if relatively less so for boys from the high school in the village (7.6%) in comparison with males from vocational school in the city (33.3%) and in the village (17.8%). The latter described their bicycle as particularly valuable.

Young men from high schools in both the city and the village considered their sports equipment (skis, skateboards, climbing equipment, fishing tackle, etc.) and computers to be important (76.2% for sports equipment and 61.9% for computers). Young people from the village high school possessed more books and records (62.5%) and listed them as more important than other subjects (18.8% for subjects from the high school in the city and 6.2% from subjects from the vocational school).

In addition, boys from vocational schools in the village (72.2%) valued their newly obtained driver's licenses very highly (boys from other groups did not report this, and 27.8% of those who listed licenses were girls from the village), whereas their female peers reported engagement rings as things of great importance (100% of the engagement rings were listed as important possessions by the girls from the vocational school in the village).

The results of this study indicate that the differences between the groups of subjects were not particularly striking. Nevertheless, they express some differences connected with gender roles and social background. Possessions treasured by young people from the vocational schools, especially in the village, reflected the respondents' pragmatic and traditional views of their social roles, whereas the subjects from the high schools, both in the city and the village, presented a more complex picture by treasuring items representing more differentiated categories.

SOCIAL INFLUENCES ON THE PATTERNS OF CONSUMPTION IN THE CONTEXT OF THE MEANING OF MATERIAL GOODS

As mentioned earlier, the individual meanings of material possessions are constructed in the process of interactions, where they serve as communicators of the personal and social characteristics of persons in intergroup and interpersonal relations within a certain cultural context. A variety of influences shape and define this process, impacting the selection and use of material goods. One of the most important of these influences is mass-mediated influence, treated by McCracken (1986) as a major instrument in the production of meaning.

The second purpose of this study was to identify factors and mechanisms influencing consumption preferences. Two types of questions were asked. The first type sought to uncover the dominant sources of influence and information about commodities for young Poles, whereas the second probed the social influence rules and principles that affect decisions concerning material goods for these Poles. The questionnaire, constructed to measure the relative weight of sources and principles of influence, consisted of 43 items related to criteria used in making consumption choices. It was based on the determinants of consumer decisions described by Engel, Blackwell, and Miniard (1990) and O'Shaughnessy (1987). For the purpose of this study, the items were assessed by 30 independent judges and ascribed to: (a) three categories of sources of influence: internal (subjects' own internalized opinions, attitudes, beliefs, values, and knowledge), external personal (other people who directly interact with subjects, such as parents, peers, etc.), and external impersonal (fashion, advertising, direct distinct stimuli provided by mass media); and (b) the six categories of social influence principles described by Cialdini (1993): reciprocity, commitment/consistency, social proof, attractiveness/liking, scarcity, and authority (of peers, parents, and celebrities not known personally by the subjects, but known mainly from mass media). The commitment/consistency principle was conceptualized here more as consistency with one's own beliefs, attitudes, and self-image, rather than as consistency with previous behavior, as stressed by Cialdini (1993).

Subjects were asked to read the items, that reflected different sources of influence and to assess, on a scale from 1 to 7, how strongly each source impacted their decisions to choose certain commodities. The results show that the internal sources of influence (beliefs, knowledge, and self-concept) appeared to be the most significant ($x = 5.08$), external impersonal second most important ($x = 3.77$)—strongly connected with an influence of mass media— and the external personal influence least important (influences of other people who directly interact with the subject); ($x = 3.32$). The differences between all pairs of means were significant at $p < .05$ per the Tukey test ($q = 4.37$).

Among the six social influence principles, commitment/consistency, , turned out to have the most impact ($x = 5.11$). This outcome is consonant with the finding reported earlier that internal sources of influence were the most important. Liking ($x = 4.25$)—or, in this case, the direct attractiveness of the goods—and the authority of significant others ($x = 4.11$) were found to be the second and third most important, respectively. The authority of parents ($x = 3.64$), social proof ($x = 3.59$), the authority of peers ($x = 3.35$), scarcity ($x = 3.05$), and reciprocity ($x = 2.8$) appeared to be least influential. Mean differences were statistically significant at $p < .05$ per the Tukey test ($q = 5.16$).

An analysis of variance (ANOVA) was performed to test whether any significant differences existed among the subgroups of subjects regarding the relative importance of the six principles. The commitment/consistency rule seemed stronger for girls than boys [$F(1,238) = 11.59, p < .001$] and for young people from the village than for their peers from the city [$F(1,238) = 18.42, p < .001$]. An interaction was found between gender and school type for the commitment/consistency principle [$F(1,236) = 7.71, p < .01$] such that boys from vocational schools tended to demonstrate more consistency than boys from high schools, whereas girls exhibited the opposite pattern.

Additional between-group differences were found for social proof, attractiveness, and authority. Social proof played a much more important role in the decisions of vocational pupils as compared with high school pupils [$F(1,238) = 33.37, p < .001$]. Girls' behavior was more impacted by attractiveness than boys' [$F(1,238) = 22.33, p < .001$]. Attractiveness was also more influential for vocational than for high schools students [$F(1,238) = 4.13, p < .05$].

The effects of authority on student preferences were quite complicated. Parents' opinions counted much more for subjects from the village than from the city [$F(1,238) = 7.15, p < .01$]. Peers were taken into consideration more frequently by pupils from vocational schools than by those from high schools [$F(1,238) = 12.25, p < .001$]. In addition, boys from vocational schools weigh peer opinion more heavily than boys from high schools, whereas girls demonstrated the opposite tendency [$F(1,236) = 4.09, p < .05$]. The authority of significant others appeared more influential for subjects from vocational schools in the village than in the city, whereas subjects from high schools in the village considered it to be less important than high school subjects in the city [$F(1,236) = 5.492, p < .05$].

DISCUSSION

The results of this study are consistent with youths' great desire to build and emphasize their identity and individuality, on the one hand, and their need to search for their place the in web of social relationships, on the other. In these respects, Polish youths do not differ from their Western peers. The possessions reported as valuable by Polish teenagers and the possessions important for young Americans and British—according to data obtained by Dittmar (1992) and Kamptner (1991)—are very similar. As Kamptner (1991) suggested adolescents' possessions are mainly activity related and self-centered. They also provide enjoyment and assurance associated with social relations.

The majority of items listed by Polish youths—as by their Western counterparts—were definitely activity related and carried clearly instrumental (mainly utilitarian and hedonistic) connotations. Things like clothes, stereos, motorbikes, computers, books, and sports equipment help youngsters to complete everyday tasks and provide enjoyment. However, the same things could also become important for noninstrumental reasons (e.g. clothes not only enable one to keep proper temperature of the body, but also serve as significant social signal that expresses the owner's personal characteristics and locate him or her within the social structure). The importance of this latter function of material possessions for Polish youths may be observed in their preferences for well-known brands. They did not simply value nice clothes. Rather, they valued clothes and accessories with certain labels. The same was true about the brands of their preferred electronics, sports equipment, and bicycles. Goods with *proper* labels, in addition to reflecting a person's self-image, provide their owner with the desired status in social circles.

The desire to develop a sense of identity while building satisfactory social links renders young people vulnerable to many types of social influences from different directions. These youths are still formally and emotionally dependent on their families, but simultaneously their peer groups exert a strong impact on their thoughts and behaviors and induce them to conform to group standards and values. In addition to personal influences, there is a significant impact of the mass media, which provide numerous models perceived by young people as important indicators of the *proper* lifestyle and value system.

The results demonstrate that Polish youths depended mainly on internal sources of information when determining their preferences and purchase decisions. This mirrors the general tendency found in consumer research in Western societies. In Poland, however, the second most important source of influence was external impersonal, mainly mass-mediated influence, which is contradictory to major findings from studies of Western consumer behavior. There, impersonal sources are typically perceived to be less impactful than personal sources (Engel, Blackwell, & Miniard, 1990). The fact that the Polish

data are different from Western data suggests that the mass media and advertising play a stronger role in shaping young Polish consumers' choices and
behavior than they do for their Western counterparts. This finding that personal
beliefs are more important than the beliefs of significant friends and relatives is
somewhat surprising given that Poland is still collectivistic at its roots
(Reykowski, 1994). However, it is supported by the additional finding that the
most influential type of authority was not the authority of personally known individuals, but rather the authority of celebrities. These results are generally consistent with research suggesting that Polish people still tend to react surprisingly
receptively to ads and weigh them very heavily when deciding whether to buy
goods (Mazurek-£opacinska, 1996).

The Polish youths' acceptance of advertising messages and mass-mediated influences could help explain the lack of differences between Polish and
Western teenagers' preferred possessions. As mentioned earlier, the desire to possess certain goods originates not only from intrinsic individual needs, but also
from extrinsic sociocultural standards that have been established partly and transmitted mainly by mass media. Mass media and advertising spread, across cultures, core elements of a certain code that uses material goods as communicators
of social standards and lifestyles (McCracken, 1986). Because advertising messages, which are sent through widely accessible media like satellite television and
the Internet, often do not differ across countries and cultures (see Kanso, 1992),
teenagers from these countries and cultures get the same picture of the *approved*
lifestyle for young people—the life style of Coca-Cola drinkers and Levi's wear-
ers. Clearly the mass media are a major factor in the socialization process (Potter,
1954) both within and across societies. However, some researchers have shown
that despite the global nature of the mass media, there persist culturally specific
differences in consumption-related phenomena. For example, Bryce and Olney
(1991) showed that the material aspirations of university students in the United
States and New Zealand were strongly influenced by culture. Similarly, Han and
Shavitt (1994) demonstrated that advertising appeals were much more effective
if they were adjusted to the collectivistic or individualistic orientation of their target societies. In both cases, the subjects were older than participants in the present research, thus the former were perhaps more resistant to the influence of the
mass media. Moreover, the older respondents were more likely to espouse the traditional values of their national culture.

Mass-mediated social influences affect the meaning of material goods
not only in their symbolic functions, but also in their instrumental functions. As
Kilbourne (1991) claimed, cultures define the standards of the accepted minimal
functional satisfaction provided by commodities. Messages about such standards
are conveyed to people primarily through the mass media and advertising.
Because the newest and most technologically advanced items dominate advertising, it is not surprising that young people more strongly desire to purchase only
the newest products available.

Intrinsic motivations for purchasing goods, such as those related to aesthetic and hedonistic values, should be relatively more independent from external influences (Bell et al., 1991). However, the media play a major role in defining, for example, what is beautiful and what is not, and thus at least partially determine the standards that are held internally. Thus, the ostensible independence of internal standards may be chimerical.

A similar argument could be made when examining the self-reported importance of the commitment/consistency principle for Polish teenagers. The consistency principle is closely connected with self-orientation and self-regulation and, on the surface, appears to work opposite from external influences, including advertising. However, contemporary ads—which also target young people—tend to promote and reinforce this self-orientation. Young people are told to *be yourself* by buying certain drinks or are convinced that *it's beautiful to be yourself* by using a certain brand of cosmetics. Other ads aimed at younger audiences show a strong differentiation between adults and youths and help to establish boundaries of self-identity inside a particular social reference system. The important point to be made here is that this notion of independence from external influences is at least partially a product of external influence. Equally important is the notion that this genre of ads actually undermines the very thing they are promoting by determining how youth should demonstrate their independence.

Unfortunately, no corresponding research exists on other populations with which to compare the present findings. However, recent related research on Poles' decisions to participate in a survey found that social proof was more potent in affecting compliance decisions than was commitment/consistency (Cialdini et al., chap. 2, this volume). As Reykowski (1994) showed, Polish society is still more collectivistically than individualistically oriented, so that the domination of social proof principle could be expected. The results of the current study reveal that the commitment/consistency principle was much more influential than the social proof principle. One of the explanations could be that there is a relatively lower level of collectivism in the younger population (Daab, 1993) than in the older population. Cialdini et al. (chap. 2, this volume) surveyed college, as opposed to high school, students. It is also possible that differences in the decision to participate in a survey (with very little ego-involvement) and the decision to purchase a material item (with much greater ego-involvement) are such that they are impacted by different types of social influences.

Another explanation for this discrepancy in the research findings may lie in the fact that the present research was based on self-reports, which are more likely to be impacted by presentation biases, thereby reflecting how participants would like to be seen, rather than how they actually think and behave. Future research based on different methodological approaches should be used to verify these results and overcome the current study's potential weakness.

CONCLUSIONS AND PRACTICAL IMPLICATIONS

The irony with much research on mass-mediated influences is that the advertising and media professionals who generate these influences often knowingly employ insights gleaned from psychological research, which (social) psychologists then study and report on. The results of the current research reveal the universality of certain values and patterns of consumption, at least among youths. Teenagers in Poland, a nation that has had a market economy for only 10 years, are deeply immersed in the global youth culture. Although the consumeristic aspects of this culture are important for economic growth, they also tend to weaken the traditional values and practices of nations like Poland.

The knowledge that Polish youths are as vulnerable to the mass media as are American youths may be used for prosocial ends, however. For instance, the anti-smoking attitudes that have become more fashionable in Western nations, and that are at least partially related to mass media campaigns, could be imported into Poland to positively impact smoking among the young (see Ohme, chap. 2, this volume).

There is one more practical implication of the present research that should be mentioned. It may be possible to establish mechanisms that influence the young to be less consumeristic and to focus instead on other methods of expressing themselves that do not involve the attainment of the newest and trendiest material possessions. For instance, one could imagine a media campaign that exhorts careful spending and breeds dislike or contempt for brand name products that serve to undermine independence while ostensibly promoting it. The inoculation paradigm of instilling resistance to persuasion would be one way to approach this problem.

REFERENCES

Beggan, J. K. (1991). Using what you own to get what you need: The role of possessions in satisfying control motivation. In F. W. Rudmin (Ed.), *To have possessions: A handbook on ownership and property*. (Special Issue). *Journal of Social Behavior and Personality, 6*, 129–146.

Belk, R. W. (1988). Possessions and the extended self. *Journal of Consumer Research, 15*, 139–168.

Bell, S. S., Holbrook, M. B., & Solomon, M. R. (1991). Combining esthetic and social value to explain preferences for product styles with the incorporation of personality and ensemble effects. In F. W. Rudmin (Ed.), *To have possessions: A handbook on ownership and property*. (Special Issue). *Journal of Social Behavior and Personality, 6*, 243–274.

Bryce, W., & Olney, T. L. (1991). Gender differences in consumption aspirations: A cross-cultural appraisal. *Journal of Social Behavior and Personality, 19*, 237–253.

Cialdini, R. B. (1993). *Influence. Science and practice.* New York: Harper Collins.
Csikszentmihalyi, M., & Rochberg-Halton, E. (1981). *The meanings of things. Domestic symbols and the self.* Cambridge, England: Cambridge University Press.
Daab, W. (1993). Indywidualizm a poglady spoteczno-polityczne [Individualism and socio-political beliefs]. In J. Reykowski (Ed.), *Wartoœci i postawy spoteczne a przemiany systemowe [Social values and attitudes and the system transformation]* (pp. 101–128). Warsaw: PAN.
Dittmar, H. (1992). *The social psychology of material possessions: To have is to be.* Hemel Hempstead: Harvester Wheatsheaf.
Dolinski, D. (1995). Etyka produktywnoœci: Czy duch kapitalizmu krazy nad Polska? [Ethics of productivity: Is the spectre of capitalism haunting Poland?] (pp. 9–21) *Kolokwia Psychologiczne,* t.IV. Warsaw: Instytut Psychologii PAN.
Engel, J. F., Blackwell, R. D., & Miniard, P. W. (1990). *Consumer behavior.* Chicago: Dryden.
Gergen, K. J. (1985). The social constructionist movement in modern psychology. *American Psychologist, 40,* 266–275.
Han, S., & Shavitt, S. V. (1994). Persuasion and culture: Advertising appeals in individualistic and collectivistic societies. *Journal of Experimental Social Psychology, 30,* 326–350.
Hirschman, E. C. (1990). Secular immortality and the American ideology of affluence. *Journal of Consumer Research, 17,* 31–42.
Kamptner, N. L. (1995). Treasured possessions and their meaning in adolescent males and females. *Adolescence, 30,* 301–318.
Kanso, A. (1992). International advertising strategies: Global commitment to local vision. *Journal of Advertising Research, 32,* 10–14.
Kilbourne, W. E. (1991). The impact of the symbolic dimensions of possession on individual potential: A phenomenological perspective. In F. W. Rudmin (Ed.), *To have possessions: A handbook on ownership and property.* (Special Issue). *Journal of Social Behavior and Personality, 6,* 445–456.
Leiss, W., Kline, S., & Jhally, S. (1990). *Social communication in advertising: Persons, products & images of well-being.* Buckingham: Open University Press.
Lunt, P. K., & Livingstone, S. M. (1992). *Mass consumption and personal identity.* Buckingham: Open University Press.
Mazurek-£opacinska, K. (1996). Wptyw œrodków promocji na zachowania konsumentów [The impact of promotion tools on consumer behavior]. *Marketing i Rynek, 11,* 123–128.
McCracken, G. (1986). Culture and consumption: A theoretical account of the structure and movement of the cultural meaning of consumer goods. *Journal of Consumer Research, 13,* 71–84.
O'Shaughnessy, J. (1987). *Why people buy.* Oxford: Oxford University Press.

Potter, D. (1954). *People of plenty.* Chicago: University of Chicago Press.

Prentice, D. A. (1987). Psychological correspondence of possessions, attitudes, and values. *Journal of Personality and Social Psychology, 53,* 993–1003.

Reykowski, J. (1994). Collectivism and individualism as dimensions of social change. In U. Kim, H. Triandis, C. Kagitcibasi, S. Choi, & G. Yoon (Eds.), *Individualism and collectivism: Theory, method, and applications* (pp. 276-292). Thousand Oaks, CA: Sage.

Wallendorf, M., & Arnould, E. J. (1988). My favourite things: A cross-cultural inquiry into object attachment, possessiveness and social linkage. *Journal of Consumer Research, 14,* 531–547.

Wicklund, R. A., & Gollwitzer, P. M. (1982). *Symbolic self completion.* Hillsdale, NJ: Lawrence Erlbaum Associates.

Part III: Culture and Moral Perspective in the Social Influence Process

Janusz Reykowski
Polish Academy of Science

Overview and Commentary

There are probably many people, who, after obtaining superficial knowledge about social influence, tend to think of it as a kind of a psychological secret weapon, and that those who possess this weapon have a powerful advantage in social games. Thus, politicians can become much better manipulators of public opinion to gain votes, salespersons can induce their clients to make purchases that are advantageous for the seller but less so for the buyer, managers can achieve better control over they employees, and so on. Even an ordinary person who is diligent enough to study available knowledge can learn how to entice his or her partners, collaborators, and others to follow his or her wishes.

In fact, this is a rather narrow-minded and shortsighted interpretation of the social influence process. Of course, knowledge about social influence (as any other kind of knowledge) can be and has been used for a variety of purposes, both noble and sinister. However, it is not the nature of the process but the nature of those who apply it that makes a difference. Part III of this volume demonstrates that such knowledge can be used for prosocial purposes.

The first chapter is an illustration of some of the ambiguity or, rather, the evaluative neutrality of the research findings in this domain. Dolinski and Kofta (chap. 13) describe a series of experiments demonstrating that the temporal organization of a message can exert a significant influence on the evaluation of the message's meaning. They found that the common media practice of separating stories concerning threatening information into two parts (a short headline and a detailed explanation, separated by a commercial break; or a brief summary on the first page and the full story somewhere inside the newspaper) can affect the evaluative judgment of the audience. In general, the isolated headline is likely to produce a certain bias in judgment, and this bias can be maintained despite that the subsequently presented full story may not support the initial conclusions drawn by the audience. The authors provide additional data showing that the strength of this effect depends on some specific factors, such as the length of the break, the type of intervening activity engaged in during the break, and the recipient's initial cognitive set (whether the recipient expected to receive follow-up information or instead believed that the headline contains all of the important information). There are probably some other factors that play a role in developing biases during the break in the story that are not discussed by the authors, such as individual dispositions (e.g., need for closure; Kruglanski & Webster, 1996).

How should one evaluate these findings? Should it be said that the obtained results provide some dishonest manipulators with a convenient and relatively undetectable tool for controlling the attitudes of the media recipients? Or should one instead conclude that the results provide a lesson about the possible unintended effects of a common media practice? Or that the findings make people aware that some apparently harmless practices can produce biased judgments that the audience would like to avoid? There is no way to escape from the possibility that new knowledge can be employed for egoistic purposes. Paradoxically, the main defense against such a turn of affairs is more knowledge.

As suggested earlier, knowledge about the mechanisms of social influence can also provide guidance regarding how to improve human conditions. One illustration of such use of this knowledge is the analysis of social influence in the political domain advanced in Pratkanis' chapter (chap. 14). This author compares two qualitatively different forms of political influence that he calls *deliberative persuasion* and *propaganda*. Deliberative persuasion is the genuine democratic form of influence and consists of reciprocal influence during a debate over a particular issue. In such debate, no one pretends to possess the absolute truth and no one tries to manipulate the other parties to accept a specific, predetermined course of action. It is, in fact, an act of discovery. In contrast, propaganda is "the use of messages that play on a target's emotions and prejudice to get the target to think and do exactly what the propagandist desires."

Pratkanis claims that deliberative persuasion was at the heart of early American political institutions. Such rights as freedom of speech, freedom of the press, right of assembly, and others were meant to provide the necessary preconditions for this kind of mutual political influence. He even suggests that early forms of the European democratic institutions, such as election rules in 16th century Poland or its legislative bodies were based on the ideal of the deliberative persuasion. At the same, time he notes that changes in contemporary politics, especially American, are leading to the increasing dominance of propaganda over deliberative persuasion. This process is related to the extensive use of the mass media in running political campaigns. Some of the characteristics of this process seem to reflect the nature of television as a form of mass communication. Pratkanis describes these characteristics in some detail and analyzes the negative consequences of this process for a democratic polity. He also recommends a number of reforms that should be instituted to reintroduce the truly democratic decision-making process—namely, deliberative persuasion.

Pratkanis' analysis indicates that, in American politics and in the politics of other countries where Americanization is taking place, deliberative persuasion is gradually being replaced by propaganda. This suggests that, in the past, a kind of a *golden age* of democracy existed that has been lost due to the harmful effects of mass media. One may wonder whether that is really the case.

First of all, can actual data be found that demonstrate that, in these earlier times, the political process involved deliberative persuasion to a greater extent than today? A superficial observation of the political life in Europe does not appear to support this view. Machiavellianism in politics is no more or less prevalent today than in the past. Historical analysis notwithstanding, one may notice that there are other reasons to doubt whether deliberative persuasion, as described by Pratkanis, could have been a common process in the past. Deliberative persuasion seems to require advanced cognitive competencies, such as a fairly high ability to articulate one's opinions and attitudes, as well as high competence in perspective taking—in other words, reduction in egocentrism in social communication (Windish, 1990). These abilities correlate with education (Reykowski, 1996). Can it be reasonably assumed that in the earlier times these abilities were more common than they are now? Probably not. Alternatively, one can speculate that the main issue is not the replacement of deliberative persuasion by propaganda, but rather the increase in the influential power of propaganda due to the effective use of the modern mass media.

As an implication of this reasoning, Pratkanis' list of reforms designed to improve the political significance of deliberative persuasion should be supplemented. What should be added are interventions that can provide people with the skills needed for effective participation in deliberative persuasion on the various levels of political debate. Of course, the characteristics of such skills as well as the conditions of their development are separate and complex issues.

The fact that social influence can be employed for the betterment of society is also illustrated in the next two chapters. Snyder and Omoto (chap. 15) describe their large-scale program of research on individuals and organizations that volunteer to help persons affected by AIDS. They outline their basic findings concerning the antecedents of volunteerism, experiences of volunteerism, and consequences of volunteerism.

As far as antecedents of volunteerism are concerned, the authors identified five groups of motives, two of which are intrinsic to volunteerism (value function, community concern), whereas the other three can be regarded as extrinsic (understanding, personal development, esteem enhancement). Knowledge of these motives is a precondition to action aimed at influencing people's inclinations to volunteer and to help them withstand the difficult moments related to their involvement. One important source of the difficulties is stigmatization resulting from association with AIDS-related activities. Stigmatization, or the threat of it, can be looked on as a social influence process interfering with the development of volunteerism. In fact, people who believe they will be targets of stigmatization are less likely to follow through on their initial intentions to become volunteers. Moreover, greater perception of the likelihood of being stigmatized is related to the increased likelihood of early termination of the services. The authors found that the presence of extrinsic motives for involvement predicted longer duration of involvement.

The last finding would suggest that an appeal to personal motives can reinforce the commitment to volunteer work. Thus, it also may help in devising procedures that can make the volunteer work more attractive. However, one should add some cautionary notes with respect to this conclusion. First of all, as the analysis presented in the first commentary might suggest, recommendations of this kind are likely to be more successful in individualistic societies than in collectivistic ones. Moreover, one may ponder about the meaning of these findings: Can it be accepted, at face value, the volunteers' declarations about their motives for volunteering in AIDS-related programs? Are people who communicate that they want to participate in the programs for intrinsic, solely prosocial reasons initially more altruistic or less sincere? If the second possibility is taken seriously, the reported findings suggest another equally valid interpretation: The prospect of longer duration of involvement in volunteer services would be associated not with the mere presence of personal motives, but with the greater awareness or openness about the volunteer's own motives.

More information is probably needed to formulate general conclusions concerning the main factors that instigate volunteerism. Nevertheless, the reported program of research serves as a rich source of knowledge about the mechanisms of helping behavior and can provide valuable suggestions regarding how volunteerism can be increased in society. Of course, one cannot be quite certain whether strategies effective in one society will be successful in another. Cultural and socioeconomic differences should be seriously considered in planning such strategies.

In the following chapter, Ohme (chap. 16) discusses another prosocial application of knowledge about social influence. Here, the main issue is the role of media in antismoking advertising. The author argues that the power of the mass media as an influence agent can be related, first of all, to its norm-establishing potential. The positive image of the nonsmoking lifestyle is likely to resonate among viewers provided that appropriate methods of influence are employed. The author discusses various psychological processes that can mediate this influence. His main point is that an effective antismoking campaign should target the three components of attitudes: cognitive (providing persuasive arguments), affective (arousing emotional reactions), and behavioral (illustrate concrete strategies designed to stop smoking). Ohme describes in some detail specific social influence techniques reflecting each of these three components that can or have been used in antismoking campaigns. He also warns that their effectiveness depends on understanding the specific concerns of target groups. He provides some examples of these concerns on the basis of his team's studies of Polish teenagers. The studies reveal that certain approaches should be avoided when dealing with this group because they would be counterproductive. Ohme describes others that are more likely to be effective. Ohme also provides examples of the social influence techniques that are employed by international tobacco companies in Poland to increase their appeal among young audience; some of them are shrewd indeed.

The case of tobacco companies attempting to influence message recipients into buying their product illustrates the application of social influence principles for egoistic commercial purposes. In modern consumer society, there are countless similar instances. Should one assume, then, that the use of social influence tactics in commercial settings is inevitably manipulative? Does this mean that those who want to sell something and who rely on social influence principles are, by definition, machiavellian manipulators who set up traps for unaware customers?

Such statements should be regarded as gross overgeneralizations. In fact, very frequently social influence tactics can be applied for the mutual satisfaction of the sellers and the buyers, as illustrated in the chapter by Cody and Seiter (chap. 17). These authors describe their empirical study of client–buyer interactions. In contrast to many other studies of this kind based on paper-and-pencil techniques, this one consisted of direct observation of the interactions between sales clerks and customers. The specially trained assistants observed the tactics employed by the sales clerks in a retail setting, the reactions of the customers, and the amount of the resulting purchases. Over 400 shoppers and 400 clerks were observed. The results demonstrate the applicability of the typology of sales tactics developed by the authors, which was derived from the social influence principles described by Cialdini (1993). However, the main conclusion of the study is that the effectiveness of sales clerks depends not only on their ability to employ particular tactics, but also on their ability to help shoppers achieve their goals by adapting to shoppers' individual needs. This is an interesting statement because it emphasizes that client–buyer interactions are not a zero-sum game where a gain for one side is a loss for the other. To the contrary, it is likely to be a cooperative endeavor where the client has a task that, quite often, is rather difficult and confusing, and the sales clerk is attempting to help him or her with the task. The more helpful he or she is, the better the outcome for the both sides.

One additional comment is needed here. The authors indicate that another important precondition for successful sales is "the ability of the sales clerk to groom an image of likability." Is this not an obvious example of a pure manipulative approach to the client–buyer interaction: the expression of false feelings to facilitate sales? Not exactly. Shoppers who have experienced indifferent or hostile clerks typical for stores in the so-called *former communist countries* would love to meet clerks who groom an image of likability. In other words, the artificial grooming of liking can be seen as an approach that makes the interaction smooth and pleasant, and this is something that most shoppers appreciate.

Furthermore, shoppers usually understand that they patronize the store not to make friends, but to make a purchase. If the behavior of the clerk makes this purchase a more enjoyable experience, the client has a good reason to prefer it. Let us stress the main point: These so-called *influence tactics* should not be seen as pure manipulative devices that permit one person to gain (economic) advantage over another. They can be part of an honest interaction involving efforts to meet the needs of potential clients and make their task easier and more pleasant. Undoubtedly, influence tactics, like most other technical devices, can be used as part of dishonest sales practices. However, there are good reasons to argue that dishonest practices not only have negative moral connotations, but also bring harmful consequences for people and institutions who employ them (Cialdini, 1996).

In conclusion, one may say that the research presented in Part III says something about the moral implications of social influence and the moral positions of at least some scholars of social influence. It shows that knowledge about social influence and its practical applications cannot be looked on solely as an instrument for the manipulation of persons or groups to the benefit of other persons or groups. In fact, it can be employed to facilitate the more effective and more satisfactory functioning of a social system. By the same token, it also shows that students of the social influence should not be perceived as hired experts who serve those possessing economic or political power: They are largely researchers who explore and reveal the mysteries of our social relations to the public. Thus, there are good reasons to argue that knowledge about the principles of social influence and the mechanisms of its successful application in social practice can play an important role in betterment of the functioning of our societies.

REFERENCES

Cialdini, R. B. (1993). *Influence: Science and practice.* New York: Harper.
Cialdini, R. B. (1996). Social influence and the triple tumor structure of organizational dishonesty. In D. M. Messick & A. E. Tenbrunsel (Eds.), *Behavioral research and business ethics* (pp. 44-58). New York: Russell Sage.
Kruglanski, A. W., & Webster, D. M. (1996). Motivated closing of the mind: "Seizing" and "freezing." *Psychological Review, 103,* 263–283.
Reykowski, J. (1996). Egocentryzm politycznego myslenia a rozwizywanie spolecznych zadan koordynacyjnych. [Egocentrism in political thinking and resolving social coordination tasks]. *Czasopismo Psychologiczne, 1,* 7–30.
Windish, U. (1990). *Speech and reasoning in everyday life.* Cambridge, England: Cambridge University Press.

13

Stay Tuned: The Role of the Break in the Message on Attribution of Culpability

Dariusz Dolinski
University of Opole
Miroslaw Kofta
University of Warsaw

ABSTRACT

Media continuously bombard their audiences with countless stories full of threatening information that often describe aversive conse-quences as the result of erroneous human action. Typically, such stories consist of two functionally different parts separated from each other by time: the headline announcement and the actual story elaboration. Headlines briefly present the actor's actions associated with highly undesirable consequences in a decontextualized manner (the news flash*). The subsequent story elaboration phase typically provides contextual knowledge about the event circumstances and other details. Three experimental studies analyzed how splitting news stories affects recipients' attributions of responsibility for the persons in the story. The main manipulation in our research con-sisted of presenting the story as either an integrated, continuous message or separating the headline from the elaboration by a time break. We found that a break in the message increased perceived responsibility and moral disapproval of the person implicated by initial information in the story. Segmentation of the news story was also associated with more punitive judgments about the accused. This highly robust effect was partly modified by a host of additional factors: attentional focus on the headline information versus an* *irrelevant task, expectations of story continuation, and length of the time delay between the story termination and the assessment of recipients' judgments. The potential cultural universality and specificity of these effects is discussed, followed by a consideration of the practical implications of the* break-in-the-news effect.

DIVIDING MESSAGES AS A COMMON PRACTICE OF MODERN MEDIA

When we learn about something bad that is happening in the world and realize that it could also happen to us, we are motivated to determine who is responsible for the event and how much responsibility that person should be assigned (Dolinski, 1992; Shaver, 1985; Thornton, 1984; Walster, 1966). Determining responsibility may help in finding the meaning of an aversive and threatening situation, regaining a sense of control over possibility of its recurrence, and ameliorating negative affect aroused by an encounter with the threatening message (Shaver, 1985; Thompson, 1981; Walster, 1966; Wortman, 1976). Nowadays, mass media (e.g., TV, radio, the print press, etc.)—a highly important element of our cultural surrounding—are the major sources of threatening stories about people's wrongdoings and the often accompanying disastrous consequences. In our research, we focus on the way such stories are presented in the media as a factor affecting attribution of culpability to persons in the story. In particular, we turn our attention to the fact that these stories are often divided into separate segments and to how this bifurcation impacts attributions of responsibility.

Cutting the message into smaller *portions* is common practice in the media all over the world, particularly in the case of sensational TV reports about negative (threatening) events. Typically, such reports consist of a *headline* (i.e., an announcement or a preview of the story) followed by the *story elaboration* (i.e., a detailed account of the event). The headline explains what happened: The event is briefly presented in a decontextualized manner exposing its most sensational aspects. The story elaboration describes how it happened: Contextual knowledge is provided about the event's circumstances, the actor's social and psychological characteristics, and the story dynamics. Most important, this part of the news presentation may provide implicating information (suggesting that the actor is at fault) or clearing information (suggesting justifications for the actor's behavior).

The story parts are often separated in time. This happens most frequently on television, where, following the headline news, the full story is presented with some delay. Temporal delays may also naturally occur when people read newspapers starting with a brief description of an event on the cover page and then later read the entire story inside the issue.

The main purpose of the present research was to examine how a few minute break in such news affects ascription of responsibility and morality to the story actor. In particular, we were interested in the effects of the story break on blaming when the story elaboration provides information inconsistent with the initial negative image of the harmdoer and thus suggests correction of the perceiver's judgment. In other words, our major question was how segmenting the threatening story affects perceivers' readiness to assimilate or reject the clearing information embedded in the story elaboration.

This focus explains the location of our chapter within the mass-mediated influences section of this volume. The mass-mediated influences examined in this chapter differ from the typical content-related influences found in other research (and in this volume) as we investigate a more formal aspect. In terms of the classic Hovland, Janis, and Kelley (1953) model of mass-mediated communication, we investigate influences occurring within the channel of communication.

Previous research on the attribution of responsibility and blame has not addressed the role of temporal breaks in the processing of social information. Yet this issue has captured researchers' attention in other areas. For example, person memory studies revealed that a short break between the stimulus presentation and subsequent memory test (usually filled by a resource-depleting interpolated task) resulted in better memory for schema-congruent material than for noncongruent material (Stangor & McMillan, 1992; Wyer & Srull, 1989). This suggests that a temporal break in a threatening story could facilitate a concentration on negative (schema-congruent) information embedded in the story headline at the cost of ignoring subsequent information. Consequently, such a process could increase the recipient's propensity to blame the story's actor for the harm observed based on the presentation of the initial information.

Convergent results can also be found in studies on consumer judgment. Hong and Wyer (1990) conducted an experiment in which they manipulated the timing of an evaluation of consumer product that was either presented as manufactured by a country known for high-quality workmanship or by a country associated with low-quality products. The origin of the product was presented to all participants at the beginning of the study, and more specific information about the product was given later, but before its final evaluation. The authors found that the reputation of the country had a greater impact on product evaluations when the evaluations were made after a 24-hour delay than when they were made immediately following presentation of the product's origin. This suggests that the information about the reputation of the producer became more important for the evaluators as time passed.

Altogether, the previously mentioned studies suggest that a time interval between the initial negative news flash and the subsequent full story might augment blaming and negative assessments of the parties involved. Thus, we hypothesize that a time break increases the weight of the initial negative information. In accordance with a full-cycle social psychology approach, suggested by Cialdini (1980), the first step in our research program was aimed at verifying whether separating the message headline from its elaboration by a time break has an influence on the judgments made by message recipients.

WHAT ARE THE CONSEQUENCES OF DIVIDING A THREATENING MESSAGE INTO TWO? THE EMPIRICAL STUDY

To test our prediction about the impact of the break in the story, we asked thirty female and 30 male university students to listen to a tape-recorded story about the unexpected death of a female student in a local hospital. The story implied that a doctor on duty at the hospital made an erroneous diagnosis. The first part of the story (the news headline) briefly presented the event as follows. A 20 year -old student complained about acute abdominal pain, which had worsened over the last few days. The doctor on duty examined her briefly, diagnosed inflammation of the ovary, and admitted her to the hospital for further observation in the morning. However, in the early hours of the morning, the patient died. The autopsy revealed a ruptured appendix.

The subsequent elaboration (the full story) provided several justifications for the doctor's actions. First of all, his diagnosis was understandable because, in a routine examination, the inflammation of ovaries presents similar symptoms to those of appendicitis. In addition, during the doctor's interview, the patient stressed that she has been suffering for several years from various gynecological problems that have been treated thus far with meager success. Additionally, although he had considered it advisable, the doctor could not operate immediately because there was no anesthesiologist on duty in the hospital at that moment.

One group of participants was exposed to the entire story without any time separation. The other group initially heard only a brief account of the event. Then the experimenter turned off the tape recorder and asked participants to write down whatever comes to their minds in response to that event. After 5 minutes, the story elaboration was delivered. In both conditions, immediately after the entire story presentation, participants assessed the physician's responsibility for the patient's death, estimated the amount of punishment the doctor deserved, and expressed an overall moral evaluation of his conduct on a series of 7-point rating scales (with four items for each composite measure).

The results show that the 5-minute break in the message was associated with ascription of more responsibility to the doctor [$F(1,56) = 37.3, p < .001$], more punitive judgments of his conduct [$F(1,56) = 7.9, p < .01$], and greater moral disapproval [$F(1,56) = 11.4, p < .01$, see Fig. 13.1]. Hence, these results unequivocally support our prediction that a break in the story would

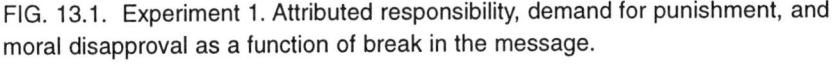

FIG. 13.1. Experiment 1. Attributed responsibility, demand for punishment, and moral disapproval as a function of break in the message.

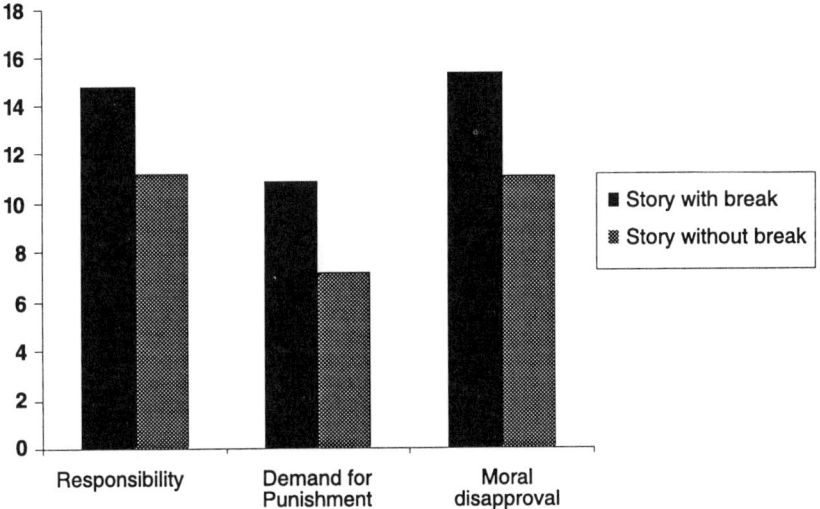

augment blaming. Presumably, separating the introductory part of the story from its elaboration by a gap of 5 minutes reduced the impact of the subsequent justification of the actor's behavior.

The overall effect that emerged on all three dependent measures is consistent with previous research (Hong & Wyer, 1990; Stangor & McMillan, 1992; Wyer & Srull, 1989). However, the exact mechanism for its occurrence has yet to be understood. Several plausible explanations are described next.

First of all, the break-in-the-message effect may depend on what people actually do during the time interval between the story segments. In some real-life occasions, people may remain mentally focused on the aversive event, as was the case in the experiment just described (in which they were directed to focus on it). On other occasions, people may fill the time with activities unrelated to the story (e.g., listening to music, paying attention to commercial ads, or engaging in a conversation). Mere thinking about a target that is initially presented in a rather negative fashion is likely to result in an even more unfavorable evaluation (Tesser, 1978). In addition, it seems plausible that mental focus on bits of initially threatening message may evoke self-defensive motives and lead to defensive attribution and increased blaming (Shaver, 1985; Thornton, 1984; Walster, 1966).

Another factor differentiating the groups in the study described previously could be that, in contrast to the continuous delivery of the story condition, participants in the break condition did not expect to hear the rest of the story. Perhaps these participants assumed that the news flash (the headline) was the entire story and felt the need to draw some conclusions (albeit premature) about the actor's responsibility and morality. Possibly this premature closure is one potential mechanism influencing the processing of subsequent information.

We decided to examine the role of these two hypothetical moderators of the break-in-the-story effect: mental concentration on either the news flash or an irrelevant task, and whether or not the audience expected to be exposed to more information about the story.

IN EMPIRICAL SEARCH OF THE MECHANISM

One hundred female university students participated in a study employing the same story as in the prior experiment. Participants in the control condition were exposed to the entire story as a continuous message. The remaining four experimental groups were all exposed to a bifurcated story as described earlier. Following the headline, the experimenter turned off the tape recorder and, by providing differential instructions to the four groups, administered the four experimental treatments.

When the tape was stopped, half of the noncontrol participants were informed by the experimenter that they would hear the continuation of the story after the proper tape was found (thereby creating an expectation of story continuation). The experimenter told some of these participants that, to not waste time, they should focus on the headline and write down whatever thoughts they had about the event in question. The remaining participants were presented with a

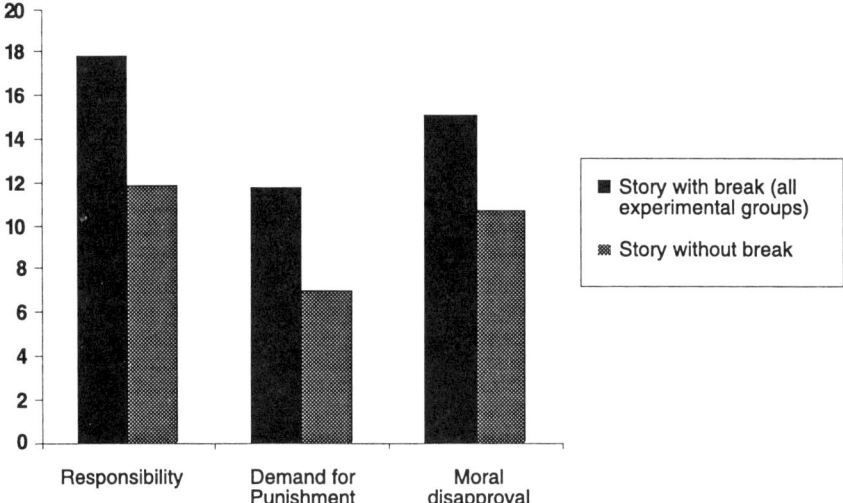

FIG. 13.2. Experiment 2. Attributed responsibility, demand for punishment, and moral disapproval as a function of break in the message.

request to perform a *favor*: to pilot research material for another study by performing a letter cancellation task. In this way, participants who expected to hear the rest of the story either engaged in a related or an unrelated task. For the other half of the participants, once the tape was stopped, the same tasks (writing about the event or working on letter cancellation test) were introduced to two different groups, this time without any excuse and comment regarding story continuation. These participants did not expect the story to continue.

In all conditions, the interpolating tasks lasted 5 minutes. After these breaks, the story elaboration was delivered from the tape recorder and all participants were instructed to listen to subsequent details of the event. Immediately after the story ended, all participants completed dependent measures that required them to make attributions regarding the physician's responsibility, to assess the degree of punishment he deserved, and to evaluate his conduct. The scales used for these dependent measures were the same as those in the first study.

The results demonstrate that participants in the experimental conditions (that encountered a story break) made more severe judgments about the physician than the continuous story baseline group [$F(1,98) = 18.23, p < .001$ for responsibility; $F(1,98) = 10.65$, p $< .002$ for punishment; and $F(1,98) = 10.30, p < .002$ for moral disapproval; see Fig. 13.2]. This experiment, then, replicated the results of our first study and similarly demonstrated the break-in-the-message effect.

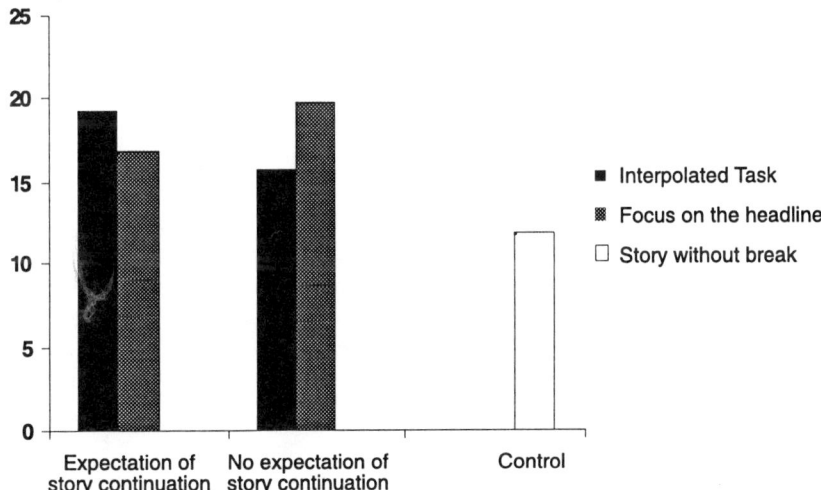

FIG. 13.3. Experiment 2. Attributed responsibility as a function of break in the message, attentional focus, and expectation of story continuation.

FIG. 13.4. Experiment 2. Demand for punishment as a function of break in the message, attentional focus, and expectation of story continuation.

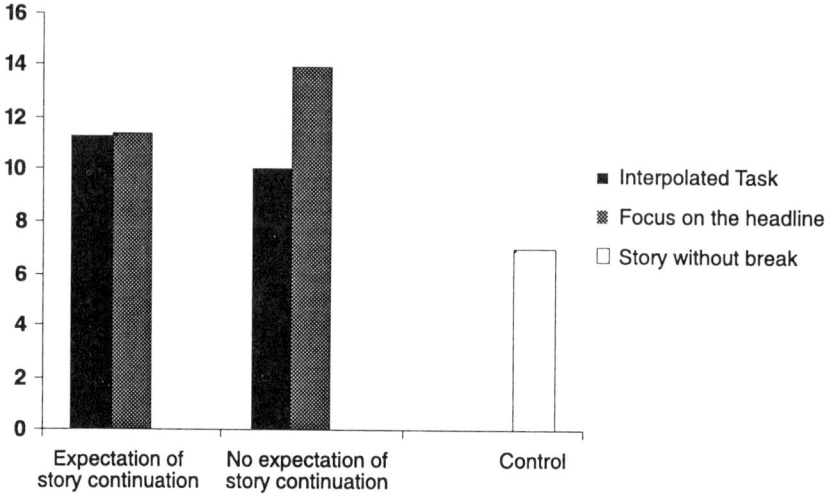

Next we tested (on the same sample) the hypothesis that focusing on the relevant task during the break would increase attributions of responsibility versus concentrating on a distracting task. On the measure of responsibility, the interaction revealed that when participants did not expect the story to be continued, they ascribed significantly more responsibility to the actor in the headline news focus condition than in the irrelevant task focus condition [$F(1,76) = 6.91, p < .01$; see Fig. 13.3]. The opposite pattern was found when the participants expected the story to continue following the break.

Somewhat similar patterns emerged for the punishment and morality judgments (see Figs. 13.4 and 13.5, respectively). In both cases, participants who did not expect the story to continue and concentrated on the headline allocated more punishment for and expressed greater moral disapproval of the doctor than their counterparts who were engaged in the irrelevant task. However, there were no significant differences between the headline news versus irrelevant task focus conditions among the participants who knew that the story would continue after the 5-minute break [$F(1,76) = 6.83, p < .02$ for moral disapproval, and $F(1,76) = 2.26$, p $< .11$ for punishment]. Thus, mental focus on the threatening news in the time interval tends to increase blaming only when people are not forewarned that the story is to be continued after interruption. This finding also implies that expectations concerning the message continuation may importantly modify the classical attitude polarization effect (Tesser, 1978).

FIG. 13.5. Experiment 2. Moral disapproval as a function of break in the message, attentional focus, and expectation of story continuation.

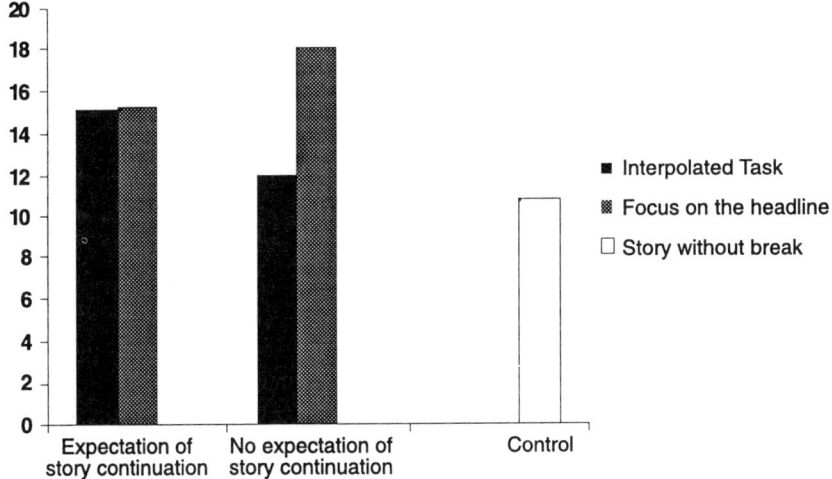

BREAK IN THE MESSAGE AND THE PSYCHOLOGY OF EVERYDAY LIFE

Although the pattern of results obtained in these two studies provides significant evidence for the break-in-the-message effect, it is not clear whether this effect would occur in a naturalistic setting. Would it appear in a nonlaboratory setting using the real media, where the message recipients are not knowingly participating in a psychology experiment? Or might it be that this effect is purely a laboratory phenomenon having little to do with everyday life? To address this question, we conducted a third experiment to examine the ecological validity of this effect.

In addition, we decided to explore the role of one more factor that may moderate the break-in-the-message effect. In the experiments described earlier, the participants were instructed to form their opinions immediately after the complete story had been presented. One might ask whether this effect would still occur when the message recipients were to form their judgments after a longer delay.

The participants in this study were 63 female university students living in a dormitory. The staff of the student radio station *Sygnaly* helped conduct the experiment by creating two types of radio hook-ups between the studio and the radio receivers permanently installed in all dormitory rooms. This technical resource provided an opportunity to present a message in two different forms via the radio. Approximately half of the dormitory rooms were fixed so that the radio message (the story) was delivered in a continuous manner. The other half of the rooms were presented with a message that was interrupted by a piece of music, which is typical for most radio transmissions.

Dormitory tenants who happened to listen that day to the radio station *Sygnaly* were informed that Magda R., a first-year university student, had reported to the police and testified that she was raped. According to her testimony, she went to a friend's birthday party on a Saturday night. Around midnight, the host left the place for a little while to buy more booze. During his absence, Marek W., who was there on a short leave from military service, lured her into an isolated room and raped her.

The participants in the continuous story condition then heard Marek W. describing this fateful night. In contrast, following this initial brief, listeners in the break-in-the-message condition were informed that the story would be continued following a musical break. Either without delay or after musical interruption, participants heard from Marek W., who explained that he had a sex with Magda, but that it was definitely consensual. He also admitted that they had an argument afterward and she accused him out of revenge.

Next the announcer informed the listeners that journalists have asked the spokesman of district police office for comments. For the sake of the investigation, he refused to say anything. However, he remarked that there was evidence both against as well as in favor of the accused. At that time, in his opinion ,it was not possible to state with certainty whether the student was indeed raped.

After the broadcast, inquirers knocked on students' doors and asked for their opinion about the incidents. The manipulation of the timing of the measurement of the attributions was achieved by approaching tenants either immediately after the story was completed or some 20 minutes later. On entering the dormitory rooms (which were selected at random), the inquirers asked the potential participants if they heard the *Signaly* broadcast and, if they had, asked them to answer the following questions on 7-point rating scales:

1. Did Marek W. really rape Magda R.?
2. To what extent is Marek W. responsible for what happened to Magda R.?
3. How severely should Marek W. be punished?
4. To what extent is Magda R. responsible for what happened?

The results reveal that participants who heard the story with the musical interruption attributed more responsibility to the accused [F(1,59) = 7.49, p < .01] and made more punitive judgements than participants who heard the story without an interruption [$F(1,59) = 9.25, p < .01$]. Not surprisingly, the listeners of the segmented story were also more certain that Marek W. has indeed raped Magda R. [$F(1,59)$ = 6.79, $p < .05$; see Fig. 13.6].

The delay in assessing blame also significantly impacted the dependent measures. Participants who were approached with at least a 20-minute delay after the completion of the broadcast attributed less responsibility to Marek W. [$F(1,59)$ = 6.82, $p < .05$; 3.61 versus 4.75, delayed versus continuous conditions, respectively]

FIG. 13.6. Experiment 3. Participants' certainty that there was a rape, attribution of responsibility, and demand of punishment as a function of break in the message.

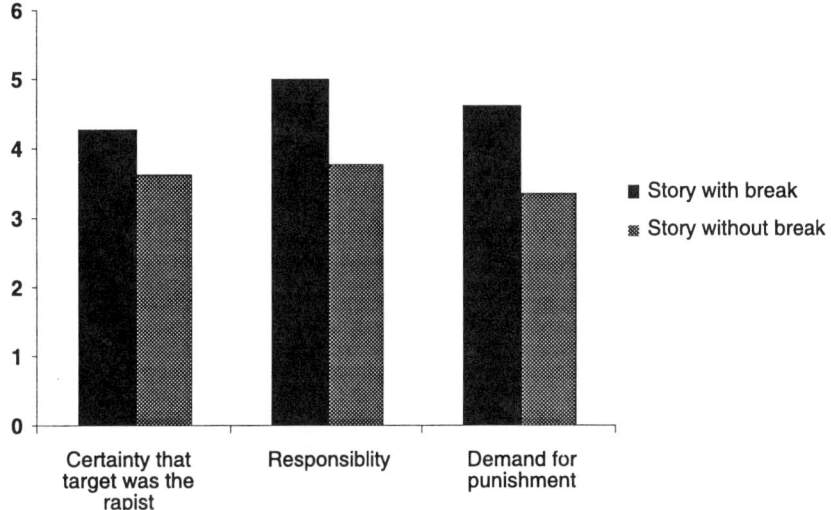

and were less punitive [$F(1,59) = 3.97, p < .05$; 3.39 versus 4.19, respectively]. The delayed and immediate response groups did not differ on the measure of certainty regarding the interpretation of the event as a rape ($F < 1$). Attributions concerning the victim's responsibility were not modified by either of the experimental manipulations ($F < 1$ for the interruption effect, $F = 1.51$ (ns.) for the delay in assessment effect, and $F < 1$ for the interaction).

The data also show an interaction between the manipulation of the story interruption and the timing of attributions on the measure assessing the target's responsibility [$F(1,59) = 5.32, p < .05$]. As depicted in Fig. 13.7, the effect of break in the story was significant for the immediate rating condition but not for the delayed rating condition.

This third study described here again successfully demonstrated the break-in-the-message effect. The person in an incriminating story was evaluated less favorably when the headline and the elaboration of the story were separated in time, as often happens in the exposure to real news in the media. However, this effect seems to be less pronounced when the attributions are made with some delay following the story termination. In fact, on the measure of the implicated person's responsibility for the event, the break-in-the-news phenomenon disappeared when assessment was delayed ($F < 1$).

This pattern of findings suggests that the emotional arousal, likely to be experienced by people exposed to threatening headline information, may mediate the impact of breaking up the story. This arousal may be evoked by the fact that one just

FIG. 13.7. Experiment 3. Attribution of responsibility to the hero of the story as a function of the break in the message and time delay between the story presentation and opinion formulation.

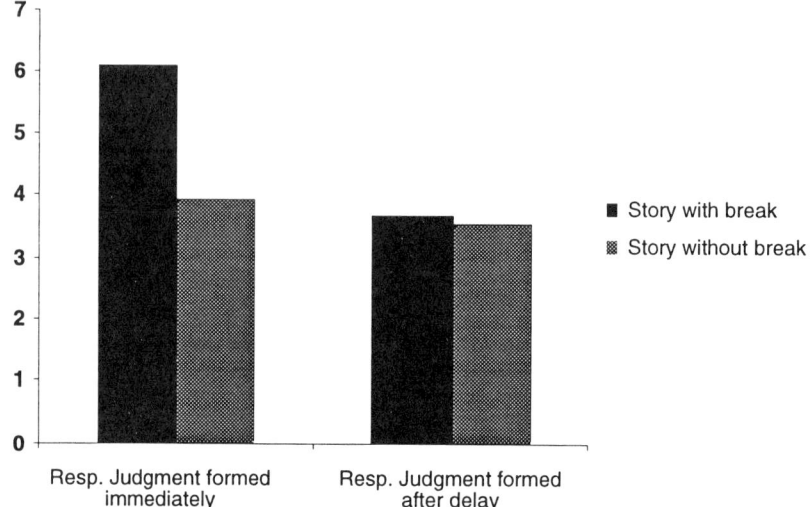

witnessed, or heard about, an event that is unjust, cruel, and potentially imminent, and this information creates a strong need for meaning and closure (for further elaboration of this point, see Discussion). Emotional arousal leads people to perceive the world in black and white colors (Dolinski, 1992; Ross & DiTecco, 1975). Because the headline often suggests that the main character in the story is guilty of an event that could happen to anyone, the recipients seem particularly influenced by the negatives implicating characterological faults in the harmdoer. Note that a few minute break between the headline and story elaboration gives the perceiver an occasion to arrive at conclusions about the actor's unsavory character. This defensive, arousal-based, evaluation likely makes the recipients less attentive, less open to, and less rational when exposed to the subsequent, more detailed information about the circumstances surrounding the target event. As with most arousal-driven phenomena, this negativity bias dissipates with time, which is consistent with the results of the manipulation of the delay in measurement of attributions.

DISCUSSION

Summing up the results of the three experiments described in the present chapter, we may state that a time interval of a few minutes between initial knowledge about aversive events and the story elaboration augments the tendency to blame the implicated harmdoer. Participants in our research behaved as if they were wedded to the headline part of the message and consequently were reticent to consider the information presented in the subsequent story elaboration. This effect seems to be quite robust, because it emerged on different measures, in different samples, and in different experimental conditions. It was reassuring to observe this effect in a natural setting, suggesting that the consequences of dividing a main message in time—a frequent practice—plays a role not only in psychological laboratories, but also in a real life.

One useful framework for understanding the break-in-the-message phenomenon might be drawn from Kruglanski's (1989, 1990; Kruglanski & Webster, 1996) concept of *need for closure*. Need for cognitive closure refers to individuals' desire for a firm answer to a question and an aversion toward ambiguity. People under a heightened need for closure experience an absence of such an answer as aversive. Kruglanski proposed two general forms in which the need for closure may manifest itself, which he called the *seizing* or *freezing phases*. During the former phase, the individual may wish to terminate the unpleasant state of lack of closure quickly by searching for information quite energetically and voluminously and thus drawing firm inferences. During the latter phase, in contrast, the person may desire to preserve or freeze on obtained knowledge and be reluctant to modify it.

The need for closure is both an individual-difference variable and a situationally induced state prompted by the perceived benefits or cost of lacking closure. The situational form is particularly relevant to the present research. What situational factors induce a motivation toward closure? According to Kruglanski, the need for closure is heightened under time pressure and under the conditions that render processing of information difficult, laborious, or aversive.

We assume that the break-in-the-message effect may be due to high motivation for cognitive closure. In the headline phase, the individual is informed that something horrible has happened. Of course, the knowledge that no one is responsible for a highly undesirable event is threatening because it implicitly suggests that "it could happen to me" (Thornton, 1984; Thornton et al., 1986; Walster, 1966). Thus, despite lack of sufficient information, an individual is motivated to find the culprit and blame him or her. To achieve this goal, the threatened individual is forced to rely on the information just obtained (seizing phase), because the emotional costs of waiting for additional, and not always more useful, data is too high. The break in the story creates an opportunity for motivated processing of the headline information and, consequently, for blaming the story actor. During the next step (the story elaboration) an individual who already has an idea about the culpability of the target becomes more reluctant to consider incoming information, hence freezing onto the headline-based interpretation of the event.

This interpretation suggests that mental focus on the threatening news during the time interval between the story segments should significantly contribute to the break-in-the-news effect. Indeed, in our second experiment, this kind of focus increased blaming the actor when participants were not forewarned that the story is to be continued after the interruption. However, mental focus does not seem to be necessary for the break-in-the-message effect to come about. If this explanation were the most parsimonious and accurate, then directing attention away from the event should have substantially reduced the effect's size or even eliminate it entirely. Yet this was not the case in our second experiment. Thus, concentration on the news flash of an aversive event and metacognitive expectations of story continuation could be better understood as variables moderating the more fundamental phenomenon rather than accounting for its emergence.

What else, then, could account for increased blaming after exposure to an interrupted story? Recent findings show that people frequently make fast, spontaneous trait inferences from behavioral data, and these inferences engage little mental capacity (for reviews, see Bargh, 1994; Fiske, 1993; Gilbert, 1995; Smith, 1994). Presumably, the break-in-the-message conditions in our experiments stimulated this type of inference, and it interfered with the assimilation of subsequent behavioral justifications that might have reduced the degree of culpability. Such a failure to discount person ascriptions with counterbalancing situationally based information is the most fundamental phenomenon observed in all of attributional research.

One may wonder whether the break-in-the-message effect is universal or dependent on cultural factors. One of the major themes of this book is the effect of culture on social influence processes. Much recent research has demonstrated the importance of understanding the role of culture in many social psychological phenomena, including, only very recently, social influence. However, the role of culture on mass-mediated influence has not received significant attention, Certainly some forms of social influence are more impacted by culture than others, as is documented in this volume. However, it seems that more formal aspects of mass-mediated influence, such as the break-in-the-message effect, may not be significantly related to culture. Rather, we suggest that, like some other formal aspects of human information processing, the phenomenon discussed here is believed to be culturally universal. However, it may be that this effect is nevertheless modified—although not erased—by such culturally specific factors as source of personal control and monochronic versus polychronic perceptions of time (Levine, 1990). As Weisz, Rothbaum, and Blackburn (1997) argued, members of Western cultures tend to prefer direct attempts at controlling existing realities. In contrast, members of Eastern cultures, such as Japan, place greater emphasis on indirectly influencing their environment by striving to accommodate to it. Weisz et al. (1997) refered to these modalities as preferences for primary and secondary control, respectively. This secondary control may overlap with the tendency for perceiving situational factors as the causes of events (Ross & Nisbett, 1991). Thus, it may be hypothesized that, at the beginning, the cause of the actor's action may be attributed to the situation more frequently in more collectivistic societies and to internal factors in more individualistic ones.

Differences in the perceived pace of time may impact the extent to which the time delay increases internal attributions. It may be that individuals with a polychronic time perspective will be less likely to seek immediate cognitive closure by assigning blame during the break—that is, less likely to engage in this type of story elaboration—than persons with a monochronic time perspective. The potential roles of emphasis on primary versus secondary control and of polychronic versus monochronic time perspectives on the break-in-the-story effect are admittedly speculative. Further research requires to clarifing whether this effect is universal or whether it is a partially generalized phenomenon with some culture-specific variations.

PRACTICAL IMPLICATIONS

The findings of the current studies shed light on the mechanisms of mass-mediated social influence. They suggest that it is not only the content of the message that is important to social influence, but also the nature of the delivery of the message. As practices common to most mass media, segmentation and time separation in the delivery of messages considerably influence the judgments of the audience.

It is likely that media viewers, listeners, readers, and those involved in producing the media are unaware of the break-in-the-message effect. Nevertheless, knowledge about this phenomenon could be of value for media producers and media audiences. If media producers would like to avoid leading the audience to premature, overconfident moral evaluation of some event or person, they should limit the headline part of the message to a brief summary or present it in a rather elaborated form, instead of utilizing the intermediate length prevalent today. On the one hand, if the headline were very short, the recipients would not have enough information to adjudge who is to blame. On the other hand, if it were rather long, the audience would receive enough information to acknowledge that the situation is complicated and unclear, which, in turn, should make them reluctant to formulate overhasty moral judgments. Despite the strategy media producers choose to adopt, newspaper readers, radio listeners, and TV viewers should be aware that they are prone to make biased moral judgments on the basis of information provided in the headline part of the message. It is not clear, however, whether simple knowledge about the break-in-the-message effect in and of itself would be sufficient to prevent it.

Although our empirical studies presented in this chapter were concentrated primarily on mass-mediated influences, one may also consider the practical implications of the break-in-the-message effect in a broader context. We would like to highlight here three different arenas in which our current research might be gainfully employed.

The first such issue concerns advertising effectiveness. Let us recall the experiment conducted by Hong and Weyer (1990) described earlier in this chapter. The product in their research was either presented as manufactured by a country known for high-quality workmanship or by country associated with low-quality goods. Either immediately following this information or after a 1-day delay, more specific information about the product was given. Participants were then asked to evaluate the product. That studied showed that information about the reputation of the producer was more important in the delay condition than in the immediate condition. It seems that advertising agencies could tailor their ad campaigns to profit from this finding. For example, it might be beneficial to begin the product presentation with a strong, positive argument and then deliver subsequent, more detailed information not immediately but rather after some delay.

The second area is stereotype formation. One of the most important sources of stereotypes is probably a direct transfer of a simplified cultural knowledge about minority groups from adults to children (e.g., in form of ready-made *truths*). Empirical data have shown, however, that this transfer is sometimes effective and sometimes ineffective (Aboud, 1988; Weigl, 1995). We suggest that effectiveness of this kind of influence may heavily depend on opportunities to validate this secondhand stereotypical knowledge through personal experience with members of the minority group. In particular, the break effect suggests that the time lapse between the message and the moment at which the subject encounters representatives of the given minority might be of importance. In line with this reasoning, Bloch and Dolinski (1998) conducted a field study on stereotypes formation. An adult confederate visited grammar school students and warned them about a newly formed group of adolescents. According to her brief statement, they were dirty, lazy, aggressive, cruel; used drugs; and were investigated by the local police. The second phase of the experiment took place almost immediately after this initial talk or one week later. The students met two well-groomed, polite children pretending to be the members of this group. While conversing with the children, they presented themselves in a positive light. Subsequently, the schoolchildren were asked to provide their opinions and judgments on questionnaires. The results reveal that a one-week delay in the meeting of the students with the representatives of the group was associated with more negative judgments of this group. This suggests that ready-made truths about certain minority groups are more dangerous and powerful when not denied immediately, and therefore that corrective responses to inappropriate and negative stereotyping should occur rapidly.

A third application of the current research regards effective coping with rumors and defamation. From time to time, politicians, movie stars, rock singers, sport heroes, and other popular figures all over the world are the target of ugly rumors by sensationalistic newspapers or dishonest rivals. The common dilemma they usually have to solve is deciding what strategy to use to counter these rumors. Should they respond immediately (but without careful preparation of the arguments) or react after scrupulous preparation of arguments (but with some delay). On the basis of the break-in-the-message effect described in this chapter, we consider the first strategy to be superior to the second. It may be that, when unflattering rumors are disseminated, one may do nothing worse than give people time to think that the rumor is true. It is enough to make the audience blind to the evidence that the rumor is false.

ACKNOWLEDGMENTS

Work on this chapter was supported by the Polish Committee for Scientific Research (Grant 1 H01F 016 10). Empirical data described in this chapter are presented in a more detailed way in Kofta and Dolinski "Details at 11.00. Blaming as a function of breaking up the story" (in preparation). We would like to thank Krzysztof Kaniasty for very helpful comments on earlier versions of this chapter.

REFERENCES

Aboud, F. (1988). *Children and prejudice*. Cambridge, MA: Blackwell.

Bargh, J. A. (1994). The four horsemen of automaticity: Awareness, intention, efficiency, and control in social cognition. In R. S. Wyer & T. K. Srull (Eds.), *Handbook of social cognition* (2nd ed., Vol. 1, pp. 1–40). Hillsdale, NJ: Lawrence Erlbaum Associates.

Bloch, B., & Dolinski, D. (1998). Rola autorytetu i niemoznosci bezposredniej weryfikacji jego opinii w procesie formowania siê stereotypow. [Role of authority and impossibility of its direct verification in the process of stereotype formation]. *Psychologia Wychowawcza, 2,* 113–124.

Cialdini, R. B. (1980). Full-cycle social psychology. *Applied Social Psychology Annual, 1,* 21–45.

Dolinski, D. (1992). *Przypisywanie moralnej odpowiedzialnosci [Attribution of moral responsibility]*. Warszawa: Wydawnictwo Instytutu Psychologii PAN.

Fiske, S. T. (1993). Social cognition and social perception. *Annual Review of Psychology, 44,* 155–194).

Gilbert, D. T. (1995). Attribution and interpersonal perception. In A. Tesser (Ed.), *Advanced social psychology* (pp. 99–147). Boston: McGraw-Hill.

Hong, S. T., & Wyer, R. S. (1990). Determinants of product evaluation: Country of origin, intrinsic attributes, and time delay between presentation and judgment. *Journal of Consumer Research, 17,* 277–288.

Hovland, C. I., Janis, I. L., & Kelley, J. J. (1953). *Communication and persuasion*. New Haven, CT: Yale University Press.

Kruglanski, A. W. (1989). *Lay epistemics and human knowledge: Cognitive and motivational bases*. New York: Plenum.

Kruglanski, A. W. (1990). Lay epistemic theory in social cognitive psychology. *Psychological Inquiry, 1,* 181–197.

Kruglanski, A. W., & Webster, D. M. (1996). Motivated closing of the mind: "Seizing" and "Freezing." *Psychological Review, 103,* 263–283.

Levine, R. V. (1990). The pace of life. *American Scientist, 78,* 450–459.

Ross, M., & DiTecco, D. (1975). An attributional analysis of moral judgments. *Journal of Social Issues, 31,* 91–109.

Ross, L., & Nisbett, R. E. (1991). *The person and the situation*. New York: McGraw-Hill.

Shaver, K. G. (1985). *The attribution of blame: Causality, responsibility, and blameworthiness*. New York: Springer-Verlag.

Smith, E. R. (1994). Social cognition: Contributions to attribution theory and research. In P. Devine, D. L. Hamilton, & T. M. Ostrom (Eds.), *Social cognition: Impact on social psychology* (pp. 77–108). San Diego: Academic Press.

Stangor, C., & McMillan, D. (1992). Memory for expectancy-congruent and expectancy-incongruent information: A review of the social and social developmental literatures. *Psychological Bulletin, 111*, 42–61.

Tesser, A. (1978). Self-generated attitude change. In L. Berkowitz (Ed.), *Advances in experimental social psychology* (Vol. 11, pp. 290–338). New York: Academic Press.

Thompson, S. C. (1981). Will it hurt less if I can control it? A complex answer to a simple question. *Psychological Bulletin, 90*, 89–101.

Thornton, B. (1984). Defensive attribution of responsibility: Evidence for an arousal-based motivational bias. *Journal of Personality and Social Psychology, 46*, 721–734.

Thornton, B., Hogate, L., Moirs, K., Pinette, M., & Presby, W. (1986). Physiological evidence of an arousal-based motivational bias in the defensive attribution of responsibility. *Journal of Experimental Social Psychology, 46*, 721–734.

Walster, E. (1966). Assignment of responsibility for an accident. *Journal of Personality and Social Psychology, 3*, 73–79.

Weigl, B. (1995). Similarity between parents' and children's social stereotypes. *Polish Psychological Bulletin, 26*, 161–174.

Weisz, J. R., Rothbaum, F. M., & Blackburn, T. C. (1997). Standing out and standing in: The psychology of control in America and Japan. In L. A. Peplau & S. E. Taylor (Eds.), *Sociocultural perspectives in social psychology: Current readings* (pp. 75–99). Upper Saddle River, NJ: Prentice-Hall.

Wortman, C. B. (1976). Causal attributions and personal control. In J. H. Harvey, W. J. Ickes, & R. F. Kidd (Eds.), *New directions in attribution research* (Vol. 2, pp. 25–52). Hillsdale, NJ: Lawrence Erlbaum Associates.

Wyer, R. S., & Srull, T. K. (1989). *Memory and cognition in its social context*. Hillsdale, NJ: Lawrence Erlbaum Associates.

14

Propaganda and Deliberative Persuasion: The Implications of Americanized Mass Media for Established and Emerging Democracies

Anthony R. Pratkanis

University of California, Santa Cruz

ABSTRACT

Today's democracies face a fundamental problem: For a democratic society to thrive, it needs free and open discussion. However, the mass media frequently translate complex problems into sound bites and images that often serve special interest groups. In other words, mass media persuasion can best be described as propaganda (simple images and slogans that play on emotions and prejudices) as opposed to deliberative persuasion (debate, discussion, and careful scrutiny of the issues) needed by a democracy. What can be done? This chapter discusses how political candidates succeed in this environment and then investigates how deliberative persuasion can be stimulated in mass-mediated political campaigns, with particular reference to American and Polish democracies.

PROPAGANDA AND DELIBERATIVE PERSUASION IN MASS-MEDIATED DEMOCRACIES

Deliberative persuasion is at the heart of the world's two oldest modern democracies—the United States and Poland. By deliberative persuasion, I mean argument, debate, discussion, and a careful appraisal of the pros and cons of a course of action. The goal of this persuasion is to lay bare the important concerns involved in an issue and to develop a social consensus on the appropriate course of action. Deliberative persuasion stands in stark contrast to propaganda that served as the basis for social control in ancient dictatorships such as the Egyptian and Mayan regimes (Marcus, 1992) to the more recent oppressive governments of Nazi Germany (Doob, 1950; Rutherford, 1978) and the Soviet Union (Benn, 1989). *Propaganda* can be defined as the use of messages (often short and heavily image-laden) that play on emotions and prejudice to get the target to think and do exactly what the propagandist desires.

The Nature of Propaganda and Deliberative Persuasion

The early work on group climate by the Poznan-born social psychologist Kurt Lewin and his colleagues reveals the conditions that foster both propaganda and deliberative persuasion (Lewin & Lippitt, 1938; Lewin, Lippitt, & White, 1939; White & Lippitt, 1960). In this research, boys were led by an adult who was trained to exhibit either an autocratic (dictates policy, determines tasks), a laissez-faire (nonparticipation), or a democratic (activity structured through leader-encouraged group discussion) leadership style.

In the autocratic regime, the elite leaders assume that they (and they alone) have special access to truth—what is good, what is bad, and what course of action should be taken next. It is the duty of the leader in such regimes to use persuasion to communicate this knowledge in simple terms to the waiting masses or as in the case of Lewin's research: The adult tells the boys what to do. The social life of the group is structured to facilitate communication to the masses of a predetermined solution of what to believe and do (Pratkanis & Turner, 1996). This communication takes the form of propaganda: It is unidirectional from the elites to the masses and is centralized in one or a few colluding sources of information; rewards and punishments are used to maintain group structure and promote leaders' status and power; authority is used to induce acceptance of leaders' wishes with the group's agenda, objectives, and task set by the elites; there are no constraints on leader behavior; rigid group boundaries (ingroups and outgroups) and social roles are maintained to limit discussion, options, and criticisms; minority and divergent viewpoints are especially discouraged through neglect, ridicule, social pressure, or persecution; and, indeed, minorities often serve as scapegoats to bear the sins and failings of the leaders. To accomplish their goals, elites must use propaganda that plays on emotions and prejudices and, if that fails, more coercive forms of social control such as terror and physical abuse. (the laissez-faire group climate can quickly become autocratic as, consistent with Michels' 1915 iron law of oligopoly, despots, and ruling cliques emerge).

In contrast, in a democracy, no one is assumed to know the absolute truth; knowledge of what is best does not reside in a single authority, but in the multiple perspectives of citizens. Persuasion is an act of discovery—finding a course of action through deliberation, debate, discussion, argument, and analysis or as in the case of Lewin's research: The adult stimulates discussion among the group as to what their objectives and tasks should be. Social life can also be structured to promote democracy (Pratkanis & Turner, 1996). Deliberative persuasion flourishes when influence is reciprocal between leaders and members and communication is decentralized with multiple sources of information; rewards and power are used to promote discussion of the group's agenda, objectives, and tasks and to move the group toward its objectives; authority and power are constrained by a system of checks and balances; there are flexible group boundaries and roles to allow additional resources to be obtained to solve problems; minority opinion is valued and encouraged as a means to obtain a better decision; and accurate feedback on the group's progress is desired.

The research of Kurt Lewin and his colleagues also reveals some of the advantages of democracy and deliberative persuasion (see also Fearon, 1998). First, deliberative persuasion can lead to productivity and better decision making. Lewin found that, although autocratic groups were productive, they also demon-- strated less initiative and were highly dependent on the leader's instructions. In contrast, democratic groups produced highly original work (laissez-faire groups produced the lowest quality and quantity of work). More recently, Nemeth (1994), in a series of experiments looking at just one aspect of democracy—the encouragement of a vigorous presentation of minority perspectives—found that minority dissent stimulates creative problem solving by inducing other group members to take in more information and think about that information in divergent ways. Second, Lewin observed that autocratic relative to democratic leadership created hostility and distrust among members, thus making it difficult to sustain long-term group effort and relationships. Third, participation in the process of decision making can lead to perceptions that the decision was fair and just (Lind & Tyler, 1988). Fourth, a deliberative discussion of the group's agenda, goals, and tasks can lead to social consensus on what should be the group's course of action; such consensus is particularly important when the action requires sacrifice on the part of one or more members. Finally, the act of discussion exposes group members to new viewpoints and thus provides an opportunity for participants to develop and grow in their moral and intellectual capacities.

The Historical Roots of Deliberative Persuasion

The significance of deliberative persuasion can be seen in early American institutions of the 1700s. The churches were small, simple structures with a pulpit placed close to the people—an ideal setting for sermons exhorting moral fortitude and for political rallies to debate the course of a revolution. Many towns developed around a town hall for holding meetings and a village green for a market where negotiations between buyer and seller took place. When the new Americans ratified their constitution and later their Bill of Rights, they gave a central role to deliberative persuasion by guaranteeing freedom of speech, freedom of the press, and the rights of assembly and of petitioning the government. The U.S. government with its three branches and two legislative houses is a system of checks and balances that demands debate, argument, and compromise. The U.S. legal system is adversarial and requires the government to prove guilt beyond a shadow of a doubt.

Similarly, deliberative persuasion was at the heart of the first experiment with democracy in Europe since the Dark Ages—the election of a Polish king in 1573. Every member of the *szlachta* (or upper class of roughly 10% of the population) could come to the Election Field outside of Warsaw to argue, debate, mull over, and finally vote for their leader (Zamoyski, 1987). Also at this time, Poland developed one of the first legislative bodies in Europe called the *Sejm*, which was responsible for discussing affairs of state and for serving as a check on the king's power. Unfortunately, this attempt at democracy failed. During this (and other) times, Poland was known for its tolerance of minorities (before WWII, Poland had the highest percentage of Jewish population in Europe). Perhaps out of respect for tolerating all viewpoints, Poland adopted the liberum veto: the principle that no legislation could be enacted without unanimity of all members of the Sejm. Although such a check on power is useful when it is acceptable not to make a decision (such as in the American jury) and can even lead to deliberative discussion in such bodies (Nemeth, 1981), it served to paralyze the Polish government at a time when it was essential to mobilize against external threats. Poland's first brush with the rule of the people died in 1793 at the hands of Catherine the Great, who found she could tolerate no more of this dangerous thing called democracy.

In the 1980s, Poland would once again find itself a leader for democracy when opposition movements such as KOR, Solidarity, and an underground press stimulated deliberative persuasion and limited the communist monopoly of information. The result was the Round Table negotiations of 1989, where members of Solidarity joined with members of the Polish communist party to establish the first free elections in the Soviet bloc. Although tensions were high, both sides of the negotiation realized the stakes and respected each other's differences (Reykowski, 1993). The deliberative discussion that ensued produced a plan for the peaceful transfer of power that has placed Poland ahead of other former-Soviet bloc countries in the transition to democracy.

The Modern Dilemma of Democracy

Given the importance of deliberative persuasion for a democracy, it is reasonable to ask: How are modern democracies faring in terms of the debate and discussion needed to make community decisions? One recent development is the widespread use of the mass media to conduct the affairs of political life. This trend has been called *Americanization* and involves political campaigns characterized by: (a) increasing reliance on TV to communicate information, (b) predominance of images over issues and substance, (c) emphasis on the personality of candidates as opposed to party platforms, and (d) the rise of professional political consultants to manage media strategies (Holtz-Bacha & Kaid, 1995a; Swanson & Mancini, 1996). Increasingly, this American-style videopolitics is being exported to other countries such as the Netherlands (Brants, 1995), Finland (Moring, 1995), and Israel (Caspi, 1996).

The rise of the American-style political campaign presents a challenge to democracy. Given the nature of the mass media, complex issues are frequently translated into sound bites and images that often serve the special interest groups that can afford to purchase expensive media time or have access to it because of their power. In other words, mass media communications take on the nature of propaganda: the dissemination from increasingly centralized sources of simple images and slogans that play on emotions and prejudices. In such cases, citizens take on a passive, spectator role of watching events unfold around them with little active involvement or self-efficacy that they can change the course of history. It is as if they are watching a made-for-TV movie because they are watching a made-for-TV movie. For those citizens who are interested in establishing the conditions for strengthening democracy, it is important to (a) look at the nature of the mass media and how political actors must perform in that environment to win an election, and (b) suggest some steps that can be taken to promote the deliberative persuasion needed for a democracy.

THE PERSUASION LANDSCAPE OF A MASS-MEDIATED CAMPAIGN

Each year the average American watches 1,150 hours of TV, listens to 1,160 hours of radio, and spends 180 hours reading newspapers and an additional 110 hours reading magazines. More than half of an American's waking hours is spent with the mass media (Pratkanis & Aronson, in press). Of course, not all political discussions in modern democracies occur via the mass media; citizens often turn to their friends, neighbors, and acquaintances for help in understanding mass-mediated content (Eliasoph, 1998; Pratkanis, 1997). However, most Americans still list the mass media, and TV in particular, as their main source of news. This is particularly true of disinterested and swing voters who make up 10% to 20% of the 50% of Americans who vote and who often determine the outcome of elections (Devlin, 1995; see Cohen & Wolfsfeld, 1995, for a similar analysis of Israel). Further, Baumgartner, Jones, and Leech (1997) found that media attention on an issue often precedes attention by Congress, which in turn stimulates more media focus on the issue. Small wonder that TV advertising now represents the biggest single expenditure for most political campaigns (West, 1993). What then is the nature of Americanized mass media and how does it impact the conduct of a modern political campaign?

The Mass Media Are a Message-Dense Environment

The average American with average media habits will see over 300 ads per day and over 7 million ads in an average lifetime. The typical TV ad runs for 30-seconds or less; magazine ads often consist of little more than a picture and a phrase. The news of the day (paid for by all those 30 second ads) comes in the form of sound bites and news snippets—short news vignettes featuring vivid images and catch phrases. In other words, the mass media are densely populated with short, catchy, and often visual messages each competing for viewers' attention.

In the political domain, the effects of this message-dense environment can be seen in U.S. presidential campaigns. According to Hallin (1992), in the average news program of 1968, a presidential candidate would speak on camera for more than 40 seconds, and it would not be unusual to hear such a candidate talk for 2 minutes or more. In the 1980s, a major political candidate could expect less than 10 seconds of speaking time, with only 4% of those appearances being 20 seconds or longer. Further, as Hallin noted, the structure of news coverage of political candidates changed dramatically from 1968 to the 1980s. In 1968, the news reporter gave a short introduction followed by a long presentation by the candidate. In the 1980s, there is a short introductory statement by the candidate followed by a lengthy presentation from the news reporter.

The message-dense environment of the political campaign presents a challenging task to the candidate. Imagine that you are at a party and would like to convince the people in the room to accept a certain position. You are allowed to speak for 8 seconds at a time with lengthy intervals between each comment. Immediately after you deliver an 8-second speech, a handful of fellow partygoers start discussing what you just said—why you said it, how it was said, who would disagree with it, and so forth. Further complicating your task, before you speak again, some of the partygoers leave the room and are replaced by others who have not heard your previous 8-second speech. The process repeats itself after your next 8-second speech. In such an environment, it is impossible to have a well-informed discussion of an issue, and persuasion must rely on vivid and catchy appeals that play on previously held prejudices and emotions—in other words, by propaganda.

The implication of such a message glut for the citizen is clear: It is difficult if not impossible to think deeply about each message. Instead, we engage in what Cialdini (1984) called the *click-whirr*. Unable to think about all these messages, we, as citizens, have developed simple rules that specify how we should act (e.g., we should reciprocate kindness, trust those who are expert and attractive, and rid ourselves of any negative emotion). The propagandist knows our rules and develops campaigns that play on the emotions and prejudices that trigger the click (activating the rule) and the whirr (executing the rule) needed to put the propagandist at best advantage.

Mass Media Campaigns Are Expensive

In the 1992 U.S. presidential election, Bill Clinton spent $1.26 per vote he received ($55 million total or 92.5 million Zwoty), George Bush spent $1.44 per vote ($55 million), and Ross Perot spent $3.12 per vote ($60 million). This does not include money spent in the primaries. In the 1996 presidential election (all phases and candidates), the Democrats spent $130 million, whereas the Republicans spent $226 million. In the early 1990s, an average candidate for a U.S. Senate seat spent $2.5 million, whereas a candidate for a seat in the U.S. House of Representatives spent $350,000 (Ansolabehere, Behr, & Iyengar, 1993). By 1998, over 60% of the candidates for the U.S. House were spending a million dollars or more ("Million-Dollar House," 1998).

Winning may depend on how much money you spend (at least in U.S. Congressional races and the presidential primary). In the early 1990s, winners spent double the amount of losers (e.g., $3.4 million to win a Senate seat (vs. $1.9 million to lose it and $410,00 to win a House seat (vs. $200,000 to lose it; see Ansolabehere et al., 1993). In the 1998 House races, 78% of those spending a million dollars or more won their races ("Million-Dollar House," 1998).

Quite simply put, mass-mediated campaigns are expensive. One of the main reasons is the high cost of purchasing media time. A typical 30-second political ad can cost between $20,000 and $250,000 to show just once on national TV. This can quickly translate into millions of dollars a day to show the ad enough times so that most American voters see it.

There are a number of implications of the high cost of campaigning. First, fundraising by the candidate takes on paramount importance. House incumbents previously spent 4 out of their 24-month term fundraising. Today it is a 24-month operation involving computer systems, direct mail, and fundraising professionals. Challengers must have a ready base of financial support to compete with the incumbents' fundraising machine. The opportunity for influence peddling has never been greater. The saliency of fund-raising can raise a difficult dilemma for elected representatives: Should I emphasize a legislative agenda that garners campaign contributions (and increase my chances of staying in office to obtain positive goals) or should I always vote my conscience (and lose my seat and chance to accomplish my goals)?

Second, given that purchasing media is so expensive, candidates attempt to obtain free media coverage or what political consultants more accurately term *earned* media. News coverage can be earned by delivering stories to reporters (on deadline) that will increase TV ratings and newspaper circulation (and thus news media profits). Such stories (a) emphasize controversy, conflict, and scandal; (b) need to be dramatic and personal; (c) are simple enough to convey in a short space and timel and (d) fit a theme that is currently prominent in the news (see Pratkanis, 1997).

In other words, campaign news must look more like the episode of a soap opera than a great debate befitting a democracy. Recent U.S. election campaigns have been marked by negative character assassinations, reports of rumors and gossip, details on campaign intrigue (who is in and who is out) and faux pas (especially those caught vividly on camera), and an emphasis on a few wedge issues such as abortion and race with built-in controversy. Given that stories must fit a theme (such as this candidate is a bumbler who cannot spell and that candidate does not appeal to men), an informational bandwagon effect occurs where news facts are filtered through a few set of themes (regardless of their veracity or triviality), thereby reinforcing the truth of the original theme. In addition, the news media's desire to report controversy and conflict leads to an emphasis on *horse-race* coverage (which candidate is ahead? will this change?) at the expense of an in-depth (and much less exciting) analysis of candidates and issues. Indeed, 27% of all campaign stories on the three major TV networks covering the 1992 U.S. presidential election were about polls and who was winning (Stanley & Niemi, 1994). Horse-race coverage means that candidates must do whatever they can to be perceived as a winner to secure campaign contributions so that they can then purchase media time to present a winning image.

Mass Media Are Immediate

Tiananmen Square, Persian Gulf war, O. J. Simpson, Monica Lewinsky, Kosovo, Columbine High School—the mass media present a series of sensational, powerful images designed to get viewers' attention and thus ratings. To keep ratings high, a vivid image must be replaced quickly with the next searing image. News cycles that were originally designed to give reporters for morning and evening papers time to prepare their stories (and their readers time to digest them) have become condensed into round-the-clock news networks, such as CNN where the next national and international tragedy or scandal is covered immediately and in real time. Once the national press core settles on a story, all other issues take a back seat. For example, at one of U.S. President Bill Clinton's first press conferences, he received 18 questions about Whitewater and his family's finances and 3 questions on policy issues (one each on health care, nuclear weapons in North Korea, and the assassination of a leading Mexican politician; see Reeves, 1997). The result is timely information—but often too timely, too trivial, and with little time for reflection.

The implications of the immediacy of mass media were clearly understood by Vice President Al Gore when he stated, "These changes are not friendly to the linear debate envisioned by the Founding Fathers" (cited in Reeves, 1997, p. xii). For the citizen, there is little time for in-depth analysis and discussion of such questions as: Where does my tax money really go? Why is there school violence? What is the impact of media mergers on the control of news? In the vacuum of real analysis, citizens much rely on their own guesses and hunches and what they are told by self-interested parties. In other words, they must rely on Cialdini's (1984) click-whirr. The result is a spiral of ignorance: To gain ratings and circulation, the mass media must present an entertaining and exciting (if not overly simple) story; this results in a less-sophisticated public that requires increasingly simplified and entertaining messages, thus further reducing the sophistication of the public at large (see Entman, 1989).

The political candidate is caught in a web of action-reaction-and-still-more reaction as the candidate attempts to manage the changing media scene to her or his advantage. As Democratic party pollster Peter Hart put it: "It is difficult to put a long-range plan into effect in a world of short-term impressions" (cited in Reeves, 1997, p. xvi). Without consensus on such a long-range plan, it becomes increasingly difficult to lead (except by manipulation) and thus address some of the difficult issues so vividly portrayed in the stream of media images.

The Low Involvement Psychology of Mass Media

In summary, the message-dense, immediate environment of the mass media makes it difficult for citizens to think deeply about an issue. To make decisions, they must rely on pieces of information, simple cues, symbols, slogans, and images that happen to break through the information clutter. In other words, the mass media encourage what Krugman (1965) called low involvement learning, what Petty and Cacioppo (1986) termed the peripheral route to persuasion, and what Cialdini (1984) labeled the click-whirr. Students of history may recognize this psychology of the masses in the theories of Adolf Hitler (1925-1971) when he wrote in *Mein Kampf* that propaganda

> must be aimed at the emotions we must avoid excessive intellectual demands on our public all effective propaganda must be limited to a very few points and must harp on these in slogans until the last member of the public understands. (pp. 180–181)

For Hitler, the masses are generally stupid and incapable of understanding complex issues. Fortunately, as Petty and Cacioppo (1986) have shown, people can also engage in a central route to persuasion that involves systematic processing of information, seeking out of information, and a more thoughtful judgment. We return to the conditions that promote this type of careful analysis after first looking at how political candidates respond to the demands of the mass media.

HOW TO WIN A MASS-MEDIATED ELECTION

How do political candidates meet the challenge of the fast-paced, expensive, message-dense environment of the mass media? For the most part, it is difficult to conduct an extended discussion with the voter on the important issues of the day. Instead, the candidate must select a few winning issues to talk about (agenda setting), look good on camera (establish an appealing image), and destroy the opposition quickly and be prepared to defend against the opposition's attack. This winning formula raises some important issues for the promotion of deliberative persuasion.

Agenda Setting

What Is Agenda Setting? In any U.S. presidential campaign, only a few issues are discussed in the mass media. To win the election, a candidate must control this agenda such that the media talks about only those issues for which the candidate is perceived as strong and capable. If successful, the candidate is seen as effective on just those issues of prominence to the nation.

The persuasive power of agenda setting can be seen in a set of ingenious experiments conducted by Iyengar and Kinder (1987). In their studies, college students watched edited evening news programs so that they received a steady dose of news about a specific problem facing the United States. For example, some students heard about the weaknesses of U.S. defense capabilities; a second group watched shows emphasizing pollution concerns; a third heard about inflation and economic matters. After a week of viewing, the results were clear: Students became convinced that those issues they had heard the most about were the most important ones for the country to solve. Further, the students acted on their newfound perceptions by evaluating more positively candidates who were perceived as strong on those issues. Similar results have been obtained in survey research that finds that the voters' perception of the importance of an issue in a campaign coincides with the amount of news coverage given that issue (McCombs & Shaw, 1972; Rogers & Dearing, 1988).

How Is Agenda Setting Used to Win an Election? Bill Clinton's two recent U.S. presidential campaigns provide textbook examples of how to use the influence tactic of agenda setting. In 1992, the economy was Clinton's winning issue (see Pratkanis, 1993, for details of the campaign). Opinion polls showed that most voters felt Clinton (compared with his opponent George Bush) was better at solving economic problems. In contrast, Bush's perceived strength was seen as foreign policy. Polls also indicated that over half of the American public perceived the economy as the number one issue facing the country—this perception helped focus media attention and thus made Clinton's rhetorical task of agenda setting that much easier. However, Clinton's campaign operatives made sure that the election served as a referendum on this issue. A sign was hung in Clinton's

Arkansas campaign headquarters that read: "The economy stupid"—a not so subtle reminder to keep the campaign focused on this issue. The Clinton forces were skilled at linking seemingly every issue to the economy. Civil rights were portrayed in terms of national productivity (we do not have a person to waste); education and welfare reform were termed investment; affordable health care was a means of reducing the budget deficit; environmental protection creates business opportunities; and change is needed because trickle-down economics does not work. Clinton's operatives were also skilled at preventing the Bush forces from refocusing the agenda by either agreeing with Bush (e.g., on the North American Free Trade Agreement), by agreeing with Bush and then raising the stakes (e.g., supporting Bush's actions in Iraq and then asking why the United States wasn't doing more in Yugoslavia), or by redefining the issue (the Republican issue of family values became valuing families and the promotion of a Democratic legislative agenda).

In 1996, Bill Clinton won reelection by limiting the campaign agenda (see Pratkanis, 1999, for details). Dick Morris, one of Clinton's key political advisors at the time, termed the strategy *triangulation*, or identifying traditional Democratic and Republican positions on an issue and then developing a third middle-of-the road position that appeals to citizens and appears to be above the fray of partisan politics. For example, traditionally Republicans seek tax cuts whereas Democrats are leery of limiting government revenues. Through triangulation, a third position is developed—limited tax cuts, for a purpose such as purchasing a first home or saving for college. From the perspective of the mass media, triangulation is really limiting the campaign agenda by removing or co-opting any issue that might appear controversial. During the campaign, Clinton forces crafted positions on traditionally Republican issues that neutralized the Republican agenda—for example, putting more cops on the street, signing welfare reform legislation, proposing a balanced budget, and favoring school prayer. What is there left to talk about in the campaign? Clinton wins by default.

The power of agenda setting can also be seen in Poland's 1989 general election—the first truly free election in Poland in decades. In the campaign, Solidarity presented a unified, consistent message (Jakubowicz, 1996). For example, broadcasts featuring Solidarity candidates spent two thirds of their time discussing general issues, especially the need for fundamental reform. In contrast, communist party candidates tried to distance themselves from the party: They spent two thirds of their airtime talking about the qualifications of specific candidates as opposed to broad party themes. Solidarity was thus able to set the agenda for Poland and was perceived as strong on this agenda. Solidarity and other opposition parties won all but one of the contested seats in this election.

What Are the Implications of Agenda Setting for Democracies? Of course, it is the responsibility of a leader to assist in setting an agenda. It is how this agenda setting is done that makes all the difference. For example, in Lewin's democracy, agenda setting is done through a collaborative group discussion as opposed to being imposed by elites. The difficulty lies in translating such group discussions to mass-mediated nations.

The current use of agenda setting presents a number of issues for those who favor the use of deliberative persuasion in a democracy. First, the effectiveness of agenda setting underscores Schattschneider's (1960) description of the American people as semisovereign—the freedom to make choices within the range of alternatives provided, in this case, by the mass media. Political power rests with those who control the nature of debate and the direction of discussion. Second, given that few if any issues receive extensive discussion in the mass media, it is difficult for an elected official to develop a nationwide consensus on many important issues. This is especially true for issues that rarely, if ever, receive the attention of the national media—for example, foreign affairs such as admitting Poland into NATO, media-sensitive issues such as the merger of media companies, and issues that cannot be readily translated into a vivid image. Finally, given that the media agenda is set at a national level, local issues are often ignored. Many of these issues, such as schooling, environmental protection in neighborhoods, and mass transportation, are major factors in the quality of life of the average citizen.

Establish a Candidate Image that Appeals to the Majority of Voters

The Importance of Image. In the 1940s, Lazarsfeld, Berelson, and Gaudet (1948) found that voters generally relied on their party affiliation to make their political choices, either by using party as a simple decision rule (e.g., vote for my party) or through the interpersonal influence of party leaders. The rise of mass-mediated campaigns in the 1960s in the United States changed the emphasis to those aspects that can be easily communicated in the mass media—in other words, the candidate's image as it appears on TV (Abelson, Kinder, Peters, & Fiske, 1982; Boiney & Paletz, 1991; Popkin, 1991). Although party identification is still a predictor of voting, party affiliation is declining (Holbrook, 1996), and candidates must increasingly present themselves in a pleasing manner. Much like a pack of cigarettes, a U.S. presidential candidate needs an image that will appeal to enough market segments to win a majority in the Electoral College. The trend from party-based elections to image-based campaigns is occurring globally as nations adopt the American-style of media. For example, in Sweden during the 1950s, less than 10% of voters switched parties (which were often class-based); today less than half of Swedish voters identify with a party (Asp & Esaiasson, 1996). A similar trend occurred in the Netherlands, where affective aspects of a candidate now dominate campaigns (Brants, 1995). In Germany, traditional social groups such as party, social class, and church have become less important as determinants of voting decision (Schoenbach, 1996) and have been replaced by candidate image. For example, in the 1990 German election, the major parties presented exclusively candidate image ads with little discussion of issues (Holtz-Bacha & Kaid, 1995b).

How to Create a Winning Candidate Image. Given the importance of candidate image for winning an election, how is such an image manufactured? One aspect of the Americanization of political campaigns is the hiring of professional media consultants to direct the campaign. In other words, with enough money, a consultant can be hired to dress and stage a politician for maximum appeal (Pratkanis & Aronson, in press). Some examples from recent elections hopefully can make the point.

In 1992, Bill Clinton faced a difficult set of political circumstances. His Democratic party was seen as too liberal and had lost the support of Southerners and the working class (so-called *Reagan Democrats*). In addition, Republicans were making inroads among young voters who were increasingly voting against the Democrats. Finally, he needed to solidify his support among Democratic strongholds such as women. Clinton met this challenge by using the granfalloon technique—adopting various social identities to suggest to voters that, "I am like you; you can trust me." For example, to reach younger voters, Clinton appeared on MTV, played his saxophone on the "Arsenio Hall Show," and joked about smoking marijuana. To reach women, he was firm on his pro-choice position. To reach Southerners, he appealed to regional pride with an all-Southern ticket (Gore is from Tennessee) and reveled in his image as a *bubba*. To appeal to Reagan Democrats, Clinton portrayed himself as a person of humble beginnings and was seen making frequent stops at local McDonald's restaurants.

To win reelection in 1996, Bill Clinton needed to appear *presidential*—to be seen as an effective leader and statesman who was "above all the petty politics" (Pratkanis, 1999). Clinton did this through a series of photo-ops (staged events for the TV cameras) in which he was seen as carrying out the will of the people. Throughout 1996, Clinton signed legislation popular to the American people, such as measures designed to upgrade meat inspection, improve drinking water, increase breast cancer research, enhance the national park system, and get tough on dead-beat dads who do not pay child support. He played the ceremonial role of leader by greeting the Endeavor astronauts, hosting Olympic athletes, and helping to rebuild an African-American church destroyed by arson. He reinforced his role as commander-in-chief by visiting troops in Bosnia and by attacking Iraq. Finally, he raised confidence in his leadership through upbeat ads and a political convention.

The significance of image can also be seen in the first round of the 1990 Polish presidential election (Jakubowicz, 1996). This six-candidate race was expected to be a two-way race between Lech Walesa and the incumbent Prime Minister Tadeusz Mazowiecki, representing two wings (workers and intellectuals, respectively) of Solidarity. However, the Walesa-Mazowiecki conflict over the direction of the Solidarity party created an image of weakness and lack of direction for these two candidates. In contrast, Stanislaw Tyminski, a little-known political figure, successfully used TV to create an image of himself as a success-ful businessman, an independent candidate uncompromised by ties to Solidarity, and a man of discipline, truth, and honesty. Unexpectedly, Tyminski placed sec-ond to Walesa, thereby forcing a run-off election.

What Are the Implications of Image-Based Campaigns for Democracies? One important task of modern U.S. presidents is ceremonial—to represent the mood and feelings of the nation in times of war, peace, and national triumph. An appealing image allows a president to serve this function. However, the emphasis on candidate image is fundamentally opposed to the dreams and intentions of the founders of America. They did not want a king or queen and took steps great (e.g., constitutional checks and balances) and small (e.g., forbidding the granting of titles of nobility to elected leaders) to prevent it. They did want a respected leader who could participate in debates and then faithfully execute the will of the people.

The mass media's fetish for candidate image results in at least two neg-ative consequences for deliberative persuasion. First, candidate image does not equal substance for a number of reasons including; (a) images and symbols often do not correlate with response, (b) the mass media serve as a filtering system, and thus some images that may be important for decision making never reach the home of the TV viewer; (c) images can be conflicting as different images are pre-pared for different social groups, thus making it impossible to know what the candidate stands for; and (d) images can be strategically manipulated as illus-trated in the movie, *Wag the Dog.* Thus, political winners are those who can hire the best image manipulators.

Second, the use of the granfalloon tactic to create an image can often serve evil purposes. Clinton, for the most part, made benign and even positive use of the granfalloon—he did not use the tactic to create outgroups and used it to reach often ignored voters (such as young people). However, this is not always the case, as illustrated in Hitler's image of a strong Aryan nation and his scapegoating of Jews, by many U.S. presidents who used racial politics as a means to get votes (O'Reilly, 1995), and today in places such as Bosnia, Yugoslavia, and the Middle East where social identities lead to destructive conflict. In such cases, granfal-looning can have negative consequences for democracies, including (a) poor deci-sion making as citizens attempt to maintain their social identity at the expense of reasoned thought (Turner & Pratkanis, 1998), (b) exclusion of minority voices that can serve as a stimulus for deliberative discussion, (c) creation of deep divisions in a society that make it difficult to reach a consensus, and (d) ethnic cleansing of citizens (Pratkanis et al., 1998).

Attack and Prepare to Be Attacked

A Negative Campaign. One way to guarantee TV ratings and newspaper circula-tion is through controversy; one way to create controversy in an election is to attack your opponent. As a result, mass-mediated campaigns tend to be divisive, using negative character assassinations and wedge issues to attack opponents. For example, American campaigns have featured such attack ads as Lyndon Johnson's "Daisy ad" raising fear about his opponents nuclear policy and George Bush's infamous "Willie Horton ad" portraying his opponent as weak on crime, especially those crimes committed by African Americans (see Jamieson, 1992). In addition, American campaigns are characterized by wedge issues designed to splinter support for the opposition. For example, Republicans use race to separate lower income Whites from Blacks in the Democratic party, whereas Democrats use abortion rights to separate moderate Republican women from the rest of the party. In the 1992 U.S. presidential election, half of the purchased media time was used for negative ads (Devlin, 1995). Similar results have been found in countries adopting the American-style campaign, including Israel where 48% of all ads in the 1992 national election were negative (Kaid & Holtz-Bacha, 1995), Germany where a third of all ads in the 1990 election focused on attacks of opponents (Holtz-Bacha & Kaid, 1995b), and Britain where 25% of the ads were negative in the 1992 campaign, including the infamous "Jennifer's Ear" describing a child waiting in pain for health services (Kaid & Holtz-Bacha, 1995; Scammell & Semetko, 1995).

One reason that campaigns are negative is that character assassination works to destroy the reputation of the person attacked. For example, Wegner, Wensalaff, Kerker, and Beattie (1981) asked subjects to rate the favorability of political candidates on the basis of a newspaper headline that could be either (a) directly incriminating, (b) questioning the candidate's participation in unseemly behavior, (c) a denial of unseemly behavior, or (d) neutral in content. Not surprisingly, candidates linked with a directly incriminating headline were perceived more negatively. However, merely questioning a candidate's involvement in a misdeed or simply denying that the candidate performed an undesirable behavior was enough to create negative perceptions of the candidate. More recently, Rucker and Pratkanis (1999) found evidence for an interpersonal projection effect. In their four experiments, a person guilty of a misdeed accuses another of doing that same deed. The results were the same across all four studies: Increased blame was placed on the target of the attack and decreased culpability of the accuser. These results occurred despite raising suspicions about the motives of the attacker, providing evidence that the attacker is truly guilty of the misdeed, and timing the projection so that it occurred after the misdeed came to light. Interestingly, White and Lippitt (1960) found that such scapegoating and personal attacks are most likely to occur under autocratic leadership.

How to Attack and Defend to Win. Once again, the presidential campaigns of Bill Clinton provide a textbook example on how to use these influence tactics (Pratkanis, 1993). In 1992, Clinton used the issue of abortion as a wedge to separate moderate Republicans (particularly women) from the fold. However, more important, Clinton forces developed three techniques for responding to the negative attacks by Republicans. First, Clinton directly countered specific alle-gations using the tactic of damn it, refute it, damn it, replace it. For example, to counter allegations that he had had an affair with Gennifer Flowers, the Clintons went on CBS's "60 Minutes" and denied the affair and further stated that they had gone through some rough times, but now things were better than ever. Second, Clinton used the tactic of inoculation (McGuire, 1964), whereby the potential recipient of a negative attack is given a mild dose of the attack to develop counterarguments for refuting later attacks. For example, early in the campaign, Clinton visited the polluted Arkansas River in his home state and defused this potential issue by noting that he had to make hard choices as gov-ernor (jobs vs. environment) under a Republican president and that was the rea-son he was seeking the presidency. Third, Clinton created the expectation that his opponent, George Bush, would attack. Such expectations placed Bush in a dilemma. If he did not attack, he looked weak; if he did attack, he appeared to be mudslinging as usual. To execute these tactics, Clinton developed a rapid response team that monitored his opponents' statements and then responded to any attack within minutes, thus preventing any negative attack from lingering in the mind of the voter.

In 1996, the Clinton campaign was less active in refuting negative alle-gations and rested more on their laurels. The continual unsuccessful attacks on the Clintons by the Republicans most likely had inoculated the American pub-lic. Given that Republicans were unable to prove the first wave of allegations to the satisfaction of the American people, there was little reason to think that the second, third, and subsequent waves of attacks were to be believed. This can be dramatically seen during the later impeachment trial of Bill Clinton, where his public approval ratings actually went up to some of the highest levels ever for a second-term president. A month or so after the trial, Clinton's approval ratings dropped to a more typical level.

The power of negative campaigns can also be seen in the second run-off round of the 1990 Polish presidential election between Lech Walesa and Stanislaw Tyminski (Jakubowicz, 1996). During the first part of the election, the Polish media had played a passive role and merely allowed candidates to present their positions. In the second part, perhaps out of fear of a Tyminski win, the Polish media took a more active role in exposing the Tyminski candidacy. The result was a series of negative portrayals of Tyminski, including a debate with Walesa where opponents attacked Tyminski's weaknesses and a background report purporting to provide evidence that Tyminski treated his wife and children poorly and refused to provide them with living expenses. The positive TV image that Tyminski had created in the first round of the election was destroyed on that same TV set, and Lech Walesa won the presidency with almost 75% of the vote. (In a turn-about-is-fair-play, it should be noted that part of Tyminski's success in the first round of the election was his negative attacks on the leadership of Tadeusz Mazowiecki.)

What Are the Implications of Negative Campaigns for Democracies? Attack campaigns create a number of problems for deliberation in a democracy. First, attack ads directly impeded deliberative discussion by focusing the agenda on a single issue (say, a wedge issue or character assassination); if the attack is not thwarted, further attempts by the candidate under attack to stimulate debate on her or his issues will be rejected. Second, negative campaigns tend to reduce voter turn-out and thus limit participation in a democracy (Ansolabehere & Iyengar, 1995). Third, negative campaigns tend to polarize the electorate into partisan camps (Ansolabehere & Iyengar, 1995) thus making it more difficult to lead and reach consensus on issues. Fourth, attack ads create cynicism about leaders who are portrayed as unable to do or be good. Such as state of affairs is difficult if the populace must trust the leader for information or for policy directions in the case of, say, war or other national emergency. Finally, a series of negative campaigns creates cynicism about the process; political candidates and the media cry wolf so many times that it becomes difficult to know when an attack is based on a real concern or just another example of partisan politics.

WHAT CAN BE DONE?

As Ben Franklin was leaving the U.S. Constitutional Convention on a warm Philadelphia day in September 1787, a young woman approached him and asked, "Dr. Franklin. What have you given us?" Ben Franklin replied, "A republic, if you can keep it." How can we develop and keep a democracy in a mass-mediated world? In other words, how can we prevent the low involvement psychology of the mass media and encourage more thoughtful analysis of the issues confronting us today? Let us look at seven ways to fulfill Ben Franklin's exhortation.

Campaign Spending Reform

Under the current matching funds formula, the American taxpayer foots the bill for much of election year campaigning—for example, spending more than $170 million to finance a typical U.S. presidential election. Why pay for propaganda? Instead of giving candidates a blank cheque to purchase misleading 30-second spots featuring attacks and slick images, why not require recipients of public funds to use the money for debates, open forums with the public, press conferences, and longer infomercials that specify the exact nature of the candidate's position on key issues?

Such regulations have already been adopted in some countries. For example, France requires most political ads to be talking heads (the candidate talks directly to the camera), thus focusing attention on what is said and away from emotion-arousing images (Johnston & Gerstle, 1995). Character assassinations of opponents are more difficult when the candidate has to deliver the message him or herself. In addition, France specifies that patriotic images (such as the French flag) cannot be used in political ads. Israel prohibits appearances on television by Knesset candidates for the 30 days before an election (Cohen & Wolfsfeld, 1995). This limits the power of incumbency (especially to set an agenda and use the image of office), but does limit access to legitimate newsmakers if they happen to be current members of the Knesset. In return, each political party receives free broadcast thus allowing lesser known parties to at least gain some media exposure. In Denmark the purchase of political advertising on public television channels (the dominant media) is prohibited (Siune, 1995). Each political party (regardless of size) is given equal access to television—a 10-minute program to present their views followed by a 30-minute program during which journalists ask questions and then a 3-minute party-produced summary statement. Recently, a new commercial TV channel has appeared and is relaxing some of these rules. Finland prohibits political ads based on negative assessments of a single person (Moring, 1995).

Media Watchdog for Campaign Ads

One recent innovation for counteracting the negative effects of an attack ad is the ad watch developed by Jamieson and her colleagues (Jamieson, 1992). In an ad watch, the news media break a political ad into its basic claims and then evaluate the veracity of each claim based on independent evidence. Jamieson created guidelines for how this information should be presented so that it does not reinforce deceptive statements in the original ad. Ad watches have proved effective in alerting viewers to the unfairness of a false ad (Cappella & Jamieson, 1994) and can even improve the perceptions of candidates who are found to tell the truth in their ads (Jamieson & Cappella, 1997).

Recently, I served as a consultant for a TV station seeking to implement an ad watch at the local level. At the time, ad watches had been conducted primarily by the national media for the U.S. presidential election. The local station sought to evaluate the truthfulness of ads used in local races for the state legislature, as well as for the California governor's race and various propositions. In conducting these ad watches, we learned at least two things. First, campaigns modify their ads in responses to the standards set by ad watches. We found that some campaigns routinely presented false and misleading ads, whereas others were generally truthful. Afraid that we may be biased, we explored how the ads were made and found that the truthful ads were produced by political consultants who had run campaigns at the national level (and thus had experience with ad watches) whereas the untruthful ads were created by consultants who lacked this experience. Second, we found that it required enormous time and resources to track down independent evidence for each claim made in an ad. Often the veracity of a claim depended on the memory of partisans for an event that had occurred 10 or more years ago. In an age when many newsrooms face budget cuts, the expense of an ad watch may discourage some reporters, especially at the local level, from conducting this much needed watchdog function.

Realistic Job Interview

In many ways, the U.S. presidential campaign is like a job interview with the public as interviewer and political candidate as job seeker. Viewed in this light, current campaign practices are all the more absurd. What company would hire a CEO on the basis of how well that person delivered innuendoes about others, divided a company into granfalloons (and thus prevented teamwork), and bleated out a few pet buzzwords? (Answer: a company you do not want to buy stock in.)

The objective of a good interview should be to discover the information needed to make a proper decision. The literature on job interviewing (Adams & Veruki, 1996; Kahn & Cannell, 1957) suggests a number of ways to structure an interview that might be adaptable to the mass media. For example, reporters could focus their stories on measurable outcomes of the candidate's past position (Where did they spend their budgets? What new programs did they implement? How did they work with others in the government?). To discover how candidates think about a problem, they can be asked how they would handle various scenarios (What would you do if nuclear weapons were found in a third world country? If the rate of inflation started to go up? If there was a breakout of school violence?). To make sure that the candidates have thought about their jobs, they can be asked about the obstacles in implementing their desired programs. If done properly, such questions can be entertaining (they contain an element of drama) and would also stimulate informed discussion as citizens pondered what is the best answer to these questions.

Deliberative Polling

Recently, political scientist James Fishkin (1995) proposed the idea of deliberative polling. In Fishkin's plan, a representative group of citizens are brought together for a conference to participate in face-to-face discussions of national issues. They also participate in sessions where they can question policy experts and political candidates. In such a forum, a wide-range of competing arguments can be evaluated and discussed, resulting in more thoughtful conclusions and recommendations. It is Fishkin's hope that such forums can be conducted at the beginning of a major campaign and, through media coverage, serve to stimulate thought and debate about key issues.

Create Involvement Devices

When issues are personally relevant, message recipients are more likely to think deeply about the message and scrutinize it carefully (Petty & Cacioppo, 1986). One way to increase personal relevancy is through involvement devices that specifically link a problem to issues and concerns the recipient feels deeply about. For example, few citizens know how their tax money is spent, thereby leaving a knowledge gap to be exploited by propagandists. Simply providing citizens with a tax receipt thanking them for paying their taxes and listing how their money was spent (e.g., $1,682 on Social Security, $1,102 on defense, $15 on student aid, etc.) would provide citizens information about budget priorities (see Pratkanis & Aronson, in press; Pratkanis & Turner, 1996 for more examples of involvement devices). Similarly, a local news show could trace where the state budget goes by vividly visiting examples of how the money is spent (e.g., describing how much money is spent on schools, legislator staff, welfare, etc). Such a report does not need to be boring (after all, advertisers are highly skilled at making the most trivial benefit seem life enhancing) and can provide an opportunity to stimulate discussion of basic governmental issues. (As an aside, Petty & Cacioppo [1986] also note that message scrutiny is more likely to occur when the recipient has the cognitive capacity to think about the message thus underscoring the observation of Thomas Jefferson on the important of public education).

Restructure the Media for Deliberative Persuasion

During the 1950s, Maier (1952, 1963; Maier & Hoffman, 1960) conducted a program of research that resulted in the development of a number of tactics for improving the quality of discussion in small groups and ultimately the quality of decisions made by these groups (see Turner & Pratkanis, 1998, for a recent application). Many of these techniques can be adapted for the mass media. For example, the two-column method, which requires that all aspects of the situation to be listed, the advantages and disadvantages of each aspect considered along with methods for securing advantages and minimizing disadvantages, can be an effective way to guide discussion of complex issues. Similarly, the developmental discussion technique whereby a discussion is broken into logical steps of soliciting opinions and then systematically appraising objectives and plans, can also provide a means of structuring news gathering and reporting that goes beyond the typical sound bite. Another approach involves multiple role playing, whereby an issue is presented from multiple roles and perspectives and provides additional sources of information to guide decision making. Finally, Maier and Solem's (1952) finding that encouraging the protection of minority opinion results in better decisions can be implemented in the mass media by providing equal time to ensure that all legitimate viewpoints in a community are expressed.

Be a Personal Watchdog for Democracy

It is the responsibility of every citizen to help maintain and develop the institutions of democracy. First, this requires that we look critically at the information we receive by asking such questions as: How credible is this information? What does the source have to gain? Is there evidence to back the claim or is it an idle rumor? Second, we should use communication style as one of the criteria for deciding who should get our vote. For example, a politician who spends most of her or his time making mean-spirited allegations and playing on our emotions does not deserve our vote. Such politicians are merely out to trick us, and we should send a message that demagoguery does not pay. Finally, we need to promote and support the social conditions that help deliberative persuasion prosper: decentralized and multiple sources of information, constraints on power, promoting group discussion, and protecting and valuing minority opinion.

A Note on Implementation

In suggesting these seven possible mechanisms, my goal is twofold: (a) to show that the situation is not hopeless and that we can start to address the dilemma of modern democracy, and (b) to serve as a catalyst for developing additional strategies for stimulating deliberative persuasion. In implementing any proposal designed to invigorate public discussion, one needs to be aware of the norms, institutions, and laws of the communities, which may make it more or less difficult to accomplish a given reform. For example, the U.S. Supreme Court has already ruled that some regulations of political campaigns would violate the constitutional requirement of freedom of speech. In developing democracies, it may be easier to institute wholesale reforms given that all such issues are on the table"and open for discussion. In countries with a strong public broadcasting system, it is reasonable to expect journalistic reform (better interviewing technique, ad watches, etc.) as part of the mission to better serve the community. However, all such efforts should be viewed as experiments in democracy with the goal of discovering what conditions are best for fostering deliberative persuasion.

A PERSONAL CONCLUSION

I had the great honor of presenting these ideas for the first time on the campus of Jagiellonian University in Krakow, Poland. It was there that Nicolaus Copernicus developed what is arguably the most revolutionary idea in human history—that the earth revolves around the sun and not the other way around.

As I looked over the beautiful Polish countryside, I eagerly basked in reflected glory: Here I stood and lectured where once the great Nicolaus Copernicus stood and lectured. My Polish hosts, recognizing my awe and excitement, graciously took me one evening to the Collegium Maius of the Jagiellonian University where the astronomical instruments of Copernicus are stored. As I stood in the courtyard, I imagined how 500 years earlier Copernicus had walked this same courtyard with a gnawing doubt that what he had been taught was wrong. In my mind's eye, I could see a young Copernicus worrying about why the earth changed seasons and why some stars varied in their positions from year to year and arguing and debating within himself and engaging in deliberative persuasion on how this can be if the earth was truly the center of the universe.

As I left the courtyard, I looked up at the corner of a nearby building, the Collegium Novum, and saw an empty room with the lights still on. Shortly after the Nazi invasion of Poland at noon on November 6, 1939, the Gestapo ordered the faculty of Jagiellonian University to this room supposedly to hear a speech on the Third Reich's approach to science and university education. Instead, the faculty were taken prisoner and later sent to the Sachsenhausen and Dachau concentration camps. Many of these professors died and were among the one in every five Poles who lost their lives at the hands of the Nazi regime. The internment of the faculty of Jagiellonian University was a harbinger of things to come. A year later and just a few kilometers away from the university in the town of Oswiecim, perhaps better known by its German name of Auschwitz, the Nazis placed into service what is arguably the most extensive and systematic death machine known to humankind. While in Poland, I also had the opportunity to visit the Auschwitz death camp; I observed the vastness and the scope of human destruction and cruelty perpetrated with such autocratic efficiency. It is here that over 2 million human beings were murdered with their ashes flushed into a nearby pond.

I could not help but be struck by the ironies. Here within the space of a few meters stood a tribute to one of the greatest accomplishments of humankind—an accomplishment that was brought about by doubt over what is the truth and an argument and deliberation that ultimately led us to a better understanding of our place in the universe. Here also stood a reminder of the destruction that we humans can bring about when we think that we have special access to the truth, when we do not respect the rights of minorities and those who disagree with us, when we are so arrogant that we force our will on others.

My visit to Poland made clear the choices we face as a species and the consequences of those choices. The great American philosopher John Dewey once noted, "With each generation democracy must be born anew." The challenge to our generation, whether we reside in established or emerging democracies, is to discover how we can best foster deliberative persuasion in our mass-mediated world and to forestall the propaganda that can result in such human destruction.

ACKNOWLEDGMENTS

I am grateful to the following people for their wise and helpful counsel on issues related to this chapter: Elliot Aronson, Guenter Bierbrauer, Jay Braun, Dariusz Dolinski, Marilyn Getas, Janusz Grzelak, Miroslaw Kofta, Zbigniew Necki, Andrezej Nowak, Janusz Reykowski, Tadeusz Tyszka, Bogdan Wojciszke, and especially Wilhelmina Wosinska.

REFERENCES

Abelson, R. P., Kinder, D. R., Peters, M. D., & Fiske, S. T. (1982). Affective and semantic components in political person perception. *Journal of Personality and Social Psychology, 42*, 619–630.

Adams, B., & Veruki, P. (1996). *Hiring top performers.* Holbrook, MA: Adams Media.

Ansolabehere, S., Behr, R., & Iyengar, D. (1993). *The media game.* New York: Macmillan.

Ansolabehere, S., & Iyengar, D. (1995). *Going negative.* New York: The Free Press.

Asp, K., & Esaiasson, P. (1996). The modernization of Swedish campaigns: Individualization, professionalization, and medialization. In D. L. Swanson & P. Mancini (Eds.), *Politics, media, and democracy* (pp. 73–90). Westport, CT: Praeger.

Baumgartner, F. R., Jones, B. D., & Leech, B. L. (1997). Media attention and congressional agendas. In S. Iyengar & R. Reeves (Eds.), Do the media govern? (pp. 349–363). Thousand Oaks, CA: Sage.

Benn, D. W. (1989). *Persuasion and Soviet politics.* New York: Basil Blackwell.

Boiney, J., & Paletz, D. (1991). In search of the model: Political science versus political advertising perspectives on voter decision making. In F. Biocca (Ed.), *Television and political advertising* (Vol. 1, pp. 3–25). Hillsdale, NJ: Lawrence Erlbaum Associates.

Brants, K. (1995). The blank spot: Political advertising in the Netherlands. In L. L. Kaid & C. Holtz-Bacha (Eds.), *Political advertising in Western democracies* (pp. 143–160). Thousand Oaks, CA: Sage.

Cappella, J. N., & Jamieson, K. H. (1994). Broadcast adwatch effects: A field experiment. *Communication Research, 21*, 342–365.

Caspi, D. (1996). American-style electioneering in Israel: Americanization versus modernization. In D. L. Swanson & P. Mancini (Eds.), *Politics, media, and democracy* (pp. 173–192). Westport, CT: Praeger.

Cialdini, R. B. (1984). *Influence.* New York: William Morrow.

Cohen, A. A., & Wolfsfeld, G. (1995). Overcoming adversity and diversity: The utility of television political advertising in Israel. In L. L. Kaid & C.

Holtz-Bacha (Eds.), *Political advertising in Western democracies* (pp. 109–123). Thousand Oaks, CA: Sage.

Devlin, L. P. (1995). Political commercials in American presidential elections. In L. L. Kaid & C. Holtz-Bacha (Eds.), *Political advertising in Western democracies* (pp. 186–205). Thousand Oaks, CA: Sage.

Doob, L. W. (1950). Goebbels' principles of propaganda. *Public Opinion Quarterly, 14*, 419–422.

Eliasoph, N. (1998). *Avoiding politics: How Americans produce apathy in everyday life*. Cambridge, England: Cambridge University Press.

Entman, R. M. (1989). *Democracy without citizens*. New York: Oxford University Press.

Fearon, J. D. (1998). Deliberation as discussion. In J. Elster (Ed.), *Deliberative democracy* (pp. 44–68). Cambridge, England: Cambridge University Press.

Fishkin, J. S. (1995). *The voice of the people*. New Haven, CT: Yale University Press.

Hallin, D. C. (1992). Sound bite news coverage: Television coverage of elections, 1968–1988. *Journal of Communication, 42*, 5–24.

Hitler, A. (1925/1971). *Mein kampf*. Boston, MA: Houghton-Mifflin.

Holbrook, T. M. (1996). *Do campaigns matter?* Thousand Oaks, CA: Sage.

Holtz-Bacha, C., & Kaid, L. L. (1995a). A comparative perspective on political advertising. In L. L. Kaid & C. Holtz-Bacha (Eds.), *Political advertising in Western democracies* (pp. 8–18). Thousand Oaks, CA: Sage.

Holtz-Bacha, C., & Kaid, L. L. (1995b). Television spots in German national elections: Contents and effects. In L. L. Kaid & C. Holtz-Bacha (Eds.), *Political advertising in Western democracies* (pp. 61–88). Thousand Oaks, CA: Sage.

Iyengar, S., & Kinder, D. R. (1987). *News that matters*. Chicago: University of Chicago Press.

Jakubowicz, K. (1996). Television and elections in post-1989 Poland: How powerful is the medium? In D. L. Swanson & P. Mancini (Eds.), *Politics, media, and democracy* (pp. 129–154). Westport, CT: Praeger.

Jamieson, K. H. (1992). *Dirty politics*. New York: Oxford Press.

Jamieson, K. H., & Cappella, J. N. (1997). Setting the record straight: Do ad watches help or hurt? *Press/Politics, 2*, 13–22.

Johnston, A., & Gerstle, J. (1995). The role of television broadcasts in promoting French presidential candidates. In L. L. Kaid & C. Holtz-Bacha (Eds.), *Political advertising in Western democracies* (pp. 44–60). Thousand Oaks, CA: Sage.

Kahn, R. L., & Cannell, C. F. (1957). *The dynamics of interviewing*. New York: Wiley.

Kaid, L. L., & Holtz-Bacha, C. (1995). Political advertising across cultures: Comparing content, style, and effects. In L. L. Kaid & C. Holtz-Bacha (Eds.), *Political advertising in Western democracies* (pp. 206–227). Thousand Oaks, CA: Sage.

Krugman, H. E. (1965). The impact of television advertising: Learning without involvement. *Public Opinion Quarterly, 29,* 349–356.

Lazarsfeld, P., Berelson, B., & Gaudet, H. (1948). *The people's choice.* New York: Harcourt, Brace.

Lewin, K., & Lippitt, R. (1938). An experimental approach to the study of autocracy and democracy: A preliminary note. *Sociometry, 1,* 292–300.

Lewin, K., Lippitt, R., & White, R. K. (1939). Patterns of aggressive behavior in experimentally created climates. *Journal of Social Psychology, 10,* 271–299.

Lind, A. A., & Tyler, T. R. (1998). *The social psychology of procedural justice.* New York: Plenum.

Maier, N. R. F. (1952). *Principles of human relations.* New York: Wiley.

Maier, N. R. F. (1963). *Problem-solving discussions and conferences.* New York: McGraw-Hill.

Maier, N. R. F., & Hoffman, L. R. (1960). Using trained "developmental" discussion leaders to improve further the quality of group decisions. *Journal of Applied Psychology, 44,* 247–251.

Maier, N. R. F., & Solem, A. R. (1952). The contribution of a discussion leader to the quality of group thinking: The effective use of minority opinions. *Human Relations, 5,* 277–288.

Marcus, J. (1992). Mesoamerican writing systems: *Propaganda, myth, and history in four ancient civilizations.* Princeton, NJ: Princeton University Press.

McCombs, M. E., & Shaw, D. L. (1972). The agenda setting function of mass media. *Public Opinion Quarterly, 36,* 176–187.

McGuire, W. J. (1964). Inducing resistance to persuasion: Some contemporary approaches. In L. Berkowitz (Ed.), *Advances in experimental social psychology* (Vol. 1, pp. 191–229). San Diego: Academic Press.

Million-dollar House races jump 24%, report shows. (1998, December 30). *San Jose Mercury News,* p. 8A.

Moring, T. (1995). The North European exception: Political advertising on TV in Finland. In L. L. Kaid & C. Holtz-Bacha (Eds.), *Political advertising in Western democracies* (pp. 161–185). Thousand Oaks, CA: Sage.

Nemeth, C. J. (1981). Jury trials: Psychology and law. In L. Berkowitz (Ed.), *Advances in experimental social psychology* (Vol. 14, pp. 309–367). New York: Academic Press.

Nemeth, C. J. (1994). The value of minority dissent. In S. Moscovici, A. Mucchi-Faina, & A. Maass (Eds.), *Minority influence* (pp. 3–15). Chicago: Nelson-Hall.

O'Reilly, K. (1995). *Nixon's piano: Presidents and racial politics from Washington to Clinton*. New York: The Free Press.

Petty, R. E., & Cacioppo, J. T. (1986). *Communication and persuasion: Central and peripheral routes to persuasion*. New York: Springer-Verlag.

Popkin, S. L. (1991). *The reasoning voter*. Chicago, IL: University of Chicago Press.

Pratkanis, A. R. (1993). Propaganda and persuasion in the 1992 U.S. presidential election: What are the implications for a democracy? *Current World Leaders, 36*, 341–362.

Pratkanis, A. R. (1997). The social psychology of mass communications: An American perspective. In D. F. Halpern & A. E. Voiskounsky (Eds.), *States of mind: American and post-Soviet perspectives on contemporary issues in psychology* (pp. 126–159). New York: Oxford University Press.

Pratkanis, A. R. et. al. (1998). Izbor savesti [A choice of conscience] (R. Mahmutcehajic, Trans.). *Dialogue: A Journal for Philosophy and Social Issues*, No. 2/3, 239–251.

Pratkanis, A. R. (1999). *Ho-humness as propaganda device in the 1996 U.S. presidential election*. Unpublished paper, University of California, Santa Cruz.

Pratkanis, A. R., & Aronson, E. (in press). *Age of propaganda: The everyday use and abuse of persuasion* (2nd ed.). New York: W. H. Freeman.

Pratkanis, A. R., & Turner, M. E. (1996). Persuasion and democracy: Strategies for increasing deliberative participation and enacting social change. *Journal of Social Issues, 52*, 187–205.

Reeves, R. (1997). The brave new world of media politics. In S. Iyengar & R. Reeves (Eds.), *Do the media govern?* (pp. ix–xx). Thousand Oaks, CA: Sage.

Reykowski, J. (1993). Resolving large-scale political conflict: The case of the Round Table negotiations in Poland. In S. Worchel & J. A. Simpson (Eds.), *Conflict between people and groups* (pp. 214–232). Chicago: Nelson-Hall.

Rogers, E. M., & Dearing, J. W. (1988). Agenda setting research: Where has it been, where is it going? In J. A. Anderson (Ed.), *Communication Yearbook 11* (pp. 555–594). Beverly Hills, CA: Sage.

Rucker, D. D., & Pratkanis, A. R. (1999, under review). Projection as an interpersonal influence tactic: The effects of the pot calling the kettle black.

Rutherford, W. (1978). *Hitler's propaganda machine*. London: Bison.

Scammell, M., & Semetko, H. A. (1995). Political advertising on television: The British experience. In L. L. Kaid & C. Holtz-Bacha (Eds.), *Political advertising in Western democracies* (pp. 19–60). Thousand Oaks, CA: Sage.

Schattschneider, E. E. (1960). *The semi-sovereign people*. Hinsdale, IL: Dryden.

Schoenbach, K. (1996). The "Americanization" of German election campaigns: Any impact on voters? In D. L. Swanson & P. Mancini (Eds.), *Politics, media, and democracy* (pp. 91–103). Westport, CT: Praeger.

Siune, K. (1995). Political advertising in Denmark. In L. L. Kaid & C. Holtz-Bacha (Eds.), *Political advertising in Western democracies* (pp. 124–142). Thousand Oaks, CA: Sage.

Stanley, H., & Niemi, R. G. (1994). *Vital statistics on American politics* (3rd ed.). Washington, DC: CQ Press.

Swanson, D. L., & Mancini, P. (Eds.). (1996). *Politics, media, and democracy.* Westport, CT: Praeger.

Turner, M. E., & Pratkanis, A. R. (1998). A social identity maintenance model of groupthink. *Organizational Behavior and Human Decision Processes, 73,* 210–235.

Wegner, D. M., Wensalaff, R., Kerker, R. M., and Beattie, A. E. (1981). Incrimination through innuendo: Can media questions become public answers? *Journal of Personality and Social Psychology, 40,* 833–832.

West, D. M. (1993). *Air wars: Television advertising in election campaigns,* 1952–1992. Washington, DC: CQ Press.

White, R. K., & Lippitt, R. (1960). *Autocracy and democracy: An experimental inquiry.* New York: Harper & Brothers.

Zamoyski, A. (1987). *The Polish way.* New York: Hippocrene Books.

15

Basic Research and Practical Problems: Volunteerism and the Psychology of Individual and Collective Action

Mark Snyder

University of Minnesota

Allen M. Omoto

University of Kansas

ABSTRACT

Volunteerism is a form of prosocial action in which people seek out opportunities to help others in need, make considerable and continuing commitments to offer assistance, and may do so in stressful circumstances without any bonds of prior obligation to the recipients of their services. In this chapter, we present a conceptual model of the processes of volunteerism that articulates the antecedents, experiences, and consequences of volunteerism. Further, we review a program of basic and applied research, conducted in the field and in the laboratory with diverse samples of volunteers and nonvolunteers, on the personal and social considerations that dispose people to volunteer and that sustain them in their ongoing helping relationships. Finally, we articulate the theoretical and practical implications of the psychology of volunteerism, and place volunteerism and other forms of citizen participation in the societal and cultural contexts in which they occur.

OVERVIEW

In this chapter, we discuss individual and collective action taken by citizens to address problems that confront and challenge their society. We do so with a special eye toward volunteer efforts in the United States, but also by considering rates of volunteerism and potential determinants of individual and collective action in different cultures and countries as well. To do so, we draw on our program of research on the psychology of volunteerism. Volunteerism is one example of the broader class of behaviors that can be called *civic participation* (e.g., see also, Kymlicka & Norman, 1994; Putnam, 1993; Verba, Schlozman, & Brady, 1995) and also includes behaviors such as voting in elections, joining professional organizations, active involvement in neighborhood groups and churches, and charitable giving. From this perspective, volunteerism and other forms of civic participation are behaviors that link individuals in dynamic fashion with the social structures of their societies, such that individuals both influence and are influenced by their societies.

The volunteer efforts of greatest concern to us have certain defining and characteristic features. Typically, they involve people choosing to help others in need. Moreover, these voluntary acts of helping are ones that have been actively sought out by the volunteers and are characterized by sustained efforts, often over extended periods of time and involving considerable expenditure of time and effort. That is, we are especially concerned with efforts in which volunteers make considerable and continuing commitments to provide assistance and to sustain these commitments. Because volunteers typically are engaged in helping others with whom they had no prior contact or association, it is helping that occurs without any bonds of prior obligation or commitment to the recipients of the services of volunteers.

We have developed a conceptual model of what we refer to as the volunteer process—a conceptual model that considers multiple levels of analysis and different stages in the life course of volunteers. Our model is informed by a functional approach to personality, motivation, and social behavior, which emphasizes the purposive and agentic nature of human action (e.g., Snyder & Cantor, 1998). This model has guided our empirical research on the personal and social motivations that dispose people to volunteer and that sustain them in their involvement in these ongoing helping relationships. We have collected data from actual volunteers and from nonvolunteers in both field and laboratory settings in a coordinated program of basic and applied investigations of the volunteer process.

In this chapter, we briefly outline the central tenets of our conceptual framework and review some of the major findings of our research program. We then expand our focus to consider other varieties of individual and collective participation in society and the characteristics of societies that may facilitate the development of a volunteer culture (one that encourages high rates of civic participation). As we see, volunteerism is a phenomenon that that is situated at, and builds bridges among, many levels of analysis—at the individual level, it involves the activities of individual volunteer and individual recipients of volunteer services; at the interpersonal level, it involves the dynamics of the helping relationships between volunteers and recipients; and at the societal level, it involves the linkages between individuals and the social structures of their societies. Throughout this chapter, furthermore, we hope to underscore the ways in which our research informs basic theory and research on helping and social influence, as well as how it contributes to solving the practical problems of how to involve and sustain volunteers in serving their communities. In this way, we seek to illustrate how a broadly defined and functionally oriented approach to the psychology of citizen participation can contribute to the building of bridges between basic research and practical problems.

VOLUNTEERISM AND OTHER FORMS OF PROSOCIAL ACTION

In our research, we have been studying people in the United States who are actively involved in doing good for others and for their society—individuals and communities who have mobilized themselves to respond to social problems, to do their part to make the world a better place. Specifically, we have been studying the phenomenon of *volunteerism*. Every year, millions of people serve as volunteers and, in so doing, devote substantial amounts of their time and energy to helping others (e.g., by volunteering to provide companionship to the elderly, tutoring to the illiterate, counseling to the troubled, mentoring to children, or health care to the sick). In fact, according to one recent survey, approximately 93 million adults in the United States perform volunteer service each year, with roughly 25 million devoting an average of over 4 hours of their time each week to volunteerism. In a purely economic sense, these volunteer services are extremely valuable ones—estimated to be worth over $200 billion (Independent Sector, 1996). Although rates of volunteerism are especially high in the United States, voluntary action and civic participation can be found in many other countries throughout the world (e.g., Curtis, Grabb, & Baer, 1992).

Volunteerism benefits the recipients of service and the broader community. As such, volunteer service is one way that people can help other people and, at the same time, help alleviate some of society's problems. Volunteer service also rewards volunteers by promoting community spirit, offering evidence of people's kindness and commitment to others, increasing feelings of helpfulness and self-worth, providing opportunities to develop and exercise different skills, and actually improving physical health (e.g., Andrews, 1990). Put in the simplest of terms, volunteer service provides individuals with opportunities to, at one and the same time, do good for other people, for society, and for themselves.

From a scientific perspective, the study of volunteerism provides opportunities for inquiring into the nature of helping and of prosocial action more generally. It also provides opportunities to explore linkages between individuals and society. In understanding the nature of helping two distinct traditions of research in psychology are relevant, each of which has investigated a specific form of helping and has focused on particular theoretical issues relevant to understanding that form of helping. As we suggest later, volunteerism is a distinctive form of helping behavior, although it shares many features and characteristics with the forms of prosocial action that have been the focus of previous theory and research. Thus, studying volunteerism, we believe, has the potential not only to inform a psychology of a distinctive form of helping, but also for illuminating issues in these other traditions in the study of helping.

One of these research traditions focuses on situations in which potential helpers are confronted with unexpected opportunities to help strangers (the classic example being bystander intervention; Latané & Darley, 1970). The help that occurs here is typically unplanned and spontaneous, is usually confined to relatively brief encounters, and generally entails neither prior acquaintance nor future contact between helper and recipient. Primary concerns of research conducted within this tradition have been to understand who helps in these circumstances and why those who help do so—or, more generally, to consider motivational and personological explanations for the occurrence of this spontaneous form of helping. Some researchers have proposed that this type of helping reflects intrinsically humanitarian concerns and altruistic personalities (e.g., Carlo, Eisenberg, Troyer, Switzer, & Speer, 1991; Rushton, 1984; Staub, 1974), whereas other researchers have made claims about ultimate motivations, including asserting that such helping is motivated by selfish concerns (such as to feel good, to boost self-esteem, or secure social recognition; e.g., Cialdini et al., 1987; Schaller & Cialdini, 1988; Smith, Keating, & Stotland, 1989) or that it reflects more purely altruistic motives to benefit others (Batson, 1998).

A second research tradition, one that has grown up relatively independent of the first, focuses on people who provide long-term and continuing assistance, care, and support to others who suffer from serious illness or chronic conditions. Most of the research in this tradition examines obligated caregivers, who, because of marital bond or blood relationship, provide assistance and services to a spouse, parent, child, or sibling suffering from ailments such as Alzheimer's disease, AIDS, arthritis, or the aftermath of a stroke or serious accident (e.g., Folkman, Chesney, Cooke, Boccellari, & Collette, 1994; Hobfoll & Lerman, 1988; Kinney & Stephens, 1989; Revenson & Majerovitz, 1990; Schulz, Williamson, Morycz, & Biegel, 1992; Thompson & Pitts, 1992). In such relationships, the impetus for assistance may reasonably be seen to flow from the legal, ethical, or familial obligations between helpers and the recipients of assistance, thereby rendering questions of personality and motivation all but moot. These helpers help because they have to, doing so for reasons related to moral, legal, or personal indebtedness.

Instead of focusing on the reasons why such helping occurs, this literature has focused on the nature of such caregiving, including the stresses, demands, and psychic and physical tolls that it extracts from the people involved. The research has generally adopted a stress-coping framework (e.g., Lazarus & Folkman, 1984) to understanding what sustains people in their helping efforts and how they are affected by their experiences as volunteers.

Volunteerism, we assert, represents a distinctive form of helping (Clary & Snyder, 1991; Omoto & Snyder, 1995; Piliavin & Charng, 1990; Smith & Macaulay, 1980) characterized by features that set it apart from the forms of helping studied in each of the research traditions just discussed. Rather than happening on situations in which help is required or having these situations thrust on them, volunteers typically seek out their opportunities to help; they may deliberate long and hard about whether to initiate volunteerism and, having decided to volunteer, about the extent and precise nature of their involvement. That is, unlike the helping that occurs in response to emergencies, there is no press of circumstance. Also, volunteers typically do not know those they help in advance because they are generally matched with recipients of service by organizations or associations. As such, volunteers are under no prior obligation to enter into personal helping relationships. That is, unlike the helping and caregiving that occurs in existing relationships, there are no bonds of commitment that obligate or mandate helping. Moreover, many forms of volunteerism entail commitments that extend over considerable periods of time and that may also include sizable personal and social costs. That is, volunteerism can be effortful, time consuming, and present *opportunity costs* to volunteers as people forego other activities and social relations in lieu of their volunteer activities. Furthermore, some volunteer activities may introduce additional social costs to and even possible rejection of those who volunteer.

Although many features of volunteerism set it apart from other forms of helping, many of its features can also be seen to make it a hybrid strain of helping. Volunteerism engages questions associated with each of the extant research traditions already discussed. It raises questions of personality (is it enacted only by individuals with altruistic dispositions?), of motivation (why, in the absence of obligation, do people volunteer?), of mechanisms for sustaining it (in what ways do personal and social resources promote long-term helping?), and of its impact on volunteers (what personal and psychic costs and benefits accrue to volunteers?).

At a theoretical level, then, understanding volunteerism requires researchers and theorists to broach questions that are also of fundamental concern in understanding other forms of helping. It should be pointed out that (and as we hope to make clear in this chapter) studying volunteerism also has the potential to contribute to broader literatures on social influence, interpersonal relationships, stereotyping and prejudice, identity development, and even organizational and community psychology. Yet despite its potential to engage a wide range of theoretical questions and disparate topic areas, there has been remarkably little psychological research on volunteerism and even less theoretical development in this area (see Clary & Snyder, 1991; Piliavin & Charng, 1990). Until recently at least, there has been little in the way of answers to questions as fundamental as: Why do some people get involved in helping others as volunteers and in participating in society? What is it that moves people to seek out opportunities to help, that guides them toward some helping opportunities and away from others, and that sustains their efforts over time and through adversity? What kinds of relationships do volunteers and recipients of service develop with each other, and how are these relationships negotiated and changed over time? What effects does volunteerism have on volunteers and on recipients of service and communities at large? These are some of the questions that we address in our research.

THE PROCESSES OF VOLUNTEERISM

In our research, we have examined the processes of volunteerism, and the dynamics of voluntary helping relationships as they occur in the real world, focusing on *real* individuals involved in *real* acts of volunteerism in real-world settings. In so doing, we have entered into a naturally occurring laboratory to investigate a phenomenon of significance for individual and collective action. Our research has been grounded in, and guided by, a conceptual model of the volunteer process that identifies three major stages of the ongoing events of volunteerism: the antecedents of volunteerism, the experiences of volunteerism, and the consequences of volunteerism. The volunteer process model, as we have articulated it, specifies psychological and behavioral features associated with each stage and speaks to activity at three levels of analysis: the individual volunteer, the organizational context in which volunteering takes place, and the broader social system, including persons living with AIDS (PWAs), friends and family members, and communities at large (for elaboration on the stages of the volunteer process and the levels of analysis in the volunteer process model, see Table 15.1). In keeping with the key features of volunteerism identified earlier, this model draws on many subdisciplines of psychology, as well as the fields of sociology, anthropology, public health, and business. In the model, volunteerism is conceptualized in terms of a process involving three interactive and sequential stages. The different levels of analysis also interact with each other. For ease of explication, however, we discuss the stages of the volunteer process separately, focusing primarily on the level of the individual volunteer (for further discussion of the volunteer process model, see Omoto, Snyder, & Berghuis, 1993; Omoto & Snyder, 1990; Snyder & Omoto, 1992a).

    In our program of research, the volunteer process model has helped frame the conceptual questions that we have asked about volunteerism and has

TABLE 15.1
Conceptual Model of the Volunteer Process

STAGES OF THE VOLUNTEER PROCESS

Level of Analysis	Antecedents	Experiences	Consequences
Organization	• Recruitment of volunteers • Training of volunteers	• Assignment of volunteers to tasks • Tracking of volunteers • Delivery of services	• Quantity & quality of services provided • Absenteeism, turnover, & reenlistment • Fulfillment of mission
Individual Volunteer	• Demographics • Prior experiences • Personality & individual differences • Resources & skills • Motivations • Identity concerns • Expectations • Social support from existing network	• Volunteer's choice of role • Volunteer performance • Relationship with client • Support from other volunteers • Organizational integration • Satisfaction	• Change in knowledge, attitudes, behaviors, & motivation • Identity development • Commitment to volunteering • Evaluation of volunteer experience • Commitment to organization • Recruitment of other volunteers • Length of service
Broader Social System	• Social & cultural climates relevant to volunteerism	• Effects on recipients of services • Effects on volunteers' social networks	• Social diffusion • Public education • Systems of service delivery

guided our empirical inquiries into volunteerism as a form of sustained, ongoing, prosocial action. Of particular concern to us, in our empirical investigations of the volunteer process model, has been the specific case of individuals involved in volunteer service programs that have emerged in the United States in response to the epidemic of HIV and AIDS (Omoto & Snyder, 1990, 1995; Snyder & Omoto, 1992a, 1992b). HIV disease, including AIDS, has had and continues to have major medical, economic, social, and societal impact throughout the world. A critical component of the societal response to the HIV epidemic in the United States has been community-based organizations of volunteers involved in caring for PWAs and in educating the public about HIV and PWAs (e.g., Chambré, 1991). In the United States, AIDS service organizations have emerged in every state, in cities large and small, and in rural areas as well. Some volunteers provide emotional and social support as "buddies" to PWAs, others help PWAs with household chores or transportation, and still others staff information and referral hotlines, make educational presentations, or engage in advocacy. AIDS volunteers donate valuable services. In fact, it has been documented that the cost of caring for PWAs is greatly reduced in areas with active volunteer programs, and AIDS-related deaths have become less likely to take place in inpatient hospital settings and more likely to occur at home or in hospices most likely because of support services provided by volunteers (Hellinger, 1993; Kelly, Chu, & Buehler, 1993; Turner, Catania, & Gagnon, 1994). Clearly, AIDS volunteerism has considerable economic, public policy, and public health impact.

In our program of research, we have used the specific case of AIDS volunteerism to inform a more general understanding of the social and psychological aspects of volunteerism. The overarching goals of this research program are to understand why people become AIDS volunteers, what sustains their volunteer activities over time and in the face of many personal costs associated with AIDS volunteerism, what volunteers and others gain from their efforts, and how volunteering affects the lives of volunteers, PWAs, and the communities in which it is embedded. In addressing these broad questions, we have conducted coordinated field-based and laboratory studies employing longitudinal and cross-sectional research methodologies and drawing from diverse populations of volunteers and nonvolunteers. We turn to some of the ways that our studies speak to key issues at each of the three stages of the volunteer process model. We do not aim to provide an exhaustive or comprehensive description of our research and its findings. Rather, for each stage of the volunteer process, we simply seek to briefly describe some of the major issues we have explored in our work as well as what we have found. We trust that this type of outline provides sufficient flavor for our research as well as grounding for additional comments on some of the connections between basic and practical issues in volunteerism and potential cultural influences on volunteerism and citizen participation.

Antecedents of Volunteerism

At the level of the individual volunteer, the antecedents stage of the volunteer process addresses the characteristics that volunteers bring to their work.

Potential volunteers may have differing personalities that may predispose them to offer certain kinds of help and have different prior histories of involvement with volunteerism or citizen participation, including with the specific form of volunteerism on which they are about to embark. Of special concern in our research are the motivations of AIDS volunteers and their expectations for their service. In exploring issues at this stage, we have utilized exploratory and confirmatory factor analytic techniques in multiple samples in identifying five primary motivations for AIDS volunteerism (Omoto & Snyder, 1995; see also Ouellette, Cassel, Maslanka, & Wong, 1995). That is, consistent with a functional approach to volunteerism and citizen participation (Clary & Snyder, 1991; Snyder, Clary, & Stukas, 2000, Snyder & Omoto, in press), we have found that AIDS volunteerism is enacted by different people to serve different goals, psychological functions, or motivations.

Based on our research, it appears that AIDS volunteerism allows some people to express their personal values and beliefs or to satisfy felt humanitarian obligations to help others; that is, it may serve a values function or motivation. Another relatively other-focused motivation expressed by volunteers is that of community concern, or volunteering out of obligation or concern about a community or particular social grouping. In the case of AIDS volunteerism in the United States, this has meant volunteering out of concern for people affected by HIV disease or the gay community (because men who have sex with men have accounted for the largest proportion of AIDS cases in the United States). The remaining three primary motivations are more self-focused in nature. Some AIDS volunteers come to their work primarily in search of greater understanding of AIDS and how people cope with HIV disease, some for reasons related to personal development such as to challenge themselves or enlarge their social networks. The final motivation is esteem enhancement, or volunteering to feel better about oneself or escape pressures and stress in other areas of one's life. In general, values motivation tends to be endorsed most strongly by AIDS volunteers and esteem enhancement least strongly; the other three motivations fall somewhere in between (see Omoto & Snyder, 1993). In short, however, it is clear that the same act of AIDS volunteerism is initiated and maintained for different, and sometimes changing, reasons.

An appreciation of the strength and variety of different motivations that lead people to do volunteer work, we believe, is necessary for developing effective methods of attracting new citizens to involve themselves in volunteer activities and associations. Rather than adopt a *one size fits all* approach to volunteer recruitment and training, organizations may be better served by creating advertisements and recruitment materials that differentially speak to the different motivations for citizen participation. This is but one example of how basic theory and research cannot only be enhanced by but also contribute to practical issues in volunteerism.

Experiences of Volunteerism

In focusing on the experiences stage of volunteerism for volunteers, we have explored the interpersonal relationships that develop between volunteers and recipients of their services (especially PWAs in buddy programs), volunteers' perceptions of their work and their volunteer organization, volunteers' perceptions of other people's reactions to their work as AIDS volunteers, and the extent to which volunteers feel that their service has met their expectations and fulfilled their needs. Illustrative of our findings at this stage, we have observed that volunteers who serve as buddies for PWAs have relatively high expectations for the quality of the relationships they will develop with client PWAs before they meet, and that actual volunteer–PWA relationships as they are experienced by volunteers fall short of these expectations (Omoto, Gunn, & Crain, 1998). Similarly, volunteer satisfaction with buddy relationships falls short of expectations, and volunteers report some stress from these relationships. The data suggest that the stress experienced by volunteers in these relationships is related to the closeness of the relationship and to the client's health; stress tends to increase with increasing relationship closeness early on, whereas being paired with a relatively healthier client is related to less stress on the part of their volunteers.

Volunteers also report feelings of stigmatization and discomfort resulting from their work as AIDS volunteers. In fact, many report that the reactions of members of their own social networks have caused them to feel embarrassed, uncomfortable, and stigmatized because of their AIDS volunteerism (Omoto, Snyder, & Crain, 1998a, 1998b; Snyder, Omoto, & Crain, 1999). This stigmatization has an ironic twist to it. National surveys in the United States indicate that the general public overwhelmingly believes that the need for charitable organizations is greater now than in the recent past and that charitable organizations help make communities better places to live (Independent Sector, 1996). Moreover, this stigmatization appears to come from volunteering to work in an AIDS-related context; hospice volunteers (who perform many of the same functions as AIDS volunteers, but with clients suffering from terminal diseases other than AIDS) report significantly lower feelings of stigmatization from the work they do (Omoto, Snyder, & Crain, 1998b). Thus, it is likely that the association of HIV disease with marginalized and already stigmatized members of society leads to spillover stigmatization of AIDS volunteers. This explanation also has been supported in some of our own laboratory research on the social costs associated with volunteerism (Omoto, Snyder, & Crain, 1998a).

Consequences of Volunteerism

Among the issues at the consequences stage, our research questions have focused on changes in attitudes, knowledge, and behavior among volunteers as a result of their service, as well as their ultimate longevity of service and their perceived and judged effectiveness as volunteers. Volunteers may play roles in changing societal attitudes and beliefs about HIV disease and PWAs and in creating new systems of service delivery; these broader social consequences are also of interest at the consequences stage. In longitudinal research with repeated measurements over time, we have found that volunteers are indeed changed by their experiences with, for example, increases in knowledge about safer sex practices, less stereotyped beliefs about PWAs, and significantly greater comfort with AIDS and AIDS-related issues (Omoto & Snyder, 1999). In their own self-reports, moreover, volunteers reveal that their experiences have powerfully affected and changed them (Omoto & Snyder, 1995).

In exploring longevity of service, we have found that the duration of service of one group of AIDS volunteers was related to their satisfaction with their work, the amount of support they perceived from their social network, and the motivations they reported for becoming AIDS volunteers (Omoto & Snyder, 1995). Specifically, volunteers served longer to the extent that they were more satisfied with their work, had less social support, and reported stronger and particularly self-focused motivation for volunteering. The fact that greater social support was actually related to shorter length of service is consistent with our findings about the stigmatization of AIDS volunteers. To the extent that being a volunteer disrupts harmonious relations with members of one's social network, and to the extent that these social network members respond negatively to this disruption and to the AIDS volunteerism that has occasioned this disruption, volunteers may be likely to quit sooner than if their work is supported by others.

In addition, we have conducted several laboratory studies and analyses of longitudinal data from AIDS volunteers, all of which converge to suggest influences of stigmatization across the volunteer process. People who believe that they will be targets of stigmatization for AIDS-related volunteerism are less likely to follow through on their initial intentions to become volunteers, and those people who expect the most negative reactions from others are least likely to even complete the training that organizations generally require before they assign volunteers to work on specific tasks in the organization. For those who complete training and become AIDS volunteers, greater perceptions of stigmatization are related to an increased likelihood of early termination of service, particularly if the experiences of stigmatization were relatively unanticipated (Omoto, Snyder, & Crain, 1998a; Snyder, Omoto, & Crain, 1999).

The findings with respect to volunteers' motivations, although initially surprising to us, are understandable in retrospect. Engaging in volunteerism for reasons related to understanding, personal development, or esteem enhancement all predicted longer duration of service, whereas ratings of the values and community concern motivations were unrelated to longevity of service. Thus, volunteers who can and did get something back from their work were likely to stay involved longer. Volunteering for relatively more other-focused reasons, however, may not sustain people in the face of the stress and stigmatization they are likely to encounter as volunteers. This finding has implications not only for the recruitment of volunteers, but also for their training and for strategies that organizations might employ to retain volunteers. Volunteers need to be inoculated against potential stigmatization they might receive because of their work and assisted in seeing the many personal (as well as societal) benefits that their volunteer work provides. Focusing on these considerations not only informs psychological theory and research on motivation and stigmatization, but also should aid in addressing the practical issue of how to increase the satisfaction of volunteers and more effectively retain them in service to aid others and society.

PRACTICAL IMPLICATIONS OF UNDERSTANDING THE PSYCHOLOGY OF VOLUNTEERISM

Clearly, the emergence of volunteer service organizations in the United States has provided us with considerable opportunities to explore the dynamics of volunteerism as a form of prosocial action and as a case example of people mobilizing themselves to respond to society's problems. The dynamics of volunteerism have also been observed in related studies of other populations of volunteers. For example, it has been possible to develop measures of volunteer motivations for use in diverse samples of actual volunteers and prospective volunteers (e.g., Clary et al., 1998), to demonstrate that persuasive messages, whether in videotape or brochure form, designed to motivate people to volunteer are persuasive to the extent that they target the motivations of individual prospective volunteers (e.g., Clary, Snyder, Ridge, Miene, & Haugen, 1994; Clary et al., 1998), to demonstrate that the satisfaction experienced by diverse groups of volunteers is predicted by the match between their motivations and the benefits that they derive from volunteering (Clary et al., 1998; Crain, Omoto, & Snyder, 1998), and that volunteers' intentions to continue volunteering both in the immediate and longer terms is predicted by the match between their motivations and the benefits that they perceive to accrue to them as volunteers (Clary et al., 1998).

Research on volunteerism, we believe, has been informative about the nature of helping, especially those forms of helping and prosocial action that are planful and sustained and that occur in the absence of bonds of obligation. In addition to these theoretical benefits of the study of volunteerism, we believe that an understanding of the psychology of volunteerism offers practical messages as well. Among the practical implications of our research are the lessons that it suggests about the practice of volunteerism, specifically about the ways that the recruitment, placement, and retention of volunteers can be enhanced. Systematic attention to the experiences and motivations of individual volunteers may go a long way in making more effective the efforts of grassroots and volunteer organizations. Specifically, to the extent that organizations dependent on the services of

volunteers can identify the motivations of prospective volunteers, they can systematically tailor their recruitment efforts to the actual motivations of potential
volunteers. To the extent that these organizations can and do attend to the motivations of their actual volunteers, they may be able to channel them toward volunteer assignments that provide opportunities to serve the particular motivations of
specific volunteers, and thereby enhance the effectiveness, satisfaction, and
longevity of volunteers' service. At a broader level still, studying volunteerism is
likely to yield valuable information of societal significance, including how to
understand and expand the roles of volunteers and volunteer organizations in confronting and surmounting many of the problems that challenge societies (e.g.,
Omoto & Snyder, 1993). Quite conceivably, a focus on the volunteers' motivations
could be one of the foundations for large-scale, mass-media-based campaigns to
promote awareness of and interest in volunteerism and other forms of involvement
of individuals in the affairs of their societies (e.g., Clary & Snyder, 1993).

THE SOCIETAL AND CULTURAL CONTEXTS OF VOLUNTEERISM AND CITIZEN PARTICIPATION

Theory and research on volunteerism, we believe, have the potential to inform us
about the links between individuals and society, particularly about the mechanisms by which individuals involve themselves in addressing the problems that
confront their communities and society. Volunteerism is but one of the ways that
people participate in society. Other examples of citizen participation are people
adopting the habits of recycling to protect the environment, neighbors watching
out for each other to reduce crime, activists pressing the case for a nuclear freeze
or against the use of land mines, community members working together to create and then staff a soup kitchen or shelter for people living on more limited
resources, and citizens participating in the political process through voting and
working on electoral campaigns. All of these and many other actions contribute
to preserving and enhancing any society's stock of social capital (e.g., Putnam,
1993, 1995)—that is, preserving and enhancing the degree to which citizens are
engaging in the affairs of their communities and building bonds of mutual trust
among themselves (e.g., Coleman, 1990). The need for and the benefits of citizen participation for society and individuals have been noted by many social
commentators (e.g., Boyte & Kari, 1996). Such citizenship behaviors are a subject of considerable study in political science and related disciplines (e.g.,
Kymlicka & Norman, 1994; Putnam, 1993, 1995; Verba, Schlozman, & Brady,
1995). Developing theory and research on volunteerism should aid in better
understanding this broader class of citizenship behavior and citizen participation.
    At several points in this chapter we have noted that, as much as our
research has focused on volunteerism in the United States, volunteerism is a phenomenon that occurs in many countries throughout the world. We step back from

our heretofore primary focus on the United States and place volunteerism and other forms of citizen participation in their larger societal and cultural contexts. To frame this discussion, we begin by noting that the type of volunteerism with which we have been concerned in our research takes place in the context of community-based organizations. This is true of many volunteer activities in the United States. It is important to recognize that these organizations are also embedded in larger social structures and systems. These layers of embeddedness, in fact, are incorporated in our conceptual model of the volunteer process (Omoto et al., 1993; Omoto & Snyder, 1995), particularly in the organizational and broader social system levels of analysis (see Table 15.1). Some social structures and cultural institutions may prescribe, foster, and sustain the work of volunteers and volunteer organizations, whereas others may create barriers and obstacles for effective volunteer efforts. In recognition of the opportunities and constraints provided by social structures and cultural institutions, let us now consider a selective set of factors that can and do differ between cultures and between societies,and how these factors might influence volunteer efforts in different cultures and societies.

The United States has long been considered a culture and nation of *joiners* one in which individual citizens typically belong to numerous formal organizations and are actively involved in community service (Babchuk & Booth, 1969; Tocqueville, 1835/1961; but see Putnam, 1993). In fact, the United States stands out in cross-national comparisons for its high rate of citizen participation, especially when this participation is broadly defined to include voluntary association memberships as well as church and union activities (Curtis et al., 1992). However, recent data from adolescents in seven different countries, including emerging and established democracies, indicate comparable rates of volunteerism among youth in the United States and youth in some of the countries of Eastern and Central Europe (i.e., Hungary, Bulgaria, and the Czech Republic). Specifically, roughly half of the youth living in urban areas in these countries who were surveyed reported that they had engaged in volunteer work, with the highest rate of volunteerism actually reported by adolescent females in Hungary (Flanagan, Bowes, Jonsson, Csapo, & Sheblanova, 1998). Thus, rates of citizen participation and voluntary association membership are high in the United States, but it appears that as countries move toward forms of government more similar to the democratic and representative traditions that characterize the United States, citizens may be expected to raise the importance of civic commitment and engage in volunteer activities to a greater extent (Flanagan et al., 1998).

In fact, a number of explanations rooted in sociological and structural factors have been offered for the relatively high rates of citizen participation in the United States and by extension in other industrialized democracies, as compared with other countries (see Curtis et al., 1992; Lipset, 1963, 1990). For example, the revolutionary history of the United States created a legacy of social and political movement that focused on self-determination and the power of citizen change through collective action. Similarly, a general Protestant religious heritage (rather than, say, a Catholic heritage) stresses personal responsibility to help others. Thus, historical and religious factors may have encouraged volunteerism in the United States and the development of a cultural ideology that promotes (and even prescribes) broad citizen participation.

Generalizing from these considerations, we would suggest that governments that are representative and democratic in nature may foster greater levels of citizen involvement than governments that are centralized and that emphasize state control (Curtis et al., 1992; Lipset, 1963). In representative and participatory democracies, equal opportunity is emphasized, and people actively take part in decision making and policy formulation through regular voting and other involvement in the political process (e.g., working on political campaigns, running for elected office, membership in interest groups, lobbying elected officials). Moreover, the concept of equal opportunity is stressed by the fact that each citizen has as much say as any other citizen (i.e., the-one citizen, one-vote principle). Centralized government control and provision of services, however, may inhibit the development of local organizations, functionally discouraging voluntary association activity and memberships. Thus, the style of government of a country may influence the nature and rates of citizen participation.

Moreover, levels of industrialization and urbanization may also partially explain higher rates of volunteerism and citizen participation in the United States relative to other countries (Curtis et al., 1992). Industrialization, and to a certain extent urbanization, may influence the opportunities for organization and association membership, may encourage social contact, and may also be related to greater amounts of leisure time. To the extent that unions and other voluntary (professional) associations exist, that social contact is relatively high, and that individuals have greater amounts of free time, rates of citizen participation and volunteerism may be higher than when relatively few professional opportunities present themselves, social contact and population density are low, and free time is scarce. With increasing industrialization and urbanization in developing countries, or the conjunction of emerging democracy in already developed countries, we would expect traditions of volunteerism and other forms of social activism and citizen participation in addressing the problems of society to take root and eventually blossom.

Thus, it would seem that there are a number of conditions, such as historical and religious traditions, form of government, and degree of industrialization, that may explain the emergence of volunteer cultures, increasing importance of association memberships, and greater citizen participation in different countries. Of course, it is unlikely that any of these conditions can be definitively proved to be the cause of citizenship behaviors and involvement. Nevertheless, it still seems worthwhile if not provocative to note the intertwining or covariation of these conditions with the history and political system of the United States, as well as to speculate on their implications for emerging democracies, such as those of Eastern and Central Europe. These conditions may, in fact, point the way to the development of cultures of volunteer service and of joiners in these emerging democracies.

However, it may be equally important to note some important differences between the history of these emerging democracies and that of the United States that may constrain the specific form that the development of a culture of volunteerism and citizen participation will take in these societies. Of particular interest are the likely motivations that will emerge to encourage any individual to participate in volunteer service activities. As state control of resources and the economy is reduced and government services are increasingly withdrawn, individual citizens may be called on to greater degrees to provide support, education, advocacy, and service functions that they have not been required to provide previously. In fact, this filling of the gaps has been the impetus for the formation and development of many different forms of volunteer services and organizations in the United States (including, not incidentally, the emergence of AIDS service organizations as grassroots community-based movements to provide services simply not available, or expected to be imminently available, from established governmental agencies).

However, the motivations associated with this filling of the gaps through volunteerism and other forms of prosocial action may emerge quite differently from the backdrop of individualistic and collectivistic cultural traditions (e.g., Triandis, 1994). In this regard, we speculate that collectivistic cultures, and especially those with state-controlled governments, may be less likely to encourage the variety of self-focused motivations for volunteerism (e.g., esteem enhancement, personal development) that we have seen among volunteers in the relatively individualistic culture of the United States (motivations that, as demonstrated in our research, are linked to longevity of service as volunteers in AIDS service organizations). To the extent that such self-focused motivations are rooted in individualistic concerns with the self, then people from more collectivistic cultures may be less likely to develop or relate to self-focused motivations for citizen participation. In a complementary fashion, however, motivations of a relatively other-focused nature, for example, and perhaps especially those related to community concern might be especially likely to emerge in collectivistic cultures. Accordingly, systematic attempts to promote a tradition of volunteerism and citizen participation in societies with collectivist cultural heritages might succeed to the extent that they appeal to community concerns and related other-focused motivations.

To be sure, much of what we have had to say about the societal and cultural contexts of volunteerism is speculative. At a minimum, however, these considerations point to a larger context for theorizing about and situating volunteerism and other forms of individual and collective (prosocial) action. In addition, attending to these considerations helps point to the larger worldwide laboratory available for research on the ways in which individuals participate in their societies and for exploring practical applications of the findings from such investigations. From such theorizing, research, and application, we fully expect a richly textured and finely nuanced understanding of the psychology of individual and collective action to emerge. This understanding is likely to be further developed and may be put to good use in informing practical efforts to encourage people to provide assistance to others and to actively participate in making their communities better places to live. As we see it, as this work progresses, it has vast potential for connecting individuals to each other, to their communities, and across cultures.

ACKNOWLEDGMENTS

The preparation of this chapter and the conduct of the research reported in it have been supported by grants from the American Foundation for AIDS Research and the National Institute of Mental Health to Mark Snyder and Allen M. Omoto.

REFERENCES

Andrews, H. F. (1990). Helping and health: The relationship between volunteer activity and health-related outcomes. *Advances, 7*, 25–34.

Babchuk, N., & Booth, A. (1969). Voluntary association membership: A longitudinal analysis. *American Sociological Review, 34*, 31–45.

Batson, C. D. (1998). Altruism and prosocial behavior. In D. Gilbert, S. Fiske, & G. Lindzey (Eds.), *Handbook of social psychology* (Vol. 2, 4th ed., pp. 282–316). Boston: McGraw-Hill.

Boyte, H. C., & Kari, N. N. (1996). *Building America: The democratic promise of public work*. Philadelphia, PA: Temple University Press.

Carlo, G., Eisenberg, N., Troyer, D., Switzer, G., & Speer, A. L. (1991). The altruistic personality: In what contexts is it apparent? *Journal of Personality and Social Psychology, 61*, 450–458.

Chambré, S. M. (1991). The volunteer response to the AIDS epidemic in New York City: Implications for research on volunteeism. *Nonprofit and Voluntary Sector Quarterly, 20*, 267–287.

Cialdini, R. B., Schaller, M., Houlihan, D., Arps, K., Fultz, J., & Beaman, A. L. (1987). Empathy-based helping: Is it selflessly or selfishly motivated? *Journal of Personality and Social Psychology, 52*, 749–758.

Clary, E. G., & Snyder, M. (1991). A functional analysis of altruism and prosocial behavior: The case of volunteerism. In M. Clark (Ed.), *Prosocial behavior: Review of personality and social psychology*, Vol. 12 (pp. 119–148). Newbury Park, CA: Sage.

Clary, E. G., & Snyder, M. (1993). Persuasive communications strategies for recruiting volunteers. In D. R. Young, R. M. Hollister, & V. A.

Hodgkinson (Eds.), *Governing, leading, and managing nonprofit organizations: New insights from research and practice* (pp. 121–137). San Francisco, CA: Jossey-Bass.

Clary, E. G., Snyder, M., Ridge, R. D., Copeland, J., Stukas, A. A., Haugen, J., & Miene, P. (1998). Understanding and assessing the motivations of volunteers: A functional approach. *Journal of Personality and Social Psychology, 74*, 1516–1530.

Clary, E. G., Snyder, M., Ridge, R. D., Miene, P., & Haugen, J. (1994). Matching messages to motives in persuasion: A functional approach to promoting volunteerism. *Journal of Applied Social Psychology, 24*, 1129–1149.

Coleman, J. S. (1990). *Foundations of social theory.* Cambridge, MA: Harvard University Press.

Crain, A. L., Omoto, A. M., & Snyder, M. (1998, April). *What if you can't always get what you want? Testing a function approach to volunteerism.* Paper presented at the annual meeting of the Midwestern Psychological Association, Chicago, IL.

Curtis, J. E., Grabb, E., & Baer, D. (1992). Voluntary association membership in fifteen countries: A comparative analysis. *American Sociological Review, 57*, 139–152.

Flanagan, C.A., Bowes, J. M., Jonsson, B., Csapo, B., & Sheblanova, E. (1998). Ties that bind: Correlates of adolescents' civic commitments in seven countries. Journal of Social Issues, 54, 457–475.

Folkman, S., Chesney, M. A., Cooke, M., Boccellari, A., & Collette, L. (1994). Caregiver burden in HIV-positive and HIV-negative partners of men with AIDS. *Journal of Consulting and Clinical Psychology, 62*, 746–756.

Hellinger, F. J. (1993). The lifetime cost of treating a person with HIV. *Journal of the American Medical Association, 270*, 474–478.

Hobfoll, S. E., & Lerman, M. (1988). Personal relationships, personal attributes, and stress resistance: Mothers' reactions to their child's illness. *American Journal of Community Psychology, 16*, 565–589.

Independent Sector (1996). *Giving and volunteering in the United States: Findings from a national survey.* Washington, DC: Author.

Kelly, J.J., Chu, S.Y., & Buehler, J.W. (1993). AIDS deaths shift from hospital to home. *American Journal of Public Health, 83*, 1433–1437

Kinney, J. M., & Stephens, M. A. P. (1989). Hassles and uplifts of giving care to a family member with dementia. *Psychology and Aging, 4*, 402–408.

Kymlicka, W., & Norman, W. (1994). Return of the citizen: A survey of recent work on citizen theory. *Ethics, 104*, 352–381.

Latané, B., & Darley, J. M. (1970). *The unresponsive bystander: Why doesn't he help?* New York: Appleton-Century-Crofts.

Lazarus, R. S., & Folkman, S. (1984). *Stress, appraisal, and coping.* New York: Springer.

Lipset, S. M. (1963). *The first new nation.* New York: Basic Books.

Lipset, S. M. (1990). *Continental divide: The values and institutions of Canada and the United States.* New York: Routledge.

Omoto, A. M., Gunn, D. O., & Crain, A. L. (1998). Helping in hard times: Relationship closeness and the AIDS volunteer experience. In V. J. Derlega & A. P. Barbee (Eds.), *HIV & social interaction* (pp. 106–128). Thousand Oaks, CA: Sage.

Omoto, A. M., & Snyder, M. (1990). Basic research in action: Volunteerism and society's response to AIDS. *Personality and Social Psychology Bulletin, 16,* 152–166.

Omoto, A. M., & Snyder, M. (1993). AIDS volunteers and their motivations: Theoretical issues and practical concerns. *Nonprofit Management and Leadership, 4,* 157–176.

Omoto, A. M., & Snyder, M. (1995). Sustained helping without obligation: Motivation, longevity of service, and perceived attitude change among AIDS volunteers. *Journal of Personality and Social Psychology, 68,* 671–686.

Omoto, A. M., & Snyder, M. (1999). [Self-reported and measured change among AIDS volunteer]. Unpublished raw data.

Omoto, A. M., Snyder, M., & Berghuis, J. P. (1993). The psychology of volunteerism: A conceptual analysis and a program of action research. In J. B. Pryor & G. D. Reeder (Eds.), *The social psychology of HIV infection* (pp. 333–356). Hillsdale, NJ: Lawrence Erlbaum Associates.

Omoto, A. M., Snyder, M., & Crain, A. L. (1998a). *Hurt because you help: Stigmatization as a barrier to social action.* Unpublished manuscript, University of Kansas.

Omoto, A. M., Snyder, M., & Crain, A. L. (1998b). *On the stigmatization of people who do good work: The case of AIDS volunteers.* Unpublished manuscript, University of Kansas.

Ouellette, S. C., Cassel, B., Maslanka, H., & Wong, L. M. (1995). GMHC volunteers and the challenges and hopes for the second decade of AIDS. *AIDS Education and Prevention, 7,* 64–79.

Piliavin, J. A., & Charng, H. (1990). Altruism: A review of recent theory and research. *Annual Review of Sociology, 16,* 27–65.

Putnam, R. D. (1993). *Making democracy work: Civic traditions in modern Italy.* Princeton: Princeton University Press.

Putnam, R. D. (1995). Bowling alone: America's declining social capital. *Journal of Democracy, 6,* 65–78.

Revenson, T. A., & Majerovitz, S. D. (1990). Spouses' support provision to chronically ill patients. *Journal of Social and Personal Relationships, 7,* 575–586.

Rushton, J. P. (1984). The altruistic personality: Evidence from laboratory, naturalistic, and self-report perspectives. In E. Staub, D. Bar-Tal, J.

Karylowski, & J. Reykowski (Eds.), *Development and maintenance of prosocial behavior* (pp. 271–290). New York: Plenum.

Schaller, M., & Cialdini, R. B. (1988). The economics of empathic helping: Support for a mood management motive. *Journal of Experimental Social Psychology, 24,* 163–181.

Schulz, R., Williamson, G. M., Morycz, R. K., & Biegel, D. E. (1992). Costs and benefits of providing care to Alzheimer's patients. In S. Spacapan & S. Oskamp (Eds.), *Helping and being helped: Naturalistic studies* (pp. 153–182). Newbury Park: Sage.

Smith, K. D., Keating, J. P., & Stotland, E. (1989). Altruism reconsidered: The effect of denying feedback on a victim's status to empathic witnesses. *Journal of Personality and Social Psychology, 57,* 641–650.

Smith, D. H., & Macaulay, J. (Eds.). (1980). *Participation in social and political activities.* San Francisco: Jossey-Bass.

Snyder, M., & Cantor, N. (1998). Understanding personality and social behavior: A functionalist strategy. In D. Gilbert, S. Fiske, & G. Lindzey (Eds.), *The handbook of social psychology* (Vol. 1, 4th ed., pp. 635–679). Boston: McGraw-Hill.

Snyder, M., Clary, E. G., & Stukas, A. A. (2000). The functional approach to volunteerism. In G. R. Maio & J. M. Olson (Eds.), *Why we evaluate: Functions of attitudes.* Mahwah, NJ: Lawrence Erlbaum Associates.

Snyder, M., & Omoto, A. M. (1992a). Volunteerism and society's response to the HIV epidemic. *Current Directions in Psychological Science, 1,* 113–116.

Snyder, M., & Omoto, A. M. (1992b). Who helps and why? The psychology of AIDS volunteerism. In S. Spacapan & S. Oskamp (Eds.), *Helping and being helped: Naturalistic studies* (pp. 213–239). Newbury Park, CA: Sage.

Snyder, M., & Omoto, A. M. (2000). Doing good for self and society: Volunteerism and the psychology of citizen participation. In M. Van Vugt, M. Snyder, T. Tyler, & A. Biel (Eds.), *Collective helping in modern society: Dilemmas and solutions.* London: Routledge.

Snyder, M., Omoto, A. M., & Crain, A. L. (1999). Punished for their good deeds: Stigmatization of AIDS volunteers. *American Behavioral Scientist, 42* (1175–1192)

Staub, E. (1974). Helping a distressed person: Social, personality, and stimulus determinants. In L. Berkowitz (Ed.), *Advances in experimental social psychology* (pp. 293–341). New York: Academic Press.

Thompson, S. C., & Pitts, J. S. (1992). In sickness and in health: Chronic illness, marriage, and spousal caregiving. In S. Spacapan & S. Oskamp (Eds.), *Helping and being helped: Naturalistic studies* (pp. 115–152). Newbury Park: Sage.

Tocqueville, A. de (1835/1961). *Democracy in America*. New York: Knopf.

Triandis, H. C. (1994). *Culture and social behavior*. New York: McGraw-Hill.

Turner, H. A., Catania, J. A., & Gagnon, J. (1994). The prevalence of informal caregiving to persons with AIDS in the United States: Caregiver characteristics and their implications. *Social Science Medicine, 38*, 1543–1552.

Verba, S., Schlozman, K. L., & Brady, H. E. (1995). *Voice and equality: Civic voluntarism in American politics*. Cambridge, MA: Harvard University Press.

16

Social Influence in Media: Culture and Antismoking Advertising

Rafal K. Ohme

Warsaw School of Advanced Social Psychology

ABSTRACT

This chapter discusses the effectiveness of antismoking ads with a special focus on teenage smoking. The classic Hovland et al. (1953) model of persuasion serves as a framework for the analysis of the major factors determining the efficacy of antismoking campaigns. Previous research, mostly conducted in the United States, is reviewed and data from the author's own research on Polish teenagers ARE presented. The research review concludes with an analysis of cultural factors that differentiate the social reality in European countries in general, and in Poland in particular, which have just recently begun antismoking campaigns from other nations, such as the United States, which have longer histories in this area. This chapter ends with a discussion of the cultural specificity of the principles of mass-mediated influences involved in antismoking campaigns and the practical implications for these campaigns in cultures with traditions of high social acceptance of smoking.

This chapter reviews the psychological factors determining the effectiveness of antismoking ads. Most of the research on this topic has been conducted in the United States on American smokers where the national history and sociopolitical reality (such as the recent acceptance of banning smoking from virtually all public places) are different from the history and sociopolitical realities in other countries in ways that impact antismoking campaigns.

American tobacco producers increasingly experiencing greater difficulty in maintaining the huge profit margins in the United States of yesteryear, and facing increasing regulation and litigation in the United States, are moving more aggressively into the Asian and European markets, including those of Eastern Europe. Large segments of the populations in Eastern European nations are fascinated with American culture. These individuals have not been inoculated against the influence of some of the tobacco industry's deadly, smoking-related symbols, such as the cartoon character advertising "Camels." If these American tobacco companies can successfully import largely American advertising campaigns into other nations to increase smoking, can the antismoking campaigns that have been effective in the United States also be efficacious in Eastern Europe?

Unfortunately, it is impossible to answer this question at the present time. Antismoking campaigns, which have lately been conducted in Poland, are limited in number and diversity. They do not borrow (or even copy) from other countries' experiences. Although the psychology of attitude change offers a great variety of persuasion forms, health promoters in Poland seem not to be aware of them. Tough, one-sided, and fear-inducing messages like "Stop smoking" or "Smoking will kill you" are fine samples of our limited arsenal in this matter. Therefore, this chapter presents the author's own ideas regarding how to fight smoking, which are research based, rather than stemming from examples of antismoking ads taken from the everyday life observations.

This chapter reviews research on the psychological and social factors determining efficiency of antismoking campaigns in the United States and presents some data from research conducted by the author and his collaborator on smoking among Polish youth. Universal versus culture-specific aspects of antismoking advertising are examined, followed by a discussion of the practical implications of these cultural differences.

In the literature review that follows, factors considered in previous research as determinants of effective persuasion were categorized into three groups, reflecting the Hovland et al. (1953) model of persuasive communication: (a) source characteristics of the mass media as an agent of influence, (b) characteristics of the message (its cognitive, affective, and behavioral components), and (c) characteristics of the target audience and especially teenagers.

WHO: THE MEDIA AS THE AGENT OF INFLUENCE

Media have the potential to promote healthy lifestyles, because they are pervasive and capable of reaching people in their natural environment (Solomon, 1983). As this author suggested, the perceived reality of the medium is intended to be a catalyst for behavior or attitude change. Moreover, media are easily accessible, whereas the use of other communication strategies (e.g., organizing communities of people) is often a difficult, lengthy, and unsuccessful process (Solomon, 1983).

Harris (1989) provided an account of several positive effects of mass media antismoking campaigns. The first positive effect is an altered perception of reality, which includes a heightened awareness of the problem addressed in the ads. For example, in the 1990s, virtually everyone in North America and Europe were aware of the dangers of smoking. We all witnessed growing restrictions toward smokers (it is hard to believe that not so long ago one could smoke inside elevators). The second positive effect is that these campaigns may increase the salience of the issue and consequently enhance the audience's receptivity to other influences. A particular televised health promotion may not necessarily lead us to immediately visit the doctor to check our cholesterol leve. However, we may attend more to subsequent messages on that topic. The third effect of media campaigns described by Harris is the stimulation of subsequent issue-related conversation with one's family, friends, or doctor. For instance, publicity about the dangers of smoking may encourage discussion between parents and children. Harris described the generation of self-initiated information-seeking as the fourth effect of media campaigns. For example, after being exposed to one or more advertisements, a person may buy a book on the topic or call a toll-free number for more details. The fifth and final effect of media campaigns is to reinforce positive attitudes and behavior, such as praising an ex-smoker for kicking the habit.

The efforts of health organizations engaged in antismoking campaigns are relatively poorly funded and supported (Harris, 1989) because these organizations cannot match the big dollars spent on promotional activities by the tobacco industry. Antismoking ads typically are not viewed or heard as frequently as tobacco ads. Public service announcements (PSAs)—for which the media source is unpaid—are generally broadcast at the low-audience hours when TV and radio stations are least able to sell lucrative advertising. Another problem is that the persons who create antismoking advertising are often less thoroughly trained to produce effective media campaigns than those conducting cigarette promotions (Harris, 1989).

A poor agent of influence may dramatically decrease the effectiveness of the persuasive attempt. Sometimes these flawed efforts at persuasion may cause a boomerang effect (i.e., by strengthening the original attitude instead of changing it; Wilde, 1993). In health promotion, the poor reputation of *bunglers of influence* (Cialdini, 1996) is likely to negatively impact perception of the intended message. To become successful agents of influence, individuals involved in mass media health promotion must construct their actions based not on intuition, but rather on the systematic knowledge of the psychological aspects of mass-mediated persuasion. Therefore, health organizations should engage in actions that are carefully prepared and executed by well-trained professionals.

Successful media campaigns furnish audiences with antismoking norms. They create a positive image of the nonsmoking lifestyle and stress that cigarette addicts are a minority that is gradually declining. This normative approach to social influence was illustrated by the cigarette advertising ban on television in the 1970s in the United States. It was then that smoking was first treated as deviant (non-normative) behavior that was tolerated but not supported.

WHAT: THE CONTENT OF
MASS-MEDIATED INFLUENCES

In health promotion (as with other persuasion attempts) through the media, it is important to properly identify the nature of recipient responses to social influence, because identical behaviors may be facilitated by different psychological processes. For instance, similar overt behavior of ex-smokers may be founded on entirely different grounds. Quitting smoking may simply be a matter of normative compliance: "I quit because nowadays smoking is passé and I don't want to be rejected by the group I belong to." Alternatively, the same behavior may be produced by identification: "I quit because my rock idols have done it and I have realized that I can still be cool—just like them—without cigarettes." A third possibility is that this change may result from internalization: "I quit because I have finally admitted to myself that I have been a nicotine addict and I decided it was not what I needed in my life."

Some mass media campaigns focus only on achieving normative compliance and do not employ identification or internalization processes. In the short run, these campaigns might be successful when measured by greater awareness of the dangers of smoking, unaided recall regarding these dangers, lower perceived attractiveness of smoking, and a reduction in smoking. However, these changes are not likely to persist once the campaign is over. Affecting all three levels simultaneously has a much greater chance of inducing enduring change. Therefore, an effective antismoking campaign should target all three attitudinal components. That is, it should (a) provide persuasive arguments, (b) energize them with appropriate affect, and (c) demonstrate how to behave to successfully stop smoking.

Influencing the Cognitive Component

Influencing the cognitive component of attitudes involves informing public opinion about the hazards of smoking and gradually building attitudes against it. The media have already succeeded in increasing awareness of the adverse effects of smoking. Three decades of information blitzing greatly increased the knowledge level about the major health effects of smoking in the general population. Interestingly, some studies show that even smokers tend to overestimate, rather than underestimate, the risk of lung cancer from smoking (Calfee & Ringold, 1992).

To change the existing attitudes of smokers or potential smokers, antismoking ads should be presented as one-sided communications (e.g., "smoking causes cancer!"). However, when the healthy lifestyle of a particular target audience is not situated at the top of its value system, it is better to first apply two-sided communications and then refute opposing arguments (Hovland et al., 1949). "You can show us ONE older person, who is in good health in spite of years of smoking. We can show you THOUSANDS who are not. Please, refrain from smoking."

Some persuasive messages should be designed to help resist the constant seduction attempts by cigarettes ads (e.g., "Lighter cigarettes—lighter pain"). The aforementioned two-sided argumentation is one method to strengthen resistance to changing newly acquired prohealth attitudes. Another approach described by McGuire (1964) is through attitude inoculation. To make former smokers immune to attempts to change their attitudes and behaviors and return to smoking, these persons should be initially exposed to small doses of counter-persuasion. Such exposure to mild counterpersuasion facilitates the development of idiosyncratic defenses and simultaneously increases intrinsic motivation not to smoke. For example, one could imagine an ad stating, "Many people think smoking is a macho thing. So did he (and here a picture of a typical 'Marlboro man' is presented). Too bad he died of lung cancer."

Prohealth messages become more appealing and thought provoking when they are framed to present benefits not as gains but as losses that could be avoided by performing a particular action. The threat of a small loss often has more impact than the promise of a small gain (Kahneman & Tversky, 1984). For example, Meyerowitz and Chaiken (1987) observed that women who received loss arguments regarding the effects of breast cancer performed breast self-exams significantly more often than those who received gain arguments.

To test whether this gain–loss approach might be useful in antismoking ads, this author and his collaborator conducted research involving Polish teenagers (Ohme & Gusztyla, 1997). We asked 105 high school students (48 boys and 57 girls) to evaluate the effectiveness of the antismoking leaflets that are frequently given away by Polish school physicians and psychologists to teenagers. There were two versions of the leaflet. In one version, persuasive messages were framed in terms of gain (i.e., "When you quit smoking your lungs will begin to heal"). In the other version, we rephrased the message in terms of loss (i.e., "When you don't quit smoking your lungs will not start to heal"). The results confirm Kahneman and Tversky's (1984) hypothesis in that both smoker and nonsmoker participants found the loss leaflet to be more effective than the gain leaflet ($F(1,104) = 10.79$, $p < .001$). Moreover, smokers found this leaflet more effective than nonsmokers ($F(1,104) = 4.42$, $p < .05$) (see Figure 16.1).

Another important issue to be considered when developing the cognitive component of antismoking ads consists of the following question: Should the media argue by appealing to statistical data or by referring to a single, illustrative case? Contrary to beliefs shared by many health marketers, a solid statistical

FIG. 16.1. Effectiveness of the antismoking leaflet[Main Effect: $F_{(2,104)}$ = 7.770, p = .001; Gain/Loss: $F_{(1,104)}$ = 10.786, p =.001; Smokers/Nonsmokers: $F_{(1,104)}$ = 4.424, p = . 038].

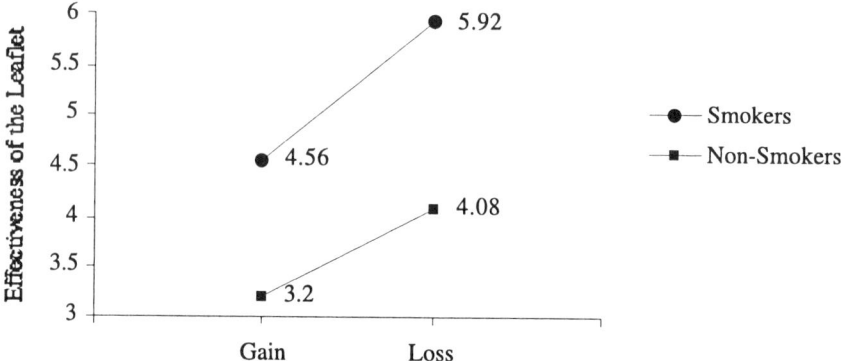

argumentation based on representative samples is a necessary but not sufficient method of influence (Górnik-Durose, 1995). Nisbett, Hamill, and Wilson (1980) posited that the vividness and psychological closeness of a single case is often more relevant to an individual than are scientific data. A message utilizing this tactic might state, "Try to remind yourself of 12 friends of yours who smoke cigarettes. One of them will die of a lung cancer. Are you there?"

Influencing the Affective Component

Despite that associations with positive emotions—sometimes accomplished by exploiting desires for luxury, beauty, and sexuality—are often employed in advertising, their effectiveness in relation to health is not clear. Swinehart (1976) found, that in a television series, stressing prevention, songs, humor, and strong emotional appeals was a poor vehicle for conveying health information. Even "Sesame Street" was not as effective as documentaries and straightforward presentations of information. Many studies on health promotion indicate that fear-inducing appeals and other negative emotional motivators (e.g., shame) can effectively reach the audience (Janis, 1967; Leventhal, Watts, & Pagano, 1967; Rogers, 1983). The threat should not be too strong, however, because then defense mechanisms may be activated and the message is likely to be tuned-out or denied (Leventhal, 1970). Bandura (1971) showed that fear-evoking appeals were effective only when combined with positive information about one's ability to overcome the addiction. A fine example of a fear-evoking appeal is a popular American 1970s public service announcement: "The minute you stop smoking, your lungs begin to heal."

Some health marketers try to fight fire with fire by creating antismoking ads that depict smoking as an ugly habit that turns people off. Such ads produced promising results: Seventh graders who saw the antismoking ads were more likely to rate smokers lower both in terms of personal appeal and common sense (Pechmann & Ratneshwar, 1994). One related ad that reflects this approach was the "Its a matter of life and breath" ad, which was widely aired in the United States in the 1970s and early 1980s (Zimbardo & Leippe, 1991). This finding implies that it is possible to use advertising to debunk myths about the glamour of smoking.

Appealing to aesthetics has been a popular theme in antismoking ads in the 1990s. In one ad shown in the United States, a young male is chewing tobacco and spitting it from time to time into a soft drink paper cup. His female friend, whose attention is absorbed by the movie they are watching, mechanically grabs the cup and reaches it to her mouth without looking inside. A scream is then heard, suggesting that the friend was horrified and disgusted when she tasted the liquid and, by extension, was also horrified and disgusted by her friend's behavior. Another example of this type of advertising was the "Ssssssssmoking sssssssstinks" billboards that were posted all across the United States. Polish TV has recently shown a quite vivid example of this strategy. In one ad, a beautiful girl is smoking a cigarette, but each time she inhales her face is covered with more and more nicotine and tar. This ad creates a huge aesthetic dissonance and shows that, regardless of how attractive you are, smoking makes you repulsive.

Influencing the Behavioral Component

The media can influence antismoking attitudes not only through emotional and informational appeals in TV ads or PSAs, but also by presenting behavioral instructions regarding how to stop smoking. Behaviorally based attitudes developed from observations of one's own (smoking) behavior toward the attitude object are considered to be highly accessible and thus more resistant to change (Fazio & Zanna, 1981). Modeling antismoking behavior becomes crucial to successful prohealth advertising. People may already know that they should stop smoking, and what they most need is to learn how to stop: Observing others performing realistic behaviors that meet that goal may encourage them to model these behaviors. In many cases, focusing on the specific behaviors that the audience may take, one small step at a time, is the best way to proceed (Harris, 1989). Imagine, for example, a set of seven short TV spots entitled "Let's quit together!" illustrating the steps in quitting smoking that are to be followed by the target audience. Janis and Mann (1965) worked on a practical application of attitude inoculation called the *role-playing technique*. It proved effective even against peer pressure to begin smoking (McAlister, Perry, Killen, Slinkard, & Maccoby, 1980). In this study, seventh graders had to respond to prosmoking logical arguments they might hear and emotional appeals they might encounter from their peers. These students were significantly less likely to smoke 3 years after the study, compared with a control group that had not participated in the program. Thus, why not utilize this technique and create an advertisement showing role playing in natural settings (i.e., responding to typical prosmoking excuses as a sort of a party game)?

Perception of self-efficacy influences a person's motivation and performance in many ways (Bandura, 1986). Antismoking messages should employ this self-efficacy-oriented approach by trying to convince people that they could be successful at achieving their goals and reducing their health risks. Fear-inducing appeals must ensure response efficacy and present strong arguments stating that the recommended actions are effective in preventing the feared outcome (Zimbardo & Leippe, 1991). An example of this tactic is the following: "In 48 hours after you quit smoking, neuronal synapses start to regenerate and you start to taste and smell properly. In 3 months after you quit smoking, your lungs start to work 30% more efficiently. In 6 months after you quit smoking" It is critical that the target audience not develop a sense of helplessness—a belief that their smoking behavior is beyond their control. If smokers do not think they are capable of achieving success in quitting, they will be less likely to try to stop or will give up their effort to quit too easily.

Keeping Antismoking Attitudes Salient

To make an antismoking message salient, it must be presented in an attention-getting and attention-keeping form. It takes as much psychological as technical expertise to design a TV ad with interesting visual and auditory components. If an antismoking attitude is highly accessible, then an encounter with a prohealth communication is more likely to activate the attitude stored in memory and consequently trigger an inference process (Fazio, 1989). Moreover, attitude accessibility partially determines how likely people are to behave consistently with their attitudes. Assuming that any message would be good enough to change behavior is far from the truth (Solomon, 1983).

To be effective, the antismoking message must stand out from the crowd in the clutter of commercial television and overcome information noise. The message to be communicated has to be stated simply and to the point. When complex messages are to be presented, television should be used to stimulate the motivation to seek information on the part of the audience rather than provide the information directly. Unfortunately, a typical communication "for more information, call" only informs and does not motivate (Solomon, 1983).

Among the most effective methods for creating salient health messages is fear elicitation, but again, it should be done with caution so as to avoid scaring people into a state of denial. Another important component of successful advertising is to make the antismoking attitude highly self-relevant for the target. Health is an important issue to most people, but people tend not pay attention to it unless something goes wrong. They often think that bad things are less likely happen to them than to others. This phenomenon is particularly common among adolescents, becaise the hazards of smoking cigarettes seem distant in time and thus do not appear to be self-relevant. Research on unrealistic optimism indicates that the average person sees him or herself as above average in general health and below average in his or her risk of disease, injury, and premature death (Weinstein, 1980). Therefore it is important that health messages overcome this insidious sense of invulnerability. To avoid inducing panic in the target audience, messages must instill the recognition that people are at risk, but can reduce their risk by acting right now (Zimbardo & Leippe, 1991). It is both surprising and unfortunate that this crucial method of persuasion has not been properly utilized in any Polish antismoking ads.

Last, influence agents sooner or later face the danger that their health warnings will become such a common motif in the advertising landscape that targets will stop processing them. We are all endlessly exhorted to act in healthy ways and bombarded with information about what is and what is not good for us, and which products are safe and which are unhealthy. When repeated constantly, some health announcements become boring and less salient and cease being persuasive. Therefore, messages should vary in style and content and should utilize the whole palette of persuasion techniques, instead of just a few of them.

TO WHOM: THE NATURE OF THE TARGET AUDIENCE

It is important to clearly define the key features of the audience and to tailor persuasive messages that will best mesh with these features. The attitudes, desires, motivations, reasonable beliefs, and skepticism of the target group may be used to help craft the message. It is important for professionals who develop the messages to try to see the issue from the perspective of the audience. Alas, many health marketers are fervently convinced of the correctness of their message and fail to believe that the issue could be viewed differently (Harris, 1989). They neglect the importance of pretesting messages and of creating messages that emphasize personal relevance and are attention grabbing.

The assumed relevance and salience of a persuasive message should be pretested by obtaining evaluations from each target group. Qualitative research is the recommended method for this purpose. One of the most popular techniques is the focus group interview (FGI), which is a guided, yet free-flowing, in-depth interview with a small group of people representing a population (for more details, see Templeton, 1994). FGI as a qualitative market research tool may also be helpful in creating or legitimizing health-promotion strategies.

Ohme and Gusztyla (1997) conducted a set of four FGIs (separately with boys and girls, 16 to 17 years of age, 8–12 persons in each group, from two different type of high schools, of whom 75% were nonsmokers). Participants were exposed to 20 different posters and 10 slogans and asked to anonymously vote for the most persuasive and appealing antismoking message. Then a structured discussion was conducted with the participants, in which they were asked to give reasons for choosing certain posters and slogans and rejecting other posters and slogans for suitability in an antismoking campaign. The results reveal that the Polish adolescents who participated in the FGIs most appreciated messages that "do not preach," "let teenagers draw conclusions for themselves," and "appeal to aesthetics." These FGIs provided an important lesson, because some of the researchers' presumably clever ideas were thoroughly dismissed. Teenage participants offered useful tips about the style of the messages as well (e.g., phrases, preferred illustrations, and slogans).

Moreover, participants' opinions and comments during the FGIs showed that health education through media should be used in tandem with other efforts, such as self-help kits, personal contact and consultation with an authority, positive reference groups, and environmental changes. Thus, it seems that behavior change in the direction of nonsmoking is not typically the result of a single source of influence, but is rather produced by the cumulative effects of several sources of influence over time.

CROSS-CULTURAL PERSPECTIVE

Cigarette smoking among adolescents has become a serious problem in Europe. As a result, antismoking campaigns and stricter regulations are increasingly being implemented. For example, cigarettes ads in France are no longer allowed on TV, at movies, on billboards, or on the radio. In Austria, teachers cannot smoke at school, and outdoor tobacco advertisements have to be placed at least 500 meters away from schools. In Slovenia, only low-tar cigarettes can be advertised, but campaigns may last no longer than 15 days. In Slovakia, ads appear only at sports stadiums (for a more detailed review, see Maison, 1997; Paczkowski, 1998). European Union (EU) executives have officially decided that new antismoking legislation is to be introduced within the next 3 years. Each EU country member will have to forbid all tobacco advertising and, beginning in 2006, cigarette manufacturers cannot sponsor any sports or cultural events. In 1995, the EU spent over 15 million ECU to promote antismoking behavior (ironically, 993 million ECU was spent to support 150,000 tobacco industry employees; Paczkowski, 1998).

In Poland, smoking has always been one of the most serious social problems. Almost 50% of adult Poles regularly smoke cigarettes. Each year approximately 2,500 cigarettes per capita are smoked, ranking Poland in the top five nations worldwide (which may be considered an improvement, because Poland was ranked first in 1976). Fortunately, social awareness of the gravity of the problem is growing in Poland, and recent legal regulations are even more restrictive than in the rest of Europe. For instance, beginning in 1998, each cigarette pack must carry a warning stating that smoking causes cancer. The warning must be placed on one of the cigarette pack's larger surfaces. In addition, the other large side of the pack must include a second message stating that smoking causes heart problems. Moreover, the label must cover at least 30% of the surface. Large labels are intended to stigmatize this carcinogenic product and to scare away children who otherwise might try smoking for the first time. A similar label law applies to outdoor advertising in Poland.

Antismoking campaigns in Poland, however, are not systematic, consistent, or well synchronized. Due to weak enforcement of the law, cigarette companies freely and successfully target adolescents. "See how our pack is having fun" reads one of the posters distributed all over the country, which depicts a group of people at a party who are clearly teenagers and who extend their hands toward a pack of Spike's. In another ad, a boy and a girl are smoking in the locker room: She has laid her head on his knee, and the ad reads, "In any position" (West). Another ad mimics a typical scene from a road movie: A fancy motorbike, leather jacketed couple is presented, and the text read, "Discover the taste of freedom" (Truly American). Yet another ad states "You can afford it" (L & M). Some outdoor billboards even refer more or less openly to "the first episodes" in each teenage life—the first alcohol, the first R-rated movie, the first party, the first love, and the first cigarette smoked in public (Uscinski, 1998).

Outdoor advertising is supported by intense direct marketing at bars and discotheques. Attractive young persons dressed in extravagant and appealing tobacco company uniforms offer free samples of cigarettes, take Polaroid pictures of bar patrons wearing a cigarette logo, conduct quasipersonality tests indicating that the customers should smoke their products, and so on. Because they are not allowed to advertise on TV and radio, tobacco companies expend huge amounts of money and effort on various sponsorships: Camel and Marlboro organize rock concerts, R1 sponsors prêt-à-porter fashion competitions, and Salem owns a network of popular boutiques.

Another interesting example of how powerful the cigarette industry in Poland has become may be found, in an antismoking TV ad. In the fall of 1998, public television aired a series of paid commercials reminding viewers that it is illegal to sell cigarettes to minors. In one of them, a beautiful woman wearing high heels enters the shop to buy a pack of cigarettes. Unfortunately she makes a wrong step, and her blond wig falls down, revealing to an amused shop owner a confused teenage girl. The campaign was entirely funded by local tobacco companies. Does the fact that this message was produced by tobacco companies mean that the smoking and antismoking forces have finally joined in mutual effort to reduce underage smoking? Not at all. This commercial is a Trojan horse offered to antismoking organizations by the tobacco companies. It shrewdly smuggles the tobacco industry's desired image of the female smoker: sexually attractive, elegantly dressed, with plenty of make-up, and full of imagination. This time, trying to illicitly obtain cigarettes did not pan out, but the attempt was fun anyway. This is quite an intriguing image to any teenager. Public relations departments at the tobacco companies and creative thinkers from the ad agency that prepared this antismoking ad should congratulate each other.

In his insightful article "Antismoking Interventions in the USA and Poland," Zielinski (1996) pointed out four cultural and social factors that led to the success of the antismoking campaign in the United States. First, Americans have realized that smoking is expensive not only because of the high price of cigarettes, but also because of the cost of medical treatment and health insurance, and, less directly, because of smoking-related impairment in work effectiveness. Second, for years American society has developed self-control and self-monitoring systems. Nowhere else has psychoanalytic counseling been so popular, and nowhere else have so many books on psychology, parapsychology, and other self-help topics been written and read. This mixture of rationality and self-monitoring gives rise to feelings of self-competence and efficacy in fighting or avoiding the addiction.

Third, a new social class was born in the United States—a knowledge class of lifestyle engineers. For this powerful group of opinion leaders, cigarettes became a public enemy. From a certain perspective, the antismoking movement is dissonant with individualistic values highly praised by American society. At least in this area of behavior, people can no longer do whatever they want. Surprisingly, Zielinski (1996) wrote, American society seems to demonstrate in this respect a more collectivistic perspective than is typically the case in America. This new approach to smoking is outwardly oriented toward common values and standards. Fourth, people in the United States have always been innovation-minded, open to scientific discoveries and ready to follow and utilize them.

Why are people in Poland less prone to adopt the habit of living without cigarettes? According to Zielinski (1996), antismoking education and persuasion is constantly confronted with simple economic reality. The price of poor-quality cigarettes is very low, and pharmacological methods used for quitting are too expensive. Chewing gum containing nicotine is four times more expensive than a pack of cigarettes, and only recently have nicotine patches been available for purchase without a prescription. However, we must remember that antismoking programs are profitable not only from a social, but also from an economic perspective. For instance, one such program conducted in Lodz cost only $8,500. Thanks to this local campaign, almost 800 persons succeeded in quitting and have not been smoking for 2 years. Now compare this $10 per capita cost to the cost of state-subsidized medical and pharmacological support that the Polish government would have had to provide instead. One can hardly disagree with Zielinski's conclusion: As long as the price of a pack of cigarettes is similar to the price of a loaf of bread, and as long as one does not have to pay for the medical treatment, the reception and internalization of the message "smoking is not good" will not become as common as in many other countries.

Zielinski (1996) posited that, in addition to these economic influences, sociopsychological factors may weaken the impact of antismoking messages in Poland. These factors, which are particularly well rooted among less educated people, are lower awareness of the dangers of smoking and the harm done to nonsmokers who inhale secondhand smoke. Smoking is still considered by many in terms of "my own health is my own business." Although Poland is generally more collectivistic than the United States, it exhibits a more individualistic tendency in this regard. There is much education needed to convince Poles that smoking is not only an individual problem, but a societal one, and to stress the possible negative effects it may have on passive smokers (e.g., members of the smoker's family, children, coworkers, etc.). Only by presenting smokers as insensitive to others' health and well-being may the target audience acquire a new perspective.

Fortunately, more and more data indicate that fighting tobacco addiction in Poland can be successful. This is partially due to years of prohealth education and observation of antismoking trends in the United States and Western European nations, whose citizens many Poles admire. In the early 1980s, 62% of men and 33% of women were smoking. Currently, the percentages are 39% and 19%, respectively. Poland and the Scandinavian countries are more motivated to quit smoking than other European nations (60% of Poles who smoke claim they want to quit); Romanowska, 1999). However, this optimistic tendency should be immediately supported by an intense nationwide advertising campaign. Institutions and individuals concerned with overcoming cigarette addiction in Poland must bear in mind a golden principle of successful business advertising: The better the sales, the more aggressive the promotion should be. Therefore, they collaborate with professionals with extensive knowledge of the psychology of social influence and attitude change. Then there will be only one thing left: To act quickly and outdo tobacco companies that freely promote the addiction to the "Generation Next."

PRACTICAL IMPLICATIONS

There are several practical implications that follow from the aforementioned research on attitude change in general and antismoking campaigns in particular. These implications should be heeded by individuals who either design antismoking campaigns or hire others to do this, whether they be compliance professionals, public health officials, government agencies, educators, or others.

First, when establishing rules regarding eligibility for government-sponsored health insurance—as is currently being done in Central and Eastern

European countries and is turning out to be very controversial—governmental agencies should deny health benefits for smoking-related diseases if patients do not quit smoking.

Second, antismoking campaigns should be based on psychological science, not on intuition. Furthermore, before presenting the ads to their target audiences, they should be pretested. Otherwise even funny and seemingly persuasive ads may boomerang, as was the case described earlier in which a teenage girl lost her wig when trying to buy cigarettes.

Third, health educators interested in antismoking campaigns should be cautious in drawing attention to the frequency of the problem in the target population. As Kenrick, Neuberg and Cialdini (1999) postulated, if the members of the target group learn how common the behavior is that they are being told not to engage in, they may consequently underestimate the danger inherent in that behavior and be more resistant to altering it.

Fourth, compliance professionals should also carefully select groups to be used as role models in antismoking campaigns. Homogeneity of groups in the Central and Eastern European societies, quite pronounced under communist rule, is no longer as prevalent. Today, Polish high school students demonstrate a much greater variety of individual identities, attitudes, and behaviors, as is found in Western nations. Therefore, it is not sufficient to simply target teens in a general sense; ads must utilize as models (and consciously aim at) multiple and divergent groups of teens. Not only may the targeting of the *general population of teens* be inefficient, it may also be counterproductive, because reactance may ensue (e.g., "If those whom I despise quit smoking—I will do the opposite").

REFERENCES

Bandura, A. (1971). *Social learning theory*. Morristown: General Learning Corp.

Bandura, A. (1986). *Social foundations of thought and action*. Englewood Cliffs, NJ: Prentice-Hall.

Calfee, J. E., & Ringold, D. J. (1992). The cigarette advertising controversy: Assumptions about consumers, regulations, and scientific debate. In J. F. Sherry, Jr., & B. Sternthal (Eds.), *Advances in consumer research* (Vol. 19, pp. 557–562). Provo, UT: Association for Consumer Research.

Cialdini, R. B. (1996). Social influence in the triple tumor structure of organizational dishonesty. In D. M. Messick & A. R. Tenbrunsel (Eds.), *Codes of conduct* (pp. 44–58). New York: Russell Sage.

Fazio, R. H. (1989). On the power and functionality of attitudes: The role of attitude accessibility. In A. R. Pratkanis, S. J. Breckler, & A. G. Greenwald (Eds.), *Attitude structure and function* (pp. 153–179). Hillsdale, NJ: Lawrence Erlbaum Associates.

Fazio, R. H., & Zanna, M. P. (1981). Direct experience and attitude-behavior consistency. In L. Berkowitz (Ed.), *Advances in experimental social psychology* (Vol. 14, pp. 162–202). New York: Academic Press.

Górnik-Durose, M. (1995). Przydatnosc modeli wplywu spolecznego dla promocji zdrowia [Usefulness of social influence models in health promotion]. *Promocja Zdrowia. Nauki Spoleczne i Medycyna*, 5-6, 22–39.

Harris, R. J. (1989). *A cognitive psychology of mass communication*. Hillsdale, NJ: Lawrence Erlbaum Associates.

Hovland, C. I., Janis, I. L., & Kelley, H. H. (1953). *Communication and persuasion: Psychological studies of opinion change*. New Haven, CT: Yale University Press.

Hovland, C. I., Lumsdaine, A. A., & Sheffield, F. D. (1949). *Experiments on mass communication* (3rd ed.). Princeton, NJ: Princeton University Press.

Janis, I. L. (1967). Effects of fear arousal on attitude change: Recent developments in theory and experimental research. In L. Berkowitz (Ed.), *Advances in experimental social psychology* (Vol. 3, pp. 166–224). New York: Academic Press.

Janis, I. L., & Mann, L. (1965). Effectiveness of emotional roleplaying in modifying smoking habits and attitudes. *Journal of Experimental Research in Personality, 1,* 84–90.

Kahnemann, D., & Tversky, A. (1984). Choices, values and frames. *American Psychologist, 39,* 341–350.

Kelman, H. C., & Hamilton, V. L. (1989). *Crimes of obedience.* New Haven, CT: Yale University Press.

Kenrick, D. T., Neuberg, S. L., & Cialdini, R. B. (1999). *Social psychology: Unravelling the mystery.* Needham, MA: Allyn & Bacon.

Leventhal, H. (1970). Findings and theory in the study of fear communications. In L. Berkowitz (Ed.), *Advances in experimental social psychology* (Vol. 5, pp. 119–186). New York: Academic Press.

Leventhal, H., Watts, J. C., & Pagano, F. (1967). Effects of fear and instructions on how to cope with danger. *Journal of Personality and Social Psychology, 6,* 313–321.

Maison, D. (1997). Paradoks reklamy papierosów [Cigarette advertising paradox]. *Marketing i Rynek, 10,* 30–34.

McAlister, A., Perry, C., Killen, J., Slinkard, L. A., & Maccoby, N. (1980). Pilot study of smoking, alcohol, and drug abuse prevention. *American Journal of Public Health, 70,* 719–721.

McGuire, W. J. (1964). Inducing resistance to persuasion. In L. Berkowitz (Ed.), *Advances in experimental social psychology* (Vol. 1, pp. 192–229). New York: Academic Press.

Meyerowitz, B., & Chaiken, S. (1987). The effect of message framing on breast self-examination attitudes, intentions and behavior. *Journal of Personality and Social Psychology, 52,* 500–510.

Nisbett, R., Hamill, R., & DeCamp Wilson, T. (1980). Insensitivity to sample bias: Generalizing from atypical cases. *Journal of Personality and Social Psychology, 39*, 578–589.

Ohme, R. K., & Gusztyla, K. (1997, August). *Positive social influence: A few tips how to create antismoking ads.* Paper presented at the conference The Practice of Social Influence in Established and Emerging Democracies, Przegorzaly, Poland.

Paczkowski, M. (1998). Swiat nie kocha palaczy [The world doesn't love smokers]. *Aida Media: Teoria i Praktyka Reklamy, 1*, 11.

Pechmann, C. & Ratneshwar, S. (1994). The effects of antismoking and cigarette advertising on young adolescents' perception of peers who smoke. *Journal of Consumer Research, 21*, 236–251.

Rogers, R. (1983). Cognitive and physiological processes in fear appeals and attitude change: A revised theory of protection motivation. In J. T. Cacioppo & R. E. Petty (Eds.), *Social psychophysiology: A sourcebook* (pp. 153–176). New York: Guilford.

Romanowska, D. (1999). Palacy problem (Smoking problem). *Wprost, 11/850*, 74–75.

Solomon, D. S. (1983). Mass media campaigns for health promotion. *Prevention in Human Services, 3*, 115–123.

Swinehart, J. (1976). Some lessons from the "Feeling Good" television series. *Consumer Behavior in the Health Market.* Lincoln, NE: Nebraska Center for Health Education.

Templeton, J. F. (1994). *The focus group: A strategic guide to organizing, conducting and analyzing the focus group interview.* Chicago: Probus.

Uscinski, K. (1998). Papierosy–promocja bez reputacji [Cigarettes—promotion without reputation]. *Aida Media: Teoria i Praktyka Reklamy, 1*, 4–7.

Weinstein, N. D. (1980). Unrealistic optimism about future life events. *Journal of Personality and Social Psychology, 39*, 806–820.

Wilde, G. J. S. (1993). Effects of mass media communications on health and safety habits: An overwiew of issues and evidence. *Addiction, 88*, 983–996.

Zielinski, T. (1996). Antytytoniowy front interwencyjny w USA i Polsce.[Antitobacco interventions in USA and Poland]. *Problemy Alkoholizmu, 6*, 10–12.

Zimbardo, P. G., & Leippe, M. (1991). *The psychology of attitude change and social influence.* New York: McGraw-Hill.

17

Compliance Principles in Retail Sales in the United States

Michael J. Cody

University of Southern California

John S. Seiter

Utah State University

ABSTRACT

A typology of verbal message tactics employed in selling encoun-ters is proposed based on Cialdini's (1993) principles of compli-ance. Trained observers recorded the use of tactics in 416 interac-tions to identify how different types of sales clerks employed the tactics. Four types of buyer–seller interaction patterns were identi-fied and described: The client-oriented clerk, the ingratiation-style clerk, the task-oriented clerk, and the passive-inactive clerk. Practical implications, cultural issues, and the validity and utility of Cialdini's compliance principles are discussed, along with the value of observing real behaviors in public settings.

Scholarly interest in the process of persuasion has changed considerably in the last few decades from a focus on one-to-many influence attempts to the study of interpersonal or one-to-one influence attempts (Gass & Seiter, 1999). This shift suggests the need to observe influence attempts as they occur in face-to-face, real-life interactions. The present study relied on such observations in one of the most common persuasive encounters in the United States: the purchasing of clothes and accessories in retail stores. In an earlier study (Cody, Seiter, & Montagne-Miller, 1995), we examined how women and men were influenced by certain sales tactics depending on their goals for shopping (i.e., browsing, gift buying, or focused shopping). Males and females differed in how they reacted to sales tactics. In addition, we found that a parsimonious set of tactics was effec-tive in influencing gift buyers. Specifically, gift buyers spent more money when clerks told them which type of gift was popular and when clerks used *opinion conformity* to help customers select a gift. However, no parsimonious results were obtained for focused or recreational shoppers largely because of the tremendous variability among the hundreds of shoppers who were browsing or seeking specific merchandise.

Our present analysis builds on this earlier work and corrects for the latter limitation. Rather than assess merely the motive of the shopper, we argue that clerks adopt particular styles of selling, which may result in different buyer–seller interactions. Client-oriented clerks use a wider range of tactics, are more engaging in their interactions, and spend more time with shoppers. For this reason, this style results in substantially greater sales than the ingratiation style (in which clerks groom an image as likable and friendly), the task-oriented style, and the passive-inactive style. We also discuss why this may be especially true in the individualistic culture of the United States.

INFLUENCE TACTICS AND THE SALES PROCESS

A considerable amount of attention has focused on the use of power or compliance-gaining tactics (e.g., Cody, Canary, & Smith, 1994; Fitch, 1994; Klingle & Burgoon, 1995; Lee, Levine, & Cambra, 1997; Wilson, Cruz, Marshall, & Rao, 1993), as well as on the use of sales tactics (e.g., Beardon, Netemeyer & Teel, 1988; Burnkrant & Cousineau, 1975; Dwyer, Schurr, & Oh, 1987; Olshavsky, 1973; Sheth, 1976; Sujan, 1986; Weitz, Sujan, & Sujan, 1986). Some projects have relied on theory (i.e., French & Raven, 1959), whereas others list a possible range of influence tactics (14, 16, or more) from which influence agents are asked to rate the likelihood of using various tactics—an approach that is open to criticism on the basis of social desirability effects and other problems.

An alternative is to observe influence tactics that are employed in real sales encounters involving face-to-face interactions between clerks and customers, and to categorize the tactics on the basis of a finite set of psychological processes underlying why people comply with requests. One viable set of processes has been presented by Cialdini (1993). He identified six processes: liking, authority, reciprocity, scarcity, commitment, and social proof. We also include the principle of anchoring and contrast effects. Our belief is that these underlying processes are parsimonious and exhaustive of the major ways in which individuals are influenced. Hence, it should be possible to categorize all clerks' tactics as attempts to impact on the principles of liking, reciprocity, and so on. A brief outline of each process and examples of tactics are provided here and in the appendix (a portion of the code sheet used in the coding). For a more complete discussion, see Bettinghaus and Cody (1994), Cialdini (1993), and our earlier work (Cody et al., 1995).

Liking. People are likely to comply with requests made by likable others (Cialdini, 1993). Tactics that promote liking include similarity, opinion conformity, general friendliness, rendering favors, and praising others (see appendix).

Helping/Reciprocity. Frequent attempts to help the shopper can make him or her feel obligated to reciprocate in some way (i.e., purchase something). Helpfulness might include offering to carry objects for a shopper, calling another store to check inventory, and so forth. Leading helpfulness involves a more active leading of a shopper toward merchandise, sales, or new items (see appendix).

Authority (or Source Characteristics). Effective sales clerks must demonstrate expertise (about what they are selling) and trustworthiness. The latter may be a difficult task considering obvious ulterior motives (e.g., to increase sales and, hence, commissions). However, one way to build trust is to appear honest to shoppers by noting limitations to the object being sold (see appendix and Cody et al., 1995),or by speaking against one's own best interest.

Commitment. People want to be consistent with what they have already done (in public; Cialdini, 1993). Once shoppers commit to a particular article of clothing, a clerk can utilize the commitment principle by recommending items that complete an ensemble of accessories—including belts, shoes, and so on.

Anchoring and Contrast. A contrast effect operates in sales when a clerk first shows customers expensive objects and then reveals substantially good values elsewhere in the store. In contrast to the expensive item, the follow-up items seem less expensive than it otherwise would have appeared.

Social Proof. There are times when shoppers rely on what others are doing to determine the correct or appropriate course of action; they join in with what the majority is buying, eating, and so on. Clerks attempt to induce the social proof principle when they inform shoppers that a particular product is a popular item.

Scarcity. Scarcity involves telling a customer that a product is in short supply or will not last long on the shelf. Its persuasiveness is based on the principle that shoppers will be motivated to buy or act quickly so they will not lose the freedom to buy or own the item when it is no longer available.

LIMITATIONS OF PREVIOUS RESEARCH

Previously, we examined both the use and effectiveness of sales tactics based on shoppers' gender and motives for shopping, which included gift buyers, recreational shoppers (browsers), and focused shoppers (those who claimed to be looking for a specific item; Cody et al., 1995). Our expectations were based on previous studies on gender and on a goal-based model of human behavior that argues

TABLE 17.1
Effectiveness of Sales Tactics Used on Recreational Shoppers (N = 106)

Tactics	Percent Used	Purchase Amount— Not Used	Purchase Amount— Used	t value	p
Liking					
Praise	20	9.21	109.42	7.76	<.001
Opinion conformity	10	18.14	132.53	6.20	<.001
Render favors	13	19.06	101.96	4.69	<.001
Friendliness	52	16.68	42.37	1.99	.050
Similarity	8	22.92	106.43	3.77	<.001
Source Competence					
Expertise	19	19.95	73.34	3.33	<.001
Honesty/trust	5	26.73	96.27	2.30	.024
Helping/Reciprocity					
Helpfulness	95	4.40	31.28	.87	.387
Leading helpfulness	32	6.92	78.91	5.90	<.001
Commitment	10	19.04	124.75	5.59	<.001
Contrast	5	26.78	95.29	2.29	.026
Social Proof	15	17.60	99.81	4.98	.001
Scarcity	12	19.71	103.69	4.59	<.001

that people (i.e., males and females) differ in the goals pursued, plans developed to achieve goals, resources committed to implementing their plans, and so forth. Indeed, in the United States, women spend more time and effort shopping, plan shopping trips. and buying economically; men are motivated to spend little time in the store and defer to the advice of women. Our conclusions included:

1. More women shopped than did men, and more women were both recreational and focused shoppers relative to men (and gift buyers were equally likely to be males or females).
2. Men spent more money and received more frequent, repeated tactics than women.
3. Men spent a significantly longer time shopping when aided by a female clerk relative to a male clerk.
4. Men were more verbally compliant (agreeing with the clerk) than women, and acceptance of sales tactics was significantly related to increased sales.
5. Shoppers were affected by tactics that (we believe) helped them

TABLE 17.2
Effectiveness of Sales Tactics Used on Focused Shoppers ($N = 256$)

Tactics	Percent Used	Purchase Amount— Not Used	Purchase Amount— Used	t value	p
Liking					
Praise	42%	62.46	141.89	4.91	<.001
Opinion conformity	16%	92.26	114.86	1.00	.317
Render favors	32%	84.18	121.46	2.09	.037
Friendliness	43%	73.76	125.45	3.12	.002
Similarity	13%	89.65	137.24	1.95	.053
Source Competence					
Expertise	50%	76.35	115.90	2.39	.018
Honesty/trust	16%	87.77	140.25	2.30	.022
Helping/Reciprocity					
Helpfulness	96%	89.82	96.25	.16	.876
Leading helpfulness	30%	75.03	143.76	3.89	<.001
Commitment	26%	73.38	161.00	4.79	<.001
Contrast	9%	92.12	133.17	1.44	.152
Social Proof	31%	84.43	121.83	2.08	.038
Scarcity	16%	90.69	122.87	1.43	.154

achieve their goals, and this was especially true of gift buyers, who were influenced by appeals to popularity (social proof) and opinion conformity (a form of ingratiation), and males, who spent significantly more money when sales clerks helped them, praised them, and used the commitment principle.

There are two important limitations in this analysis. First, some buyer–seller interactions were engaging and highly interactive, with sales clerks and their clients engaged in communication for longer than an hour; other encounters ended within minutes. The analysis based solely on the shoppers' motives of gift buying, focused intentions, or recreational shopping does not fully capture the different types of buyer–seller interactions. Some clerks may have self-presentation styles that make them appear more likable, competent about what they are selling, and so forth, and different sequences of interactional patterns may follow when shoppers appreciated or reacted neutrally to the self-presentations of the clerks. Thus, additional analyses, other than one based simply on shoppers' motives, are necessary.

Second, there was substantial variability in the data for both the recreational and focused shoppers, both in time spent shopping and number of tactics employed. Note that a simple, parsimonious outcome was obtained for gift buyers. However, no simple or straightforward outcome emerged for the large group of recreational shoppers (106 shoppers, 25% of the sample) and focused shoppers (257 shoppers, 62% of the sample). The results reproduced in Tables 17.1 and 17.2 indicate that nearly all of the tactics were effective in increasing sales. The conclusion, based on these analyses, is that clerks who do nothing sell less, whereas clerks who use any tactic (beyond merely helping; see tables) can significantly increase sales. A more informative analysis stems from examining different patterns of buyer–seller interactions.

CULTURE, PRODUCT TYPE, AND PERSUASIVE APPEALS

In a previous study, Han and Shavitt (1994) examined the persuasiveness of advertising appeals in individualistic and collectivistic cultures (i.e., the United States and Korea, respectively). Their results indicate that, although people's cultural backgrounds influence how persuaded they are by certain appeals, product characteristics may also be a moderating variable. Specifically, personal products (e.g., fashion apparel) are sold more effectively through the use of individualistic appeals (i.e., demonstration of personal benefits to the buyer), whereas shared products (e.g., furniture, appliances) are sold most effectively through the use of collectivistic appeals (i.e., appeals emphasizing cultural values and group benefits).

Although Han and Shavitt (1994) focused on product types (i.e., shared vs. personal) and the content of appeals (i.e., individualistic vs. collectivistic) rather than on customer goals and tactic types (the focus of our previous study), parallels can be drawn between the two projects. First, people buying shared products and people buying gifts are comparable because, when shopping, both must consider others besides themselves. Interestingly, in both studies, these types of consumers were most persuaded by tactics and appeals that took others' needs or values into consideration. Specifically, people buying shared products were influenced by collectivistic appeals (Han & Shavitt, 1994), wheres gift buyers were most persuaded by social proof and opinion conformity—the two tactics in our typology that suggest others in the culture besides the buyer (i.e., the public and the clerk) find value in the product (see appendix).

Second, people buying personal products and focused/recreational shoppers are comparable because these types of consumers are making purchases for themselves. Thus, following Han and Shavitt (1994), focused and recreational shoppers should be persuaded by individualistic messages. We assume that personal wants and needs may be highly idiosyncratic. In the same way, preferences for certain persuasive tactics may vary greatly from person to person. If this is the case, it is not surprising that, in our study, a wide variety of tactics appealed to focused and recreational shoppers (Cody et al., 1994).

With this in mind, one implication is that, when selling to focused and recreational shoppers (the majority of shoppers in our sample), clerks who are able to assess individual customers' needs and adapt by choosing and implementing the proper or preferred tactic, should be more successful than clerks who cannot perform such tasks. This should be especially true in the United States, where people tend to find individualistic appeals more persuasive (see Han & Shavitt, 1994).

DIFFERENT TYPES OF BUYER–SELLER INTERACTIONS

Previous studies have focused on different types of sales clerks in buyer–seller interactions, but the literature is far from extensive. First, such research has proposed that some clerks are more customer oriented than others (Busch & Wilson, 1976; Evans, 1963; Saxe & Weitz, 1982; Williams & Spiro, 1985). Customer-oriented workers help shoppers make satisfactory purchase decisions, help customers assess their needs, describe products accurately, and adapt their sales presentation to the customers' interests (Saxe & Weitz, 1982). Self-oriented workers, however, are preoccupied with their own welfare and display little interest in the needs of others (Williams & Spiro, 1985). Williams and Spiro (1985) also suggested a three-part typology consisting of individuals with a task-oriented style (those concerned with minimizing cost, time, and effort), interaction-oriented style (those concerned for personal/social aspects of a situation), and self-oriented style.

A serious limitation of previous studies is their reliance on paper-and-pencil, self-report data (Williams & Spiro, 1985). What clerks report and how they behave may not be congruous. Our project overcame this limitation by categorizing salesclerks on the basis of direct observations of behaviors. The expectation is that task-oriented clerks will offer assistance, but will not attempt to manipulate liking or source competence,\ and rarely use inducements like commitment, contrast, social proof, or scarcity. Incontrast, a self-oriented clerk should rely heavily on bolstering hisor her own level of credibility (expertise, honesty/ trustworthiness) and use source competence tactics more than other tactics. Client-oriented clerks should be motivated to use any and all of the tactics,and, for the reasons noted earlier, will sell more than other types of clerks.

THE CURRENT STUDY

Twelve pairs of observers were trained to code the statements clerks communicated to shoppers and the shoppers' reactions, which included acceptance, rejection, postponement, or neutral reactions (see appendix). Observers worked in pairs to record the communication exchanges as accurately as possible. Most exchanges were brief, with a mean of 7.02 tactics employed per shopper. Three or fewer tactics were employed in 26% of the cases, whereas 25% of the cases involved nine or more tactics.

Thirty-two stores were selected, all paying clerks on a commission basis, and the locations ranged from northern Los Angeles County (Santa Monica's 3rd Street Promenade and the Beverly Center) to northern Orange County (South Coast Plaza, Fashion Island). Coders watched and listened to the sales interactions,\ and wrote, on preformulated code sheets, only the details dealing with tactics, reactions, and total amount of purchases. Shoppers included 322 females and 94 males. Salesclerks included 284 females and 132 males. The median estimated age of shoppers was 25.370, and the median estimated age of the clerks was 25.077.

Training

One graduate student and 23 senior Honors students, who had read all Cialdini (1993) committed 10 hours per week for 8 weeks to observe sales exchanges. Three two-hour sessions were employed to train coders how to identify different sales tactics and customer reactions (see appendix). This training included defining tactics and reactions, identifying the psychological principles that account for the tactics' use and effectiveness, and illustrating the use of the code sheets that were to be employed. The training also asked all participants to generate clear and accurate examples of how each tactic might be phrased in actual sales encounters, and to discuss how they would code expressions that are ambiguous (i.e., should a particular statement be coded as a praise or as friendliness?). Finally, two tests were employed to assess the reliability of the coding. Each test contained a multiple-choice section and a paragraph description of a sales encounter that coders had to unitize and code (*unitizing* means that the coders broke down the sequence of exchanges [tactics-reactions] in the same way). After the first test and more training, the second test was administered. The coders averaged 93% agreement on the multiple-choice section (82%–100%), 86% on the unitizing section (69% –100%), and 81% on the coding of the unitized coding (73%–91%). Data for one pair of coders was low (69% unitizing and 73% coding), and additional training was scheduled and completed. After all data were collected, one of the authors and a graduate student read all coded data for all participants to assess consistency in the coding, and discussions were held with one another and with the coders to resolve any questions about the coding.

TABLE 17.3
Sales Tactics Used by Four Types of Buyer–Seller Interactions

Tactics	Client-Oriented ($N = 20$)	Ingratiator ($N = 68$)	Task-Oriented ($N = 167$)	Passive/Inactive ($N = 161$)
Liking/ ingratiation	8.45	3.48	1.96	.66
Source competence	3.70	1.38	.90	.28
Helping/ reciprocity	10.35	5.94	3.40	1.81
Commitment	1.05	.46	.29	.09
Contrast	.02	.13	.13	.03
Social proof	1.00	.49	.34	.12
Scarcity	.45	.28	.14	.10
Reactions				
Accept	13.80	7.59	4.09	1.29
Reject	1.75	1.06	.80	.87
Postpone	.55	.10	.16	.16
Neutral	5.10	1.57	.66	.39
Purchase amount	$213.82	$141.07	$88.86	$20.58

Results

Helping/reciprocity tactics were the most common (used 3.39 times per sales encounter), followed by liking/ingratiation attempts (1.91 times). Source competence tactics were employed an average of .87 times per sales encounter; social proof, .31, commitment, .28, scarcity, .16, and contrast, .10. Our discussions with the clerks indicate that they did not use the latter two tactics often for strategic reasons. First, in an urban setting such as Los Angeles, to claim scarcity (few in stock, only one of its kind) carries little weight, because there are so many other places to shop in Los Angeles. Second, clerks claimed that using contrast (taking shoppers to the most expensive items first) wasted time for both the clerk and the shopper. They voiced the opinion that most shoppers buy clothes similar to those they already own. It is more economical to lead shoppers to the same quality of clothing than try the contrast tactic.

Strategic Use of Tactics: Types of Buyer–Seller Interactions

K-means cluster analysis (SPSS) was utilized to identify particular types of buyer–seller interactions based on tactics and reactions observed during selling. Two- , three- , four- , five- , and six-cluster solutions were obtained. A four-cluster solution was judged as an adequate solution for three reasons. First, it was parsimonious. Second, the four clusters were easily interpretable. Third, the two-, three-, five-, and six-cluster solutions produced a number of clusters that differed substantially in size, with some of the clusters being very small indeed. The three-cluster solution included 27, 120, and 269 interactions; the four-cluster solution 20, 68, 167, and 161 interactions; the five-cluster solution 12, 25, 160, 149, and 70 interactions; and the six cluster solution 12, 25, 45, 147, 54, and 133 interactions.

Two multivariate analysis of variance (MANOVAs) were computed— one for tactics and purchases and one for reactions. We report here the significant univariate analyses, and Table 17.3 shows the means for each tactic and reaction for the four groups, along with the purchased amount. The four groups differed significantly in terms of acceptance [$F(3,412) = 621.71, p = .001$], liking [$F(3,412) = 228.80, p = .001$], helping [$F(3,412) = 227.3, p = .001$], authority [$F(3,412) = 74.84, p = .001$], neutral reaction [$F(3,412) = 58.02, p = .001$], commitment [$F(3,412) = 25.00, p = .001$], social proof [$F(3,412) = 22.87, p = .001$], scarcity [$F(3,412) = 7.75, p = .001$], rejection [$F(3,412) = 6.21, p = .001$], postponement [$F(3,412) = 4.58, p = .004$], and contrast [$F(3,412) = 3.20, p = .023$]. The four groups also differed significantly in terms of amount purchased [$F(3,412) = 36.82, p = .001$].

The four groups were labeled *client-oriented, ingratiation-oriented, task-oriented,* and *passive-inactive.* Client-oriented interactions involved significantly more tactics (and reactions) than other patterns, whereas *ingratiation-oriented* exchanges were characterized by reliance on friendly, helpful tactics (high levels of helping and liking tactics), with infrequent use of commitment, contrast, social proof, and scarcity. These two active types of styles were not common, because there were only 20 client-oriented clerks (approximately 5% of all buyer–seller interactions) and only 68 ingratiation-oriented clerks (16% of the sample). The *task-oriented* approach involved high levels of helping tactics ($M =$ 3.04), a modest amount of liking tactics ($M = 1.69$), and infrequent use of the other tactics (the 167 task-oriented clerks represent 40% of the sample). The *passive-inactive* exchanges were characterized by minimal helping tactics (M = 1.82) and no other type of tactic (the 161 passive clerks represent 39% of the sample).

The *client-oriented* clerk is an active user of all the tactics and, relative to the *ingratiator*, used significantly more helping tactics [$t(86)$ = 5.68, p = .0001], authority tactics [$t(86)$ = 5.68, p = .0001], liking tactics [$t(86)$ = 8.69, p = .0001], commitment tactics [$t(86)$ = 3.11, p = .003], and social proof [$t(86)$ = 3.18, p = .002]. The *client-oriented* exchange also involved significantly more of each type of reaction. Shoppers spent more (M = 213.82) with the client-oriented clerk relative to the ingratiator [M = 141.07; $t(86)$ = 2.05, p = .044].

The Ingratiator differed from the Task-oriented type of exchange in regards to liking tactics [$t(233)$ = 8.42, p =.001], authority tactics [$t(233)$ = 3.00, p = .003], helping [$t(233)$ = 11.30, p = =.001], and scarcity tactics [$t(233)$ = 2.45, p =.015]. Ingratiators also received, from their shoppers, more frequent acceptances [$t(233)$ = 17.36, p = .001] and neutral reactions [$t(233)$ = 4.22, p = .001] compared with task-oriented clerks. Ingratiators sold more than task-oriented clerks [$t(233)$ = 2.96, p = .003].

Significantly fewer sales tactics were employed by passive-inactive clerks compared with the client-oriented or task-oriented clerks (generally speaking). Passive-inactive clerks sold less than the client-oriented clerks [$t(179)$ = 11.32, p = .001], ingratiators [$t(227)$ = 10.98, p = .001], and task-oriented clerks [$t(326)$ = 6,72, p = .001].

DISCUSSION AND PRACTICAL IMPLICATIONS

This study proposed a typology of sales tactics and examined the impact of the tactics in a specific setting. Clerks preferred to use helpfulness and ingratiation tactics (i.e., praising, conforming opinions, rendering favors, being friendly, and inducing similarity) frequently and were less likely to use commitment, contrast, and scarcity. There are at least three reasons that the latter tactics were used infrequently. For one, liking and helping were more strongly related to purchase amounts (r = .36, .34) relative to other tactics (e.g., social proof; r = .20, scarcity, r = .13; contrast, r = .09). It is likely even probable that practitioners learn to use tactics that are effective (see Cialdini, 1993). Second, certain tactics may involve simple, one-step attempts to influence (e.g., "Let me help you," "That looks great on you"), whereas other tactics require more effort to implement (i.e., anchoring and contrasting). Third, statements within the categories of scarcity (This is the last one in blue) and social proof (This is what all high school students are wearing) may simply be less believed than other tactics because there is no direct proof available and the clerk may be perceived as simply trying to increase sales. Also, using certain statements associated with scarcity may be a poor strategy in image management: That's the last one in your size implies that the store is not well stocked. In a competitive market area, some shoppers will resent this type of message and move onto the next store.

What practical implications do our projects have and what do they reveal about social influence processes? First, it is clear that there is a direct relationship between thousands of statements that hundreds of clerks communicate daily and a parsimonious, finite set of psychological principles. This conclusion speaks volumes for the face validity and utility of relying on the use of such underlying principles as organizing guidelines for categorizing messages. We say this in part to contrast our current approach (behaviors and reactions in various public settings) with research 10 years ago, which involved listing various message tactics and asking individuals to rate the likelihood of using the tactics (see Cody et al., 1994). This approach is open to criticism on the basis of social desirability effects, evaluation apprehension pressures, or simply on the grounds that providing lists of tactics may contaminate the research because it provides a list of tactics individuals may not be aware of or use on their own initiative (Burleson & Wilson, 1988; Cody, 1982). However, our observers were not trained to seek out any new tactics or ploys, although some noted that effective clerks also engaged a shopper's friend or child during the interaction. Indeed, some clerks were effective when boosting the esteem of mothers' children or praising a boyfriend for shopping with and paying for a girlfriend's clothes. Although lacking in experimental control, we are strong advocates of field experiments and observations of real behaviors in sales encounters, traffic courts (Cody & McLaughlin, 1988), or during any number of public, accessible events such as bake sales, blood drives, or charity drives (Burger, 1986; Cialdini, 1993).

Second, for practitioners interested in improving sales, our projects indicate that effectiveness depends on the ability of the sales clerk to (a) help shoppers achieve their goals; (b) engage and adapt to shoppers' needs and reactions; and/or (c) groom an image of being likable. More specifically, while trying to appear likable, sales clerks should assess whether customers are shopping for a gift, recreational purposes, or for a particular item. If the customer's goal is to purchase a gift, sales clerks should be more successful when they point out the popularity of the item (social proof) and agree with the customer about positive aspects of the item (opinion conformity). If the customer is browsing or wants to buy a specific type of merchandise, clerks are advised to be customer-oriented, using a wide variety of adapting tactics to suit the customer's preferences.

This conclusion is consistent with timeworn principles of persuasion and interpersonal effectiveness, which advise communicators to adapt to their audiences and/or to be other oriented. Despite the apparent obviousness of this conclusion, the truth is that 39% of sales clerks were passive-inactive, selling on average only $20.58 per customer. This finding suggests that a worthwhile endeavor for businesses that depend on sales is increased attention to training clerks about the nature of customer orientation. We should point out, however, that customer orientation may depend on factors other than training. One of the limitations of the present project, for instance, is that we did not study sales encounters over time (e.g., what might have happened early in the buyer–seller interaction that prompted both clerks and shoppers to engage in an extended client-oriented encounter?). Similar questions can be asked about other types of buyer–seller interactions. For instance, what are effective ways to approach a recreational shopper? When a recreational shopper announces I am just browsing, successful clerks will have a way to reengage the shopper (friendliness, similarity, etc.).

Finally, we noted earlier that certain approaches to selling may be more effective in some cultures than in others. Although we suggested that the ability to adapt selling appeals and tactics to individual customers' wants and needs might be especially effective in individualistic cultures like the United States, we imagine that such skills would be beneficial in any culture. For example, Han and Shavitt (1994) found that, when considering personal products (e.g., clothing), subjects from both individualistic and collectivistic cultures tended to be more persuaded by appeals emphasizing individualistic benefits. Research further suggests that conformity is much higher in collectivistic cultures than in individualistic cultures (Bond & Smith, 1996). Thus, the use of a tactic such as social proof, which indicates that a product is popular in a culture, may be a simple and effective approach to sales in collectivistic cultures. Future research should explore this possibility and other issues noted in this chapter.

REFERENCES

Beardon, W. O., Netemeyer, R. G., & Teel, J. E. (1988). Measurement of consumer susceptibility to interpersonal influence. *Journal of Consumer Research, 15*, 473–481.

Bettinghaus, E. P., & Cody, M. J. (1994). *Persuasive communication* (5th ed.). New York: Holt, Rinehart & Winston.

Bond, R., & Smith, P. B. (1996). Culture and conformity: A meta-analysis of studies using Asch's (1952b, 1956) line judgment task. *Psychological Bulletin, 119*(1), 111–137.

Burger, J. M. (1986). Increasing compliance by improving the deal: The that's not all technique. *Journal of Personality and Social Psychology, 51*, 277–283.

Burleson, B. R., & Wilson, S. R. (1988). On the continued undesirability of item desirability: A reply to Boster, Hunter and Seibold. *Human Communication Research, 15*, 178–191.

Burnkrant, R. E., & Cousineau, A. (1975). Information and normative social influence in buyer behavior. *Journal of Consumer Research, 2*, 206–215.

Busch, P., & Wilson, D. T. (1976). An experimental analysis of a salesman's expert and referent bases of social power in the buyer seller dyad. *Journal of Marketing, 13*, 3–11.

Cialdini, R. B. (1993). *Influence: Science and practice* (3rd ed.). New York: HarperCollins.

Cody, M. J. (1982). A typology of disengagement strategies and an examination of the role of intimacy, reactions to inequity and relational problems play in strategy selection. *Communication Monographs, 49*, 148–170.

Cody, M. J., Canary, D. J., & Smith, S. W. (1994). Compliance-gaining goals: An inductive analysis of actors' goal types, strategies, and successes. In J. M. Wiemann & J. A. Daly (Eds.), *Strategic interpersonal communication* (pp. 33–90). Hillsdale, NJ: Lawrence Erlbaum Associates.

Cody, M. J., & McLaughlin, M. L. (1988). Accounts on trial: Oral arguments in traffic court. In C. Antaki (Ed.), *Analyzing everyday explanation: A casebook of methods* (pp. 111–126). London: Sage.

Cody, M. J., Seiter, J., & Montagne-Miller, Y. (1995). Men and women in the market place. In P. J. Kalbfleisch & M. J. Cody (Eds.), *Gender, power, and communication in interpersonal relationships* (pp. 305–329). Mahway, NJ: Lawrence Erlbaum Associates.

Dwyer, R. F., Schurr, P. H., & Oh, S. (1987). Developing buyer–seller relationships. *Journal of Marketing, 51*, 11–27.

Evans, F. (1963). Selling as a dyadic relationship: A new approach. *American Behavioral Scientist, 6*, 76–79.

Fitch, K. L. (1994). A cross-cultural study of directive sequences and some implications for compliance-gaining research. *Communication Monographs, 61*, 185–209.

French, J. R. P., & Raven, B. (1959). The bases of social power. In D. Cartwright (Ed.), *Studies in social power* (pp. 150 167). Ann Arbor, MI: University of Michigan, Institute for Social Research.

Gass, R. H., & Seiter, J. S. (1999). *Persuasion, social influence, and compliance gaining*. Boston, MA: Allyn & Bacon.

Han, S., & Shavitt, S. (1994). Persuasion and culture: Advertising appeals in individualistic and collectivistic societies. *Journal of Experimental Social Psychology, 30*, 326–350.

Helson, H. (1964). *Adaptation level theory: An experimental and systematic approach to behavior*. New York: Harper & Row.

Klingle, R. S., & Burgoon, M. (1995). Patient compliance and satisfaction with physician influence attempts: A reinforcement expectancy approach to compliance-gaining over time. *Communication Research, 22*, 148–187.

Lee, C. R., Levine, T. R., & Cambra, R. (1997). Resisting compliance in the multicultural classroom. *Communication Education, 46*, 29–43.

Olshavsky, R. W. (1973). Customer salesman interaction in appliance retailing. *Journal of Marketing Research, 10*, 208–212.

Saxe, R., & Weitz, B. A. (1982). The SOCO scale: A measure of the customer orientation of salespeople. *Journal of Marketing Research, 19*, 343–351.

Sheth, J. N. (1976). Buyer–seller interaction: A conceptual framework. *Advances in Consumer Research, 15*, 382–386.

Sujan, M. (1986). Smarter versus harder: An exploratory attributional analysis of salespeople's motivations. *Journal of Marketing Research, 23*, 41–49.

Weitz, B. A., Sujan, H., & Sujan, M. (1986). Knowledge, motivation, and adaptive behavior: A framework for improving selling effectiveness. *Journal of Marketing, 50*, 174–191.

Williams, K. C., & Spiro, R. L. (1985). Communication style in the salesperson customer dyad. *Journal of Marketing Research, 22*, 434–442.

Wilson, S. R., Cruz, M. G., Marshall, L. J., & Rao, N. (1993). An attributional analysis of compliance-gaining interactions. *Communication Monographs, 60*, 352-372.

APPENDIX

Sales Technique Instruction Sheet

Sequencing. You will notice that the sales interaction is divided into phases. You will find situations that do not meet this sales interaction model perfectly (e.g., only two strategies or no postsale follow-up), but code the salesperson's comments into this format to the extent that it makes sense. You should keep track of how many minutes are spent in these phases. For example, the initiation phase may take less than 1 minute; but if the following conversation is based on some similar experience, it may take several minutes.

Code/Customer Response. Each logical set of statements by the sales clerk should be coded according to the codes at the bottom of the code sheet. By logical set, we mean a grouping of statements that all can be coded with one label. For example, if a sales clerk says, "You know those are really going fast. We got a shipment in the other day and they're almost gone. I can't believe how fast they have been snapped up," this set of statements can be coded with a single *scarcity* label. You should also note whether the technique seems to have been accepted or rejected by the customer.

It should also be noted that, for each clerk attempt, there is a response by the customer. The customer may (a) accept the statement (e.g., simple agreement with the comment made by the clerks; seeming to go along with the clerk's statement; following the clerk to the dressing room), (b) reject the attempt (e.g., disagreement with the comments of the clerk; simply continue looking), (c) postpone (e.g., "I'll be along in a minute," or even continue to looking for a few minutes and later go along to the dressing room), or (d) act neutral (i.e., neither accept, reject, nor postpone the attempt). You must try to interpret these reactions as closely as possible, inserting the codes of accept (A), reject (R), acting neutral (N), or postponing (P).

Technique Coding

Contrast Effect CON. This technique is used when the clerk leads the customer to the most expensive items first and then works down to the less expensive. The clerk will be contrasting price and features (e.g., "Well, these are a bit cheaper, but…Well, we do have some less expensive ones, but…").

Commitment CMT. This is similar to the foot-in-the-door technique. The clerk starts off with small commitments from the customer first (e.g., accessories, hosiery, ties) and moves up to more expensive, bigger ticket items or simply attempts to add on more (e.g., "Oh, do you know what would go great with that? We have the perfect belt… Would you like the matching X that goes with that?").

Scarcity SCR. This is an attempt to lead customers into fast action by making them think that if they do not act now, they may not have the chance later (e.g., "Boy, these are almost gone. They've been selling so fast! This is the last pair of blue ones in your size. We're not going to ever get another shipment like these").

Similarity SIM. This technique draws the clerk and customer closer together by making the customer think that the two have something in common. It is one of the three strategies used to increase liking (e.g., "Oh, I lived [ate, worked, vacationed, etc.] there! I bought one like that last week.; My husband [wife, friend, etc.] has one just like that").

Friendliness FRN. This is the second way salespeople create liking. It is simple conversations about nonsales-related issues (e.g., "Hello, how are you? Welcome to X. Is it still crowded (rainy, sunny, etc.) out there? Have you seen [pop movie], etc.?").

Praise PRA. This is the third way salespeople increase customer liking of them. It is any complementary statement (e.g., "You did a good job of coordinating that. That looks great on you. You're so thin you can really wear something like that").

Expertise EXP. These are statements designed to enhance the credibility of the salesperson by setting him or her up as a person knowledgeable of the item's attributes (fashion, designer, material, care, etc.; e.g., "You know, that was made by X. These are better for your feet than X. That's made out of X, so it doesn't have to be dry cleaned").

Opinion Conformity OPN. This is any form of agreement with what the customer has said in an effort to be liked. It may sound like one of the other categories such as praise, but the difference is that this statement follows a customer's statement (e.g., " Yes, I know what you mean. I agree, that color looks good on you.

Rendering Favors FAV. Extra action on the part of the salesperson beyond making the sale is the fifth and final way clerks induce liking (e.g., "Can I gift wrap that for you?; We can have that tailored here.; Here, let me put you in the big dressing room, the one that's usually saved for formals.

Social Proof SOC. This technique is designed to heighten the image of the item by showing its popularity (e.g., "Everyone is buying these. Boy, we just got these in and everyone seems to want one").

Trustworthiness/Honesty HON. Usually these take the form of a straw man criticism followed by a better alternative. It is any attempt by the salesperson to appear honest and nonpushy (e.g., "This is dry clean only, but it looks fantastic. This can never get wet, but it is so cute").

Helpfulness HLP. Simple, sales-related questions that provide assistance in some way (e.g., "Do you need some help with that? May I answer any questions for you? Would you like to try that on?").

Leading Helpfulness LED. Although this still qualifies as helpfulness, it is a bit more forceful and action oriented. Most such statements are phrased as a statement and are accompanied by an action on the part of the salesclerk (e.g., "Here, come see what we have on sale (as clerk walks to store front). Let me look for that in your size").

Author Index

Subject Index

  effectiveness, 328t, 329t, 333, 334–335
  tactics for, 326–327, 340, 341
  workplace obligation, 98, 110
    China, 107
    Germany, 108, 115
    Spain, 108–109, 111–112, 115
    United States, 105–106, 110–111, 114–115
Low involvement psychology, 267
Marginalization, 191–192, 194, 195–196
Mazowiecki, Tadeusz, 272, 275
Media influences, see Advertising,
    antismoking; Advertising, Polish
    consumption and; Campaigns,
    mass-mediated; Message breaks
Message breaks
  assessment delay
    morality attribution, 250–252
    punitive judgment, 250–252
    responsibility attribution, 250–252
  characteristics
    headline, 242
    newspapers, 242
    story elaboration, 242
    television, 242
    temporal delay, 242
  closure need theory
    freezing phase, 253
    seizing phase, 253
  continuous message
    morality attribution, 244–245, 246–249,
      250–252
    punitive judgment, 244–245, 246–249,
      250–252
    responsibility attribution, 244–245,
      246–249, 250–252
  cross-cultural research, 254–255
  divided message
    morality attribution, 243–245, 246–249,
      250–252
    punitive judgment, 244–245, 246–249,
      250–252
    responsibility attribution, 242, 243–245,

      246–249, 250–252
    follow-up information and
      morality attribution, 245–246, 248, 249
      punitive judgment, 248
      responsibility attribution, 245–246, 247f,
        248
    intervening activity and
      morality attribution, 245, 248
      punitive judgment, 248
      responsibility attribution, 245, 248
    morality attribution
      assessment delay, 250–252
      continuous message, 244–245, 246–249,
        250–252
      divided message, 243–245, 246–249
        250–252
      follow-up information and, 245–246, 248,
        249
      intervening activity and, 245, 248
    practical applications, 255–256
      advertising effectiveness, 255–256
      defamation strategy, 256
      stereotype formation, 256
    primary vs. secondary control, 254–255
    punitive judgment
      assessment delay, 250–252
      continuous message, 244–245, 246–249,
        250–252
      divided message, 244–245, 246–249,
        250–252
      follow-up information and, 248
      intervening activity and, 248
    responsibility attribution
      assessment delay, 250–252
      continuous message, 244–245, 246–249,
        250–252
      divided message, 242, 243–245, 246–249,
        250–252
      follow-up information and,
        245–246, 247f, 248
      intervening activity and, 245, 248
    study overview, 235–236, 241–242
    hypotheses, 243–244, 246, 248, 249